On the Path to Genocide

ON THE PATH TO GENOCIDE

Armenia and Rwanda Reexamined

Deborah Mayersen

berghahn
NEW YORK · OXFORD
www.berghahnbooks.com

Published in 2014 by

Berghahn Books

www.berghahnbooks.com

© 2014 Deborah Mayersen

Library of Congress Cataloging-in-Publication Data

Mayersen, Deborah.
  On the path to genocide : Armenia and Rwanda reexamined / Deborah Mayersen.
  pages cm
  Includes bibliographical references and index.
  ISBN 978-1-78238-284-3 (hardback : alk. paper)—ISBN 978-1-78238-285-0 (ebook)
  1. Armenian massacres, 1915–1923.   2. Armenians—Crimes against—Turkey.
3. Genocide—Turkey.   4. Turkey—Ethnic relations.   5. Rwanda—History—Civil
War, 1994—Atrocities.   6. Tutsi (African people)—Crimes against—Rwanda.
7. Genocide—Rwanda.   8. Rwanda—Ethnic relations.   I. Title.
  DS195.5.M3738 2014
  956.6'20154—dc23   2013029905

British Library Cataloguing in Publication Data
A catalogue record for this book is available from the British Library

Printed on acid-free paper

ISBN 978–1-78238–284–3 hardback
ISBN 978–1-78238–285–0 ebook

For Jennie and Mary
with deep gratitude

CONTENTS

ACKNOWLEDGEMENTS

I am deeply grateful to Professor Peter McPhee (University of Melbourne) for his superb guidance in the course of this project. I could not have had a better historian to guide my path. Sincere thanks to Professor Ben Kiernan, under whom I was privileged to have a visiting fellowship to Yale University's Genocide Studies Program, where I spent a semester researching this book. Professor Kiernan's support and assistance, both whilst I was at Yale and subsequently, have been invaluable. My thanks also to Professor Vahakn Dadrian and Professor Stephen Feinstein, of blessed memory, for tremendously helpful feedback on an earlier draft of this book. I am grateful to the editors and production team at Berghahn Books for their invaluable assistance in bringing this volume to fruition, and I would especially like to thank Adam Capitanio, Elizabeth Berg and Caitlin Mahon.

During the course of this project I was fortunate to receive funding from numerous sources. These include funding from The University of Melbourne, the Australian Federation of University Women (South Australia and Victoria), B'nai B'rith Victoria and the Jewish Community Council of Victoria. The funding I received was instrumental to the successful completion of this project, and my sincere thanks to all the organizations and people that made this possible. Special thanks also to Mary Mass for making this project possible in a very practical way.

ABBREVIATIONS

APROSOMA	L'Association pour la Promotion Sociale de la Masse
BBTG	Broad-based transitional government
CDR	Coalition pour la Défense de la République
CUP	Committee of Union and Progress
FAR	Rwandan Armed Forces
GDP	Gross domestic product
GNP	Gross national product
IMF	International Monetary Fund
JEM	Justice and Equality Movement
MDR	Mouvement Démocratique Républicain
MDR/PARMEHUTU	Mouvement Démocratique Rwandais/Parti du Mouvement et de l'Émancipation Hutu
MRND	Mouvement Révolutionnaire National pour le Développement
NGO	Nongovernmental organization
NRA	National Resistance Army
PARMEHUTU	Parti du Mouvement et de l'Émancipation Hutu
PDC	Parti Démocrate-Chrétien
PL	Parti Libéral
PSD	Parti Social-Démocrate
RADER	Rassemblement Démocratique Ruandais
RPF	Rwandan/Rwandese Patriotic Front
RTLM	Radio Télévision Libre des Mille Collines
SLM/A	Sudan Liberation Movement/Army
TRAFIPRO	Coopérative Travail, Fidelité, Progrès
UN	United Nations
UNAMIR	United Nations Assistance Mission for Rwanda
UNAR	Union Nationale Rwandaise

'THE SYMPTOMS OF AN EXPLOSIVE SITUATION'
The Temporal Model of Genocide

Introduction

The United Nations (UN) received its first official warning of the risk of genocide in Rwanda in 1962—technically speaking, some thirty-two years of advance
notice. UN Commissioner Majid Rahnema, after returning from an observer mission, declared that the nation exhibited 'the symptoms of an explosive situation'.[1]
The 'social and political tension' there, he believed, 'may result either in the gradual
extermination of the majority of the Tutsi population, or it may at any moment
degenerate into violence and, possibly, civil war'.[2] Certainly, there was some cause
for concern during the decolonization process of the early 1960s. Yet within a
decade or so, the risk appeared to have passed. By the mid-1970s, experts on
Rwanda were predicting a bright future of ethnic unity.[3] In the 1980s the volatile
issue of regionalism, rather than ethnicity, dominated the political agenda; even in
1991 some Rwandans 'openly scoffed' at the idea of 'ethnic' politics.[4] For many of
the thirty-two years between Commissioner Rahnema's counsel and the eruption
of genocide, his warning seemed overstated and alarmist. Then suddenly it became
prophetic. Between April and July 1994 the most intense genocide of the twentieth century tore through Rwanda, leaving close to a million Tutsi and moderate
Hutu dead in its wake. Commissioner Rahnema's prediction had eventuated. And
yet why thirty-two years later? Why did the genocide erupt in 1994 rather than
1964, or, for that matter, 1974 or 1984? Was Commissioner Rahnema's warning
in 1962 really portentous, or just an accident of history?

The objective of this book is a simple one. It is a quest to provide a greater understanding of why genocide occurs *when* it does. Why did the Armenian genocide

erupt in Turkey in 1915, only seven years after the Armenian minority achieved civil equality for the first time in the history of the Ottoman Empire? How can we explain the Rwandan genocide occurring in 1994, after decades of relative peace and some cooperation between the Hutu majority and Tutsi minority? In the wake of the seeming explosion of genocides that have marked the twentieth century, scholars in the field of comparative genocide studies have identified and modelled preconditions and risk factors for genocide. Yet there is only a very limited historical understanding of how such determinants develop over time. Does the risk of genocide develop over decades or generations, or can a nation escalate from a low risk to a high risk of genocide very quickly? Can the risk of genocide wax and wane, or is the progression a linear one?

Integral to understanding the processes that culminate in genocide is a conception not only of the escalatory factors, but the inhibitory factors that may delay or prevent its onset. Why did the Hamidian massacres of 1894–96, in which more than one hundred thousand Ottoman Armenians were slaughtered, not escalate into an attempt to eliminate the minority entirely? If the invasion of second-generation Tutsi refugees into Rwanda in 1990 triggered the events that led to the 1994 genocide, why did a similar refugee invasion in 1963 not trigger a genocidal response? The role of constraints in inhibiting genocide may be as significant as that of preconditions in provoking it. Moreover, the preconditions and constraints that impact upon risk of genocide are subject to change in surprising ways.

This book offers fresh insight through a detailed investigation of how risk of genocide develops over time and in varying circumstances. It presents the temporal model, a new model of the risk factors for genocide that is the first to consider the nonlinear manner in which they may develop over time. It also offers new research into the role of constraints in inhibiting genocide. Through careful historical research and theoretical analysis, this book enables greater understanding than ever before of the path that leads to genocide.

The book also comprises a comprehensive account of the history of the Armenian minority in the Ottoman Empire, from the internationalization of the 'Armenian question' to the genocide itself, and of the history of Rwanda, from the precolonial period to the 1994 genocide. The Armenian and Rwandan genocides were the culmination of long processes of intergroup division, exclusion, discrimination and intermittent outbreaks of violence. While the genocides themselves have been the focus of much scholarly attention, the long history that preceded them has often been overlooked. Yet in each case, a deep historical understanding of the roots of the violence provides essential context for understanding its culmination. It is also vital history in its own right. There is surprisingly little research on the Hamidian massacres, for example, which—while overshadowed by the subsequent genocide—were of a magnitude to merit far more attention than they have received. Similarly, the long history of relatively peaceable coexistence between Hutu and Tutsi in Rwanda is often subsumed by the far more dramatic episodes of violence. This book seeks to redress this imbalance through a careful examination of these historical periods.

Defining Genocide

It is somewhat odd that a crime well-known in biblical times, one that has occurred since antiquity, had to wait until the twentieth century to acquire a label.[5] This is even more surprising when it is the 'crime of crimes'—the destruction of entire peoples. Yet, as Winston Churchill witnessed the unfolding horrors of Nazi Europe, he could only describe Hitler's barbarity as the 'crime without a name'.[6] The dubious honour of rectifying this nomenclatural omission fell to Polish Jewish scholar Raphael Lemkin, even as he observed his own community fall victim to it. Lemkin publicly coined the term 'genocide' in 1944, combining the Greek *genos* (race, tribe) with the Latin *cide* (killing).[7] In 1946, it was largely as a result of Lemkin's determined lobbying that the issue of the prevention and punishment of genocide was first addressed at the United Nations.[8] The combination of Lemkin's determined lobbying and a world reeling in horror from the Holocaust led to remarkably rapid action at the United Nations.

On 9 December 1948, the Convention on the Prevention and Punishment of the Crime of Genocide was adopted by the UN General Assembly. The crime of genocide was defined as:

> Any of the following acts committed with intent to destroy, in whole or in part, a national, ethnical, racial or religious group, as such:
> (a) Killing members of the group;
> (b) Causing serious bodily or mental harm to members of the group;
> (c) Deliberately inflicting on the group conditions of life calculated to bring about its physical destruction in whole or in part;
> (d) Imposing measures intended to prevent births within the group;
> (e) Forcibly transferring children of the group to another group.[9]

Genocide, conspiracy to commit genocide, direct and public incitement to commit genocide, attempt to commit genocide and complicity in genocide were all declared punishable. Contracting parties, nations ratifying the convention, confirmed genocide as a crime under international law, 'which they undertake to prevent and to punish'.[10] The convention came into effect in 1951, after being ratified by the minimum of twenty nations, and remains in effect and unmodified today, ratified by the vast majority of states.[11]

Arriving at a convention upon which there was general agreement, however, had meant considerable wrangling over what constituted genocide. As the definition was drafted and debated in the United Nations, political groups came to be excluded from the definition.[12] The question of defining intent was problematic, and was eventually resolved without defining the grounds on which it would be necessary for the crime to constitute genocide.[13] The final, legal definition of genocide was achieved through negotiation and compromise between UN member states. Whilst this was a remarkable achievement, there is widespread agreement amongst genocide scholars that it is not without significant flaws. The narrowness of the definition has meant that a number of atrocities have not 'qualified' as genocide—in particular, the destruction of political groups and social classes. The requirement that genocidal acts must be committed with 'intent' also poses great difficulties, as intent is very difficult to prove conclusively.[14]

The flawed UN definition of genocide contributed to a split between scholars in the burgeoning field of genocide studies, between those who adopt the UN definition of genocide and those who work with an alternative definition.[15] Scholars who have abided by the UN definition, such as Ben Kiernan and Leo Kuper, do not deny its shortcomings, but point to its status as an internationally recognized definition of this odious crime.[16] This is the definition nations acknowledged when they ratified the Convention on the Prevention and Punishment of the Crime of Genocide, and as such it is of enormous significance. Scholars such as Frank Chalk and Kurt Jonassohn, however, have advocated the use of an alternative definition of genocide, contending that it allows the phenomenon to be defined—and therefore studied—with greater clarity and precision. Chalk and Jonassohn have defined genocide thus: 'A form of one-sided mass killing in which a state or other authority intends to destroy a group, as that group and membership in it are defined by the perpetrator.'[17] Utilizing this alternative definition overcomes the inconsistency associated with the convention's exclusion of political and social groups as potential victims of genocide. More recently, there has been greater acceptance within genocide studies of definitions based upon, but more inclusive than, the definition in the Genocide Convention.

The present study adopts the stance of the journal *Genocide Studies and Prevention*, subscribing to 'a broad concept of genocide consistent with but not necessarily limited to the United Nations Convention definition'.[18] It resists, however, the recent trend amongst scholars of comparative genocide to consider an expanded range of massacres as further examples of genocide, or genocidal massacres. That is, in accordance with most of the scholarship that pertains specifically to the Armenian genocide, and similarly to the Rwandan genocide, neither the Armenian massacres of 1894–96 nor the Rwandan massacres of 1963–64 will be considered genocide. Whilst quantitative scholars in particular have sought to expand the category of 'genocide' to include limited outbreaks of massacres, this study focusses upon genocide as massive outbreaks of violence with clear eliminationist intent.

The Aetiology of Genocide

Following ratification of the Genocide Convention, the topic of genocide received very little scholarly attention for almost a quarter of a century. In 1976, when Irving Louis Horowitz addressed the subject in *Genocide*, he lamented the failure of modern social science to grapple with the crime.[19] When, shortly thereafter, that failure began to be rectified, very quickly the study of the aetiology of genocide—that is, the study of the causes and factors that lead to it—became a key focus of the field. Over the past three decades, scholars have utilized several different approaches within their investigations. Many scholars, such as Kuper, Fein and others, have utilized a qualitative approach to identify preconditions for genocide, with several outlining models of the preconditions. Others, including Bauman and Levene, have proposed singular overarching factors to explain the explosion of genocides in the past century. More recently, Harff, Krain and others have presented models of the antecedents of genocide based on quantitative research. Comparatively few scholars have taken the approach of including nongenocidal examples amongst their case studies to understand why genocide is much less common than more limited outbreaks of violence. Each of these approaches has yielded valuable insights into the aetiology of genocide, and together they form the basis of our understanding of the causes of genocide. Yet it is an understanding that remains far from complete.

The Qualitative Approach

Leo Kuper, often regarded as the doyen of comparative genocide studies, laid much of the early groundwork for understanding the aetiology of genocide.[20] Kuper's early analysis identified the 'plural society' as the structural basis for genocide. He defined a plural society not simply as a society with a diversity of racial, ethnic and/or religious groups, but rather as a society with persistent and pervasive cleavages between these sections.[21] Kuper identified ideological legitimation as a further precondition necessary for genocide to occur.[22] Perpetrators use legitimizing ideologies to shape a dehumanized image of the victims in the minds of their persecutors, breaking down inhibitions against killing. Kuper noted several preconditions for what he termed 'domestic genocides', that is, genocides that arise on the basis of internal divisions within a society and not in the course of international warfare. First, he observed that in many cases there have been differences of religion between the aggressors and the victims. Second, Kuper highlighted that the catalyst is often a situation of change and of threat. Periods of war or their immediate aftermath seem to facilitate, or provide the opportunity for, large-scale massacres of civilian populations and genocide. Decolonization has also been a predisposing factor for genocide. Finally, Kuper also observed that genocide is committed mostly, but not exclusively, by governments.

Helen Fein, in a number of studies examining the causes of genocide, has further theorized on this topic. Whilst Kuper focussed predominantly upon events at a societal level, Fein's analyses explore both the role of society and that of government.[23] Fein's model of the preconditions for genocide proposed that '[t]he sequences of preconditions, intervening factors, and causes that lead towards genocide'[24] are as follows:

1. The victims have previously been defined outside the universe of obligation of the dominant group. This is an essential, but not sufficient condition for genocide.
2. The status of the state has been reduced by defeat in war and/or internal strife. This is a predisposing condition toward a political or cultural crisis of national identity in which the third step becomes more likely to occur.
3. An elite that adopts a new political formula to justify the nation's domination and/or expansion, idealising the singular rights of the dominant group, rises to power. Adoption of such a formula by a ruling elite is a necessary but not sufficient condition for premeditated genocide.
4. The calculus of costs of exterminating the victim—a group excluded from the circle circumscribed by the political formula—changes as the perpetrators instigate or join a (temporarily) successful coalition at war against antagonists who have earlier protested and/or might conceivably be expected to protest persecution of the victim. This calculus changes for two reasons: the crime planned by the perpetrators becomes less visible and they no longer have to fear sanctions.[25]

According to Fein, the third and fourth conditions taken together constitute necessary and sufficient conditions or causes of premeditated genocide.

Fein took issue with Kuper's assertion that the plural society forms the structural basis upon which genocide can occur.[26] She highlighted the fact that some plural societies that have integrated different groups into a democratic state, such as Canada and Belgium, have not been marked by intergroup violence, despite long-standing intergroup conflicts. In contrast to Kuper, Fein proposed that the status of the potential victim group as 'alien' within a society is an essential precondition of genocide against the group. Furthermore, it is the charter and structure of the state itself that may warrant or negate genocide.[27] Fein suggested a number of precipitants that may trigger genocidal responses. They include challenges by the victim to the structure of domination, opportunities for internal development impeded by the presence or habitual mode of life of the victim, and ideological strains within the worldview or utopia of the dominant group that demand social homogeneity and sacrifice of groups that do not fit the idealized image.[28]

A number of genocide scholars have built upon the theoretical analyses of authors such as Kuper and Fein through the use of a range of case studies. Florence Mazian analysed the Holocaust and the Armenian genocide to develop a six-stage model.[29] In addition to the preconditions of 'outsiders', 'internal strife' and the role of a genocidal leadership, akin to those of Fein, Mazian highlighted the role of 'destructive uses of communication', 'organization of destruction' and 'failure of multidimensional levels of social control'.[30] 'Destructive uses of communication' highlights the crucial role of propaganda in facilitating genocide, while the 'organization of destruction' incorporates the challenging pragmatics of organizing mass murder. Importantly, the 'failure of multidimensional levels of social control'—a factor not incorporated within other models—highlights the role of the failure of normally inhibitory factors in contributing to the outbreak of genocide. These factors can include social control by the state, the role of religious institutions, the international oversight of other nations and international bodies and even the victim group's ability to defend itself.

Robert Melson conducted an examination of the processes that led to the genocides in Armenia and Nazi Germany.[31] He presented largely complementary findings to those of Mazian; however, his conclusions include two further important factors. First, Melson highlighted that, in each case, the minority group experienced something of a renaissance in the years preceding the genocide. Both the German Jewish people and the Turkish Armenians adapted with relative success to the modern world, and experienced progress in the social, economic, cultural and political spheres. This social mobilization created new tensions between the minority and segments of the majority, who found this progress unacceptable and threatening to the old order based on inequality. Second, in each case the victimized group came to be identified, either geographically or ideologically, with the enemies of the larger society and state. Melson suggested that this identification may be real or may be falsely attributed to the minority, but the important factor is that a link is established between an external and an internal threat.

Scholars working from a psychological perspective have also sought to understand the factors that lead to genocide. Ervin Staub conducted a comparative study of the Holocaust, the Armenian genocide, the Cambodian genocide and the mass killings in Argentina, from which he developed a model of the preconditions of genocide from a psychological perspective.[32] Staub identified 'difficult life conditions', such as economic or political strife, as one of the origins of genocide. Resulting actions to cope with the psychological stresses of difficult life conditions may lead to a progression along a continuum of destruction.[33] Initial acts that cause limited harm result in psychological changes that make further destructive actions possible. Gradually lost are any deeply ingrained, socially developed feelings of responsibility for others' welfare, and inhibitions against killing. Particular cultural-societal characteristics may determine whether and how difficult life conditions lead to progression along the continuum of destruction. For example, Staub cites a cultural sense of superiority interacting with an underlying (and often unacknowledged) collective self-doubt as a combination with a particularly high potential to result in genocide.[34] Strong respect for authority and a strong inclination to obedience are other predisposing characteristics for genocide, which he found in each case study. The role of bystanders is particularly important to the progression of the continuum of destruction. Indifferent bystanders facilitate the continuum, while bystander opposition can restrain or break it. Each of Staub's case studies also featured a cycle of increasing violence prior to the genocide/mass killing. It is significant that while Staub writes from a psychological perspective, the factors he identifies as preconditions for genocide are similar and complementary to those proposed by Kuper, Fein, Mazian and others.

The psychologist Israel Charny has taken a very different approach to understanding the antecedents of genocide. Rather than focussing on preconditions, Charny identified ten 'Genocide Early Warning Processes' 'that define a series of natural psychocultural processes . . . [that] may be turned by society toward support of life, or they may be turned towards momentums of increasing violence toward human life, culminating in genocide'.[35] These processes form part of a proposed 'Genocide Early Warning System'. The ten major early warning processes include such general factors as how a society values human life, the quality of human experience, and its use of power. More specific processes include machinery for managing escalations of threat, orientation towards force for self-defence and solution of conflicts, and overt violence and destructiveness. It is only in the latter part of the model that processes more closely related to genocide are elucidated, including dehumanization of the victim group, its vulnerability, and legitimization of the victimization by authorities. The model also includes an interesting process largely omitted elsewhere: namely, 'perception of victim groups as dangerous'. This process acknowledges that victim groups, at the same time as being dehumanized and targeted, are often strangely also perceived as dangerous and threatening.[36] Charny's model identifies ten contributory processes, reflecting the complexity of genocide as a crime, and enabling a wide range of factors to be considered.

In recent years, Gregory Stanton's 'The Eight Stages of Genocide' model of the preconditions for genocide has become well-known, utilized by Genocide Watch as the basis for its list of countries at risk of genocide, politicide or mass atrocities. According to Stanton: 'Genocide is a process that develops in eight stages that are predictable but not inexorable . . . The later stages must be preceded by the earlier stages, though earlier stages continue to operate throughout the process.'[37] Stanton identified 'classification'—the classification of social groups into 'us versus them'—as the first stage of genocide.[38] Interestingly, however, he acknowledged that 'all cultures have categories to distinguish people into "us and them"', suggesting that 'bipolar societies that lack mixed categories . . . are the most likely to have genocide'.[39] The second stage is symbolization, in which groups are given names and symbols, rendering them distinguishable. Again, however, Stanton commented: 'Classification and symbolization are universally human and do not necessarily result in genocide.'[40]

The third stage 'is where the death spiral of genocide begins'.[41] Dehumanization involves the equation of the victim group with animals, vermin or diseases and the use of vilifying propaganda, each with the purpose of overcoming 'the normal human revulsion against murder'.[42] Stage four is organization, such as the training of militias; stage five is polarization. Extremists target those adopting a moderate position, eliminating opportunities for a middle ground. During the preparation stage (stage six), genocidal plans are made, and trial massacres conducted.[43] Stage seven is extermination, as the genocide itself is conducted, whilst the final stage is denial, which can occur both during and after the genocide. Stanton's model is further enhanced by his approach of suggesting preventative strategies at each stage, 'to prevent and stop the genocidal process'.[44]

Sociological Explanations

Of particular concern to a number of sociologists has been the seeming explosion of instances of genocide in the twentieth century. Rather than focussing upon the risk factors for individual occurrences of genocide, these sociologists have sought to understand the broader mechanisms that made 'the century of genocide'. For Zygmunt Bauman, then, modernity itself is the overarching risk factor.[45] According to Bauman, the Holocaust (and by extension, genocide) was not an aberration or atavistic event in contemporary society. Rather, it represented an extreme manifestation of modernity. At the heart of modern society is the drive for control, to design and cultivate our surrounds and subject them to rational organization. The Holocaust, according to Bauman, was the ultimate attempt to achieve a fully designed, fully controlled world.

Mark Levene, by contrast, has identified nationalism, rather than modernity, as the 'one great ideological underpinning' of genocide.[46] According to Levene, whilst there is a relationship between genocide and modernity, it is more indirect than that posited by Bauman. Levene viewed genocide as particularly related to 'states which are new, or are heavily engaged in the process of state and nation building, or are redefining or reformulating themselves in order to operate more autonomously and effectively within an international system of nation states'.[47] Particularly at risk are states that possess an acute anxiety about the wide and ever-increasing gap between themselves and the global leaders within the international system. 'The genocidal mentality . . . is closely linked with agendas aimed at accelerated or force-paced social and economic change in the interests of "catching up" or alternatively avoiding, or circumventing, the rules of the system leaders.'[48] Levene has recognized that specific instances of genocide are bound up with the social and ethnic composition of a state's population, and questions 'at what point does this become toxic?'[49] The answer appears to be in crisis situations, when a regime's conscious effort to break out from its perceived fetters encounters obstacles that recall some previous failure, either its own or committed by a predecessor. At that point, the state will seek to blame its misfortune on the traditional internal scapegoat, which has popularly been held responsible for earlier failures. Levene highlighted how in this way: 'State organized genocide is actually constructed not from the top down, but bottom-up from hate models provided by grass-roots societal phobias . . . The group is accused of *actively* disrupting or polluting the state's drive to transcend its limitations.'[50] The regime's attempt to realize the unrealizable has resulted in a crisis whereby it has boxed itself into a corner from which it is unable to retreat. The only recourse becomes massive violence. While such broad mechanisms cannot singularly explain genocide, the contributory role of modernity and nationalism in facilitating the crime is recognized by many scholars in the field of genocide studies.[51] Other overarching explanations, although somewhat less compelling, include those surrounding resource scarcity and overpopulation.

Quantitative Models

Increasingly, scholars researching the aetiology of genocide are utilizing quantitative approaches to identify its antecedents. One of the major challenges of a quantitative approach, however, has been building a valid data set. Genocide is a relatively rare event, yet quantitative researchers require a substantial number of instances of genocide to analyse in order to have reasonable prospects of obtaining statistically significant findings. To achieve this, researchers have often employed very inclusive definitions of genocide and politicide. Included within the data sets, therefore, are many examples of much more limited outbreaks of violence than have hitherto been considered 'genocide'. Whether these events are 'genocidal' is arguable; however, one of the consequences of their inclusion is that research findings from studies utilizing this approach identify preconditions not only of major outbreaks of genocide, but also of much smaller, localized incidents of targeted violence. Quantitative models, therefore, may be identifying the preconditions for massacres, smaller events previously conceptualized as 'genocidal massacres', or less targeted forms of mass killing as much as the larger events of genocide that have typically been the focus of genocide studies. Nevertheless, with appropriate awareness of these factors, quantitative studies can offer valuable insights into the antecedents of these crimes.

A pioneer of quantitative research into genocide and mass killing is Rudolph Rummel. After extensive statistical analysis, Rummel concluded that government type is the crucial factor in determining a nation's propensity to genocide.[52] Utilizing his concept of 'democide'—defined as 'the intentional killing of people by government'—Rummel concluded that democracy is inversely related to genocide, and that the level of centralization of power is the best way to predict propensity to democide:[53]

> Among a variety of social diversity (eg. Race, ethnicity, religion, language), socio-economic, cultural, geographic, and other indicators, the best way to account for and predict democide is by the degree to which a regime is totalitarian along a democratic-totalitarian scale. That is, the extent to which a regime controls absolutely all social, economic, and cultural groups and institutions, the degree to which

its elite can rule arbitrarily, largely accounts for the magnitude and intensity of genocide and mass murder.[54]

Rummel's work has been criticized by a number of scholars, who have taken issue with the estimates of death tolls in his data, the breadth of the concept of democide and his failure to adequately conceptualize the relationship between genocide and democide. Additionally, although Rummel's data may explain under which regimes one may expect to find genocides, it does not attempt to explain at what point during these regimes' lifetimes one should expect to find them.[55] Nevertheless, as Gregory Stanton has remarked, 'Rudy Rummel's meticulously documented conclusion that democracies do not commit genocide against their own enfranchised populations had often been challenged, but never refuted.'[56] It offers a very valuable contribution to the scholarship.

The political scientist Barbara Harff has conducted extensive quantitative research to identify predictors of genocide and politicide.[57] Much of Harff's work is focussed around the development of structural models of the antecedents of genocide and politicide. In a major study, Harff analysed 126 instances of internal war and regime collapse between 1955 and 1997 in an attempt to empirically differentiate between those episodes that led to genocide or politicide (thirty-five, according to her inclusive definitions of genocide and politicide) and those that did not.[58] Harff's most recent findings identify seven factors that significantly increase the risk of genocide or politicide.[59] These include prior genocides and politicides, the ethnic character of the ruling elite (that is, whether the ruling elite represents a minority communal group), the ideological character of the ruling elite and the existence of an autocratic (rather than democratic) regime. The role of trade openness is interesting, with low trade openness significantly increasing the risk of genocide or politicide, while high international interdependence decreases risk.[60] Other factors include state-led discrimination and instability risk. Harff has utilized these findings to tabulate annual lists of nations at high risk of future genocide or politicide.[61]

Further work by Harff has concentrated upon whether the escalation of a high-risk situation into genocide, such as what occurred in Rwanda in 1994, can be empirically anticipated in the year preceding the eruption of violence.[62] In order to determine this, all accelerators, triggers and deaccelerators that influenced conditions in Rwanda in the year prior to April 1994 were categorized and documented. Two matched control situations of high risk that did not eventuate into genocide, namely, Burundi in 1993 and (then) Zaire in 1990–92, were similarly documented. Harff found significant differences between the cases:

> Zaire at times shows high levels of conflictual activities, but cooperative activities rarely ever cease . . . Burundi's relatively low levels of conflictual events are accompanied by relatively high levels of cooperative events. By contrast, in Rwanda,

cooperative activity is highest six months prior to the conflict and ceases almost entirely four months prior to the outbreak of genocide . . . Thus in Rwanda . . . [there is] clearly a much sharper increase of accelerators accompanied by a steady decrease in de-accelerators in late 1993.[63]

The ultimate goal of this empirical approach adopted by Harff and others, such as Ted Gurr in the Minorities at Risk Project, is to provide early warning of risk of genocide and other conflicts.[64] This valuable approach has already contributed much to our understanding of risk factors for genocide, and has the potential to contribute much more.

Research Utilizing Nongenocidal Case Studies

Relatively few scholars have examined nongenocidal nations to explore the factors that may mitigate genocide. For Kuper, this was an integral component of understanding the aetiology of genocide.[65] Kuper identified a number of structural conditions that mitigate genocide, such as a religiously, ethnically and racially homogeneous society (which does not account for class or political differences). In multicultural societies, restraints on destructive conflicts may arise from the complex web of social relationships, and of interdependence, that cut across racial, ethnic and religious divisions.[66] A further model of the nongenocidal society is one in which ethnic or other divisions are frankly accepted, and ethnic/racial/religious identity is used as the basis for a balanced accommodation, either in terms of the constitution or by virtue of understandings in the conduct of the affairs of the nation.

Kuper also analysed two examples of seemingly 'at-risk' societies to determine why each had not descended into genocide. Both South Africa under apartheid and Northern Ireland exhibited many of the risk factors for genocide Kuper identified, being plural and deeply divided societies with a long history of conflict. In each case, he suggested, there were powerful restraints that inhibited genocide. In South Africa, he pointed to the dependence of the economy on nonwhite labour as one such restraint. The demographic composition of the country, with the white population forming a minority of less than 20 per cent, is also significant. Explanations of restraining factors in Northern Ireland include the presence of the British army as a peacekeeping force (although Kuper is unsure just how effective this may have been), the interdependence of Protestants and Catholics in an industrialized society and the fact that the violence seemed to operate within set limits accepted by each side (for example, the inappropriateness of targeting women and children).[67] Here, Kuper has highlighted the importance of examining high-risk but nongenocidal societies to discover the role of inhibitory factors. An examination of such societies appears as important as an examination of genocidal societies to determine the conditions that are most likely to culminate in or mitigate genocide.

Few scholars have taken up Kuper's challenge to study seemingly high-risk but nongenocidal societies in order to determine the restraining factors that may prevent genocide.[68] The political scientist Manus Midlarsky is one such scholar, having examined a number of cases where genocide might have been expected to occur but did not eventuate, 'in order to establish valid causal inference'.[69] Midlarsky's analysis focusses upon two key features of at-risk but ultimately nongenocidal societies. The first is the 'absence of loss'. According to Midlarsky, therefore, the behaviour of Bulgaria and Finland in refusing to cede their Jewish populations to Nazi control in the Second World War, in contrast to the behaviour of other European nations in this respect, can be explained through:

> the absence of territorial loss and its accompanying refugee influx. Without the large number of refugees of like ethnoreligious identity [experienced by nations that have suffered loss], sympathy can actually be extended to others of a different identity, who, through no fault of their own, are subject to deportation and a probable death.[70]

The second feature of such societies, according to Midlarsky, is the 'affinity condition'. Further expanding on Charny's concept of victim vulnerability as a risk factor for genocide, Midlarsky has identified that potential victim populations may be protected by large affine populations or governments with substantial influence, often in neighbouring countries.[71] War, however, 'may invert the affinity condition'.[72]

Midlarsky's contribution is complemented by that of Daniel Chirot and Clark McCauley. Taking a more theoretic approach, Chirot and McCauley have explored the question, 'Why is limited warfare more common than genocide?'[73] They have proposed three broad explanations. The first is that 'competing groups, be they families, clans, tribes, ethnicities, or nations, can work out rules of conflict and conciliation that dampen violence and make the complete destruction of any of the competing parties less likely'.[74] Second, 'exchanges are worked out between competing groups that give them an interest in maintaining rules of conflict to limit damage'.[75] Whether such exchanges consist of exogamy, commercial trade or ritualized interactions, they are effective mitigating strategies. The third explanation is the role of ideology. Whilst certain ideologies are far more dangerous than others, Chirot and McCauley have commented: 'As the modern world's competing groups have become larger, and technologies of communication and destruction have rapidly improved, dangerous ideological currents have vastly increased the dangers of genocide'.[76] Like Midlarsky, Chirot and McCauley conclude their contribution with an examination of factors and strategies that may potentially limit or prevent genocidal violence.

The Path to Genocide

In the past three decades, there has been tremendous progress in understanding the factors that lead to genocide. Scholars have taken a range of approaches and made a large number of findings, providing an excellent overall indication of the origins of genocide. Researchers who have focussed specifically on identifying the necessary and sufficient preconditions for genocide have developed a number of models, and they are notable for their multiple points of commonality and complementarity. Despite differing terminology and foci, a number of preconditions appear repeatedly. The existence of an outgroup, for example, whether described as 'outsiders', through 'classification' and 'polarization', or as an 'available' victim group, is a common feature of many models. Similarly, the role of propaganda is widely recognized, whether labelled as a 'dehumanization' process, 'destructive uses of communication' or 'ideological legitimation' of genocidal goals. Several models also recognize the contributory role of internal strife and a powerful dictatorial leadership. Other factors may be recognized in only one or two models, but nevertheless offer valuable insight into the risk factors for genocide. Melson, for example, has explored the role of the social mobilization or success of a potential victim group; others have examined colonial conquest and decolonization, sociocultural characteristics, and the approach of the dominant authority towards power. Many of the broad predisposing risk factors for genocide have now been identified, and their role explored.

Nevertheless, there remain substantial gaps in our knowledge of the path that leads to genocide. Current models of the preconditions for genocide, for example, offer very little information as to how these factors develop over time. Many of the predisposing factors that have been identified can be fairly stable characteristics of a society. For example, groups of outsiders such as Jews and Armenians have existed with relative stability in particular societies for centuries; a strong tradition of obedience to authority is also a stable feature of many cultures. Do such factors need to exist for some time in a society before genocide becomes likely? Or can a society progress from a very low risk of genocide to a very high risk within a short period? There is a sparse scattering of temporal information within the models: for example, Staub has identified a continuum of destruction along which societies progress, while Levene has suggested that a traditional scapegoat in society will be targeted at a time of crisis. Times of political upheaval after the emergence of a new leadership, even democratization, have also been pinpointed as potentially risky.[77] Yet there is surprisingly little information regarding the likely time period of the risk escalation process. Is a progression through the risk factors for genocide likely to be linear? Do certain risk factors cluster together closely in time? Can societies stagnate at a certain level of risk, or even experience a decline in it? Current models of the preconditions for genocide have not adequately addressed such questions.

Current models of the aetiology of genocide also lack predictive capacity. The specific role of, and distinction between, predisposing and precipitating factors for genocide is not often clearly delineated. Models have typically focussed on a small number of predisposing factors, and at times also identified one or two precipitating factors, but failed to distinguish which type of factor is under discussion. Yet this distinction is essential for identifying the catalysts that will transform a high-risk situation into genocide. Additionally, the breadth of some preconditions can make it difficult to identify their presence and severity in specific contexts. 'Internal strife', for example, can take many forms. Is an acute crisis of particular concern, or is a confluence of multiple difficulties more likely to increase the risk of genocide?

Many, if not most, societies will experience one or more of the identified risk factors for genocide at some level. The overwhelming majority of these societies will not experience genocide. Ideally, a robust model of the aetiology of genocide would offer a level of specificity that can contribute to at least some predictive capacity. Potentially, it could identify the seriousness of the risk of genocide at certain points, and at what point along 'the continuum of destruction' various forms of intervention may be required to prevent an occurrence of genocide.

As scholars such as Midlarsky, Chirot and McCauley have recognized, examining constraints that inhibit genocide is crucial to developing our understanding of the aetiology of the crime. For genocide to occur, not only must certain risk factors be present, but inhibitory factors must also be absent. Mazian's model, for example, identified 'failure of multidimensional levels of social control' as the final determinant of genocide, which encompasses the failure of religious institutions and other nations to effectively restrain the potential perpetrators. Similarly, Fein's model considered the role of war. War facilitates the onset of genocide through effectively removing the powerful restraint of potential international scrutiny or intervention. Largely, however, models have refrained from clearly delineating the specific role of inhibitory factors, and from differentiating between the removal of a constraint and the addition of a risk factor or precipitant. The study of the specific role of constraints in inhibiting genocide is still very much in its infancy. Yet arguably, the role of constraints may prove as important as that of preconditions in the aetiology of genocide. Moreover, investigating constraints may be of great value in the area of genocide prevention.

The Temporal Model

The temporal model of the preconditions of genocide has been developed to offer new insights into the timing of genocide and the role of precipitants and constraints. It extends previous models of the preconditions for genocide to elucidate a model that includes temporal progression as a component. It includes a strong focus on the specific factors that trigger risk escalation. It considers the complex dynamics that can influence escalatory and deescalatory processes, and recognizes that the process of risk escalation that culminates in genocide is often nonlinear. It also offers a limited predictive capacity in its later stages. The eight stages of the temporal model are briefly outlined below:

1. The presence of an outgroup. This can be defined as a relatively powerless minority, with whom relations are politicized, and which is subject to legal discrimination.
2. Significant internal strife. Significant, ongoing destabilization that affects the dominant group and the outgroup, and for which there is no clear solution.
3. The perception of the outgroup as posing some kind of existential threat to the dominant power.
4. Local precipitants and constraints determine the nature and time of the dominant group's response. A violent response is typical, with the onset of massacres quite likely.
5. A process of retreat from the intensity of the circumstance, or further escalation. While the process is commonly one of retreat, repeated cycles of escalation through the preceding stages followed by retreat ultimately facilitates further escalation.
6. The emergence of a genocidal ideology within the dominant power, typically accompanied by concerted efforts by the dominant group to further augment their power, and a deepening perception of the outgroup as posing an existential threat.
7. An extensive propaganda campaign, a key component of which features attempts to present the victim group as a grave threat to the dominant power.
8. Case-specific precipitants and constraints determine the precise timing of an outbreak of genocide.

The temporal model was developed following substantial research into the events that culminated in the 1915 Armenian genocide and the genocide in Rwanda in 1994. These two particular examples of twentieth-century genocide were carefully chosen for specific reasons. Arguably, the Armenian genocide is a paradigmatic instance of twentieth-century genocide, and as such, is worthy of particular attention.[78] Also paradigmatic to many scholars, the 1994 Rwandan genocide occurred subsequent to the publication of several of the models of the preconditions for genocide. It therefore offers a fresh challenge to our current understanding of the aetiology of genocide. The primary reason for the selection of these cases, however, is that in each case, more limited massacres of the victim group occurred, which started and stopped decades prior to the outbreak of genocide. Each case, therefore, has a matched control, where genocide did not erupt (earlier) despite a seemingly high risk. Additionally, the case studies were selected for their dissimilarities, to facilitate the development of a model likely to be widely applicable. These dissimilarities are substantial, with the genocides occurring in different continents and at the opening and closing of the twentieth century. While issues of race and ethnicity dominated in Rwanda, religion was a primary issue in the Armenian case. The Armenian genocide occurred in the context of global war, in contrast to the Rwandan genocide. Each featured very different levels of pregenocidal propaganda as well.

The following chapters present the case study analysis that provides the empirical basis for the temporal model. Historical investigation into the events leading to the Armenian and Rwandan genocides covers the period from the emergence of minority identity as a political issue to the genocide itself. The focus of the investigations revolves closely around the development of the risk of genocide over these periods. The study tracks the emergence of individual risk factors within each society, their ongoing operability and whether or not they cease to be operable during the period under study. The presence and effectiveness of constraints will also be closely examined. The study identifies triggers for risk escalation, along with any deaccelerators that may ameliorate risk. It highlights how the temporal model provides greater understanding of these processes. It also utilizes the wisdom of multiple models, investigating individual risk factors as they become salient within each case study. Such an approach allows for maximum flexibility in identifying those factors of most impact upon the temporal progression of risk of genocide. Following the historical investigations, the temporal model is further elucidated in chapters 7–9.

Notes

1. United Nations. 1962. *Question of the Future of Ruanda-Urundi: Statement Made by Mr. Majid Rahnema, United Nations Commissioner for Ruanda-Urundi, at the 1265th Meeting of the Fourth Committee,* A/C.4/525, 23 January, 17–18.
2. Ibid.
3. R. Lemarchand. 1975. 'Recent History' in section on 'Rwanda', in *Africa South of the Sahara, 1974,* London: Europa Publications, 1975, 660, quoted in M. Mamdani. 2001. *When Victims Become Killers: Colonialism, Nativism, and the Genocide in Rwanda,* Princeton, NJ: Princeton University Press, 140.
4. B. Jones. 1999. 'Civil War, the Peace Process, and Genocide in Rwanda', in T. Ali and R. Matthews (eds), *Civil Wars in Africa: Roots and Resolution,* Montreal: McGill-Queen's University Press, 60; Mamdani, *When Victims Become Killers,* 154.
5. For an excellent discussion of biblical references to genocide, see B. Kiernan. 2007. *Blood and Soil: A World History of Genocide and Extermination from Sparta to Darfur,* New Haven, CT: Yale University Press, intro.
6. S. Power. 2003. *"A Problem from Hell": America and the Age of Genocide,* London: Flamingo, 29.
7. For further information on Lemkin's conception of genocide, see R. Lemkin. 1944. *Axis Rule in Occupied Europe: Laws of Occupation, Analysis of Government, and Proposals for Redress,* Washington, D.C.: Carnegie Foundation for International Peace.

8. L. Kuper. 1981. *Genocide: Its Political Use in the Twentieth Century*, New Haven, CT: Yale University Press, 23.
9. United Nations. 1948. Convention on the Prevention and Punishment of the Crime of Genocide.
10. Ibid., Article I.
11. For a list of these states, see the United Nations Treaty Collection. Retrieved 9 April 2013 from http://treaties.un.org/Pages/ViewDetails.aspx?src=UNTSONLINE&tabid=2&mtdsg_no=IV-1&chapter=4&lang=en#Participants
12. F. Chalk and K. Jonassohn (eds). 1991. *History and Sociology of Genocide*, New Haven, CT: Yale University Press, 10.
13. Kuper, *Genocide*, 33.
14. UN, Convention on the Prevention and Punishment of the Crime of Genocide; S. Feinstein. 2002. 'Understanding the "G" Word', in C. Rittner, J. Roth and J. Smith (eds), *Will Genocide Ever End?*, St. Paul, MN: Paragon House, 41–42.
15. For a more detailed discussion of some of the issues surrounding the definition of genocide, see D. Harris [Mayersen]. 2001. 'Defining Genocide: Defining History?', *Eras Online Journal* 1(1). Retrieved 2 October 2007 from http://www.arts.monash.edu.au/eras/edition_1/harris.htm
16. Kiernan, *Blood and Soil*, 11; Kuper, *Genocide*, 39.
17. Chalk and Jonassohn, *History and Sociology*, 23.
18. Email communication from Henry Theriault, co-editor, *Genocide Studies and Prevention*, 9 October 2007.
19. I.L. Horowitz. 1976. *Genocide: State Power and Mass Murder*, New Brunswick, NJ: Transaction Publishers.
20. Kuper, *Genocide*, passim.
21. Ibid., 57–58.
22. Ibid., 84.
23. H. Fein. 1984. 'Scenarios of Genocide: Models of Genocide and Critical Responses', in I. Charny (ed.), *Toward the Understanding and Prevention of Genocide*, Boulder, CO: Westview Press; H. Fein. 1979. *Accounting for Genocide: National Responses and Jewish Victimization during the Holocaust*, New York: Free Press.
24. Fein, *Accounting for Genocide*, 9.
25. Ibid.
26. Fein, 'Scenarios of Genocide', passim.
27. Ibid., 6.
28. Ibid., 7.
29. F. Mazian. 1990. *Why Genocide? The Armenian and Jewish Experiences in Perspective*, Ames: Iowa State University Press.
30. Ibid., ix–x.
31. R. Melson. 1992. *Revolution and Genocide: On the Origins of the Armenian Genocide and the Holocaust*, Chicago: University of Chicago Press.
32. E. Staub. 1989. *The Roots of Evil: The Origins of Genocide and Other Group Violence*, Cambridge: Cambridge University Press.
33. Ibid., 17.
34. Ibid., 18–19.
35. I. Charny. 1999. 'Genocide Early Warning System (GEWS)', in I. Charny (ed.), *Encyclopaedia of Genocide*, Santa Barbara, CA: ABC-CLIO, 257.
36. Ibid., 259.
37. G. Stanton. 1998. *The Eight Stages of Genocide*, Washington, D.C.: Genocide Watch. Retrieved 30 January 2012 from http://www.genocidewatch.org/genocide/8stagesofgenocide.html

38. G. Stanton. 2004. 'Could the Rwandan Genocide Have Been Prevented?' *Journal of Genocide Research* 6(2), 213.
39. Stanton, *The Eight Stages of Genocide*.
40. Ibid.
41. Stanton, 'Could the Rwandan Genocide Have Been Prevented?', 214.
42. Stanton, *The Eight Stages of Genocide*.
43. Stanton, 'Could the Rwandan Genocide Have Been Prevented?', 216.
44. Ibid., 213.
45. Z. Bauman. 1991. *Modernity and the Holocaust*, Ithaca, NY: Cornell University Press.
46. M. Levene. 2000. 'Why Is the Twentieth Century the Century of Genocide?', *Journal of World History* 11(2), 332.
47. Ibid., 317.
48. Ibid., 319.
49. Ibid.
50. Ibid., 324–25.
51. For example, see E. Weitz. 2003. *A Century of Genocide: Utopias of Race and Nation*, Princeton, NJ: Princeton University Press; N. Naimark. 2001. *Fires of Hatred: Ethnic Cleansing in Twentieth-Century Europe*, Cambridge, MA: Harvard University Press, 5–11.
52. R.J. Rummel. 1984. *Death by Government: Genocide and Mass Murder since 1900*, New Brunswick, NJ: Transaction Publishers.
53. R.J. Rummel. 1995. 'Democracy, Power, Genocide, and Mass Murder', *Journal of Conflict Resolution* 39(1), 3.
54. Ibid., 24.
55. M. Krain. 1997. 'State-Sponsored Mass Murder: The Onset and Severity of Genocides and Politicides', *Journal of Conflict Resolution* 41(3), 332.
56. G. Stanton. 2005. 'Early Warning', in D. Shelton (ed.), *Encyclopaedia of Genocide and Crimes Against Humanity*, Detroit, Mich.: Macmillan Reference, 271–73. Retrieved 4 October 2007 from http://www.genocidewatch.org/aboutus/stantonearlywarningarticle.htm
57. See, for example, B. Harff. 1987. 'The Etiology of Genocides', in I. Wallimann and M. Dobkowski (eds), *Genocide and the Modern Age: Etiology and Case Studies of Mass Death*, New York: Greenwood Press, 41–60; B. Harff. 2003. 'No Lessons Learned from the Holocaust? Assessing Risks of Genocide and Political Mass Murder since 1955', *American Political Science Review* 97(1), 57–73; B. Harff. 2001. 'Could Humanitarian Crises Have Been Anticipated in Burundi, Rwanda, and Zaire?', in H. Alker, T. Gurr and K. Rupesinghe (eds), *Journeys Through Conflict: Narratives and Lessons*, Lanham, MD: Rowman and Littlefield, 81–102; B. Harff. 1998. 'Early Warning of Humanitarian Crises: Sequential Models and the Role of Accelerators', in J. Davies and T. Gurr (eds), *Preventive Measures: Building Risk Assessment and Crisis Early Warning Systems*, Lanham, MD: Rowman and Littlefield, 72–80; B. Harff. 2012. 'Assessing Risks of Genocide and Politicide: A Global Watchlist for 2012' [electronic version], in J.J. Hewitt, J. Wilkenfield and T.R. Gurr (eds), *Peace and Conflict 2012*, Boulder, CO: Paradigm. Retrieved 12 October 2011 from http://www.gpanet.org/webfm_send/120
58. Harff, 'No Lessons Learned from the Holocaust?', 57–73.
59. Harff, 'Assessing Risks', 54.
60. Ibid.
61. See, for example, http://www.gpanet.org/webfm_send/120
62. Harff, 'Could Humanitarian Crises Have Been Anticipated?', 81–102.
63. Ibid., 99.
64. See http://www.cidcm.umd.edu/mar
65. Kuper, *Genocide*, passim.
66. Ibid., 189.

67. Ibid., 204–5.

68. M. Lund. 2001. 'Why Are Some Ethnic Disputes Settled Peacefully, While Others Become Violent? Comparing Slovakia, Macedonia, and Kosovo', in Alker, Gurr and Rupesinghe, *Journeys Through Conflict*, 129. There are some exceptions; for example, studies such as T. Gallagher. 2001. 'The Northern Ireland Conflict: Prospects and Possibilities' and A.M. Tripp and C. Young. 2001. 'The Accommodation of Cultural Diversity in Tanzania', both in D. Chirot and M. Seligman (eds), *Ethnopolitical Warfare: Causes, Consequences, and Possible Solutions*, Washington, D.C.: American Psychological Association; J.L. Brain. 1973. 'The Tutsi and the Ha: A Study in Integration', *Journal of Asian and African Studies* 8(1–2), 39–49.

69. M. Midlarsky. 2005. *The Killing Trap: Genocide in the Twentieth Century*, Cambridge: Cambridge University Press, 325.

70. Ibid., 328–29.

71. Ibid., 335.

72. Ibid., 364.

73. D. Chirot and C. McCauley. 2006. *Why Not Kill Them All? The Logic and Prevention of Mass Political Murder*, Princeton, NJ: Princeton University Press, 95–148.

74. Ibid., 96.

75. Ibid.

76. Ibid., 97.

77. Krain, 'State-Sponsored Mass Murder', 332.

78. A number of scholars have made this suggestion; see, for example, R. Melson. 1996. 'Paradigms of Genocide: The Holocaust, the Armenian Genocide and Contemporary Mass Destructions', *Annals of the American Academy of Political and Social Science* 548, 156–68.

Part I

THE ARMENIAN GENOCIDE

Chapter 1

'TRYING DESPERATELY TO ESCAPE HISTORY'
The Armenian Question

The Armenians are an ancient people, based in the lands now referred to as Eastern Anatolia and Transcaucasia. In the fourth century of the Common Era they
adopted Christianity as their state religion, one of the first peoples to do so. At
various times throughout their history they have ruled their own kingdoms, while
at other times they have been subjugated by foreigners, often suffering persecution
because of their faith. Ultimately, most of their lands came under the control of
the rising Ottoman Empire, although the eastern portion came under Persian and
then Russian rule. Ottoman Armenians were concentrated primarily in Anatolia (Asia Minor), where they formed a scattered but sizeable minority, and were
closely intermingled with the Turkish population. Most were farmers, residing in
small villages, although there were also merchants, traders, artisans and members
of the professions. While this chapter often considers the Armenians collectively
as a people, it is important to acknowledge the vast diversity within this category.
The historical experiences of Armenian groups and individuals differed markedly
in different places and in different time periods, as did levels of Armenian self- and
communal identification, fluidity of identity and acculturation.[1]

Under Ottoman rule, the Armenian people were regarded as *giaours*, or infidels.
This official status, inferior to that of the Moslem population, meant Armenians
were subject to legal discrimination and occupied a position of relative powerlessness within Ottoman society—two of the features associated with an 'outgroup' at
risk of genocide. By the nineteenth century, such discrimination against the Armenian minority was entrenched, and worsening. Conditions were worst in Armenia
proper, and particularly so in rural areas. There, the special taxes and disabilities
imposed on Armenians were at their harshest, and least able to be borne by the
poor and disenfranchised villagers. Ordinary government taxes were so high that

a peasant's share of his crop was only 33 per cent.[2] In addition, Christians were subject to a capitation tax, for the right to live from year to year, and a tax in lieu of military service, imposed on all males from three months old and above. There were extraordinary additional taxes for specific temporary purposes, which often became permanent. Sometimes Christians were obliged to pay taxes in advance, but then those same taxes were demanded again at the usual time.[3] The system of 'farming of taxes' exacerbated the situation even further. In these cases, an 'official'—often a dubious character—would pay a specified fee upfront for the right to collect as much taxes as could be squeezed from the inhabitants of a particular region. These taxes rarely went towards infrastructure improvements, or even the salaries of civil administrators. Roads were poor or nonexistent in rural areas, there were very few bridges and the only railway had been built by foreign enterprise.[4] Corruption was endemic, with the absence of officials' salaries being compensated for by the collection of 'fees'.[5]

A major hardship was the inadmissibility of Christian evidence in courts of law, and the resulting lawlessness it encouraged. There were regular incidents between the Kurds and the Armenians, whereby cattle or property might be stolen, Armenians might be set upon and injured or even killed, or women subjected to rape and abduction. An example of the many cases recorded in official British documents was an 1867 report from Vice-Consul Sankey:

> In a court of justice, when a Turk is plaintiff or defendant, Christian testimony is not received . . . in the district of Toultcha . . . a Christian peasant last winter lost three horses, which horses he afterwards saw in the possession of a Musulman belonging to another village. The case came before the Cadi and Judicial Medjliss. The plaintiff was desirous to produce witnesses to prove that the horses belong to him. He offered the testimony of every man in his village, any of whom could swear to the horses. He must produce two Turks. It was in vain that he insisted that no Turks lived in his village. No Turks, no horses.[6]

The result of this law was aptly described by British consul Lloyd: 'In all crimes of violence of which the Christians have been the victims during the past year in the Province of Erzeroum no one has been punished.'[7]

Furthermore, Christians were forbidden to bear arms. As one author put it, 'The Armenian subjects of the Sultan are thus literally as defenceless as a flock of sheep surrounded by wolves.'[8] Consul Lloyd summed up the impossible predicament of the Armenians in the following official communication:

> Since the receipt of your Excellency's telegram, I have heard of the commission of several very serious crimes and outrages upon the Armenians, which shall be reported when details reach me. In a country such as this lawlessness is to be expected, but unfortunately in nearly every instance armed and ungoverned Kurds are the aggressors, and the unarmed and unprotected Armenians the victims.

Though it is well known that the Kurds live by plundering the Christians, no effort is made by the Turkish Government either to disarm them or to afford protection to the Christians, the law against the latter carrying arms or having arms being at the same time strictly enforced.[9]

Perhaps the worst of the depredations endured by the Armenians was the *Gazdalik*, or hospitality tax. This law provided that a Christian householder must give three days gratuitous hospitality to every Moslem traveller or official who requested it. Travellers could simply demand this 'hospitality' at any time, choosing the best houses, demanding to be fed and to sleep wherever they wished. It was not uncommon for wives or daughters to be raped by these travellers. In the period from January to June 1891, British consuls in Armenian regions reported on four separate incidents in which Turkish travellers, utilizing the *Gazdalik*, murdered and/ or raped their hosts. None appear to have been punished. The British consul at Erzeroum reported the following incident in January 1891:

> A band of thirty mounted police which were on the march were billeted for the night in a small Armenian village of ten houses, a few hours distant from Bitlis. Four of them were quartered in the house of a young married Armenian. Overhearing them discussing plans against his wife's honour, he secretly sent her to the house of a neighbour. When the *zaptiehs* learnt this they ordered him to send for her, and, on his refusing to do so, beat him most cruelly. He fled to a neighbour's house, but, two days later, died from the effects of the ill treatment which he had received . . . In the houses where the other *zaptiehs* were quartered their designs against the female members of the family were carried out without resistance.[10]

In comparison to the subsequent mass outbreaks of violence, however, the period up to the Russo-Turkish War of 1877–78 might be considered relatively stable and calm.[11] There was a recognized (albeit inferior) place for the Armenian minority within the multinational and multireligious empire, as a *millet*, or national community.[12] Indeed, the Armenians were often referred to by the Ottoman authorities as the 'most loyal *millet*'.[13] Moreover, while most Armenians suffered from some discrimination, those in Constantinople and other major centres were significantly advantaged compared to their provincial kin. Indeed, historians have noted that one almost cannot speak of 'the Armenians' during this period, so great was the disparity between urban and rural conditions.[14] For urban, professional Armenians, this period became a time of cultural and intellectual renaissance, and increasing prosperity. European notions of enlightenment, reform and romanticism began to reach the community, with profound effects.

The beginnings of this cultural revival can be traced to the 1700s. Foreign travellers exposed Armenia to European influence, and Europe to the Armenians. The first foreign missions in Armenia date back to about 1720, and over the following century both Roman Catholic and Protestant missions became widespread. The missions established a network of schools, which gradually spread throughout the region. By the 1850s, not only were thousands of Armenian children attending elementary school, even in the more remote areas, but secondary schools were also opened in major towns. Girls were not excluded from education, with a number of girls' boarding schools being established. By the 1880s, almost every community with one hundred or more families had a school.[15] Colleges were established in the Ottoman Empire, and Armenian students began to travel to Russia, Germany, Italy, Switzerland, France and even the United States for a university education.[16]

As the education of the Armenian population increased, so too did literature and journalism. At the Benedictine monasteries in Venice and Vienna, monks collected and translated Armenian manuscripts from classical to modern Armenian, published grammar books and dictionaries for modern Armenian, and spread Armenian culture in Europe.[17] This important work prepared the ground for novelists, poets, historians and journalists to adopt modern Armenian as the written language, it having already been the vernacular for centuries.[18] Modern Armenian literature was thus born in the nineteenth century: a rich, romantic and patriotic literature that tells of the sufferings and struggles of Armenia. The first enduring periodical, a monthly published by American missionaries, commenced publication in 1839. Some ninety periodicals began between 1840 and 1870, and the establishment of an Armenian press saw fourteen newspapers published in Constantinople between 1820 and 1866, along with others in Transcaucasia.

The increased education and exposure of Armenian youth saw the rise of an intellectual class within the Armenian community.[19] Primarily this was confined to the urban and professional milieu. In Constantinople a wealthy class of traders and bankers was able to send their sons to Europe to finish their education, while sons from other cities were sent to Constantinople. Returning home, they were struck by the backwardness and injustices. They were conscious that, while some effects of the Armenian renaissance had diffused into the villages, conditions remained very poor. They were also aware of improving conditions in Russian Armenia, where during this period there was internal stability, protection for middle-class Armenians and increasing prosperity.[20] The difficulties of the Armenians, previously accepted as fate, became a cause of growing distress and unhappiness. An embryonic nationalism began to grow.[21]

In contrast to the renaissance unfolding in Armenian communities across the Ottoman Empire was the decline of the empire itself. 'Internal strife' is widely recognized as a precondition for genocide, and aptly describes conditions in the nineteenth-century Ottoman Empire. The Ottoman government's administrative, financial and military structure struggled under the weight of both internal corruption and external pressures.[22] The empire was unable to compete with the growing capitalistic system in Europe and, as a multinational empire with a religious foundation, it was at odds with the new concept of nationalism.[23] Europe had long been interfering in Ottoman internal affairs, and a system of 'capitulations'—that is, a series of legal and commercial privileges governing relations with foreign nations—was firmly in place.[24] The empire's troubles only worsened as the nineteenth century wore on. In 1821 Greece declared independence. Other national minorities were agitating for a similar future. It became clear that the empire would eventually break up, but the competing powers in Europe made efforts to preserve it as a weak buffer state, which was in their own immediate interests.[25] Britain, in particular, believed the empire could be maintained through administrative reform. Several major reform edicts were issued, and other commitments were made via treaty obligations, and in response to European threats of intervention. The reality of the reform era, however, was one of increasing administrative corruption, exploitation of the populace and 'virtually no improvement in the daily life of the common person'.[26] The oppressive tutelage of the European powers increased still further when the Ottoman Empire, long in financial ruin, went bankrupt in 1876. In the same year, Sultan Abdul Hamid II took the throne in a palace revolution.

As part of the overall reforms, in 1829, 1839 and 1856 sultans had all committed themselves to reforms for the Christian subjects in the empire. Conditions had not improved. In fact, according to authors Chaliand and Ternon:

> Every proposal for reform strengthened Muslim solidarity and the demands of ambassadors and consuls had the effect of exacerbating the hostility of provincial administrators and the Kurds towards the Armenians without in any way modifying the unchanging relations between Turks and *gyaurs*.[27]

These external pressures focussing upon relations between the Moslem majority and Armenian minority within the empire were accompanied by increasing internal movement in the same direction. As the Armenian minority found its own voice of protest during the Armenian renaissance, relations between the groups were increasingly politicized. The rising levels of prosperity, education and culture experienced by the Armenians stood in contrast to the deteriorating conditions experienced by many other inhabitants of the empire, and became a source of resentment.[28] Through their progress, the Armenians themselves unwittingly contributed to the increasing antipathy of the general population towards them during this period. The deteriorating conditions in the empire also contributed to increased levels of intolerance and exploitation of the Armenians.

This period of the nineteenth century was a particularly significant one for the development of early risk factors for genocide. The Armenians could already be regarded as an 'outgroup' in many respects, being a relatively powerless minority subject to legal discrimination. As the century progressed, however, cleavages between Ottoman government and society and the Armenian community deepened. Relations between the dominant group and the Armenian minority became increasingly politicized, and all three components indicative of an outgroup at risk of genocide—legal discrimination, relative powerlessness and politicized intergroup relations—are clearly present together for the first time. At the same time, the empire struggled through significant internal strife that threatened its financial, geographic and political integrity. The presence of these two risk factors for genocide contributed to deteriorating conditions for some Armenians—particularly those in rural areas—and an increased level of vulnerability. These were long-term processes, developing over decades. Whilst an historical perspective enables us to infer a process of destabilization, there was no rapid escalation of violence or abrupt change in circumstance. These two factors are present as broad, predisposing preconditions. It took further events to dramatically change the Armenians' risk profile for genocide—events that were just about to unfold.

The Impact of the Treaty of Berlin

In 1877, following the Turkish massacres in Bulgaria, Russia declared war on the Ottoman Empire, achieving victory within a year. In defeat, the *Sublime Porte* (Ottoman government) had little choice but to accept the Treaty of San Stefano. Bulgaria and Macedonia were created, while Serbia, Romania and Montenegro gained complete independence. Russia also kept some territory. Article 16 of the Treaty of San Stefano made the following provision for the introduction of reforms in Armenia:

> As the evacuation by the Russian troops of the territory which they occupy in Armenia, and which is to be restored to Turkey, might give rise to conflicts and complications detrimental to the maintenance of good relations between the two countries, the Sublime Porte undertakes to carry into effect, without further delay, the improvements and reforms demanded by local requirements in the provinces inhabited by the Armenians, and to guarantee their security from Kurds and Circassians.[29]

However, pro-Turkish British prime minister Benjamin Disraeli successfully pressured for the treaty to be submitted to a European congress.[30] The result was the Treaty of Berlin, signed in 1878. While substantially similar to the Treaty of San Stefano, the promises of Article 16 were replaced by much weaker statements. No longer would the evacuation of the Russian troops be made conditional upon implementation of reforms for the Armenian people. Article 16 of the original agreement was replaced by Article 61 of the Treaty of Berlin:

> The Sublime Porte undertakes to carry out, without further delay, the improvements and reforms demanded by local requirements in the provinces inhabited by the Armenians, to guarantee their security against the Circassians and Kurds. It will periodically make known the steps taken to this effect to the Powers, who will superintend their application.[31]

Article 62 is also of great importance, although often overlooked by historians. This article concerns religious liberty for all Ottoman subjects, and reads in part:

In no part of the Ottoman Empire shall difference of religion be alleged against any person as a ground for exclusion or incapacity as regards the discharge of civil and political rights, admission to the public employments, function, and honours, or the exercize of the various professions and industries. All persons shall be admitted, without distinction of religion, to give evidence before the tribunals.[32]

The period in the immediate aftermath of the signing of the Treaty of Berlin can clearly be identified as one of dramatic risk escalation for the Armenian minority within the empire. As Viscount James Bryce, coeditor of the seminal British blue book *The Treatment of the Armenians in the Ottoman Empire*, commented:

> Before the Treaty of Berlin the Sultan had no special enmity to the Armenians, nor had the Armenian nation any political aspirations. It was the stipulations then made for their protection that first marked them out for suspicion and hatred, and that first roused in them hopes of deliverance whose expression increased the hatred of their rulers.[33]

Indeed, it is perhaps here that a fundamental turning point was reached, and the path towards massacre, and eventual genocide, became substantially more likely. A number of keen observers of the situation expressed such concerns. British consul Sir Layard commented as early as 1879 that '[u]nless the *Porte* takes care, and acts with prudence and forethought, there will some day be an Armenian question in Asia, similar to the Bulgarian question in Europe, from which the last war arose'.[34] French ambassador Paul Cambon also traced the beginning of the Armenian question, and Armenian desires for autonomy, to this period.[35] Cambon believed that, in the aftermath of the Treaty of Berlin, Turkey was actively antagonizing the Armenian population, and not just passively inept.[36]

Rolin-Jaequemyns, president of the Belgian Institute of International Law and keen observer of Ottoman affairs, expressed a more extreme view. In articles published in the Belgian *International Law Review* in the 1880s (that is, well before the 1894–96 massacres), Rolin-Jaequemyns all but accused the Ottoman government of genocide.[37] The basis for his accusation was twofold. First, he discussed the Turkish response to the huge immigration of Circassians into Ottoman territory following the Russo-Turkish war. Between 1878 and 1880, tens of thousands of immigrants poured into the Armenian districts. While some certainly migrated of their own volition, there is evidence that the Turkish government both enticed and compelled many thousands to come.[38] Yet it made almost no provisions for their survival (despite extensive promises to the contrary), and forbade both the immigrants and resident Armenians from leaving the districts, despite deplorable conditions.[39] The immigrants, allowed to bear arms, preyed on the Armenians for their survival. Rolin-Jaequemyns concluded that:

> it could not but be foreseen that this . . . body of immigrants, arriving quite unprovided with the necessaries of life in a country where no preparation had been made

to receive them, would obey no other law but that of self-preservation, and that in order to live they would rob and kill wherever they had the chance.[40]

He further opined: 'How can the conviction be resisted that . . . the consequences [of the immigration were] singularly aggravated, by the negligence, the unwilling-ness . . . of the Turkish authorities.'[41] Another observer, the Reverend Ohan Gaid-zakian, went even further, stating that the sultan intended for such consequences to occur, and had a 'deliberate policy of extermination'.[42]

The second premise of Rolin-Jaequemyns' accusation concerns the famine of 1879–80 that ravished Asia Minor. While in Constantinople and London private relief committees were formed to raise aid money, the response of the Turkish government was to demand three years' arrears of taxes from the districts most affected by the war.[43] Taxes were demanded on sheep stolen by the Kurds or that had perished due to the lack of fodder, and in one district the government even tried to demand taxes in advance.[44] The British vice-consul at Erzeroum reported:

> Half ruined by the war, and lately reduced to beggary and starvation by the failure of the crops, the unfortunate people have nevertheless been inexorably pursued by the taxgatherers, and imprisoned by the authorities when unable to pay, and this not-withstanding that the Government owed many of these same people considerable sums of money for supplies furnished during the war.[45]

Furthermore, local authorities in some places refused to release government stores of wheat, even when offered 'almost unheard-of' prices for it.[46] In other loca-tions authorities sold the wheat at exorbitant rates, pocketing the profits.[47] Rolin-Jaequemyns contended:

> If these proceedings are considered in conjunction with the encouragement given to the disastrous invasion of the Circassian immigrants, the singular toleration shown to Kurdish brigandage, is not the conclusion irresistible that there is something more at work than stupidity or administrative greed? Do they not once more suggest the idea of a settled plan to slowly exterminate the Christian element for the sake of the Moslem?[48]

While it can be difficult to gauge the extent to which the central government was involved versus the extent of depredation imposed by corrupt local authorities, evidence such as the central government's choice to demand taxes from these dis-tricts, and of consular communications to the *Porte* containing detailed reports of the state of affairs in various districts (which did not serve to bring about change), suggests at the very least considerable complicity at the highest levels of the Otto-man government.

If the Ottoman government was willing to allow the Armenians to be deci-mated through lawlessness and famine in the 1878–80 period, it must be ques-tioned why there was no outbreak of massacres at this juncture. In fact, there were several powerful restraints against such a course of action. First, the sultan was new and inexperienced. The empire had just been defeated in war and lost considerable territory, and was not at all in a position of strength. Furthermore, the war had been precipitated by the Bulgarian massacres—and the spectre of further European intervention in the event of Armenian massacres loomed large. Both the Circassian immigration and the famine in Asia Minor, however, were relatively easy to present as being beyond governmental control. In reality, human malevolence is always involved in famine, and the consequences of famine can be functionally equivalent to those of genocide.[49] Arguably, the actions of the sultan during this period were about as aggressive as possible without attracting further undesirable attention from Europe.

What then, in the Treaty of Berlin or the processes surrounding it, provoked such a major change in the Ottoman government's attitude towards its Armenian population to lead to such aggression? Moreover, how can these events be located within the context of the development of risk of genocide? The answer, it seems, lies in the role of the Treaty of Berlin in triggering—for the first time—a perception within the *Sublime Porte* that the Armenian minority posed a serious existential threat to the integrity of the empire. To understand how the Treaty of Berlin was interpreted by the Ottoman government in this way, however, requires an understanding of the religious basis of the Ottoman Empire.

The Ottoman Empire was ruled from a religious, Islamic foundation. Islam, as it was interpreted at the time, had little tolerance for non-Moslems. An official Islamic prayer used throughout Turkey in this period can be translated as:

> I seek refuge with Allah from Satan, the accursed. In the name of Allah the Compassionate, the Merciful! O Lord of all Creatures! O Allah! Destroy the infidels and polytheists, thine enemies, the enemies of the religion! O Allah! Make their children orphans, and defile their abodes! Cause their feet to slip; give them and their families, their households and their women, their children and their relations by marriage, their brothers and their friends, their possessions and their race, their wealth and their lands, as booty to the Moslems, O Lord of all Creatures![50]

This is just one of a number of inflammatory religious passages in use during this period.[51] Non-Moslems in the Ottoman Empire were infidels, subject to the rule and the mercy of Moslem society. There was a place for non-Moslems under the *millet* system, but it was a clearly inferior position. Turkish Moslems had long been taught to look down on Christians.

From an outsider's perspective, attempting to understand hatred, and particularly the massive intergroup hatred that leads to massacres and genocide, can be challenging. Nevertheless, there are some facets of Ottoman society that can provide insight into how so many Armenians ultimately became the targets of such loathing. The pluralist Islamic model that was the foundation of Ottoman society, and the resulting Moslem outlook upon relations with non-Moslem inhabitants, was a crucial aspect of this process. From the Islamic perspective of the time, Christians were to be endured and tolerated, their presence accepted 'so long as they accept the authority and superiority of Muslims and the Islamic order'.[52] The very basis of the plural society, therefore, was built around a Moslem concept of their superiority over the *giaour*.[53] The reforms of the nineteenth century—directly challenging this core belief regarding Moslem-Christian relations—were particularly conducive to provoking antipathy and resentment. Innate opposition was magnified by a propaganda campaign by Moslem leaders in the 1850s, 'pointing to the erosion of religion and the decline of the state, which was due to the influence of Christian customs'.[54] The primacy of religion as an identifier during this period must also be considered.[55] For example, while the common attitude of most Turks and Kurds towards Armenians during this period might seem surprising from a contemporary perspective, it was religious rather than national identity that was predominant. Thus, while anti-Armenian sentiment ebbed and peaked due to specific factors across the period under consideration, the role of these long-standing, core beliefs in facilitating the mass hatred that ultimately led to the genocide cannot be underestimated.

The accepted position of the Armenians as a *millet* within the Ottoman Empire became increasingly precarious during the second half of the nineteenth century. There was a growing perception that the Armenians had violated their place in society in multiple ways and therefore no longer had the right to live and have property under this system.[56] From a Turkish perspective, the Armenian renaissance, increase in prosperity, higher education levels and Armenian business and financial acumen conflicted with their status as *giaours*. As the Armenians flourished despite their hardships, the *millet* system served to provide a legitimate religious framework for the resentment and jealousy this created.[57] This was particularly so following Sultan Abdul Hamid II's ascension to the throne. The sultan's focus upon reinvigorating Islam within Ottoman society brought to the fore the paradigm of Moslem superiority and the infidel status of the Armenians.[58] Accordingly, Robert Melson has commented upon the conservative ideology of the sultan as a most important predisposing and magnifying factor for the 1894–96 massacres.[59]

The Armenians were seen to have further acted outside their correct place as a *millet* through their perceived disloyalty in appealing to Europe for international intervention to improve their conditions of life in the empire. The reforms demanded by the Treaty of Berlin, however, stretched beyond any capacity of the Islamic system to accommodate the changing circumstances. Article 62 called for the civic equality of the Christian Armenians. This was a demand that violated a fundamental tenant of Islam as it was interpreted at the time.[60] According to Greene, from the Turkish standpoint, the civil equality of Christian and Moslem 'would imperil the foundation of the State'.[61] The two conflicting paradigms could not coexist peaceably, and, as Melson put it so aptly, 'something had to give'.[62] That is, the Armenian minority, through the Treaty of Berlin, now came to be closely associated with a perceived existential threat to the empire. This treaty irrevocably changed the context of Armeno-Turkish relations, resulting in an increasingly destructive sequence of events.

There were three further profound effects of the Treaty of Berlin. Each was unintended; each also ultimately exacerbated the tensions between the Ottoman government and the Armenian people. The first of these was the treaty's effect on Armenian expectations of their circumstances. The magnitude of this impact can be seen from the following excerpt of a speech given by the Armenian patriarch (religious leader) Nercès in response to the treaty:

> Let all those unfortunate people whom misery has driven from their firesides return; famine, pestilence, and oppression are going to cease in Armenia; no longer will life, property, and honour be outraged there. Henceforth Armenia will have her roads and canals; mills will spring up; English capital will seek investment there; let our capitalists go there also, and commence to work together from to-day. Let us combine to establish schools in every town and every village; let us unite and extend our commerce and develop our industry; let all the Armenians in India, Armenia, England, Turkey and Russia, Austria and Persia, join hands and unite in this work of progress.[63]

The impact of the treaty on the Armenian psyche can hardly be overestimated. Wrote one traveller concerning Article 61 of the treaty: 'Many a time has that precious paragraph been quoted to me in the wilds of Kurdistan by common Armenian artisans and ignorant villagers. They had welcomed it as a second evangel, and believed the word of England as they did the Gospel.'[64]

The Armenian renaissance, the nationalist awakening throughout Europe and increased Armenian exposure to outside influences led to a new collective self-consciousness developing amongst Armenians during the second half of the nineteenth century.[65] The Treaty of Berlin substantially increased Armenian expectations—and when these expectations were met with only worsening conditions, at least some Armenians were no longer willing to quietly endure their ongoing oppression. In the wake of the Treaty of Berlin, a number of Armenian fraternal organizations and secret societies began to evolve into revolutionary political parties. In 1885 the Armenakan party was founded in Van, with the aim of 'gain[ing] for Armenians, by revolution, the right to govern themselves'.[66] The Hunchak party was founded in 1887, with a socialist and nationalist platform. The Dashnaktsutiun, or Armenian Revolutionary Federation, emerged in Russia in 1890, with a less prominently socialist bent. It stressed civil and political rights, and expressed a willingness to remain within the Ottoman Empire if granted communal autonomy.[67] These parties were heavily influenced by Armenians in Europe and Russia. While they gained some supporters within the Ottoman Empire, particularly amongst the educated classes, there was much opposition to them among wealthy and influential Armenians, and they were not popular amongst the rural Armenians.

There is considerable discussion in the literature surrounding the Armenian revolutionary movement. The primary reason for this is the 'provocation thesis', whereby the Armenian massacres of 1894–96 are discounted and the events are described as a justifiable response to Armenian insurrection. First put forth by the sultan in a letter to the British ambassador following the massacres in Sassoun, this thesis has been adopted in various guises by revisionist historians and expanded to encompass the Armenian genocide as well. There is little credence to such claims. The available evidence indicates that the influence of the Armenian revolutionary parties was limited in the period before the massacres.[68] They were newly formed, and a few protests notwithstanding, they did not constitute a serious threat to the Ottoman Empire. Melson has suggested, however, that the reality of the threat posed by these groups may be less important than the level of threat that Sultan Abdul Hamid II perceived in them. It was clear that the sultan linked the Armenian agitations to the earlier Bulgarian disturbances—which with British assistance had led to the creation of autonomous Bulgarian provinces.[69] Perhaps, Melson has suggested, from the vantage point of the *Porte* and given the context of the times, these parties were credibly perceived to represent an 'intolerable danger'.[70] Bloxham, too, has commented regarding the nationalist parties that 'their very existence intensified Abdülhamid's paranoia of imperial collapse'.[71]

Other historians and observers have taken a more cynical approach. Yves Ternon has argued that 'here again the Ottoman government had the role of exploiter: it used the revolutionary movement to achieve its own ends'.[72] Ternon has argued that the Ottoman government knew the risks presented by the Armenians were negligible, and schemed to drive the Armenians to revolt through excesses of oppression.[73] 'Justified in the eyes of the world by the duty of any government to re-establish order, the authorities were [then] free to use the excuse of this revolution to crush an entire race of people.'[74] Indeed, both the French and British ambassadors at the time of the massacres commented on the Ottoman government's oppression of the Armenians as seemingly driving them towards sedition.[75] One consul remarked upon 'the efforts of the Turkish authorities, at times frantic efforts, to discover sedition among the Armenians'.[76] Another observer, an American travelling through the region in the wake of the massacres, commented wryly:

> When I say that the Armenian massacres were caused by the Armenian revolutionists, I tell a truth, and a very important truth, but it is not the whole truth. It would be more correct to say that the presence of the revolutionists gave occasion and excuse for the massacres. That the Turks were looking for an occasion and an excuse, no one can doubt who has traversed that country.[77]

The Armenian revolutionary movement, despite the conjecture, was not a significant threat to the empire, but rather was utilized as a convenient excuse through which to attempt to justify the massacres. Whatever threat there was of possible future Armenian claims for autonomy, or of future intercessions by the Great Powers on behalf of the Armenians, it had little to do with the nascent Armenian revolutionary movement.

The second major but unintended effect of the Treaty of Berlin was a considerable hardening of attitudes towards the Armenians at the official level.[78] It rapidly became clear that the Ottoman government did not intend to implement Articles 61 or 62 of the Treaty of Berlin. Its only action in the year after the treaty was signed was that of dispatching a 'Commission of Enquiry' into the district of Erzeroum, with a view to identifying the difficulties there and preparing a plan of reforms.[79] According to one observer, however, this was more a tactic of the *Porte* to gain time rather than a genuine response.[80] Rather than the raft of improvements promised, the reality for Armenians was a steady deterioration in conditions. Civil restraints against the population increased. Armenian officers were gradually removed from their positions.[81] Some Armenian schools and churches were ordered closed on trifling grounds, requests to repair others were denied, and it became very difficult to gain permission to establish a new church or school.[82] Religious and educational leaders and other prominent community figures were imprisoned without justification, and sometimes tortured.[83] School textbooks and programs were closely examined, and many were declared seditious and prohibited.[84] Correspondence became increasingly difficult, and in some areas impossible.[85] Travel also became difficult, and was forbidden in some places. Armenians who possessed official passports for Turkish cities such as Constantinople or Smyrna found themselves arrested along the way, and either imprisoned or sent back to their hometown.[86] Furthermore, in 1891 regulations were changed such that Christians wishing to travel had to obtain certificates from the Moslem chiefs of their district before even being issued with a passport.[87] Emigration to foreign countries was very difficult, and forbidden in some cases.[88] Nevertheless, many Armenians accepted great risk and substantial loss of property and wealth to emigrate out of the provinces at this time.[89]

As rapidly as it became clear that the *Sublime Porte* did not intend to implement the Armenian reforms within the Treaty of Berlin, it became equally apparent that the European powers did not have the political will to enforce them. In 1879, the British ambassador wrote confidentially to an embassy official: 'Her Majesty's Government by no means intends under present circumstances to press the *Porte* to apply to their full extent the reforms which the latter has promised to make in the administration of the Asiatic provinces of Turkey.'[90] Admittedly, this statement was followed by caveats that the obligations could not be forgotten, and that the reforms should at least be commenced.[91] Yet coming only eleven months after the signing of the treaty, this statement is surprising. Nevertheless, in the public domain protocol was followed, with various communications between the Great Powers and the Ottoman government, to little effect. In September 1880, the six powers sent a 'Collective Note' to the Ottoman government, discussing at some length its failure to act and stating:

> It is absolutely necessary to carry out, without loss of time, the reforms intended to secure the life and property of the Armenians; to take immediate measures against the incursions of the Kurds; to carry out at once the proposed system of finance; to place the Gendarmerie provisionally on a more satisfactory footing; and, above all, to give to the Governors-General greater security of office and a more extended responsibility.[92]

They received only an evasive reply from the sultan. A further attempt by the British in early 1881 to initiate joint action on this matter was unable to gain the unanimous support required.[93] The issue essentially dropped off the international agenda; Britain's response was simply to suspend the publication of diplomatic information on Armenian affairs. Thus, this third outcome of the Treaty of Berlin took some time to become fully apparent, but perhaps proved most dangerous of all for the Armenians. Not only did the European powers fail to enforce Articles 61 and 62, but as conditions continued to deteriorate for the Armenians, they would remain unwilling to intervene.

To summarize, therefore, the Treaty of Berlin can be regarded as a key event in Ottoman Armenian history. The treaty triggered a perception of the Armenian minority as posing an existential threat to the Ottoman Empire—a perception that left the Armenians at dramatically increased risk of being targeted as a vulnerable minority. In the immediate aftermath of the treaty, this led to the Ottoman government's callous disregard of the impact on Armenians of the massive Circassian immigration into Armenian districts. Similarly, the government made no attempt to ameliorate the effects of the famine in Asia Minor in 1879–80. Yet there was no immediate outbreak of massacres in the wake of the Treaty of Berlin. Rather, subsequent events were determined by the influence of local precipitants and constraints. This was because the threat of European intervention served initially as a highly effective constraint. Over time, however, the effect of this constraint weakened, as it became increasingly clear that the European powers did not have the political will to intercede on behalf of the Armenians. At the same time, the ongoing perception of the Armenian minority as posing an existential threat to the integrity of the empire served as a constant driver of escalation. Indeed, more than one scholar has asserted a belief that the sultan began planning for an Armenian massacre immediately following the Turko-Russian war.[94] This was further exacerbated as Sultan Abdul Hamid II's conservative religious ideology diffused through the empire, reinforcing a legitimizing context for massacre. By the late 1880s, the balance between precipitants and constraints that had previously impeded any further escalation had significantly changed. By 1894, it would take only a string of the most minor precipitating incidents to trigger the first massacre in Sassoun.

Notes

1. U.U. Ungör. 2012. *The Making of Modern Turkey: Nation and State in Eastern Anatolia, 1913–1950*, Oxford: Oxford University Press, 51.
2. 1860. *Consular Reports*, 55, in M. MacColl. 1895. *England's Responsibility Towards Armenia*, London: Longmans, Green, 8.
3. Ibid.
4. O. Gaidzakian. 1898. *Illustrated Armenia and the Armenians*, Boston: n.p., 191; M.G. Rolin-Jaequemyns. 1891. *Armenia, The Armenians, and the Treaties*, London: John Heywood, 81–82.
5. Gaidzakian, *Illustrated Armenia*, 190.
6. 1867. *Reports from Her Majesty's Consuls relating to the Condition of Christians in Turkey*, 4, in MacColl, *England's Responsibility*, 9.
7. 1890–91. *Turkey*, no. 1, 81, in MacColl, *England's Responsibility*, 11.
8. Ibid., 12.
9. 1890–91. *Turkey*, no. 1, 35, 40, in MacColl, *England's Responsibility*, 13.
10. 1892. *Turkey*, no. 1, 9, in MacColl, *England's Responsibility*, 17–18.
11. T. Akçam. 2007. *A Shameful Act: The Armenian Genocide and the Question of Turkish Responsibility*, London: Constable, 3–4; R. Hovannisian. 1986. 'The Historical Dimensions of the Armenian Question, 1878–1923', in R. Hovannisian (ed.), *The Armenian Genocide in Perspective*, New Brunswick, NJ: Transaction Publishers, 20.
12. D. Lang. 1981. *The Armenians: A People in Exile*, London: George, Allen and Unwin, 2; Akçam, *A Shameful Act*, 7–9.
13. N. Naimark. 2001. *Fires of Hatred: Ethnic Cleansing in Twentieth-Century Europe*, Cambridge, MA: Harvard University Press, 19.
14. D. Bloxham. 2005. *The Great Game of Genocide: Imperialism, Nationalism, and the Destruction of the Ottoman Armenians*, Oxford: Oxford University Press, 44.
15. A.E. Redgate. 1998. *The Armenians*, Oxford: Blackwell Publishers, 268.
16. Hovannisian, 'The Historical Dimensions', 21.
17. G. Chaliand and Y. Ternon. 1983. *The Armenians: From Genocide to Resistance*, London: Zed Press, 26.
18. Ibid.
19. Redgate, *The Armenians*, 268.
20. Bloxham, *The Great Game*, 44; J. Missakian. 1950. *A Searchlight on the Armenian Question, 1878–1950*, Boston: Hairenik, 3.
21. Bloxham, *The Great Game*, 16.
22. Akçam, *A Shameful Act*, 10.
23. Hovannisian, 'The Historical Dimensions', 20.
24. Akçam, *A Shameful Act*, 10.
25. Ibid., 21; Chaliand and Ternon, *The Armenians*, 24.
26. Hovannisian, 'The Historical Dimensions', 21.
27. Chaliand and Ternon, *The Armenians*, 24–25.
28. Bloxham, *The Great Game*, 41.
29. Missakian, *A Searchlight*, 8.
30. Ibid., 8.
31. Ibid., 10.
32. Rolin-Jaequemyns, *Armenia*, 39.
33. J. Bryce. 1896. *Transcaucasia and Ararat: Being Notes of a Vacation Tour in the Autumn of 1876*, rev. 4th ed., London: Macmillan, 523.

34. 1879. 'Dispatch from Sir A. H. Layard to the Marquis of Salisbury', 12 June, *Blue-Book*, Turkey, no. 10, 93, in Rolin-Jaequemyns, *Armenia*, 52.

35. France, Ministère des Affaires Étrangères. 1897. *Documents diplomatiques: Affaires arméniennes: Projets de réformes dans l'empire ottoman, 1893–1897*, Paris: Imprimerie Nationale, 10–13; V. Dadrian. 1989. 'Genocide as a Problem of National and International Law: The World War I Armenian Case and Its Contemporary Legal Ramifications', *The Yale Journal of International Law* 14(2), 251–52.

36. Ibid.

37. Rolin-Jaequemyns, *Armenia*, 70. Of course, the term 'genocide' was not yet invented; however, Rolin-Jaequemyns accused the Ottoman government of 'a settled plan to slowly exterminate the Christian element for the sake of the Moslem'.

38. Ibid., 62–65; Gaidzakian, *Illustrated Armenia*, 205.

39. Rolin-Jaequemyns, *Armenia*, 62–65.

40. Ibid., 64.

41. Ibid.

42. Gaidzakian, *Illustrated Armenia*, 205; see also B. Papazian. 1918. *The Tragedy of Armenia: A Brief Study and Interpretation*, Boston: Pilgrim Press, 72–73. Papazian stated: 'Once the Russian forces were withdrawn, the Sultan, as might have been expected, immediately began to inaugurate a policy of reprisals which had for its aim nothing less than the total impoverishment and final extermination of the Armenian population.'

43. Rolin-Jaequemyns, *Armenia*, 69.

44. Ibid., 67, 69.

45. 1880. Report sent from Erzeroum on 23 September by Vice-Consul Everett. *Blue-Book*, no. 6 (1881), 185, in Rolin-Jaequemyns, *Armenia*, 66.

46. 1879. Note sent to the Porte by British ambassador Sir A.H. Layard, 23 December. *Blue-Book*, Turkey, no. 23 (1880), 15, in Rolin-Jaequemyns, *Armenia*, 70.

47. 1880. Report sent from Erzeroum on 23 September by Vice-Consul Everett. *Blue-Book*, no. 6 (1881), 185, in Rolin-Jaequemyns, *Armenia*, 66; see also Rolin-Jaequemyns, *Armenia*, 71.

48. Rolin-Jaequemyns, *Armenia*, 70.

49. D. Marcus. 2003. 'Famine Crimes in International Law', *American Journal of International Law* 97(2), 248, 250–51.

50. F. Greene. 1896. *Armenian Massacres or The Sword of Mohammed*, n.p.: American Oxford, 434.

51. S. Bey. 1898. *Islam, Turkey and Armenia and How They Happened*, St. Louis: C.B. Woodward, preface; Gaidzakian, *Illustrated Armenia*, 183.

52. Akçam, *A Shameful Act*, 7.

53. R. Davison. 1954. 'Turkish Attitudes Concerning Christian-Muslim Equality in the Nineteenth Century', *The American Historical Review* 59(4), 855.

54. Akçam, *A Shameful Act*, 18.

55. Davison, 'Turkish Attitudes', 844.

56. Bryce, *Transcaucasia and Ararat*, 505; Akçam, *A Shameful Act*, 9.

57. Akçam, *A Shameful Act*, 9.

58. M.S. Anderson. 1966. *The Eastern Question 1774–1923: A Study in International Relations*, London: Macmillan, 223.

59. R. Melson. 1992. *Revolution and Genocide: On the Origins of the Armenian Genocide and the Holocaust*, Chicago: University of Chicago Press, 63.

60. Ibid., 65; Bryce, *Transcaucasia and Ararat*, 458.

61. Greene, *Armenian Massacres*, 435.

62. Melson, *Revolution and Genocide*, 65.

63. 1878. *Discours prononcé par la Sainteté Nercès, Patriarche arménien, à la séance du 21 Juillet/2 Août, 1878, de l'Assemblée des représentants*, Aramian, Constantinople, 19–20, quoted in Rolin-Jaequemyns, *Armenia*, 40.

64. Gaidzakian, *Illustrated Armenia*, 209.
65. H. Fein. 1978. 'A Formula for Genocide: Comparison of the Turkish Genocide (1915) and the German Holocaust (1939–1945)', *Comparative Studies in Sociology* 1, 276.
66. Y. Ternon. 1981. *The Armenians: History of a Genocide*, Delmar, NY: Caravan Books, 75.
67. Fein, 'A Formula for Genocide', 277.
68. Melson, *Revolution and Genocide*, 50.
69. 1894. Great Britain, House of Commons, *Correspondence Relating to the Asiatic Provinces of Turkey*, Sessional Papers, c. 7894, inclosure 1 in no. 35, 4 November, in Melson, *Revolution and Genocide*, 59.
70. Melson, *Revolution and Genocide*, 64.
71. Bloxham, *The Great Game*, 16.
72. Ternon, *The Armenians*, 83.
73. Ibid.
74. Ibid.
75. Ibid., 83; 1894. Doc. No. 6, M.P. Cambon, French Ambassador at Constantinople, to M. Casimir-Perier, Cabinet Minister, Ministry of Foreign Affairs, 20 February, in France, Ministère des Affaires Étrangères, *Documents diplomatiques*, 10–11.
76. 1895. Turkey, no. 3, 10, quoted in G. Douglas. 1896. *Our Responsibilities for Turkey—Facts and Memoirs of Forty Years*, London: John Murray, 128, reprinted in V. Ghazarian (ed.). 1997. *Armenians in the Ottoman Empire: An Anthology of Transformation 13th-19th Centuries*, Waltham, MA: Mayreni Publishing, 657.
77. G. Hepworth. 1898. *Through Armenia on Horseback*, New York: E.P. Dutton, 339.
78. J. Pierce (ed.). 1896. *Story of Turkey and Armenia: With a Full and Accurate Account of the Recent Massacres written by Eye Witnesses*, Baltimore: R.H. Woodward, 447.
79. Rolin-Jaequemyns, *Armenia*, 51.
80. Ibid.
81. Bey, *Islam, Turkey and Armenia*, 189.
82. Ibid.; E. Pears. 1911. *Turkey and Its People*, London: Methuen, 277.
83. MacColl, *England's Responsibility*, 35; Bey, *Islam, Turkey and Armenia*, 189.
84. Bey, *Islam, Turkey and Armenia*, 189; Pears, *Turkey*, 277; Greene, *Armenian Massacres*, 181–82.
85. 1891. 'Inclosure 3 in No. 18, Acting Consul Hampson to Sir W. White', Erzeroum, 4 April, F.O. 424/169, nos. 42–43, in B. Simsir (ed.). 1990. *British Documents on Ottoman Armenians*, vol. 3, Ankara: Turk Tarih Kurumu Printing Office, 35.
86. Bey, *Islam, Turkey and Armenia*, 190.
87. 1891. 'Inclosure in No. 27, Acting Consul Hampson to Sir W. White', Erzeroum, 2 May, in Simsir, *British Documents*, 63.
88. 1891. 'Inclosure in No. 24, Acting Consul Hampson to Sir W. White', Erzeroum, 2 May, in Simsir, *British Documents*, 59; Bey, *Islam, Turkey and Armenia*, 90.
89. 1891. 'Inclosure in No. 24, Acting Consul Hampson to Sir W. White', Erzeroum, 2 May, in Simsir, *British Documents*, 59.
90. 1879. Communication from British ambassador at Constantinople to Sir A. Sandison (Oriental secretary to the British Embassy at Constantinople). *Blue-Book*, Turkey, no. 10, 94, in Rolin-Jaequemyns, *Armenia*, 53.
91. Ibid.
92. 1880. 'Collective Note', 7 September, sent to the Sublime Porte by Ambassadors Hatzfeldt, Novikow, Goschen, Corti, Tissot and Calice, reprinted in Rolin-Jaequemyns, *Armenia*, 93.
93. Rolin-Jaequemyns, *Armenia*, 97–100.
94. Gaidzakian, *Illustrated Armenia*, 205; J. Bryce and A. Toynbee. 2000. *The Treatment of Armenians in the Ottoman Empire, 1915–1916*, uncensored ed., edited and with an introduction by Ara Sarafian, Princeton, NJ: Gomidas Institute, 634 (originally published 1916).

Chapter 2

'A SETTLED PLAN TO SLOWLY EXTERMINATE'
The Hamidian Massacres

> People were crowded into houses which were then set on fire. In
> one instance a little boy ran out of the flames, but was caught on a
> bayonet and thrown back. Children were frequently held up by the
> hair and cut in two, or had their jaws torn apart. Older children
> were pulled apart by their legs.[1]

The above description, penned by a missionary who witnessed the Hamidian massacres, is horrific. It was spring 1894 in the Armenian region of Sassoun, and
the events formed part of the first of a series of massacres that claimed well over
one hundred thousand lives during the following two years.[2] While these massacres have been largely overshadowed by the subsequent 1915 genocide and have
received relatively little scholarly attention, they provide an opportunity to understand the dynamics of hatred and violence that characterized Armeno-Turkish
relations during this period. Examining the massacres and the events that triggered
them provides insight into the increasing vulnerability of the Armenian minority
in the late nineteenth century. Even decades prior to the 1915 genocide, this can
clearly be identified as a community at grave risk.

The Hamidian Massacres

There is evidence of the sultan and the *Sublime Porte* making concrete preparations
for massacre as early as 1890.[3] At this time, Kurdish attacks upon Armenians
increased in both number and ferocity.[4] Furthermore, the Kurdish perpetrators
openly declared that their actions had the approval of the Ottoman government.[5]

The targeted nature of these attacks was clear, as related by the British consul at Erzeroum:

> I regret to state the Armenian peasantry in the Passen Plain and the Valley of Alash-gird have suffered severely from the attacks of the neighbouring Kurds. I believe that every Christian village in the Passen Plain has been plundered . . . the Musulman villages are reported to have been exempt from the visits of these robbers.[6]

Counsel Lloyd, speaking of the Turkish response to these events, went on to remark: 'There is a want of foresight and earnestness displayed in all matters connected with the protection of the Christian people which is difficult to reasonably account for.'[7]

Despite the numerous and continued complaints regarding Kurdish attacks on Armenians, many from official diplomatic sources, in 1891 Kurdish horseback riders, long known for living on the edge of the law, were organized into irregular cavalry regiments that became known as the *Hamidieh* regiments. Resistance to the Kurds became rebellion against the sultan. Consul Lloyd described the response to this measure in Erzeroum:

> This measure of arming the Kurds is regarded with great anxiety here. This feeling is much increased by the conduct of the Kurds themselves, many of whom openly state that they have been appointed to suppress the Armenians, and that they have received assurances that they will not be called to answer before the Tribunals for any acts of oppression committed against Christians.[8]

Indeed, as early as May 1891, the situation was so severe that British acting consul Hampson reported that '[a] very small spark is all that is necessary to put the whole place in a blaze'.[9]

By the spring of 1894 it is fair to say that the villagers of Sassoun were expecting trouble. There had been a number of skirmishes with bands of Kurds the previous year, and they had refused to give up an activist to the authorities.[10] Yet the Armenians felt quite confident that they would repel the Kurds, having successfully done so many times previously.[11] The assault of 1894, however, was not a typical Kurdish attack. This time, the Kurds attacking Sassoun were supported by a well-armed and well-supplied Turkish regular army. The Armenians were unable to resist the onslaught. Over a period of three weeks massacres swept through the region, and over half of the sixty villages were destroyed.[12] Village after village was burnt to the ground, thousands of Armenians were slaughtered, others tortured or raped. In an official diplomatic account of the massacre in Sassoun, the British diplomat Shipley stated, 'The Armenians were massacred without distinction of age or sex . . . it is not too much to say that the Armenians were absolutely hunted like wild beasts, being killed wherever they were met.'[13]

It is difficult to ascertain the precise trigger for the Sassoun massacres. Some accounts suggest that it was a government response to the Sassounlis refusing to pay their taxes twice—once to the Kurds under the tax farming system, and then again directly to the government.[14] Other accounts refer to the Armenians' refusal to give up one or more Armenian revolutionaries believed to be in the region.[15] There was also the issue of the Armenians' strength in the district. Kurdish raids were being easily repelled by the Armenians, to the extent that Kurdish irregular troops became reluctant to conduct operations there. The Kurds, after one unsuccessful raid, had carried the bodies of two of their comrades to the nearby garrison town of Moush, reporting the insubordination of the Armenians and the armed strength of the peasantry.[16] One or more of these issues had apparently reached the ears of the sultan, and an order was dispatched 'directing that the Sassounlis be killed and their villages destroyed'.[17]

Some sources have suggested that the extent of government planning and involvement in the Sassoun massacre is disputable. William Howard, however, an American newspaper correspondent who travelled to Armenia in December 1894 to investigate the massacre, found 'ample proof' that the massacre was planned by the sultan several months before it occurred.[18] He and others referred to large volumes of kerosene sent to the region in the months prior to the massacre, which were subsequently used in burning down villages. Several accounts also mention significant numbers of soldiers and Kurdish tribes concentrating in the region, well in advance of the atrocities. What actually occurred was probably a combination of both planning and response. The Armenians of Sassoun defended themselves mightily, and as the planned campaign met stronger than expected resistance, further troops were brought to the region, further orders issued, and the targeted raids progressed to 'the bitterest attack'.[19] According to one survivor:

> At this time all pretence of revolution was thrown aside. Villages against which no charge of disloyalty had ever been made, where there had been no trouble of any sort, suffered equally with those where there had been contests. The receipt of taxes amounted to absolutely nothing. On every hand it was proclaimed that there must be a clean sweep; that the whole population of the Armenian district must be exterminated.[20]

The first report of these events in the British record is on 31 August 1894. In the dry official language of diplomacy, British ambassador Currie stated that 'the Armenians at Talori, in the Vilayet [province] of Bitlis, have risen, and that in order to quell the revolt a small number of troops are being sent to the scene'.[21] By 4 September, British enquiries had elicited a Turkish response that the commander sent to quell the insurrection had been 'specially instructed to allow no excesses'.[22] The British government had good reason to seek such assurances. The conditions in which the Armenians lived under Ottoman rule had become an international issue in 1878, and with the Treaty of Berlin Great Britain had committed itself to an international responsibility for them. Yet none of the signatories had insisted upon the requisite improvements being made, and conditions for the Armenians had steadily deteriorated. Already at this early juncture it appeared the Ottoman government was employing its common tactics of falsifications and obfuscations, for in the same report Ambassador Currie noted conflicting information from the official Turkish sources compared to that from British consular officers.[23] A flurry of communication followed. In early October, a request by Vice-Consul Hallward to visit the area to determine what occurred was denied by Turkish authorities, on the pretext that a sanitary cordon had been imposed due to an outbreak of cholera. Continued protests by the European powers led to the sultan appointing a commission of enquiry that met from January to July 1895 in Moush.[24] However, the commission refused to hear testimony from Christians (and therefore Armenians), and the terms of the commission were limited to enquiring 'into the criminal proceedings of the Armenian brigands'.[25] Commander Zekki Pasha, who had led the Turkish troops, was decorated for his participation in the massacres.[26]

In protest, British, French and Russian consular officials travelled to Sassoun, and independently heard evidence of the atrocities. Despite Turkish attempts to conceal the evidence of massacre and present the events as a reasonable response to an Armenian rebellion, the commissioners found ample evidence that the Armenian actions were defensive, and that a massacre claiming the lives of approximately six thousand Armenians had taken place.[27] As a result, the Memorandum and Project of Armenian Reforms was drawn up by the ambassadors of Great Britain, France and Russia and presented to the Sultan on 11 May 1895.[28] Essentially, these reproduced the reforms that had earlier been agreed upon in the treaties of San Stefano and Berlin in 1878, but that had never been implemented.[29] A period of negotiation ensued, leading to a final 'Scheme of Armenian Reforms' being agreed upon between Great Britain, France, and Russia and the Ottoman government. The reforms included the appointment of 'non-Moslem' deputies to assist provincial governors and other civil administrators, civil officials to be selected 'without distinction of religion', and proportionate representation amongst administrators of various kinds.[30] Numbers of Moslem and non-Moslem police and gendarmerie were to be proportionate to that of the population, judicial inspectors 'who shall be Mussulmans and non-Mussulmans [*sic*] in equal number' were to be appointed, the Kurds were to be brought under control, and political prisoners released.[31] Furthermore, a permanent 'Commission of Control' was to be appointed to 'see to the strict carrying out of the reforms'.[32]

The Scheme of Armenian Reforms was still awaiting signature more than a year after the Sassoun massacres. In protest at the delay, a large number of Armenians marched through Istanbul on 30 September, intending to present a petition to the government.[33] The procession was set upon by the gendarmerie, and the attack on the protestors quickly descended into riots. Several hundred Armenians were killed by Turkish forces.[34] After three days of violence, the situation was barely under control when reports came in that the disturbances had spread to other locations. The reforms were sanctioned by imperial irade on 17 October 1895, but were precluded by the launching of widespread massacres of Armenians throughout the areas in which they were to be implemented. The Reverend Greene, a missionary in the Armenian provinces, commented upon events:

> The Sultan professed to accept the reforms which for more than five months the Powers had urged upon him in vain. What he really did, as subsequent events demonstrate beyond a doubt, was to sign the death-warrant of the Armenians who were to have profited by the reforms. He had darkly hinted that this would follow if he were pushed too hard, but no one believed that he would that he would really prove so vindictive or so foolish as to carry out the threat . . . from this time on reform by massacre was the order of the day.[35]

Trebizond was an early target of massacre. The city had been in a state of extreme tension for nearly a week when the first blow fell on the morning of 8 October. The signal to commence was given by a trumpet, upon which 'the Moslem population flooded into the Armenian quarters, and, often helped by the company of troops, gave itself up to countless massacres and scenes of pillage'.[36] About one thousand Armenians were killed—almost exclusively men, and representing approximately half of the adult male population of the Armenian community.[37] Extensive looting of Armenian shops and homes followed. Bands of armed Moslems then left the town and spread through the countryside to undertake the same work.[38] Thirty-four villages in the surrounding area were destroyed, and around twenty-one hundred Armenians were murdered.[39] A further three to four thousand Armenians were left completely destitute by the looters.[40] Consuls later established that 'there had been no provocation of any kind from the Armenians', and there was also clear evidence that the attack was premeditated and enjoyed the connivance of the authorities.[41]

In the *villayet* (province) of Erzeroum, the massacres were extensive. In the town of Erzeroum itself, the local Turkish population prepared for massacre quite openly, but the consuls there were unable to persuade the authorities to intervene.[42] Indeed, officers and soldiers assisted the populace in their attack on 30 October. Twelve hundred Armenians were killed (compared to only twelve Turks), and about fifteen hundred shops and several hundred houses were plundered.[43] In the town of Erzingjan in the *villayet*, seven hundred Armenians were killed, while a particularly brutal massacre in Baiburt killed over one thousand, and left all but twenty Armenian men either killed or imprisoned.[44] Almost every single Armenian village in the region was attacked, with the murder of men, the plunder of shops and homes, and the rape of women endemic.[45] Many of the survivors were forced to convert to Islam.

A further example of the massacres occurred in Ourfa between 28 and 29 October, and again on 28 and 29 December. Immediately after the Armenian demonstration in Constantinople, orders were received in Ourfa from the central government 'to the effect that should the Armenians attempt any disturbance, it was to be at once sternly quelled, and in the event of their offering resistance, they were to receive a terrible lesson'.[46] British vice-consul Fitzmaurice, stationed in Ourfa, wrote of these orders:

> The central government must have known, or ought to have known, the disastrous consequences which, in view of Mussulman feeling against the Armenians, such instructions were certain to have in the provinces, and it incurred a very grave responsibility in sending them.[47]

In a tactic common in these massacres, a minor incident, which the authorities could have resolved with ease had they desired, was instead allowed to escalate and thereby precipitate the massacre.[48] Events in Ourfa were distinctive, however, in that the local Armenian population attempted to defend itself from the onslaught. At the onset of the massacre most Armenians withdrew into the Armenian quarter of the city, the entrances to which were defended. The attackers were beaten back, and initially turned their attention to plundering several hundred Armenian shops and homes on the outskirts of the quarter.[49] Armenians found outside the quarter were attacked, and the males slain. Then the Armenian quarter was besieged, the water supply cut off, and no food permitted to enter. This state of siege continued for almost two months, as the Armenians struggled for provisions and to defend themselves. On 28 December the quarter was stormed, and all the males within were targeted.[50] Trumpets were sounded to commence the assault on both 28 and 29 December, with trumpets also being sounded at the end of each day. Following the trumpet on the final day, notables went around the quarter announcing that the massacre had ended and there would be no more killing.[51] For approximately eight thousand Armenians, however, it was too late.[52]

There are innumerable accounts of the use of torture and rape as weapons of aggression. Horrific incidents of torture, and of excruciatingly painful deaths, are reported in almost every description of the massacres. In Ourfa, for example, close to three thousand people were burnt to death as they sought refuge in the Armenian cathedral.[53] In another incident, young men were tied hand and foot, laid in a row, covered with brushwood and burnt alive.[54] Common forms of torture included beatings, the use of hot irons of fire to burn or the hacking off of limbs. Stead, who witnessed the Sassoun massacre, reported:

> The Kurds killed people with bullets and daggers, but the soldiers delighted in torture. They put some to death with scissors, cutting them and opening veins in the neck. Others were sawed, others had their tongue cut out, eyes gouged out, and several fingers removed before death. I saw men and women thus mutilated, and they lay about the camp for two hours before they were killed.[55]

There is evidence that rape was not just incidental to the massacres, but a deliberate tactic. Several accounts of the massacres refer to the soldiers specifically being ordered to rape Armenian women.[56] One journalist in the region reported:

After the massacres the Kurds and Turks began an orgy of lust which has seen no cessation, day or night. It is their deliberate purpose to utterly debase and degrade Armenian women, and so hasten the destruction of the Armenian nation . . . It is not merely that a maiden's virtue is taken in wanton lust and wickedness . . . but now this same girl is violated again and again, from day to day, by different men, until life is worse to her than death.[57]

The perpetrators of the massacres can be categorized into four main groups—soldiers, civil administrators, Kurds and members of the Turkish populace. There is widespread evidence that significant numbers of soldiers from regular army units participated in the massacres.[58] Dr. Johannes Lepsius, a German Protestant pastor who became a prominent author on the plight of Ottoman Armenians, described the role of the military as being to arm the populace and offer reserves where required, and to assist the Kurdish *Hamidieh* (irregular cavalry regiments), police and Turkish population when there was resistance, or if the massacre was not proceeding along planned lines.[59] The role of civil officials and administrators was more complex. They were responsible for the preparation required before the massacres, but at the same time a level of deception had to be maintained towards the fearful Armenian population.[60] Preparations included a drive to strictly enforce the decree that Armenians were forbidden to bear arms, so as to ensure they were unable to defend themselves.[61] Where possible, 'the fanaticism' of the Moslem population was to be aroused, and the perpetrators were to receive a guarantee that there would be no punishment.[62] There is also evidence that lists were prepared by provincial governors detailing Armenian men of influence who were to be specifically targeted within particular massacres.[63]

Kurdish *Hamidieh*, the general Kurdish populace and the Turkish populace were also heavily involved in the perpetration of the massacres. The motives of the Kurdish and Circassian populations that participated in the massacres were perhaps the simplest. These groups were traditionally the enemies of the Armenian people, and had a long history of preying upon them. Under the rule of Sultan Abdul Hamid II, such actions had rarely been punished, and in some cases were actively encouraged. Kurdish *Hamidieh* regiments boasted of instructions to kill and plunder in the Armenian villages. Other Kurdish bands were equally confident that not only would their actions go unpunished, but in fact they were officially sanctioned. According to Greene, 'Plunder was the chief motive [of the Kurds and Circassians], who swept over the country like a swarm of locusts, everywhere declaring that they had received authorization for their raids.'[64] The Turkish population, too, had received reassurances that there would be no punishment for participation in the massacres, and plunder also proved a strong immediate motivation. A further motivation was that in many villages there were Armenian moneylenders to whom Turks owed money. The massacres effectively made these debts unrecoverable.[65] The lack of punishment for plunder, a situation that had largely endured since

the 1850s, was so widespread that Sir Edwin Pears could report: 'There was . . .
a traditional feeling among their [the Armenians'] Moslem neighbours that they
had the right to plunder Christians.'[66] The missionary and author Reverend Edwin
Bliss believed that the massacre in Sassoun also further encouraged plunder:

> It whetted the appetite for plunder and also showed that that appetite could be
> gratified with no evil results to the plunderers. The facts that no-one was punished
> and that the leaders were rewarded were well known throughout the empire. Longing
> eyes were cast upon Christian shops and houses and upon Christian women, and
> threatening glances turned upon the owners of the former and the protectors of
> the latter. If they could be got rid of safely, property and sex could be appropriated
> without danger.[67]

The issue of whether the sultan ordered the massacres, tolerated but did not
initiate them, or was something of a powerless figurehead, unable to stop them as
they transpired, was a highly contentious one at the time. Even today, there is no
final consensus. Robert Melson, author of a modern analysis of the massacres,
refrained from coming to any conclusion on this matter—stating repeatedly only
that the sultan 'initiated or tolerated' the massacres.[68] While there is no definitive
proof that the sultan ordered the massacres, Melson's position is a very cautious
one. Akçam, by contrast, has asserted: 'From reports of the various diplomatic
missions in Istanbul and eyewitness accounts, it is clear that the massacres of
1894–96 were centrally planned.'[69] Account after account of the massacres, written in their immediate wake, also concluded that they were ordered by the sultan.[70]
The evidence presented for this conclusion is extensive. First, the system of government was such that the sultan was very clearly the centre of power within the
empire.[71] He was very industrious, took personal cognizance of the smallest details
of his government and empire, and, according to one source, held minute control
over its internal administration.[72] Second, reports of the massacres are littered with
accounts of officials acting upon orders to massacre, and military personnel boast-
ing that they have official authority for their actions. The structured nature of the
massacres also provides very strong evidence for their central organization.[73] Most
massacres adopted a similar course, with men specifically targeted to be killed, and
universal plunder and rape. The burning of houses and the reprieve given to Armenians who converted to Islam were also common features. Each massacre lasted
from one to a few days, indicating that the maximum length for which a massacre
was allowed to continue had been centrally prescribed.[74] In particular, the orderly
cessation of each massacre—occasionally even followed by a religious procession
through the area—is indicative not of a frenzied mob, but of the soldiers' ongoing
control of the situation.[75]

Further evidence of central organization can be found by examining the locations of the massacres, with the vast majority occurring in the six provinces in which

the reforms were to be introduced.[76] The focus of the massacres was uniform—non-Armenian Christians were spared, and foreigners were actively protected from harm. According to Lepsius, this was a result of orders being given regarding the nationality of the victims.[77] Greeks in particular were carefully protected from harm, because it was known in Constantinople that Russia would interfere if anyone belonging to the Greek Orthodox Church was injured.[78] A further source of evidence that the massacres were deliberate policy is the continued persecution of the Armenians following their cessation. Perhaps the most telling evidence, however, is that in some cases there is evidence of officials who refused to participate in massacres being punished. For example, the provincial governor in Amasia was nearly killed for refusing to obey a command to order a massacre—he ultimately ceded.[79] In Van, attempts by the governor to prevent massacres were thwarted when a special ambassador of the sultan arrived, ostensibly as a peacemaker.[80] Following the massacres, this ambassador was rewarded with the governorship of the district. Near the city of Malatia, an entire Kurdish village that had refused to participate in the massacres was set upon by regular army troops, who destroyed and burnt it as though it were an Armenian village.[81] Finally, it must be remembered that massacre was not an exceptional event within the Ottoman Empire. Indeed, as one author described it, it is an event with 'abundant precedent'.[82] Within the nineteenth century, there had already been four massacres in which over ten thousand victims perished, and three smaller massacres in different locations in the empire.[83] The last of these, the Bulgarian massacres, had occurred under the reign of Sultan Abdul Hamid II. Perhaps Lepsius summed up this issue best:

> It is beyond question that the Turkish people, the military and the Kurds, knew that they were acting, not only under the direction of subordinate officials, who had promised them exemption from punishment, but by the command and in the name of the Sultan himself.[84]

Massacre was widespread throughout the empire from October to December 1895, but especially in the six provinces of Erzeroum, Bitlis, Van, Harpout, Sivas and Diyarbekir, where the Scheme of Armenian Reforms had been slated to go into effect.[85] Massacres were perpetrated in fifteen major locations in October, twenty major locations in November, and five major locations in December.[86] In addition, literally hundreds and hundreds of villages were laid waste.[87] By the coming of the New Year, there had been a massacre in almost all of the towns and villages in the six provinces, and in many other additional areas where there was an Armenian population. While the situation remained extremely tense, the massacres largely abated, and there were only sporadic instances of massacre in the first half of the year.

Beginning on 24 August 1896, however, there was one final large-scale massacre of Armenians. On that day, the Dashnaktsutiun Armenian revolutionary party seized the Imperial Ottoman Bank in Constantinople to protest against the

massacres, and to prompt external intervention.[88] While negotiations with the cap-
tors meant the hostages were released, and the insurgents were permitted to leave
the country unmolested, their action was followed by a large massacre in Constantinople in which approximately six thousand Armenians were killed.[89] There were
reports, such as that by Washburn, that the Turkish government knew about the
plan to take over the bank many days in advance and 'the Minister of Police had
made elaborate arrangements, not to arrest these men or prevent the attack on the
bank, but to facilitate it and make it the occasion of a massacre of the Armenian
population of the city'.[90] The massacre raged for two days, easing on the third.
Again, men were the primary targets, and looting was widespread.[91] Long after the
massacre, there remained extensive persecution of Armenians in Constantinople,
and indeed of Ottoman Armenians generally.

The estimates of numbers killed in the Armenian massacres vary widely.
Johannes Lepsius, working immediately after the massacres, compiled the statistics
from each province to come up with a figure of 88,243 'Armenians and other
Christians' killed.[92] More modern estimates usually suggest a higher figure. Richard Hovannisian estimated that between 100,000 and 200,000 were massacred,[93]
while Louise Nalbandian suggested an estimate of 50,000 to 300,000.[94] Chaliand
and Ternon proposed a figure of 300,000.[95] Robert Melson cited such figures
as amounting to between 2 and 12 per cent of the Armenian population being
killed in the massacres.[96] Beyond those killed, the enormous toll on those left
alive must be considered. Lepsius estimated that some 2,500 towns and villages
were plundered, 645 churches and monasteries were plundered and destroyed, 328
churches were turned into mosques and 646 villages were forcibly converted to
Islam.[97] Bliss estimated that approximately 40,000 individuals were forced to convert.[98] While Lepsius was unable to come up with a total figure of houses and
shops plundered and destroyed, Bliss conservatively placed the figure at 12,600
burnt and 47,000 plundered (this figure being calculated prior to the final massacre at Constantinople).[99] Statistics as to the number of incidents of rape and torture are unobtainable. Bliss also suggested that some 350,000 to 500,000 persons
were left destitute, while Lepsius provided a figure of 546,000.[100] The particular
focus of the massacres, which specifically targeted men for destruction, left large
numbers of women and children destitute and with no obvious means of recovery.

The Hamidian Massacres and the Temporal Model

The temporal model provides a framework through which the events leading up
to and during the Hamidian massacres can be analysed, enabling fresh insight into
their causes and timing. The preceding analysis (in chapter 1) has revealed that,
in many respects, the Armenians were a long-standing 'outgroup' in the Ottoman Empire. The Armenian minority was relatively powerless and faced legal

discrimination, yet had a legitimate if inferior place as a *millet*. This was a stable feature of Ottoman society for some time, suggesting it may best be described as something akin to Stanton's initial stages of genocide: classification and symbolization.[101] As Stanton has elucidated, these stages are a common societal feature, and not necessarily indicative of heightened risk of genocide. Indeed, the Armenian minority's status as an outgroup in the sense meant by Fein and Mazian, that is, as truly indicative of some risk of genocide, only crystallized in the course of the nineteenth century.[102] This occurred as Ottoman-Armenian relations became increasingly politicized. The three defining features of an outgroup at risk of genocide as outlined in the temporal model—legalized discrimination, relative powerlessness and politicized intergroup relations—became progressively more marked as the century progressed.

At the same time, the Ottoman Empire came under significant internal strife. It faced serious threats to its geographic, political and financial integrity, which only worsened as the nineteenth century wore on. Both of these preconditions for genocide, therefore, emerged slowly and well in advance of both the Armenian massacres and eventual genocide. Moreover, even when fully present, they did not provoke a sudden outbreak of violence.

Instead, it took a further factor to sharply increase the vulnerability of the Armenian minority. The Treaty of Berlin triggered an Ottoman perception of the Armenians as posing an existential threat to the empire—leading to rapidly deteriorating intergroup relations and a callous disregard for Armenian life. As the temporal model elucidates, this suggests that a perception by the dominant group that an outgroup poses an existential threat to its power is an important precondition in understanding how risk of genocide progresses over time. Even then, however, the outbreak of the massacres was strongly influenced by the interaction of local precipitants and restraints. The threat of potential European intervention and the weak position of the empire in the 1880s forestalled any immediate outbreak of anti-Armenian violence. As Sultan Abdul Hamid II consolidated his rule, however, and the prospect of European intervention grew gradually more remote, the continued perception of the Armenian minority as posing an existential threat to the empire provoked a more aggressive response.

The Armenian massacres are typically thought of, and discussed, as one event. Yet they occurred in three very distinct phases: the Sassoun massacres in 1894, the main outbreak of massacres from October to December 1895, and the final large-scale massacre in Constantinople in August 1896. The vulnerability of the Armenian minority as a whole, as a result of the factors outlined in the preceding sections is clearly evident. Yet each phase of the massacres had a specific and individual constellation of triggering events, which can be instructive to understanding the risk escalation process. As mentioned in the beginning of this chapter, there were very specific, albeit almost trivial, triggers for the Sassoun massacre.

While other Armenian districts had been somewhat subjugated through impoverishment, lawlessness and official discrimination, the Armenians in Sassoun
formed a greater proportion of the population than in other regions, and were
particularly able to successfully repel Kurdish attacks and some of the depredations experienced elsewhere.[103] Once all the broader preconditions were in place,
paradoxically, it was through these local conditions of strength that the Sassounlis
became an obvious target.

What, then, sparked the massacres in province after province in 1895? While
there is no doubt the situation was very ominous, the specific precipitants for those
massacres did not develop until after the Sassoun massacre. Indeed, the immediate
precipitants to the massacres in 1895 can be viewed as arising almost exclusively
from the European response to the Sassoun massacres. In the pamphlet *England's
Responsibility towards Armenia*, the Reverend MacColl wrote in July 1895:

> The impunity which the *Porte* has enjoyed for the horrors of Sassun has encouraged
> the Sultan and his advisors to organize a crescentade [*sic*] in Asia Minor; and I have
> good evidence for saying that if Europe do not intervene speedily, the Armenian
> question will soon be settled by the extermination of the Armenians.[104]

Very little action followed the initial protests of the Great Powers in response to
events in Sassoun. The Scheme of Armenian Reforms, while much more specific
than the Treaty of Berlin, contained little that the sultan had not already committed to in 1878, and that he had already proved through sixteen years of insolence
that the Great Powers would not enforce. Furthermore, Great Britain, France and
Russia tolerated the sultan's protests, objections and delays regarding the signing
of this document. Great Britain, at least, was well aware of the dangers of pursuing reform without the intent of carrying it through. The British ambassador at
Constantinople, Sir Phillip Currie, reported in November 1894:

> The Sultan, I am told, declared quite recently to a foreign Representative that noth-
> ing would induce him to introduce reforms into his Asiatic provinces, and it is not
> likely that he would yield without the employment of force. If the attempt were
> made without being carried through to a successful issue, the position of the Arme-
> nians would become even worse than it is at present.[105]

The failure of the Great Powers to mount a concerted response to the Sassoun
massacres meant that the threat of European intervention was not seen as a genuine one. It therefore did not form an effective constraint, and could not prevent
further escalation of the violence.

Not only did the European response to the Sassoun massacres fail to con-
strain further violence, but the nature of the response itself exacerbated the situation. Through attempting to resolve the 'Armenian question' by the granting of
rights to Armenians, it accentuated the Ottoman perception of the minority as

posing an existential threat to the empire. As was discussed in chapter 1, the provision of civic equality to non-Moslems within the empire was in direct conflict with its religious basis. The reforms also declared that the governors in the six provinces most heavily populated with Armenians were to be elected according to the proportions of the population. In some areas, this effectively meant an Armenian governor would be the first representative.[106] As the missionary Frederick Greene commented:

> By insisting that the Armenians should have a proportionate representation in the administration of certain provinces, the Powers placed a price on the head of every Armenian. By failing to protect them in this critical position with a prompt and decisive use of force, they are guilty of a share in their destruction.[107]

Indeed, a statistical analysis of the massacres in 1895 reveals that about 90 per cent occurred within the six provinces to which the Scheme of Armenian Reforms applied.[108]

So inadequate was the European response to the events in Sassoun that a number of contemporary commentators held the Great Powers responsible for the subsequent massacres that occurred. The Reverend Bliss, writing in 1896, asserted: 'The Powers might, if they had taken the right steps, have prevented the massacres, at least those of 1895.'[109] Johannes Lepsius went as far as to claim, 'The painful truth must become universally known that it was the policy of the Christian Powers, and this alone, that has brought about the frightful annihilation of the Armenian people.'[110] Certainly, had there been no international response to the Sassoun massacres whatsoever, further massacres would most likely have followed. But the nature of the European response, and particularly how readily it became apparent that European protests would not be backed with force or enforcement, shaped the nature and ferocity of the massacres in 1895.[111]

The final major massacre in Constantinople in 1896 appears, at least superficially, to be a direct response to the actions of the Dashnaktsutiun Armenian revolutionary party, which seized the Imperial Ottoman Bank to protest the previous massacres. As mentioned above, there may have been an opportunity for the *Sublime Porte* to prevent the attack, but instead it was utilized as an occasion for a further massacre. Coming as it did several months after the largest outbreak of massacres, it is likely that the purpose of this massacre was to 'remind' any recalcitrant Armenians of the power of the empire, and of their precarious position within it. It was also not clear at the time that this would be the last large-scale massacre. Yet the massacre, 'occurring under the very eyes of the Ambassadors and the European residents', roused the attention of Europe in a way that the previous massacres had not done, and 'a cry of horror arose in England'.[112] For a short time at least, there was a real fear of European intervention.[113] This was undoubtedly an influential factor contributing to the cessation of the mass killing.

The Aftermath of the Hamidian Massacres

There was no defining event that marked the cessation of large-scale massacres in 1896, or that led to a rapid reduction in tensions. Indeed, as Bliss put it in late 1896, 'Massacre has been followed by persistent persecution, less prominent, perhaps, but not less effective.'[114] Following the massacres, the authorities arrested thousands of male survivors and imprisoned them for extended periods.[115] Conditions in the prisons were deplorable, and torture was commonplace.[116] Attacks on Armenians, plunder and rapes continued to occur. Armenian fields and lands were taken by force in many villages.[117] There were also reports of the government assessing the taxes of the dead upon the survivors, and of tax collectors targeting the recipients of relief.[118] According to one resident in Constantinople:

> The massacre of the Armenians came to an end . . . but the persecution of them which went on for months was worse than the massacre. Their business was destroyed, they were plundered and blackmailed without mercy, they were hunted like wild beasts, they were imprisoned, tortured, killed, deported, fled the country, until the Armenian population of the city was reduced by some seventy-five thousand, mostly men, including those massacred . . . Since that time it is very difficult for an Armenian to get permission to come to Constantinople from the interior. The poverty and distress of those left alive in Constantinople was often heartrending, and many women and children died of slow starvation . . . this persecution still continues in a milder form.[119]

Starvation, exposure and sickness claimed the lives of many Armenians.[120] By the end of 1896 a famine 'of the most gigantic proportions' was underway in Ottoman Armenia.[121] An estimated five hundred thousand Armenians were completely destitute, and unable to provide for themselves.[122] Initially, the *Sublime Porte* forbade European relief committees and missionaries from distributing provisions.[123] The government itself did provide some relief; however, by all accounts it was woefully inadequate, sporadic and usually took the form of only a few days' worth of bread.[124] Similarly, government attempts to return plundered property to its rightful owners were farcical—although enthusiastically reported to the European powers. In one village, twelve thousand sheep had been stolen from the Armenians; following government intervention, two of those sheep were returned.[125]

After some time, and following the intercession of the British ambassador, relief was gradually allowed to flow in from Europe and America. The testimony of the missionaries, who were the primary distributors of relief, portrays the pitiful condition of the Armenian people. Worst affected were the six provinces to which the reform scheme applied, although the provinces of Trebizond, Angora, Aleppo and Adana were also affected to a lesser extent.[126] Missionary accounts tell of the extraordinary extent of the plunder and destruction of villages. J. Rendel and Helen Harris, two missionaries who toured through Harpout and attempted to provide relief, visited village after village where almost every Armenian home had been systematically burnt down.[127] Survivors of the massacres very often possessed only the rags in which they were clad, and lived either in the burnt-out remains of their homes or slept in orchards and out in the open. Simply feeding the survivors was an enormous challenge for the missionaries. There were reports of survivors eating grass to prevent starvation, while others survived on meagre relief rations of bread and corn. In these deplorable conditions, epidemics of typhus, smallpox and cholera broke out.[128] There was also a great deal of hopelessness and despair. Armenian survivors were too terrified to rebuild their houses, 'for fear we might be attacked again'.[129] Peasants no longer had livestock, seeds with which to plant crops or the tools required to tend them. Merchants had lost the tools of their trade and their stock, and did not have the capital to buy anew. Furthermore, the destitution of the Armenian people meant that there was no longer a viable economy in which to trade.

While it is difficult to obtain accurate figures, there was considerable emigration from Ottoman Armenia during this period. Some 20,000 Armenians had sensed the gathering storm clouds and emigrated to Russia in 1892–93; 12,500 went to the United States between 1891 and 1898.[130] Between 1899 and 1914, almost 52,000 Armenians (some from Russia) emigrated to the United States.[131] For those who remained within the Ottoman Empire, the conditions under which they lived following the massacres remained pitiful. Captain Townshend, a military consul in Turkey between 1903 and 1906, described Armenian villages: 'As a rule the people are even poorer than in a Moslem village and have quite a different bearing, for which fear is largely responsible. If a European were to strike an impertinent Moslem he would be paid back in kind, but an Armenian would become cringing; his spirit is broken by centuries of oppression.'[132] Townshend passed through Marash, a large town with a mixed population, which 'like most similar places . . . has been the scene of massacres of Armenians in recent years':[133]

The Christians are always in a state of apprehension. When I arrived there in November 1903 . . . I found all the Armenian shops closed and none of the Christians abroad in the streets . . . when the word had gone round that a foreigner, a Consul, had arrived, shops were opened, and in a few hours the market was thronged with Armenians who had not left their houses for days. The begged me to walk through the bazaar, as they had an idea that my presence would insure tranquillity . . . It seemed that the authorities were collecting taxes for, I think, the previous seventeen years, and according to the Armenians all these taxes had already been paid, but many of the receipts had been burned in a big fire which had occurred a few years previously in the bazaar . . . consequently when an Armenian went to the Bazaar a zaptieh appeared and took him to the Konak [Government buildings], where he had either to pay up or go to prison.[134]

Of the town of Kaisariyeh, in which Turks were the majority, Townshend observed:

The Moslem population . . . keep the Armenians . . . in absolute subjection. No Christian would dare to walk through the Moslem bazaar at any time, nor would he leave his house if he could possibly help it after dark, and if compelled to do so would never go alone. In spite of the large number of Christians, the latter are quite unable to stand up for themselves. They are not allowed to have any arms, whilst the Moslems are always well equipped in that respect.[135]

Townshend described the missionaries to the Armenians as working under 'the ever-present fear of massacre', and remarked that 'every possible obstruction is put in the[ir] way, such as the forcible closing of schools and refusals to grant the smallest favour'.[136]

Clearly, the Armenians remained in a very vulnerable position. Following the cessation of the Hamidian massacres the Ottoman government maintained a great deal of hostility towards the minority. There was only a very gradual retreat from this position. According to Ternon, the government returned 'to a discreet policy of endemic persecutions and small-scale massacres'.[137] Kurdish brigandage and lawlessness continued. The Armenians' movements were restricted, severely hampering commerce; they were taxed heavily, imprisoned on the slightest pretext and forbidden from bearing arms.[138] In 1900 a massacre instigated by Kurds killed over two hundred Armenians at Khassdur.[139] In 1904, there was further unrest in Bitlis. The grand vizier reported to the British ambassador that some twenty-five villages in the region had been burnt or destroyed, although he blamed Armenian insurgents for this destruction.[140] (The British ambassador found this explanation 'almost incredible'.[141]) Armenian revolutionary activity increased, however, as the hope of reforms faded. Indeed, 'in the provinces reform was considered a dead issue'.[142]

The Ottoman government attempted to reduce Armenian strongholds, such as Sassoun and Zeitoun, by stationing large numbers of troops in these areas. The idea of forced relocations of Armenians from the mountains of Sassoun to the plains of Moush—where they could be more easily controlled—was floated in 1904, but did not proceed.[143] British diplomatic records even report the sultan as stating: 'The Armenians fancy that they are protected by the Powers, but if they provoke us we will kill all the Armenians before the Powers can intervene at all. After all, what can the Powers do? I am an old man.'[144] This contained more than a kernel of truth. According to Ternon, 'Already by the end of 1896 the Armenian question had been relegated to chancellery files . . . the Powers had agreed not to intervene ever again in Armenia.'[145] The Armenians thus very definitely still constituted a minority at great risk of being subjected to further violence. They remained an outgroup, and the precondition of significant internal strife within the empire also continued to be operable. In many respects, however, they could hardly continue to be perceived as posing an existential threat to the empire. In the absence of a renewed threat, or any further precipitants, the situation remained relatively stable until 1908.

Notes

1. F. Greene. 1896. *Armenian Massacres or The Sword of Mohammed*, n.p.: American Oxford, 22.

2. A more detailed discussion of the number of victims is presented below.

3. M. MacColl. 1895. *England's Responsibility Towards Armenia*, London: Longmans, Green, 26.

4. Ibid.

5. Ibid.

6. 1890. Despatch from Mr. Clifford Lloyd, British consul at Erzeroum, to Sir W. White, 1 October, *Turkey*, no. 1 (1890–91), page number not provided, in MacColl, *England's Responsibility*, 27.

7. Ibid., 28.

8. 1891. Despatch from Mr. Charles Hampson, British consul at Erzeroum to the British ambassador at Constantinople, 28 February, *Turkey*, no. 1 (1892), 23, in MacColl, *England's Responsibility*, 29.

9. 1891. 'Inclosure in No. 27, Acting Consul Hampson to Sir W. White', Erzeroum, 2 May, in B. Simsir (ed.). 1989. *British Documents on Ottoman Armenians*, vol. 3, Ankara: Turk Tarih Kurumu Printing Office, 64.

10. E.A.B. Hodgetts. 1896. *Round about Armenia: The Record of a Journey across the Balkans through Turkey, the Caucasus and Persia in 1895*, London: Sampson Low Marston, 90.

11. Ibid., 89–90.

12. Ibid., 111–12; E. Bliss. 1896. *Turkey and The Armenian Atrocities*, Boston: H.L. Hastings, 374; W. Spry. 1895. *Life on the Bosphorus-Doings in the City of the Sultan: Turkey Past and Present, Including Chronicles of the Caliphs from Mahomet to Abdul Hamid II*, London: H.S. Nichols, 281, reprinted in V. Ghazarian (ed.). 1997. *Armenians in the Ottoman Empire: An Anthology of Transformation 13th–19th Centuries*, Waltham, MA: Mayreni Publishing, 624.

13. W. Stead (ed.). 1896. *The Haunting Horrors in Armenia*, London: 'Review of Reviews' Office, 31.

14. Bliss, *Turkey and the Armenian Atrocities*, 370.

15. Ibid., 369, 374; Hodgetts, *Round about Armenia*, 90.

16. Bliss, *Turkey and the Armenian Atrocities*, 370; Hodgetts, *Round about Armenia*, 91.

17. W. Howard. 1896. *Horrors of Armenia: The Story of an Eye-witness*, New York: Armenian Relief Association, 33.

18. Ibid., 31.

19. Bliss, *Turkey and the Armenian Atrocities*, 371.

20. Ibid., 371–72.

21. 1894. 'Sir P. Currie to the Earl of Kimberley', Constantinople, 31 August, F.O. 424/178, *Turkey*, no. 1 (1895), Part 1, no. 193, reprinted as document 261 in Simsir, *British Documents*, 376.

22. 1894. 'Sir P. Currie to Earl of Kimberley', Therapia, 4 September, F.O. 424/178, *Turkey*, no. 1 (1895), Part 1, no. 206, reprinted as document 265 in Simsir, *British Documents*, 379.

23. Ibid.

24. J. Lepsius. 1897. *Armenia and Europe: An Indictment*, London: Hodder and Stoughton, 2.

25. Ibid.

26. R. Melson. 1992. *Revolution and Genocide: On the Origins of the Armenian Genocide and the Holocaust*, Chicago: University of Chicago Press, 45.

27. Spry, *Life on the Bosphorus*, 281–82, reprinted in Ghazarian, *Armenians in the Ottoman Empire*, 624–25; R. Hovannisian. 1986. 'The Historical Dimensions of the Armenian Question, 1878–1923', in R. Hovannisian (ed.), *The Armenian Genocide in Perspective*, New Brunswick, NJ: Transaction Publishers, 25.

28. Spry, *Life on the Bosphorus*, 316, reprinted in Ghazarian, *Armenians in the Ottoman Empire*, 629.

29. Melson, *Revolution and Genocide*, 46.

30. Spry, *Life on the Bosphorus*, 325–26, reprinted in Ghazarian, *Armenians in the Ottoman Empire*, 639–40. This contains a reproduction of the full text of the Scheme of Armenian Reforms.
31. Ibid., 641–43.
32. Ibid., 643.
33. Ibid., 626.
34. S. Bey. 1898. *Islam, Turkey and Armenia and How They Happened*, St. Louis: C.B. Woodward, 200–1.
35. Greene, *Armenian Massacres*, 33.
36. F. Surbezy. 1911. 'Les Affaires d'Arménie et l'Intervention des puissances européennes (de 1894 a 1897)', Ph.D. diss., Université de Montpellier, 20; Lepsius, *Armenia and Europe*, 4.
37. Bey, *Islam, Turkey and Armenia*, 201; Greene, *Armenian Massacres*, 32.
38. Surbezy, 'Les Affaires d'Arménie', 20.
39. Lepsius, *Armenia and Europe*, 5.
40. Ibid.
41. Ibid.
42. Ibid.
43. Ibid.
44. Ibid., 6.
45. Ibid., 6–7.
46. G.H. Fitzmaurice, extract from Blue Book no. 5, *Turkey*, in Lepsius, *Armenia and Europe*, 157.
47. Ibid., 157–58.
48. Ibid., 158–61.
49. Ibid., 161.
50. Ibid., 168–69.
51. Ibid., 172.
52. Ibid., 173.
53. Ibid., 171–72.
54. Greene, *Armenian Massacres*, 22.
55. Stead, *The Haunting Horrors*, 29.
56. Ibid., 28; Howard, *Horrors of Armenia*, 5; Bliss, *Turkey and the Armenian Atrocities*, 373.
57. Howard, *Horrors of Armenia*, 5.
58. 1896. *Turkey*, no. 2 (1896), no. 403, quoted in G. Douglas. 1896. *Our Responsibilities for Turkey: Facts and Memoirs of Forty Years*, London: John Murray, 117, reprinted in Ghazarian, *Armenians in the Ottoman Empire*, 657.
59. Lepsius, *Armenia and Europe*, 47.
60. Ibid., 48.
61. Ibid., 49.
62. Ibid., 48.
63. Ibid., 81; Bey, *Islam, Turkey and Armenia*, 208.
64. Greene, *Armenian Massacres*, 436.
65. G.H. Fitzmaurice, extract from blue book no. 5, *Turkey*, in Lepsius, *Armenia and Europe*, 174.
66. 1911. E. Pears, *Turkey and Its People*, London: Methuen, 276.
67. Bliss, *Turkey and the Armenian Atrocities*, 556–57.
68. Melson, *Revolution and Genocide*, 43–69.
69. T. Akçam. 2007. *A Shameful Act: The Armenian Genocide and the Question of Turkish Responsibility*, London: Constable, 33.
70. MacColl, *England's Responsibility*, 38; Lepsius, *Armenia and Europe*, 76; Bey, *Islam, Turkey and Armenia*, 207; Hodgetts, *Round about Armenia*, 37; Pears, *Turkey and Its People*, 278; A.W. Williams and M.S. Gabriel. 1896. *Bleeding Armenia: Its History and Horrors Under the Curse of Islam*, New York: Publishers' Union, 347; Bliss, *Turkey and the Armenian Atrocities*, 567; J. Pierce (ed.). 1896. *Story of Turkey*

and Armenia: With a Full and Accurate Account of the Recent Massacres written by Eye Witnesses, Baltimore: R.H. Woodward, 445.

71. J. Bryce. 1896. *Transcaucasia and Ararat: Being Notes of a Vacation Tour in the Autumn of 1876*, rev. 4th ed., London: Macmillan, 460. The sultan himself had changed the system of government so as to significantly reduce the power of the grand vizier (prime minister) and ministers of the *Porte*.

72. Bliss, *Turkey and the Armenian Atrocities*, 564–66; O. Gaidzakian. 1898. *Illustrated Armenia and the Armenians*, Boston: n.p., 188.

73. Bey, *Islam, Turkey and Armenia*, 208.

74. Ibid.; Lepsius, *Armenia and Europe*, 83.

75. Lepsius, *Armenia and Europe*, 82.

76. Ibid., 77; Bey, *Islam, Turkey and Armenia*, 207–8.

77. Lepsius, *Armenia and Europe*, 80.

78. Ibid.

79. Ibid., 55.

80. Ibid., 185.

81. J.R. Harris and H. Harris. 1897. *Letters from the Scenes of the Recent Massacres in Armenia*, London: n.p., 174.

82. Greene, *Armenian Massacres*, 432.

83. Ibid., 432–33.

84. Lepsius, *Armenia and Europe*, 83.

85. Melson, *Revolution and Genocide*, 46.

86. Ibid.

87. Lepsius, *Armenia and Europe*, 18.

88. Melson, *Revolution and Genocide*, 46.

89. Ibid.

90. G. Washburn. 1909. *Fifty Years in Constantinople and Recollections of Robert College*, Boston: Houghton Mifflin, 246, reprinted in Ghazarian, *Armenians in the Ottoman Empire*, 717; R. Hovannisian. 1997. 'The Armenian Question in the Ottoman Empire 1876 to 1914', in R. Hovannisian (ed.), *The Armenian People From Ancient to Modern Times*, vol. 2, *Foreign Dominion to Statehood: The Fifteenth Century to the Twentieth Century*, New York: St. Martin's Press, 225.

91. Washburn, *Fifty Years*, 247, reprinted in Ghazarian, *Armenians in the Otttoman Empire*, 717.

92. Lepsius, *Armenia and Europe*, 320–31. This figure was compiled prior to the massacre in Constantinople in August 1896.

93. R. Hovannisian. 1967. *Armenia on the Road to Independence, 1918*, Berkeley: University of California Press, 28.

94. L. Nalbandian. 1963. *The Armenian Revolutionary Movement: The Development of Armenian Political Parties through the Nineteenth Century*, Berkeley: University of California Press, 206.

95. G. Chaliand and Y. Ternon. 1983. *The Armenians: From Genocide to Resistance*, London: Zed Press, 28.

96. Melson, *Revolution and Genocide*, 47.

97. Lepsius, *Armenia and Europe*, 330–31.

98. Bliss, *Turkey and the Armenian Atrocities*, 554.

99. Ibid.

100. Ibid.; Lepsius, *Armenia and Europe*, 331.

101. G. Stanton. 1998. *The Eight Stages of Genocide*, Washington, D.C.: Genocide Watch. Retrieved 9 January 2012 from http://www.genocidewatch.org/genocide/8stagesofgenocide.html

102. H. Fein. 1979. *Accounting for Genocide: National Responses and Jewish Victimization during the Holocaust*, New York: Free Press, 9; F. Mazian. 1990. *Why Genocide? The Armenian and Jewish Experiences in Perspective*, Ames: Iowa State University Press, ix–x.

103. E.J. Dillon. 1896. 'Armenia: An Appeal', *The Contemporary Review*, in Institute for Armenian Studies (ed.). 1987. *The Armenian Genocide: Documentation*, vol. I, Munich: Institute for Armenian Studies, 161.

104. MacColl, *England's Responsibility*, iii.

105. 1894. 'Sir P. Currie to the Earl of Kimberley', Pera, 26 November, no. 305, in Simsir, *British Documents*, 423–24.

106. Bey, *Islam, Turkey and Armenia*, 179.

107. Greene, *Armenian Massacres*, 435.

108. Ibid., 438.

109. Bliss, *Turkey and the Armenian Atrocities*, 560.

110. Lepsius, *Armenia and Europe*, 102.

111. For a further discussion of the role of Europe in the Armenian massacres, see D. Mayersen. 2007. 'Intermittent Intervention: Europe and the Precipitation of the Armenian Massacres of 1894–1896', in S. Koehne and B. Mees (eds), *Terror, War, Tradition: Studies in European History*, Unley, SA: Australian Humanities Press, 247–70.

112. Bryce, *Transcaucasia and Ararat*, 517.

113. Ibid., 518.

114. Bliss, *Turkey and the Armenian Atrocities*, 567.

115. Lepsius, *Armenia and Europe*, 104.

116. Ibid., 113–18; Williams and Gabriel, *Bleeding Armenia*, 348.

117. Lepsius, *Armenia and Europe*, 129.

118. Ibid., 108; Harris and Harris, *Letters*, 153.

119. Washburn, *Fifty Years*, 248–49, reprinted in Ghazarian, *Armenians in the Ottoman Empire*, 718.

120. Williams and Gabriel, *Bleeding Armenia*, 425.

121. Lepsius, *Armenia and Europe*, 118.

122. Ibid.

123. Ibid., 109.

124. Ibid., 105–7.

125. Ibid., 108.

126. Pierce, *Story of Turkey and Armenia*, 451.

127. Harris and Harris, *Letters*, 147–79.

128. Lepsius, *Armenia and Europe*, 135–36.

129. Ibid., 126.

130. A.E. Redgate. 1998. *The Armenians*, Oxford: Blackwell Publishers, 271.

131. Ibid.

132. A.F. Townshend. 1910. *A Military Consul in Turkey*, London: Seeley, 92.

133. Ibid., 116.

134. Ibid., 116–17.

135. Ibid., 120.

136. Ibid., 153.

137. Y. Ternon. 1981. *The Armenians: History of a Genocide*, Delmar, NY: Caravan Books, 127.

138. Ibid., 127–28.

139. Ibid., 128.

140. R. Lister. 1904. 'Confidential Memorandum respecting Armenia', printed for the use of the Foreign Office, August 1904, 8227, compiled in part from communications from Sir N. O'Conor, no. 90, 16 May, Sir N. O'Conor, no. 92, 19 May, Sir N. O'Conor, no. 392, 24 May, reprinted in A. Burdett (ed.). 1998. *Armenia: Political and Ethnic Boundaries 1878–1948*, Chippenham, UK: Archive Editions, 230.

141. Ibid.

142. Ternon, *The Armenians*, 127.
143. Lister, 'Confidential Memorandum', 8227, in Burdett, *Armenia*, 231–32.
144. T.R. 'Confidential Memorandum Respecting the Armenians', printed for the use of the Foreign Office, December 1905, 8556, compiled in part from communication from Sir N. O'Conor, no. 655, 26 September, in Burdett, *Armenia*, 240–41.
145. Ternon, *The Armenians*, 127.

Chapter 3

'THEY WILL HAVE TO BE DESTROYED'

From Massacre to Genocide

In July 1908, the Young Turks came to power in an almost bloodless revolution. This ushered in a period of wild optimism and crushing despair for the Ottoman Armenian minority. The period between 1908 and 1912 was marked by strong fluctuations in the conditions of life experienced by Armenians. Elation at the provision of legal equality was tempered by a renewed outbreak of massacres. Greater rights did not prevent ongoing persecution. Moreover, contradictory indications from the new Committee of Union and Progress (CUP) government appeared to suggest a deep ambivalence regarding the 'Armenian question'. Arguably, the position of the Armenians in the period between the 1908 Young Turk Revolution and the 1912–13 Balkan Wars is reflective of an empire floundering in the face of overwhelming challenges.

Upon their seizure of power, the Young Turks promised democracy, restoration of the constitution and the ideals of liberty, equality and fraternity. All peoples of the empire were to be full citizens, with equal rights and duties. What followed has been described as a 'general love feast'.[1] There was exuberance on the streets, and weeks of celebrations for the new government, the reforms, and the reconciliation of Turkish peoples. Armenians and Turks embraced publicly.[2] Leaders of the new government visited Christian churches, schools, and even cemeteries, where tribute was paid to those Armenians killed in the massacres.[3] CUP leader Enver Pasha declared: 'Henceforth we are all brothers. There are no longer Bulgars, Greeks, Romanians, Jews, Moslems; under the same blue sky we glory in being Ottomans.'[4] (Despite the expression of a universal spirit, however, neither Armenians nor Christians were specifically mentioned.) Moreover, concrete changes were enacted almost immediately. The constitution was published, Armenians previously forbidden from bearing arms were now encouraged to do so and

Armenians were enrolled in the army equally with Moslems.[5] At least initially, the Armenians were wholeheartedly enthusiastic about the new regime.[6] The euphoria of the Young Turk victory did not last long, however. At the elections, the Armenians received only ten seats in the parliament, despite being formally promised a larger number.[7] The CUP had not penetrated the provinces, and local officials maintained their discriminatory practices.[8] In the eastern provinces, Kurdish crime, onerous taxation and lawlessness continued.[9] Moreover, it soon became apparent that preparations were afoot for a massacre.[10]

The Cilician Massacres

The massacres that occurred in Cilicia in 1909 are difficult to characterize, and perhaps it is for this reason that many scholars of this period have made only passing reference to the events. As Yves Ternon stated, 'In 1909 killing broke out in Cilicia, and no one can say whether it was the last gasp of the traditional hamidian policies or a prelude to the 1915 genocide.'[11] These massacres, however, bear close scrutiny. In a two-week period between 14 and 27 April 1909, it is estimated that twenty-five thousand Armenians were massacred—up to one-quarter of the figure massacred in the entire 1894–96 period.[12] Moreover, these massacres occurred after the Young Turk government had come to power, and just six years prior to the genocide. A closer examination of events will provide significant insight into Ottoman society, the Young Turk government and the international situation at the time.

As with the massacres in 1894–96, the Cilician massacres were not unexpected. Tension had been building in the region for months, and by February 1909 the province was 'in a complete state of anarchy'.[13] Hostility increased still further as the harvest season approached, when around five thousand workers—Kurds, Turks and Armenians—came down into the plain of Adana to harvest the crops.[14] By mid-March, following a string of local incidents, Armenians and Turks alike sought arms, as they sensed the approaching massacres.[15] Two instances of interracial murders brought the temperature to boiling point in early April, and many Armenians who were able left for the relative safety of the nearby port city of Mersina.[16] On 14 April, a Wednesday, the first battle erupted in the city of Adana, the most important town on the Cilician plain. The Armenians, who formed about one-third of the forty thousand residents of Adana, rapidly retreated to their quarter of the city as the Turks took possession of the streets. Having expected the massacre for some time, they were well prepared with arms and a strategy for self-defence.[17] The battle raged all day and night. Police and soldiers aided the Turkish populace in their attack.[18] The provincial governor, frightened that the Armenian self-defence was rapidly turning the planned massacre into a drawn battle (in which the Turks themselves were suffering significant losses), called in further soldiers of the Turkish army.[19] After a further day of fierce fighting, by Thursday evening the exhausted Armenians began to run low on ammunition. A proposal for a ceasefire and a request for government protection were sent to the provincial governor. On Friday morning, with the aid of the British consul from Mersin, a truce was negotiated, and the fighting ceased.[20]

In the meantime, massacres had erupted in many of the surrounding villages. In these smaller villages, the Armenians had much less capacity to offer resistance and fared very badly. In Injerlik, for example, every single Armenian house was burnt to the ground.[21] At Missis, the entire Christian quarter was destroyed, and all of the men except for two were massacred.[22] In the town of Hamidieh and its surrounds, the slaughter continued for twenty-two days, during which over fifteen hundred people were killed.[23] Two French cotton mill owners fed and protected a further nine hundred Christians at Hamidieh, despite Turkish threats. In the village of Abdul Oglou, Armenians formed the majority of inhabitants. Here, the two Turkish village leaders promised the Armenians that no harm would befall them, and police were sent to provide reassurance.[24] Thus, all remained quiet until the Turkish leaders had summoned further support, when the Armenians were gathered together and massacred.[25] In Antioch, the local authorities provided soldiers with arms and ammunition, as the governor simultaneously assured the Armenians that there was nothing to fear.[26] In the ensuing massacre, 135 men and boys (out of a male population of 157) were killed.[27] In addition, six women were killed, and Armenian homes were systematically robbed of all their valuables. In several villages the Armenians were able to put up a determined resistance until assistance arrived, or until they could evacuate to Adana during a cessation in hostilities.[28] Altogether, more than two hundred villages were attacked.[29] Looting was extensive, as was the burning of Armenian homes and businesses. Men were the primary targets, while women were raped, and some kidnapped for Turkish harems.

There was considerable local variation in the massacres, and some areas escaped without harm. While the smaller villages fared worst, the town of Tarsus (the third most important town in the region) was also attacked. The leader of the mob that led the massacre in Tarsus was a prominent Young Turk.[30] Around five hundred Armenians perished in and around Tarsus, a comparatively low death toll.[31] Here, government officials assisted the Armenians to reach safe harbours, and provided a small number of guards for them. Soldiers actually brought wounded Armenians to the American missionary school to receive medical treatment.[32] In Tarsus it appeared the primary motive of the attackers was to loot and destroy Armenian homes; after systematic pillaging, houses were then set alight with kerosene.[33] In a number of areas in Cilicia, no massacres took place. In Alexandretta, Marash, Mersina and Ourfa, local governors took measures to keep the peace.[34] Some of these towns nevertheless suffered, as many of the breadwinners had travelled to the Adana plain to bring in the harvest and were caught up and killed in the atrocities.[35] While the massacres remained restricted to the *villayets* of Adana and Aleppo, the fear of massacre spread throughout almost all of the Armenian regions.[36] It was a realistic fear: plans for a massacre in Harpout were only scuttled after the provincial governor was able to prevent their outbreak, and Van and Caiserea also only narrowly escaped massacre.[37]

As the villages burnt, the uneasy truce held in Adana, despite a number of suspicious fires in the Armenian quarter. The quarter had not been entirely destroyed, and the Armenians began to look after one another and treat the wounded.[38] Many of those whose homes had been plundered or burnt gathered in refugee camps established in churches, schools and factories. There they were joined by large numbers of rural Armenians, who had escaped the massacres in their villages and fled to Adana for refuge.[39] The warships of no less than seven nations—Britain, France, Italy, Austria, Russia, Germany and the United States—steamed into the waters of Adana's port city of Mersina, their presence (though they took no action) giving the community some degree of confidence.[40] The Young Turks, meanwhile, dispatched two regiments to Adana to quell the disturbances. Yet after ten days of armistice, almost as soon as the troops arrived they themselves opened fire on the Armenian quarter.[41] Again, it is unclear precisely what the provocation was, but the soldiers, who were unhappy at having to protect Armenians against Turks, were persuaded to turn their guns on the Armenians they were there to protect.[42] Almost as soon as the gunfire commenced, the situation exploded. The Armenians, who had disarmed as part of the truce agreement, were now defence-less.[43] Soldiers and Turkish plunderers rushed into the Armenian quarter. Incendiary bombs set much of the district alight. Armenians were slaughtered, butchered and burnt alive.[44] According to Yves Ternon, 'A veritable storm of blood and fire raged through Adana'.[45] Professor Vahakn Dadrian, one of the foremost scholars of the Armenian genocide, described it as 'one of the most gruesome and savage bloodbaths ever recorded in human history'.[46] The frenzy of rage—as the Turks avenged their earlier losses—continued until 27 April. It was not until early May that the murders and fires completely ceased.[47]

It is difficult to determine the precise causes of the outbreak of massacres in Cilicia. Both local and national elements were involved, but unlike the massacres of 1894–96, this outbreak was not instigated by the central government. Despite the involvement of soldiers and police, there is no real evidence to implicate the central body of the CUP in the massacres.[48] Indeed, occurring simultaneously with the outbreak of massacres was a countercoup against the CUP government. Conservative elements, including Islamic fundamentalists, CUP opponents and loyalists to Abdul Hamid II, attempted to reinstate the sultan to his former position of power, but were defeated when the Ottoman third army retook Constantinople after ten days, restoring the CUP regime to government. According to one theory, the Cilician massacres were organized by these conservative elements to occur simultaneously with the countercoup. Such elements were particularly strong in the Adana region, and enjoyed the protection and support of both the new provincial governor and the military commander.[49] Like much of the rest of the Moslem population, these leaders resented the idea of regarding Armenians, *giaours*, as equal citizens.[50] Furthermore, they were supported by many administrative officials, who were resentful of the new regime and apprehensive about their jobs under it.[51]

The Armenians, meanwhile, were ardent and vocal supporters of the CUP and its constitutional liberties, and at times flaunted their newfound freedoms rather ostentatiously.[52] During the months preceding the counterrevolution and the massacres, these factors considerably increased tensions in the local area. There is also considerable evidence of reactionary officials in the region repeatedly spreading rumours and propaganda in the lead-up to the massacres.[53] In particular, these rumours were often to the effect that the Armenians were plotting to rebel and massacre the Moslems, and establish an independent Kingdom of Armenia.[54] Many Turks believed that this was a real threat, although it is hard to judge their perception regarding the seriousness or imminence thereof.[55] Whether the officials spreading such rumours were acting in concert to plan the Adana massacres as part of a general uprising with the counterrevolution, or whether the causes were more local, is unclear. What is clear is the unchanging attitude of the populace towards the Armenian minority, despite the cries of 'Liberty! Equality! Fraternity!' only nine months earlier. Dormant suspicions, combined with fresh resentment and rumour, easily roused the population to massacre. Finally, it is worth noting that Cilicia was one of the few regions that escaped massacre between 1894 and 1896.[56] The Armenians in the region were comparatively prosperous, and jealousy and the desire for loot almost certainly played a role.[57]

The international reaction to the Cilician massacres was again dismal. The British consulate at Mersina had some involvement in negotiating the initial ceasefire in Adana, and numerous warships had sailed to Mersina upon news of the massacres. The French and British commanders of their warships did disembark and make enquiries regarding the situation. When the massacre recommenced in Adana, however, there was no order given for the combat sailors to intervene. The international powers were unable to determine a joint response with the speed required, and the state of international politics regarding the region was such that no power wished to act unilaterally.[58] Once again, the international powers played the role of spectator to a slaughter of Armenians. According to Dadrian, the failure of the powers to intervene 'emboldened the perpetrator group considerably', and was 'an incentive to renew the carnage with even greater ferocity'.[59]

The newly restored Young Turk government appeared to have difficulty in determining an appropriate reaction to the massacres. Initially, a court of enquiry was composed; however, it consisted largely of local officials, and one of its first activities was to begin arresting Armenians.[60] After protestations from the Armenian patriarch and others, a number of courts-martial were established that could claim a greater degree of independence. A parliamentary commission also investigated the massacres. Both the courts-martial and the commission were deeply flawed by today's standards. Nevertheless, they were genuine attempts to investigate the massacres, and to try and punish the guilty.[61] Ultimately, 124 Turks and 7 Armenians were hanged. Dadrian has claimed that the Armenians were hanged 'to mollify Moslem sentiment', while author H. Charles Woods suggested that at least three of those seven were 'entirely innocent'.[62] There were also cases of senior officials—including both the provincial governor and the military commander of Adana—being given unreasonably inadequate punishments.[63] Yet there were numerous prominent local politicians, religious leaders and wealthy men amongst the hanged.[64] Whilst acknowledging the flawed nature of the courts-martial and the commission, the hanging of Moslems for murdering Christians was a momentous transformation.

The Young Turk government also made efforts to provide relief and reparations to the Cilician Armenians, and to reduce the tensions in the area. In early May it passed a resolution expressing regret for the events at Adana, and allocated funds for the relief of victims there.[65] At the same time, however, it sought to minimize the recorded number of victims, and formally denied that any soldiers participated in the second massacre in Adana.[66] Later, this was retracted, and the Young Turks adopted a more conciliatory approach.[67] Relief was also provided by the International Committee of Relief, who, three months after the massacres, reported that nearly eighty thousand people required relief, of whom five thousand were orphans.[68] Some effort was made to collect and return the plunder taken from Armenian houses, but according to one author, this was 'farcical'.[69] The initial relief monies provided by the government were mismanaged, and it was not until August that this relief was properly administered and began to reach the Armenians.[70] Further funds were allocated at this time. In August, the government also promised to introduce reforms and resolve domestic issues that caused hardship to Armenians.[71] The contradictions in the government's stance, and the dubious validity of the courts-martial, however, led to continuing Armenian uneasiness.[72] Six months later, Armenians in Adana remained highly fearful of a new massacre.[73] Furthermore, the previously prosperous region was now ruined economically.[74]

The Cilician massacres reveal a government, and a society, at a crucial crossroad. The first flush of enthusiasm for the Young Turks had subsided, and they now had to determine a path to manage the very significant challenges ahead. The populace had echoed the joyous cries of 'Liberty! Equality! Fraternity!', but the massacres exposed the deep divisions within Ottoman society. The Young Turk government's response to the massacres showed that there was still a commitment to the new, liberal principles. Yet the contradictions within this response—a blatantly biased enquiry, initial attempts to minimize the disaster, failure to adequately punish the two most senior perpetrators and mismanagement of relief—reveal the tenuousness of this commitment. The Young Turks had just survived a counter-revolution, and desperately needed to consolidate their power. Whether or not this could be achieved with a reformist agenda unpopular with much of the Turkish populace was a very real question. From the Armenian perspective, the Cilician massacres were a crushing blow. The belief that they could not be massacred under the new regime was shattered, and faith in the new government had suffered a severe shock. Furthermore, it is of crucial importance that, despite the change of government and the promulgation of equality, most of the predisposing factors for massacre and genocide remained firmly in place.[75] Officially, Armenians were now citizens of the empire, but the highest levels of government still referred to them as *giaours*, and believed true equality to be an 'unrecognizable ideal'.[76] Within the Turkish populace there remained a deep suspicion of the Armenians, and many harboured increased resentment of their 'fellow citizens' under the new regime. The massacres probably remained as limited as they were because, without central organization, local authorities had a significant influence. While the authorities in Adana were willing to perpetrate massacre, as was a portion of the populace, once the CUP regained power, local authorities in other areas realized that there was no central support for such actions, and that massacre was in conflict with the ideology of the new government. Furthermore, the presence of international war-ships may have been a constraint, although their forces made no attempts to stop the violence. Thus, without precipitants, the massacres ceased. Yet clearly, despite the regime change, and despite their official status as equal citizens, in 1909 the Armenians remained a minority at very high risk of being targeted.

How, then, can the Cilician massacres be understood within the context of the development of preconditions for genocide over time? Like the Hamidian massacres of the 1890s, the Cilician massacres occurred at a midpoint along what Staub has referred to as the 'continuum of destruction' that culminates in genocide.[77] That is, both episodes of massacre occurred when some, but not all of the pre-conditions for genocide were present. In many aspects, the events that led to the Cilician massacres mirrored those that resulted in the Hamidian massacres, but were contained at a more local level. In particular, there are strong parallels between events in Sassoun in the early 1890s and events in Cilicia in 1908–9. In both cases, underlying predisposing factors were present, and the situation was exacerbated by perceptions of the Armenians as an existential threat to those in a position of power. Localized precipitants contributed to the eruption of massacres. Following the massacres, there was a period of retreat. While the danger lessened, however, it certainly did not disappear, as tensions, threats and lesser outbreaks of vio-lence continued. These findings highlight the cyclic element in the way that risk of genocide progresses over time—with periods of escalation being followed by partial retreats. How such a process might ultimately escalate to genocide will be considered next.

Change and Uncertainty

The period between 1908, when the CUP took power, and 1915, when the Armenian genocide commenced, is a vital one for exploring the temporal progression of risk of genocide. From an Armenian perspective, the first major event after the revolution was the Cilician massacres, which appeared to bode rather badly. At the time of the massacres, however, the CUP had been in power for only months, and had barely consolidated its rule in Constantinople, let alone been able to hold sway in the provinces. In the following years, the regime would consolidate its power, but also be buffeted by strong internal and external pressures. These would significantly affect the lives of Armenians, both urban and rural. By 1912, the first effects of Young Turk policies could clearly be seen in the Armenian provinces. The British travellers Noel Buxton, a member of parliament, and the Reverend Harold Buxton, provided a snapshot of conditions in Armenia in the 1912–13 period. An account of their extended journey through Armenia, *Travel and Politics in Armenia*, was published in 1914, and provides an important record of local conditions. Buxton and Buxton divided Armenian grievances into two categories, those caused by the deliberate policies of the government and those largely out of governmental control.[78] They also documented how much, and yet how little, had changed with the new constitutional government.

There were a number of areas in which conditions of life improved considerably for Armenians following the Young Turk Revolution. Freedom of association was much greater, with Armenians able to talk to foreigners without fear of retribution.[79] Schools and clubs were being built, and progress was being made in education.[80] The mail service was much more reliable, and there was considerably less censorship of both mail and newspapers.[81] Travel was permitted without a passport, and many roads were now much safer.[82] Armenians were now active members of both the police and the army.[83] Furthermore, while taxation was still onerous, some of the worst practices had abated.[84]

Despite these seeming improvements, however, conditions remained precarious on a number of fundamental levels. The ongoing failure of the justice system to protect the Armenian people exacted an enormous toll. Buxton and Buxton recounted the case of an Armenian peasant who appealed to the court for the recovery of his stolen lands.[85] (These lands had been appropriated by Kurds when the peasant had fled following a massacre.) The appeal was granted, but the Kurdish response was simply to murder the peasant and his family. No arrests were made.[86] In Van, a nine-year-old girl was raped by a Kurd. Following consular complaint, the Kurd was imprisoned for a few days but then released.[87] Two policemen witnessed a group of unarmed Armenians requesting payment from an armed Kurd for some grain purchased some weeks earlier. The Kurd admitted the debt, saying he would pay 'later on'. When the Armenians became more insistent, the police response was to charge the group with their horses and whip the 'insolent Christians'.[88]

Indeed, what Buxton and Buxton termed the 'pro-Kurdish policy' of the Young Turks was a major source of Armenian discomforts. Kurdish brigandage continued unpunished. The authors narrated an incident whereby a Russian consul with police escort came upon a caravan being robbed by Kurdish brigands.[89] The governor of the district was present at the scene, but was taking no action. When the consul demanded the arrest of the brigands, the district governor refused, stating that it was 'quite impossible' to interfere with Kurds.[90] The consul then had his own police escort intervene, capturing two of the men involved. They were later acquitted at trial, however, which the authors describe as 'generally the result of a trial where Kurds are concerned'.[91] Kurds were now in the employ of the government, both as police and military officers, yet effectively could act with impunity. One such Kurdish police officer, riding with the Buxtons as an escort, offered this example of the prevailing lawlessness: 'Look at that village. I could go there and kill half a dozen people. Who would punish me? I am a Kurd.'[92] There is also evidence of systematic, government-organized removal of Armenians from their homes in some border areas at this time, in order to provide accommodation for Kurds newly arrived from the Russian side of the border.[93]

The Armenians themselves dealt with their situation in a number of ways. The Buxtons' impressions of the Armenians during this period were of an optimistic, resilient, enterprising people, able to maintain their morale and vitality despite their debilitating life conditions and the insecurity under which they lived.[94] Yet the massacres of 1894–96 still weighed heavily on the Armenian consciousness. Throughout their travels, they met large numbers of Armenian survivors of and witnesses to the massacres, and it is clear that their wounds were still fresh and raw.[95] Furthermore, 'the argument that under the new regime such things cannot happen has perished'.[96] According to the Buxtons, while a 'powerful section' of the Armenians still worked towards a productive alliance with the Young Turks, many now believed that the progressive ideals of the Young Turks had given over to their 'native chauvinism'.[97] Already, by 1912, there was little faith in the idea of internal reforms.[98] The 1908 revolution had brought a period of hopefulness, and also of improved conditions, when the Kurds initially desisted from crime, fearing possible punishment.[99] However, only four years later, the situation was 'in some respects . . . more intolerable now than before the Constitution. The hopes that were then raised have been extinguished by subsequent events. The spread of education and enlightenment makes the yoke heavier and the misery more acute.'[100] For many Armenians, the ultimate hope was for executive control by the Great Powers, and Russian intervention.[101] In the meantime, however, a policy of self-defence and armed resistance was increasingly taking over from the earlier passivism.[102] Furthermore, emigration, particularly to Russia, was becoming more and more common. At one frontier post with Russia, over seven thousand Armenian emigrants had passed in a period of ten months.[103] Perhaps, as the Buxtons suggested—writing prior to the genocide—many had come to realize that the Young Turks were 'more dangerous than Abdul Hamid himself'.[104]

The Impact of the Balkan Wars

The conditions in the Armenian provinces reflected the state of flux in which the empire floundered. Some reform had improved the lives of Armenians, but it was already obvious to many that the liberal reformist agenda was no longer operative. Whilst technically the Armenians were now full citizens of the empire, in practice they remained an outgroup, only slightly less disadvantaged than previously. The empire continued to be subject to severe internal strife. Between 1908 and 1913 it lost vast swathes of territory, and the government was powerless to prevent the secession of many minority groups. Shortly after the Young Turk Revolution in 1908, Bulgaria had proclaimed independence, and Austria annexed Bosnia and Herzegovina, which it had occupied since 1878. The same day, Crete announced that it would unite with Greece. In 1911, the Italians captured Libya. The Balkan Wars of 1912–13 were devastating to Turkey, both geographically and psychologically.[105] Almost all of the empire's European territory was lost, except for a strip to protect the straits of Istanbul. Between 1908 and 1914, the Ottoman Empire lost one-third of its territory, and 20 per cent of its population.[106]

These losses and defeats, especially those of the Balkan Wars, directly and indirectly affected the Armenians in a number of ways. In 1911–12, troops were taken from the Armenian provinces to Tripoli and the Balkans, leaving the Armenian peasantry with much reduced military protection.[107] Following the war, tens of thousands of Turks fled the Balkans. Destitute and miserable, they harboured an intense animosity towards 'all Christians' as a result of the defeat.[108] The Young Turk policy involved resettling these refugees in Anatolia, largely into homes that had previously belonged to Armenians.[109] According to one author, not only was this resettlement carefully prepared and promoted, but the anti-Christian hatred of the refugees was also encouraged and inflamed by the government.[110] Large numbers of agents were sent into the Armenian provinces, inciting violence and spreading propaganda against Christians.[111] Dadrian has suggested these policies reflected the changing ideology of the Young Turk government, and were a portent of what was to come.[112]

As unpleasant as these immediate and tangible effects were, they were perhaps the least important of the effects of the Balkan Wars. As Robert Melson has elucidated:

> Of profound significance for the Armenians was the fact that the loss of the European provinces, in effect, destroyed the multinational and multireligious character of the Ottoman Empire. The Greeks and then the Balkan Christians had seceded,

leaving the Armenians as the last of the great Christian minorities still under Ottoman rule.[113]

As the only significant Christian minority left in the empire, the Armenians were
now in a very vulnerable position. This was made even more dire by the location
of the Armenian provinces, in what was perceived as the Turkish heartland. The
events of the Balkan Wars resulted in Armenians being considered suspect for their
minority status alone. Moreover, as Vahakn Dadrian has noted, there were striking
similarities between the Balkan situation and that of the Armenians. Article 23 of
the Treaty of Berlin had stipulated reforms for Macedonia; the government, being
unwilling to implement these reforms, had also perpetrated massacres against the
Macedonian population.[114] Subsequently, the First Balkan War saw the former
subject nationalities in the region triumph through the direct and indirect assistance of the Great Powers, and especially Russia.[115]

The continuity of the first two preconditions for genocide in Ottoman Turkish
society, therefore, left the Armenians in a precarious position. It was a renewed perception of the minority as representing an existential threat to the empire, however,
that once again led to a rapid risk escalation process. As the Young Turks grappled
with their shocking defeat in the Balkans, the spectre of Armenian reforms would
be raised yet again. According to Dadrian:

> The reviving of the Armenian Reform issue, in the aftermath of the crushing mil-
> itary defeat the Ottoman army suffered in the course of that first Balkan War in
> 1913, sent shock-waves through the ranks of the CUP . . . the spectre of a repeat
> Balkan disaster in eastern Turkey galvanized these leaders. They were driven to con-
> sider drastic new measures to avert by all means a recurrence.[116]

Akçam, too, has remarked that

> [f]ollowing their shocking defeat in the Balkan War, 1912–13 . . . a deep belief
> developed [amongst the Young Turks] that it was impossible to live side-by-side
> with the empire's remaining Christian population, or even worse, that Ottoman
> Christians posed a threat to the empire's very survival.[117]

The Armenian Reform Agreement

After fifteen years of international inactivity, in 1912 Russia resurrected the
'Armenian question' at the international level. Serge Sazonov, Russian minister for
foreign affairs, cited in his memoirs 'a purely humanitarian interest in the fate of an
unfortunate Christian people, [and] the desire to maintain order in the most rest-
less of our border provinces' as the reasons for the Russian initiative.[118] Certainly,
there were many disturbances in the border provinces, and it was feared that the

situation could escalate and lead to war between Russia and Turkey. The Russian government 'wished at all costs to avoid' such a development.[119] However, Russian motives were rather more complex. At the beginning of 1912 Russia had changed its policy towards its own Armenians, moving from a policy of forced Russification to one of confidence and friendship.[120] Russia wished to avoid its own, newly appeased Armenians being caught up in disturbances arising from over the border.[121] Furthermore, this would aid in regaining the loyalty of Russian Armenians.[122] While Russia was not desirous of war in 1912, it certainly had plans for future expansion, for which, according to Hovannisian, 'Russia needed a loyal Transcaucasia and a peaceful Turkish Armenia'.[123] Finally, the Russian government feared German economic infiltration in this region, and wished to prevent it.[124]

Late in 1912, Russia therefore took the initiative regarding a new set of reforms for Turkish Armenia. Preliminary discussions were held with the other Great Powers, and Armenian leaders submitted their own proposals.[125] Turkey, wishing to neutralize the international powers, announced in March 1913 its own proposal of reforms for all of its *villayets*.[126] By June, however, the Russians had prepared a draft proposal of reforms for the Great Powers to consider. Again, in a countermove, the *Porte* issued on 1 July a further reform scheme, sending it to the Great Powers.[127] During July, the Great Powers held a conference on the proposed reforms, but were unable to reach agreement. The conference clarified the positions of all involved, however, and after six months of further negotiation, an agreement was reached by all six powers.[128] While the *Porte* was excluded from preliminary talks, the German ambassador represented Turkish interests to some extent.[129] The final agreement was signed by Russia and the Ottoman Empire on 8 February 1914. Two provinces would be created in Anatolia, each under the supervision of a foreign inspector.[130] The inspectors were the centrepiece of the reforms. Each would have the power to appoint and replace government officials, excepting those of a senior rank.[131] Chosen by the Great Powers for a term of ten years, inspectors would direct military forces to implement the reforms.[132] The police force was to be commanded by a European and recruited as a mixed Turkish and Armenian force, with the Kurds excluded.[133] Christians and Moslems were to be equal before the law, and the Armenian language would be permitted in court and in public administration.[134] There were to be no restrictions on the creation of Armenian schools.[135]

These reforms represented the most viable reform program proposed since the internationalization of the Armenian question in 1878.[136] But as in 1878, the Ottoman government had been presented with a virtual fait accompli, and its resentment was clear. During the period of slightly over a year in which the Great Powers negotiated the agreement amongst themselves, the Young Turk government had employed a multitude of tactics to derail the proposals. These included presenting two reform proposals of its own, and an attempt to set Russia and Great Britain at odds with each other with respect to the Armenian question.[137] These tactics—surprisingly similar to those previously employed by Abdul Hamid II—continued after the agreement was signed. A clause was inserted in the inspectors' contracts of engagement that enabled the government to discontinue them at any moment, upon the payment of one year's salary.[138] This was in flagrant violation of the agreement. Similarly, the list of government officials of 'superior rank' to the inspectors—whom they could therefore not replace—was inflated enormously.[139] Additionally, the Young Turk government attempted to reduce the inspectors' salaries to slightly over half the amount originally proposed, and bickering over their contracts of engagement continued for many weeks.[140]

The Russian minister for foreign affairs, Serge Sazonov, described in his memoirs the Turkish attitude towards the scheme of reforms as one of 'undisguised ill-will'.[141] But beneath the Turkish recalcitrance lay a perception that the Armenian Reform Agreement of 1914 was an attack on Ottoman sovereignty.[142] Sazonov recalled, 'The pressure that Russia had exerted to secure reforms in the Armenian *vilayets* [sic] was particularly unwelcome to the Young Turk Government, *which regarded it as an attempt on Turkish independence.*'[143] Indeed, there is evidence that the ultimate annexation of the affected territories was probably contemplated by Russia.[144] The Young Turk government strongly resented the Armenian Reform Agreement, and was enraged that the Armenians had again obtained foreign intervention.[145] The clause establishing the Armenian language as an official language—able to be used in the courts and public offices—was also viewed with bitterness by the Young Turk nationalists.[146] The inspectors were just about to commence duties at their posts when the First World War broke out. Although Turkey was not yet involved in the war, the government promptly denounced the contracts of the inspectors and suspended the scheme of reforms.[147] Thus, once again, an international attempt to improve conditions of life for Ottoman Armenians was unsuccessful. Once again, the Great Powers of Europe left the Armenians unprotected at a crucial juncture.

Both Bryce and Toynbee linked the February 1914 agreement with the subsequent genocide of the Armenian people. In *The Treatment of the Armenians in the Ottoman Empire, 1915–1916,* Toynbee wrote:

> Thus, at the close of 1914, the Armenians found themselves in the same position as in 1883. The measures designed for their security had fallen through, and left nothing behind but the resentment of the Government that still held them at its mercy. The deportations of 1915 followed as inexorably from the Balkan War and the Project [Reform Agreement] of 1914 as the massacres of 1895–6 had followed from the Russian War and the Project [Treaty of Berlin] of 1878.[148]

Vahakn Dadrian has also suggested the massacres and genocide were 'consequences' of the failed reform programs.[149] Like the Treaty of Berlin in 1878 and the Scheme of Armenian Reforms in 1895, the Armenian Reform Agreement of 1914 resulted in the Ottoman government perceiving its Armenian inhabitants as a serious existential threat to the empire. Previously, this had led to a rapid escalation of risk, culminating in massacres of the Armenians. This time, however, the process of risk escalation would have even more dire consequences.

The renewed perception of the Armenians as posing an existential threat to the empire was unwittingly aggravated by the Armenians themselves. Armed with their newfound status as full-fledged Ottomans, members of the Armenian community were increasingly active in the public domain, in politics, in demands for reform and in protestations regarding injustices. Following the restoration of the constitution after the Young Turk Revolution, Armenian revolutionary groups became legitimate political institutions, heavily involved in parliamentary processes. The Young Turk government now had to actively manage its relationship with these parties and their reform agendas. For example, it is believed that the Armenian Revolutionary Federation may have continued to support the Young Turk government in the wake of the Cilician massacres only after negotiations in which the government agreed to a formal reform program.[150] When conditions stagnated and then deteriorated, the Armenian protests regarding the situation did little other than aggravate the authorities. The Armenian minority was thus more visible than ever before, inadvertently contributing to its own increasing vulnerability as the Young Turks traversed the ideological spectrum from liberal government to genocidal regime. A destructive dynamic developed, as the continual petitions of various consuls and the Armenian political parties themselves kept Armenian issues high on the agenda of the Turkish government. This was exacerbated by the international intervention associated with the Armenian Reform Agreement. Similarly, the populace was highly suspicious of the (entirely legitimate) activities of the Armenian political parties, and displays of Armenian freedoms appeared only to increase resentment.[151]

The Rise of Turkish Nationalism

The Young Turk government had an enormous task in running the empire, and it was beset with huge challenges from the moment it took power. To quote the German expert on Near and Middle Eastern affairs, Ernest Jackh, who first visited Turkey during 1908:

> Any Pan-Ottoman or Pan-Turkish movement was bound to accentuate the historic conflict between the centripetal and the centrifugal forces within the empire—not to mention the magnetic pull on the peripheral provinces and nationalities exerted by the powers and conationalities outside. Trying desperately to escape history, the Young Turks had set themselves the task of squaring the circle.[152]

The Young Turks had to address the consequences of the empire's failures and frustrations, and at the same time attempt to preserve it. Very quickly it became apparent that constitutional democracy and liberalism would not alleviate polit-ical, economic or international pressures.[153] In particular, the military failures of the new regime had 'critical consequences for the evolution of the ideology of the Young Turks'.[154] The initial Ottoman pluralist and liberalist platform on which the Young Turks had seized power was undermined by the secession of the minori-ties and military defeats—not only had these minorities themselves declared it unsatisfactory, but the very fact of their secession largely removed the rationale behind Ottomanism.[155] The Young Turks also flirted with pan-Islam for a short while, but the rebellion and secession of Moslem peoples in Albania and Macedo-nia critically compromised this concept.[156]

The ideology that came to dominate the Young Turk government, and which would lead to the genocide, was 'pan-Turkism', or Turkish nationalism.[157] Accord-ing to author Gerard Libaridian, 'It is possible to argue that the critical period when the fundamental change occurred was between 1909 and 1911.'[158] Initially, this abandonment of pan-Ottomanism and the reform agenda was replaced by plans for the 'coercive homogenization of Turkey'.[159] The programme became one of 'Turkish nationalization, of "Turkifying" the multifarious Ottoman nationali-ties—instead of "Ottomanizing" the Turks'.[160] This was outlined by Young Turk leaders as early as 1910 under the euphemism of 'the complete Ottomanization of all Turkish subjects'.[161] British ambassador Lowther referred to this policy as 'one of pounding the non-Turkish elements in a Turkish mortar'.[162] And by Novem-ber 1910, the CUP had already resolved to use military force to settle barriers to Turkish unity if peaceable measures failed.[163]

Over the period between 1910 and 1914, however, the ideology of Turkish nationalism adopted by the CUP evolved into a much more sophisticated and extreme ethos. The Ottoman defeats in the Balkan Wars and the renewed percep-tion of the Armenian minority as an existential threat undoubtedly contributed heavily to this radicalization. Also critical to this process was the appointment to the central committee of the CUP—the heart of power in the Young Turk government—of Ziya Gökalp, the 'father of Turkish nationalism', and the fanatic nationalists Doctor Nazim and Ömer Naci.[164] Gökalp's ideal was that of a homo-geneous Turkish nation.[165] According to this ideology, all Turkish-speaking peo-ples shared a common culture and glorious past, and should be unified into a political entity.[166] This included peoples in the Russian Caucasus, Central Asia, Kazan and the Crimea, thereby embedding significant expansionist goals within the ideology. Gökalp's definition of the nation, as 'a society consisting of people who speak the same language, have had the same education and are united in their religious and aesthetic ideals', excluded the Armenians and other minorities.[167] The doctrine of Turkish nationalism thus fundamentally changed Turkish per-ceptions of the Armenians. No longer were they a *millet* with the associated rights and a legitimate—if inferior—place within Ottoman society; they were now an alien group.[168] Moreover, they were an alien group occupying the very heartland of Turkey, and 'a major obstacle to the Pan-Turkic ideal of a homogeneous Turan [greater Turkish nation] stretching from Anatolia to the borders of China'.[169]

Between 1908 and 1913 the pan-Turkish movement penetrated the empire. Numerous periodicals were established explaining and expounding the virtues of Turkism. Many associations were formed, where thousands of Turks met to discuss the new ideology. Intellectuals crystallized pan-Turkish thought, while poets and novelists gave it creative expression. The teaching of Turkish history and literature was reformed at all levels of the school curriculum.[170] Universities established chairs in Turkish studies, with an emphasis on pan-Turkism.[171] In addition, the ideology spread to the peasant and working classes, and for the first time they began to identify themselves as 'Turkish'.[172] In 1912 this led to a boycott of foreign shops, which lasted for several months. While higher-priced and poorer-quality goods eventually undermined the embargo, it spelt the ruin of hundreds of Greek and Armenian tradespeople.[173] The American ambassador at Constantinople, Henry Morgenthau, believed that this was an 'official boycott'—evidence of the rapidly changing government attitude towards minorities.[174] In 1913, in a further coup, the ultranationalistic faction of the Young Turk party gained control of the government. A powerful triumvirate, composed of Enver Pasha, minister of war; Talaat Pasha, minister of the interior and subsequently grand vizier; and Jemal Pasha, military governor of Constantinople, now dominated the government, and would effectively control it until after the end of the First World War. Both Enver and Talaat were intellectually influenced by Ziya Gökalp.[175] Talaat, as minister of the interior, selected officials of all kinds on the basis of their pan-Turkish fervour.[176] Enver passionately believed in pan-Turkism's expansionist doctrine, and as minister of war, formulated major military objectives based on this ideology.[177] Turkish nationalist ideology now pervaded both the Ottoman government and the populace. It would culminate in 'an explosion of racial fanaticism'.[178]

The Path to the Armenian Genocide

During this period, risk of genocide escalated rapidly. The Turkish nationalist ideology permeating the empire provided the ideological foundation for the genocide. Models of the preconditions for genocide widely recognize the importance of an ideology that enables or facilitates genocide. Fein, for example, refers to the elite's adoption of a new political formula to justify the nation's domination and idealize the singular rights of the dominant group, while Kuper refers to 'ideological legitimation'.[179] The temporal model highlights that alongside the emergence of a genocidal ideology is often a deepening perception of the outgroup as posing an existential threat. The international intervention leading to the Armenian Reform Agreement in 1914 strongly increased such a perception of the Armenians, particularly in the wake of the Balkan Wars. Additionally, the promulgation of pan-Turkish ideology throughout the Ottoman government and the populace effectively functioned as an extensive propaganda campaign, both supporting the superiority of the dominant group and justifying the active exclusion of the Armenian minority from participation in Turkish society. The key role of propaganda as a precondition that escalates risk of genocide is widely recognized, including within the temporal model. The rapid emergence and progression of these later preconditions for genocide is in stark contrast to the stability and longevity of earlier preconditions.

The swift accumulation of risk factors for genocide continued with the outbreak of the First World War. This is consistent with Kuper's identification of war as a catalyst for genocide; with Fein's final precondition, the changing costs of exterminating the victim as a result of war; and with Krain's finding of war as a significant predictor of genocide.[180] The links between the Armenian minority and the Great Powers were now links with the enemies of Ottoman Turkey. Rather than viewing the outbreak of the First World War as the fulfilment of a precondition for genocide or as a precipitant, however, it can be more accurately characterized as the removal of the most powerful constraint against genocide—a constraint that had been present since the very genesis of the Armenian question. With the outbreak of the First World War, the threat of international intervention effectively disappeared. A crucial constraint was no longer operable.

The threat of international intervention was a major restraining factor for Sultan Abdul Hamid II's regime during the massacres in 1894–96. The threat, and the reality, of international intervention continued to be a major factor affecting both internal and external politics under the Young Turk government. From the perspective of hindsight, given the complete failure of the international powers to prevent the mass slaughter of the Armenian people, it is easy to overlook the importance of this threat. At the time, however, the impotence of the European powers was not at all clear. A number of minorities had seceded with varying levels of international involvement, taking vast tracts of Ottoman territory with them. Moreover, as Feroz Ahmad asserted, 'it is impossible to exaggerate the impact' of the Balkan Wars on the Young Turks.[181] The Young Turks viewed the Armenian Reform Agreement of 1914 as an abrogation of their sovereignty, and feared that it was a step towards a repeat of the Balkan disaster and that Russia had designs upon the very heartland of Turkey.[182] Perhaps James Gidney put it most aptly: 'The complete uselessness to the Armenians of both European and American friendships must have ultimately surprised the Turks as much as anyone else.'[183]

Just how seriously the Young Turks perceived the threat of international intervention can be inferred from the example of their response to the Bitlis rebellion in March 1914. In this case, almost as soon as there were signs of Kurdish unrest in the region, troops began patrolling the city streets and the government imposed a 6.00 P.M. curfew.[184] When the Kurds rioted, the government immediately put all its forces towards suppressing the riot and capturing the rebel leaders.[185] Troops were called in from surrounding regions, and the government went so far as to distribute arms to the Armenians so that they could fight the Kurds and defend themselves.[186] While one Armenian paper interpreted this as a sign 'the Government has complete confidence in the Armenians', in fact it indicates just how fearful the government was of Russian intervention.[187] At this point—just months before the genocide would commence—the Young Turks perceived the threat of Russian intervention—and the potential loss of Anatolia—in response to the Bitlis rebellion as so serious that they were willing to arm the Armenians in response.[188]

Christopher Walker has described the First World War as providing 'a thick black velvet arras, behind which the Young Turks could act with impunity'.[189] Indeed, there is a consensus amongst both primary and secondary sources that the outbreak of the First World War was a crucial factor in determining the onset of the genocide.[190] Vahakn Dadrian described the opportunity provided by the war as the 'catalyst' for the genocide.[191] According to Dadrian, 'The presence or absence of effective external deterrence on behalf of a potential victim group is perhaps the most crucial determinant in the calculus of genocide.'[192] Miller and Miller, authors of *Survivors: An Oral History of the Armenian Genocide*, went so far as to suggest that it is doubtful a genocide (as opposed to localized massacres and persecution) would have occurred in the absence of the First World War context.[193] There is no doubt that Turkey's entry into the war effectively removed the threat of international intervention, the major restraining factor that had been protecting the Armenians from the full force of the Young Turks' wrath. Turkey's entry into the war, however, cannot be considered a cause of the genocide. The war removed the powerful restraining factor of the threat of international intervention, but almost all other factors that would lead to the genocide were already in place prior to its outbreak. As Bryce and Toynbee concluded in *The Treatment of the Armenians in the Ottoman Empire, 1915–1916*, 'It is evident that the war was merely an opportunity and not a cause—in fact, that the deportation scheme, and all that it involved, flowed inevitably from the general policy of the Young Turkish government.'[194] Indeed, Vahakn Dadrian has contended that the desire of the CUP leadership to 'solve the Armenian Question' was of considerable influence in their decision to enter the war.[195]

The Armenian Genocide

It is difficult to pinpoint exactly when the decision was made to exterminate the Armenians, and how long after that it was before a concrete plan was developed. Dadrian has suggested that 'the outlines of a genocidal scheme' were in place by the close of 1910.[196] Indeed, despite the inevitable secrecy and use of euphemisms, between 1910 and the commencement of the genocide there were a number of reports from disparate and seemingly reliable sources that referred to the CUP's determination to annihilate the Armenians.[197] In contrast to Dadrian's position, Ternon has contended that the central committee of the CUP probably only decided upon the genocide in January or February of 1915.[198] Ronald Suny, too, has dated the decision at this late juncture.[199] While the exact timing of the decision to commit genocide is contentious, there is no doubt that such a decision was made. Despite the claims and obfuscations of denialists and Turkish revisionist historians, there is overwhelming evidence that the Armenian genocide was a clear case of state-sponsored mass murder. Such evidence includes telegrams from Talaat Pasha transmitting orders regarding the genocide, official CUP documents regarding the genocide, innumerable witness accounts, survivor accounts, reports by European and American consuls and ambassadors (including those of Turkey's allies during the war) and even evidence from the postwar courts-martial in Turkey itself. Talaat's proud boast to his friends—'I have accomplished more toward solving the Armenian problem in three months than Abdul Hamid accomplished in thirty years'—is an accurate indicator of the Young Turks' genocidal campaign.[200]

On 2 August 1914 Turkey proclaimed a general mobilization, announcing that it would pursue a status of armed neutrality. Under this general mobilization, Armenian males were conscripted into the army. Yet within weeks of this conscription—which would eventually encompass all Armenian males aged fifteen to sixty—an order was given to disarm all Armenian soldiers and form them into 'labour battalions'.[201] These Armenian *amélés* were assigned to tasks such as the construction of roads, labouring and, once Turkey entered the war, the carrying of provisions for Turkish troops. The conditions under which the labour battalions survived were often terrible, and many conscripts died from hunger and exhaustion.[202] In early 1915 the first reports emerged of groups of fifty to one hundred *amélés* being taken to isolated places and executed.[203] This quickly became the fate of almost all the conscripted Armenians. For Armenian civilians, meanwhile, the outbreak of war led to further deteriorations in their conditions of life. Turkish troops moving towards the Russian front took lodging in Armenian homes, and robbery and rape were common.[204] The army's requisitioning of supplies for the war effort disproportionately affected Armenians, and in many areas descended into veritable looting.[205] In the early months of the war, there were a number of local massacres of Armenians, and Armenian civil servants were fired and their passports permitting movement within the empire were cancelled.[206] All weapons belonging to Armenians were confiscated. In this way, the preparations for genocide were quietly completed.

Both Dadrian and Ternon have remarked upon the Young Turks' careful application of the lessons learned from previous Armenian massacres.[207] Zeitoun, an Armenian stronghold during the massacres of 1894–96, was the first major target of the genocide. In late March 1915, a large contingent of troops was sent to Zeitoun. The leaders of the community were summoned for talks and then summarily arrested. A small Armenian offensive was quickly overcome, and the first of the deportations commenced.[208] Within a month, approximately twenty-three thousand Armenians had been exiled from Zeitoun and its surrounding villages. Zeitoun appears to have been used quite deliberately as a 'trial run' by the CUP, with some deportees being sent to the marshy swampland of Konya and others to Der-el-Zor in the Syrian Desert.[209] Der-el-Zor was deemed the best destination for the deportations, and became a major terminus in the following months.[210]

Van, too, was an early target during the genocide. After a number of local incidents, soldiers attacked Van on 20 April. The Armenians, however, were well prepared for the assault, having watched the surrounding villages being set ablaze.[211] The attack developed into a siege, and the Turks publicized widely that there was an Armenian rebellion at Van.[212] In reality, the Armenian actions at Van were entirely defensive.[213] The battle for Van was fierce, as testimony by one soldier indicates: 'I have rarely seen such furious fighting as took place at Van, it was an uninterrupted combat, sometimes hand to hand or with only a wall between. Nobody gave quarter or asked it.'[214] For the Armenians, it was a desperate battle for their lives. Outnumbered, outgunned and with dwindling supplies of food and ammunition, their only real hope was to hold out in the hope of rescue by the Russian army.[215] Incredibly, the Armenians of Van were able to maintain their defence for some four weeks, until the Turkish forces fled upon the approach of Russian troops.[216] They then came under Russian protection, and remained in Van until the Russian withdrawal from there on 31 July. Russian General Nikolaev ordered all Armenians in the province to retreat with the Russian army.[217] The retreat was chaotic, and thousands of Armenians died of hunger and exhaustion along the way, and of epidemics in the refugee camps established over the Russian border. Nevertheless, approximately 210,000 Van Armenians survived by escaping to Russia, and became one of only two surviving groups of any size from Turkish Armenia.[218]

On 24 April, the arrests of hundreds of Armenian intellectuals and community leaders in Constantinople commenced. This marked the beginning of the most intensive phase of the genocide, and Armenians and others around the world commemorate this day each year in remembrance. The procedure of arrests and deportations was similar in many places. First, the men of a town or village would be summoned to be present at the government building. There, they would be arrested and imprisoned for a day or two. Told they were to be deported on a long journey, they would then be marched out into the countryside, completely unequipped for travel. At the first isolated place along their journey, they would be executed.[219] Prisons were also cleared of previously incarcerated Armenians in this way. A few days following the disappearance of the men, an announcement would be made that all remaining Armenians were to be deported. Usually, but not always, the women were given a few days to prepare for the journey. The exiles were then gathered into convoys, which varied in size from two hundred to several thousand. Each convoy was provided with a detachment of police—ostensibly for protection—and would begin its long journey to Der-el-Zor, Aleppo or another desert location.[220] However, the purpose of the deportations was not to arrive at a destination, but rather to decimate the exiles along the journey. Deportees were systematically robbed, murdered, raped and left without food or water. Only a small fraction ever made it to their destination, and those that did found themselves forced on further and subject to appalling conditions and a complete lack of provisions. In this way, during the course of 1915, the Armenian population of Turkey was destroyed.

The following account, by a missionary who witnessed the exile of the Armenians of Zeitoun, gives some idea of the horrors of deportation:

> These poor exiles were mostly women, children and old men, and they were clubbed and beaten and lashed along as though they had been wild animals, and their women and girls were daily criminally outraged both by their guards and the ruffians of every village through which they passed as the former allowed the latter to enter the camp of the exiles at night and even distributed the girls among the villagers for the night. These poor victims of their oppressors' lust and hate might better have died by the bullet in their mountain home than to be dragged about the country in this way. About two thousand of them have passed through Ourfa, all more dead than alive: many hundreds have died from starvation and abuse along the roadside, and nearly all are dying of starvation, thirst, of being kidnapped by the Anaza Arabs in the desert where they have been taken.[221]

Deportees were typically kept away from cities and villages, both to prevent them from getting access to food and water and to prevent them from being seen by those who 'would wonder what was going on'.[222] Many were marched through the mountains and deserts for months. One survivor summarized it as such: 'Walk, walk, walk; the world didn't seem to end.'[223] Most were robbed of everything in the course of their journey. They had no shoes, no tents and were even robbed of their clothing.[224] Many arrived at their destination completely naked and nearly black from sunburn.[225] But the majority did not arrive at all. One survivor recounted that so many bodies were strewn along the deportation route that 'we used to try to avoid stepping on them'.[226]

The genocide targeted all Armenians, but there was a significant difference in the treatment of men and women. For men, the marked features were torture and rapid extermination. In particular, the community leaders in each area, arrested prior to the deportations, were often subjected to torture, to force (usually false) admissions of revolutionary activity and to reveal the secret locations of their arms. For women and children, the primary method of extermination was through deportation. Yet, as one witness revealed, there was no sparing the cruelty to which the women were subjected:

> Women with little children in their arms, or in the last days of pregnancy were driven along under the whip like cattle. Three different cases came under my knowledge

where the woman was delivered on the road, and because her brutal driver hurried her along she died of haemorrhage.[227]

The rape of women and girls was so widespread during the genocide that it is a feature of almost every account. Gendarmes were reportedly told that they 'may do as they wish with the women and girls'.[228] Indeed, German consul Bergfeld believed rape to be part of the plan for 'the virtually complete extermination of the Armenians'.[229] Also common was the kidnapping of girls and young women, either for the purposes of forced marriage to Turks, for Turkish harems or for a booming slave trade.

The perpetrators of the genocide fell into a number of different categories. The gendarmerie was heavily involved, arresting, torturing and murdering the men, and organizing and accompanying the deportations. Provincial governors, local party leaders and civil authorities also played key roles in the organization of the genocide.[230] In 1914, the 'Special Organization' was created by the Young Turks. Consisting of bands of criminals released from prisons throughout the empire, the *chété*, as they were known, were charged with attacking the caravans and the actual butchering of deportees.[231] Kurdish tribal groups were similarly encouraged to attack the columns of defenceless women, children and old men.[232] Finally, the Turkish rural populace also played a significant role, participating primarily in the extensive plundering and the raping and kidnapping of women and girls. As Morgenthau has stated, 'Every caravan had a continuous battle for existence with several classes of enemies—their accompanying gendarmes, the Turkish peasants and villagers, the Kurdish tribes and bands of *chétés* or brigands.'[233]

There were numerous motives that influenced the participation of these groups. The diffusion of pan-Turkish ideology into all levels of Turkish society provided an exclusivist rationale that justified the genocide in the eyes of adherents. Moreover, it complemented the previous paradigms of *millet* and *giaour*—sufficient justification for previous massacres—and thus, to some extent, the population was already desensitized and primed to massacre, regardless of the ideology. While there was no separate propaganda ministry within the CUP government, the Young Turks did engage in extensive propaganda.[234] Rumour was also used extensively, and was a particularly powerful tool. The CUP repeatedly spread rumours of an impending Armenian rebellion, of Armenian stockpiles of hidden weapons and of instances of Armenian disloyalty and treason.[235] The Armenian Reform Agreement of 1914 was falsely characterized, and presented particularly to the Turkish refugees from the Balkans 'as a Christian gimmick to subdue and crush Muslims'.[236] The rumour of Armenian rebellion, and the prospect of Armenians ruling over Moslems, was particularly effective in inciting violence. The events at Zeitoun and Van were publicized as Armenian rebellions, both to inflame the Turkish population and to provide justification to foreign powers for the Young Turk response. Beyond ideology and rumour, however, two very powerful motives combined. These were the prospect of plunder, and the reassurance that there would be no punishment for any actions taken against Armenians. According to Dadrian, 'the Armenian genocide was punctuated by prodigious pillage'.[237] All the categories of perpetrators were heavily involved, with senior officials reaping vast sums of gold, money and jewellery, gendarmes taking the most valuable items from Armenian houses, Turkish women and children following them in to take whatever else they could, and peasants, *chétés* and Kurds stealing everything the deportees carried with them. Finally, perpetrators were secure in the knowledge that any action against Armenians, be it murder, rape or theft, would go completely unpunished.

There were very few opportunities for resistance to the genocide, either by the Armenians or Turks opposed to the genocide. In what appears as meticulous planning, the genocide first involved the conscription of able-bodied men, the disarming of the civilian population and the removal of community leaders, followed by the separation of men from their families. This progression, combined with the demographic reality of the majority of the Armenian population existing as minorities within small villages, made resistance all but impossible. It must also be noted that communication in the empire, and especially in remote parts, was slow. Armenians did not immediately perceive the breadth and severity of the genocidal plan to which they fell victim.[238] Nevertheless, there were some attempts at self-defence. The events at Van described earlier constitute the most notable case of Armenian resistance. In Ourfa, Armenians also decided to fight, but were quickly overpowered by Turkish troops.[239] The battle for Sassoun was fierce but ultimately futile, and there was also resistance at Zeitoun (as mentioned above) and Musa Dagh.[240] From the Turkish perspective, there were few bystanders who actively opposed the genocidal policies. Again, however, the government had acted so as to forestall any opportunities for intervention on behalf of the Armenians. Officials known to be friendly or lenient towards Armenians were either sent off on another task while the Armenians in their areas were murdered and deported, or removed from their post and replaced with more cooperative officials.[241] Furthermore, the punishment for assisting Armenians was the death penalty.[242] While the vast majority of the Turkish population acquiesced in the genocide, there were many individual cases of Turks, Kurds and Arabs risking their lives to help and save Armenians.[243]

The deportations swept through all the Armenian provinces with astonishing speed. In May and June, Erzeroum was targeted, while deportations from Sivas, Harpout, Trebizond and Samsun commenced in June. In July there were deportations from the Cilician region, including Antioch, and from Aintab and Ankara. August saw the focus move to western Anatolia, Marash and Konya. Deportations from Broussa were in early September, and Adrianople was targeted in mid-October. The process was so well controlled that American consul Leslie Davis commented in a letter to Ambassador Morgenthau that '[t]he entire movement seems to be the most thoroughly organized and effective massacre this country has ever seen'.[244] Some areas were singled out for special treatment. In July, in Bitlis, Moush and Sassoun the military—with the assistance of the Kurds—exterminated rather than deported most of the Armenian population, on account of their proximity to Van and the advancing Russian forces.[245] From some metropolitan districts and the northwest, deportees were transported to Aleppo by rail rather than foot. These deportees suffered no less hardship—packed into cattle wagons, their journey was incredibly slow, and at every stopping place they were turned out without food or shelter.[246] These deportees also had to traverse the two breaks in the Baghdad Railway, the ranges of the Taurus and Amanus Mountains, on foot.[247] For other deportees, their journey involved a river crossing, often the Euphrates, and these river crossings were occasions for 'wholesale murder'.[248] In Constantinople and Smyrna, many Armenians were exempted from deportation. While most of the community leaders that had been arrested in late April were killed or deported, there were many protests in the capital due to the proximity of foreign embassies. For this reason, many of the remaining Armenians there were spared.[249]

The speed of the genocide was such that by early August Talaat Pasha could tell American ambassador Morgenthau, in response to a plea for the Armenians: 'It is no use for you to argue, we have already disposed of three-quarters of the Armenians; there are none at all left in Bitlis, Van and Erzeroum.'[250] Indeed, the death rate was so high that thousands of bodies were strewn across the deportation routes. The problem became so severe that Talaat himself had to send out several telegrams ordering their disposal.[251] As the genocide progressed, the goal of the complete destruction of the Armenian people became even more extreme. Talaat forbade any conversions of Armenians to Islam, except of those 'removed to their place of exile'.[252] Whereas previously children under seven were to be spared, this instruction was reviewed to include only children under five.[253] Even this was abandoned, as orphanages that had been established to bring up the young children as Turks were closed, and the children either killed or sent to their death via deportation.[254]

Yves Ternon has estimated that around one-third of those deported survived to reach the deportation camps.[255] The main congregation points were at Damascus, south of Aleppo, and Der-el-Zor, on the Euphrates. Yet there was no destination in reality:

> It was very easy to push this mass of humanity made up of women and children from one camp to another 'until thousands are reduced to hundreds and hundreds to a tiny group and this group pursued until it no longer exists. And thus the end of the voyage is reached.' And thus the last of the Armenians were swallowed up by the desert sands.[256]

There were no provisions made for the deportees. Instead, they were robbed, raped, starved and exposed to the elements, and they died daily by the hundreds. One survivor from Marash described the scene he witnessed when approaching Der-el-Zor:

We saw a lot of Armenians who had gotten there much earlier than us, and they had turned into skeletons. We were surrounded with skeletons so much that it felt like we were in hell. They were all hungry and thirsty, and they would look for familiar faces to help them. We became terribly discouraged, so hopeless that it is hard to explain exactly how we felt. From grief my father became ill.[257]

For those who insisted upon surviving, the government ordered three large massacres at the deportation camps.[258] By the end of 1916, the genocide of the Armenians had claimed the vast majority of its victims.

It is very difficult to estimate the number of victims of the Armenian genocide. Toynbee estimated around six hundred thousand Armenians were killed up to the point of his writing, in early 1916.[259] Following the war, in the brief period when the Turkish government recognized the genocide and when the courts-martial were in progress, the Turkish interior minister admitted that eight hundred thousand Armenians were killed throughout the deportation process.[260] Robert Melson has estimated around one million were killed, while Christopher Walker has suggested a figure of 1.5 million for the period between the outbreak of the First World War and 1922.[261] Gerard Libaridian has estimated 1.5 million were killed during the genocide; Yves Ternon put the total death toll at between 1.2 and 1.5 million.[262] Altogether, it can be concluded that approximately half of the Armenian population of Turkey, and one-third of the Armenian population globally, died as a result of the genocide.[263]

The Armenian Genocide and the Temporal Model

Historians have often referred to the Hamidian massacres of 1894–96 as a 'dress rehearsal' for the subsequent genocide. But did these events differ only in scope, or can they be regarded as qualitatively different? Many commentators writing immediately after the genocide believed that, despite the regime change, the main difference between the massacres and genocide should be regarded as the level of success of the perpetrators. Toynbee, for example, while acknowledging the ideological differences between Sultan Abdul Hamid II and the Young Turks, believed that the CUP essentially 'clothed the same evil in a more clearly-cut and infinitely more dynamic form'.[264] In contrast, Melson has suggested that the massacres and genocide were qualitatively different, pursued for distinct purposes:

> Although some of the same factors that precipitated the massacres also led to the genocide, the latter instance of violence was qualitatively different. In the first instance the regime of Abdul Hamid II used massacre against the Armenians not to destroy the community but to restore an old order; in the later genocide the regime of the Committee of Union and Progress used genocide to eliminate the Armenians from the Turkish social structure.[265]

Helen Fein, too, has commented that the policies of each regime were only 'superficially' similar.[266] Yet Dadrian has contended there are much deeper connections:[267] 'In the final analysis . . . what emerges here as a single common denominator is the ethos of massacre, prevalent in the regimes of both Sultan Abdul Hamit and Ittihad [CUP].'[268]

The temporal model enables the massacres and genocide to be analysed within a new analytical framework. It highlights genocide as the culmination of an often cyclic process of risk escalation followed by retreat. Within this framework, the massacres can be understood as a peak within the cyclic process that ultimately led to the genocide—a point characterized by the fulfilment of some but not all preconditions for genocide. This facilitates due recognition of both the commonalities and unique elements associated with each violent episode. It also places the Cilician massacres within a context previously lacking. The Cilician massacres can be difficult to characterize, and are often largely omitted from analyses as a result. Yet within the framework of the temporal model, a localized process of risk escalation can be identified. The Cilician massacres form another peak within the cyclic process of temporal progress of risk of genocide.

The temporal model also provides a context through which the ongoing vulnerability of the Armenian minority can be understood, despite the 1908 regime change, and despite the very different ideological frameworks through which each regime operated. The Armenian case study highlights that a change of government—even a revolutionary one—may not itself be of great import for a nation's risk of genocide. This is consistent with a historical examination of outgroups generally, many of whom have been long-standing targets of violence and discrimination under successive regimes and in different locations (Jews and Roma, for example). Indeed, despite the discrete ideological frameworks through which the Abdul Hamid II and Young Turk regimes operated, it is clear that many of the same elements of conflict propelled both the massacres and the genocide.[269] Each regime was presented with the problem of the 'Armenian question'. Each regime, at least at times, associated the Armenians with an existential threat to its continued dominance. Each regime, within the unique constellation of precipitants and constraints under which it operated, chose to address the 'Armenian question' through massive violence.

The rapidity with which the later preconditions for genocide succeeded each other is in stark contrast to the longevity and stability of the earlier preconditions. The period between 1910 and 1915 was one of dramatic escalation of risk, culminating in the outbreak of genocide in April 1915. While closely linked temporally, a number of distinct factors influenced this process. Russia's resurrection of the issue of Armenian reforms in the wake of the Ottoman defeat in the Balkans once again triggered perceptions of the Armenian minority as being closely associated with a serious existential threat to the integrity of the empire. This risk factor substantially increased the risk of an outbreak of violence. At the same time, the new ideology of pan-Turkism emerged. Turkish nationalism actively excluded the Armenian minority, effectively making it an ideology that enabled and facilitated the subsequent genocide. During the period in which the Armenian reforms were negotiated, this ideology became increasingly radical, and increasingly took hold in both the Young Turk government and society. In a society already primed with anti-Armenian sentiment, the diffusion of this ideology effectively functioned as a propaganda campaign that would justify ideologically the genocide to come.

Utilizing the concepts of precipitants and inhibitory factors in analyzing the Armenian massacres and genocide particularly highlights the significant role of Europe in both restraining and precipitating the outbreaks of violence in a way that previous analyses have not. As we have seen, Europe's role regarding the Treaties of San Stefano and Berlin, and particularly its failure to enforce the Treaty of Berlin, was instrumental in precipitating the Armenian massacres. Indeed, numerous observers at the time commented that if it were not for the Treaty of Berlin, the Armenian massacres would not have occurred. Following Sassoun, the ill-conceived and ill-fated Scheme of Armenian Reforms precipitated the major outbreak of massacres in 1895, and shaped their timing, location and nature. Europe's failure to impose any sanctions or punishments upon the empire in the wake of the massacres contributed to the 'legacy of impunity' that facilitated the Armenian genocide.[270] Furthermore, the Armenian Reform Agreement of 1914 once more exacerbated tensions while failing to benefit the Armenians in any way. According to Dadrian: 'The issue of Armenian Reforms emerges here as the central and abiding issue around which the Turko-Armenian conflict crystallized throughout the eras of Abdul Hamit and the Young Turk Ittihadists.'[271] Europe's intermittent intervention in Armenian affairs was key to the development and progression of the entire conflict. While it was intended to be benign (although not purely altruistic), and certainly for some periods restrained the outbreak of violence, the consequences of Europe's meddling were overwhelmingly negative. Arguably, had Europe never interfered in Ottoman Armenian affairs, the oppression of the Armenian people may never have evolved into genocide. As Dadrian has elucidated: 'When international actors intervene in response to persecutions in another state without firm coordination and commitment, any actions they take may actually do more harm than good.'[272] The Armenian tragedy contains many lessons on the dangers of intermittent, insufficient and ineffective intervention, lessons still of great relevance today.

This chapter, therefore, offers insight into the processes that lead to genocide and their development over time. Previous explorations of the risk factors for genocide have led to a number of models of the necessary and sufficient preconditions. Whilst extremely valuable, they offer little information as to how these preconditions develop over time. Through a historical examination of the development of risk of genocide in Ottoman Armenia, however, my analysis has sought to contribute to our understanding of the temporal progression of these preconditions.

A number of significant findings have emerged: the stability and longevity of early preconditions; the role of perceptions of the outgroup as an existential threat in provoking risk escalation processes; the presence of a cyclic process whereby risk escalation is followed by partial retreat; the role of precipitants and constraints; and finally, the very rapid coalescence of the later preconditions for genocide. The question arises, however, as to if the way in which risk of genocide emerged over time in the Ottoman Empire was idiosyncratic, or if it exemplifies a common pattern. To explore this question, I will now turn to a very different example of genocide: that of Rwanda in 1994.

Notes

1. H. Morgenthau. 1918. *Ambassador Morgenthau's Story*, New York: Doubleday, Page, 188.
2. Ibid.
3. Ibid., 188; G.S. Graber. 1996. *Caravans to Oblivion: The Armenian Genocide 1915*, New York: J. Wiley, 46.
4. Graber, *Caravans to Oblivion*, 45.
5. Morgenthau, *Ambassador Morgenthau's Story*, 188.
6. J. Bryce and A. Toynbee. 2000. *The Treatment of Armenians in the Ottoman Empire, 1915–1916*, uncensored ed., edited and with an introduction by Ara Sarafian, Princeton, NJ: Gomidas Institute, 625 (originally published 1916).
7. Y. Ternon. 1981. *The Armenians: History of a Genocide*, Delmar, NY: Caravan Books, 162.
8. Ibid.
9. Ibid.
10. Ibid.
11. Ibid., 162–63.
12. V. Dadrian. 1995. *The History of the Armenian Genocide: Ethnic Conflict from the Balkans to Anatolia to the Caucasus*, Providence, RI: Berghahn Books, 182; Graber, *Caravans to Oblivion*, 48, estimated thirty thousand; R. Hovannisian. 1986. 'The Historical Dimensions of the Armenian Question, 1878–1923', in R. Hovannisian (ed.), *The Armenian Genocide in Perspective*, New Brunswick, NJ: Transaction Publishers, 27, estimated twenty thousand; D. Miller and L.T. Miller. 1993. *Survivors: An Oral History of the Armenian Genocide*, Berkeley: University of California Press, 63, estimated twenty thousand, as did D. Bloxham. 2005. *The Great Game of Genocide: Imperialism, Nationalism, and the Destruction of the Ottoman Armenians*, Oxford: Oxford University Press, 60.
13. Ternon, *The Armenians*, 164.
14. Ibid.
15. Ibid.
16. H.C. Woods. 1911. *The Danger Zone of Europe: Changes and Problems in the Near East*, Boston: Little, Brown, 129.
17. Dadrian, *The History of the Armenian Genocide*, 182.
18. Ternon, *The Armenians*, 165.
19. Ibid.; Dadrian, *The History of the Armenian Genocide*, 182–83; Woods, *The Danger Zone*, 134.
20. Dadrian, *The History of the Armenian Genocide*, 183; Woods, *The Danger Zone*, 133–34.
21. Woods, *The Danger Zone*, 155.
22. Ibid.

23. Ibid., 155–56.
24. Ibid., 159.
25. Ibid.
26. Ibid., 159–60.
27. Ibid., 160.
28. Ibid., 160–64.
29. Graber, *Caravans to Oblivion*, 48.
30. Woods, *The Danger Zone*, 147.
31. Ibid.
32. Ibid., 148.
33. Ibid., 147–48.
34. Ternon, *The Armenians*, 165.
35. Woods, *The Danger Zone*, 164.
36. Ibid., 164–65.
37. Ibid., 165.
38. Ibid., 135.
39. Ibid.
40. Ibid.; Dadrian, *The History of the Armenian Genocide*, 183.
41. Graber, *Caravans to Oblivion*, 48.
42. Ternon, *The Armenians*, 166–67.
43. Dadrian, *The History of the Armenian Genocide*, 183.
44. Ternon, *The Armenians*, 166.
45. Ibid.
46. Dadrian, *The History of the Armenian Genocide*, 183.
47. Ibid.
48. Woods, *The Danger Zone*, 174.
49. Ternon, *The Armenians*, 164.
50. Dadrian, *The History of the Armenian Genocide*, 182; Woods, *The Danger Zone*, 175; Bloxham, *The Great Game*, 60.
51. Dadrian, *The History of the Armenian Genocide*, 182.
52. E. Pears. 1911. *Turkey and Its People*, London: Methuen, 293.
53. F. Ahmad. 1982. 'Unionist Relations with the Greek, Armenian, and Jewish Communities of the Ottoman Empire, 1908–1914', in B. Braude and B. Lewis (eds), *Christians and Jews in the Ottoman Empire: The Functioning of a Plural Society*, vol. I, *The Central Lands*, New York: Holmes & Meier Publishers, 420.
54. Woods, *The Danger Zone*, 170–71; Bloxham, *The Great Game*, 61.
55. Ibid.
56. This was probably due to the proximity of foreign consuls, and the presence of international warships that patrolled the nearby coast.
57. Woods, *The Danger Zone*, 176; Bloxham, *The Great Game*, 61.
58. Dadrian, *The History of the Armenian Genocide*, 183; Ahmad, 'Unionist Relations', 421.
59. Dadrian, *The History of the Armenian Genocide*, 183.
60. Woods, *The Danger Zone*, 180.
61. Ibid., 188.
62. Ibid., 183; Dadrian, *The History of the Armenian Genocide*, 182.
63. Woods, *The Danger Zone*, 185–86. Woods believed that the Young Turk government feared the general or local effect of punishing these leaders more severely.
64. Ibid., 188; Ahmad, 'Unionist Relations', 421.
65. Ahmad, 'Unionist Relations', 421.
66. Ternon, *The Armenians*, 167.

67. Ibid.
68. Pears, *Turkey and Its People*, 293–94.
69. Woods, *The Danger Zone*, 140.
70. Ibid., 143.
71. G. Libaridian. 1987. 'The Ultimate Repression: The Genocide of the Armenians, 1915–1917', in I. Wallimann and M. Dobkowski (eds), *Genocide and the Modern Age: Etiology and Case Studies of Mass Death*, New York: Greenwood Press, 210.
72. Woods, *The Danger Zone*, 178.
73. Ibid.
74. Ternon, *The Armenians*, 168.
75. V. Dadrian. 2003. 'The Armenian Genocide: An Interpretation', in J. Winter (ed.), *America and the Armenian Genocide of 1915*, Cambridge: Cambridge University Press, 53.
76. Dadrian, *The History of the Armenian Genocide*, 180; T. Akçam. 2007. *A Shameful Act: The Armenian Genocide and the Question of Turkish Responsibility*, London: Constable, 70.
77. E. Staub. 1989. *The Roots of Evil: The Origins of Genocide and Other Group Violence*, Cambridge: Cambridge University Press, 17.
78. N. Buxton and H. Buxton. 1914. *Travel and Politics in Armenia*, New York: Macmillan, 42.
79. Ibid., 109.
80. Ibid., 109–10.
81. Ibid.
82. Ibid.
83. Ibid.
84. R. Davison. 1948. 'The Armenian Crisis, 1912–1914', *The American Historical Review* 53(3), 482.
85. Buxton and Buxton, *Travel and Politics*, 45.
86. Ibid.
87. Ibid., 113.
88. Ibid., 47.
89. Ibid., 48.
90. Ibid.
91. Ibid.
92. Ibid., 112.
93. Ibid., 117; Davison, 'The Armenian Crisis', 482–83.
94. Buxton and Buxton, *Travel and Politics*, 36–37.
95. Ibid., 118.
96. Ibid.
97. Ibid., 111–12.
98. Ibid., 50.
99. Ibid., 110.
100. Ibid., 42.
101. Ibid., 50–51.
102. Ibid., 50.
103. Ibid., 45.
104. Ibid., 109.
105. R. Melson. 1986. 'Provocation or Nationalism: A Critical Inquiry into the Armenian Genocide of 1915', in Hovannisian, *The Armenian Genocide in Perspective*, 71–73; U.U. Ungör. 2012. *The Making of Modern Turkey: Nation and State in Eastern Anatolia, 1913–1950*, Oxford: Oxford University Press, 43.
106. Melson, 'Provocation or Nationalism', 71–73; Graber, *Caravans to Oblivion*, 49.
107. Davison, 'The Armenian Crisis', 483.

108. V. Dadrian. 1998. *Warrant for Genocide: Key Elements of Turko-Armenian Conflict*, New Brunswick, NJ: Transaction Publishers, 112; Ternon, *The Armenians*, 170.

109. F. Mazian. 1990. *Why Genocide? The Armenian and Jewish Experiences in Perspective*, Ames: Iowa State University Press, 51.

110. F. Nansen. 1928. *Armenia and the Near East*, London: George Allen and Unwin, 296–97, quoted in Dadrian, *Warrant for Genocide*, 112; F. Nansen. 1928. *L'Arménie et le Proche Orient*, Paris: Librairie Orientaliste, 330–31, quoted in Dadrian, *Warrant for Genocide*, 145.

111. 1913. Report of British consul at Erzeroum, Consul Moynahan, 28 August 1913, quoted in Dadrian, *Warrant for Genocide*, 146.

112. Dadrian, *Warrant for Genocide*, 145.

113. Melson, 'Provocation or Nationalism', 72.

114. Dadrian, 'The Armenian Genocide', 58.

115. Ibid.

116. Ibid., 58–59.

117. Akçam, *A Shameful Act*, xvii.

118. S. Sazonov. 1928. *Fateful Years: 1909–1916: The Reminiscences of Serge Sazonov*, London: Jonathan Cape, 141.

119. Ibid.

120. Ternon, *The Armenians*, 174.

121. W.J. van der Dussen. 1991. 'The Question of Armenian Reforms in 1913–1914', in Institute for Armenian Studies (ed.), *The Armenian Genocide*, vol. 3, Munich: Institute for Armenian Studies, 391; Davison, 'The Armenian Crisis', 487.

122. Ibid.; Ahmad, 'Unionist Relations', 423.

123. Ibid.

124. Ibid.; Davison, 'The Armenian Crisis', 489.

125. Ahmad, 'Unionist Relations', 424; Bryce and Toynbee, *The Treatment of Armenians*, 633.

126. Van der Dussen, 'The Question', 393; Davison, 'The Armenian Crisis', 493.

127. Van der Dussen, 'The Question', 395.

128. Ahmad, 'Unionist Relations', 424.

129. Ibid.

130. Ternon, *The Armenians*, 176.

131. Ibid., 177.

132. Ibid.

133. Bryce and Toynbee, *The Treatment of Armenians*, 633.

134. Ibid.; Ternon, *The Armenians*, 177.

135. Bryce and Toynbee, *The Treatment of Armenians*, 633; Ternon, *The Armenians*, 177.

136. Ternon, *The Armenians*, 177.

137. Van der Dussen, 'The Question', 394; Davison, 'The Armenian Crisis', 493.

138. Bryce and Toynbee, *The Treatment of Armenians*, 633.

139. Ibid.

140. L.C. Westenenk. 1991. 'Dairy Concerning the Armenian Mission', in Institute for Armenian Studies, *The Armenian Genocide*, vol. 3, 418, 403–58.

141. Sazonov, *Fateful Years*, 145.

142. Ternon, *The Armenians*, 178; Akçam, *A Shameful Act*, 101–2.

143. Sazonov, *Fateful Years*, 136, italics added.

144. Davison, 'The Armenian Crisis', 488–89; Ahmad, 'Unionist Relations', 424; van der Dussen, 'The Question', 392.

145. Dadrian, *The History of the Armenian Genocide*, 194.

146. Bryce and Toynbee, *The Treatment of Armenians*, 633.

147. Ibid., 634.

148. Ibid.
149. Dadrian, *The History of the Armenian Genocide*, 198.
150. Libaridian, 'The Ultimate Repression', 210–11.
151. Woods, *The Danger Zone*, 169.
152. E. Jackh. 1944. *The Rising Crescent: Turkey Yesterday, Today and Tomorrow*, New York: Farrar and Rinehart, 94.
153. Melson, *Revolution and Genocide*, 160.
154. Ibid., 161.
155. Ibid., 163.
156. Ibid.
157. This ideology is also referred to as pan-Turanism.
158. Libaridian, 'The Ultimate Repression', 210.
159. Dadrian, *The History of the Armenian Genocide*, 179.
160. Jackh, *The Rising Crescent*, 94.
161. Dadrian, *The History of the Armenian Genocide*, 179.
162. 1910. Report written by British ambassador Lowther, 6 September, doc. no. 181 in G.P. Gooch and H.W.V. Temperley (eds), *British Documents on the Origins of the War 1889–1914*, vol. 9, part I, quoted in Dadrian, *The History of the Armenian Genocide*, 179.
163. Dadrian, *The History of the Armenian Genocide*, 180.
164. Ternon, *The Armenians*, 150.
165. Melson, *Revolution and Genocide*, 165; Ungor, *The Making of Modern Turkey*, 35.
166. Melson, *Revolution and Genocide*, 164, 166.
167. Ibid., 166.
168. Ibid., 169.
169. Ibid., 168.
170. Ternon, *The Armenians*, 158.
171. Mazian, *Why Genocide?*, 71.
172. Ternon, *The Armenians*, 157.
173. Mazian, *Why Genocide?*, 17–18.
174. Morgenthau, *Ambassador Morgenthau's Story*, 50.
175. Melson, *Revolution and Genocide*, 165.
176. Ternon, *The Armenians*, 158.
177. Melson, *Revolution and Genocide*, 167.
178. Ternon, *The Armenians*, 156.
179. H. Fein. 1979. *Accounting for Genocide: National Responses and Jewish Victimization during the Holocaust*, New York: Free Press, 9; L. Kuper. 1981. *Genocide: Its Political Use in the Twentieth Century*, New Haven, CT: Yale University Press, 84.
180. Kuper, *Genocide*, passim; Fein, *Accounting for Genocide*, 9; M. Krain. 1997. 'State-Sponsored Mass Murder: The Onset and Severity of Genocides and Politicides', *Journal of Conflict Resolution* 41(3), 331–60.
181. F. Ahmad. 1988. 'War and Society Under the Young Turks', *Review: Fernand Braudel Center* 11(2), 266.
182. Ahmad, 'Unionist Relations', 424; Ternon, *The Armenians*, 178.
183. J. Gidney. 1967. *A Mandate for Armenia*, Kent, OH: Kent State University Press, quoted in N. Ravitch. 1981. 'The Armenian Massacre', *Encounter* 57(6), 76.
184. Ahmad, 'Unionist Relations', 424.
185. Ibid.
186. Ibid.
187. 1914. *The Orient* 5(4), 131, quoted in Ahmad, 'Unionist Relations', 425; Ahmad, 'Unionist Relations', 424–25.

188. Ahmad, 'Unionist Relations', 424.
189. C. Walker. 1980. *Armenia: The Survival of a Nation*, New York: St. Martin's Press, 200, quoted in Mazian, *Why Genocide?*, 63.
190. For example, Mazian, *Why Genocide?*, 63; R. Smith. 1994. 'Introduction: The Armenian Genocide: Perpetration, Denial, Documentation', *Journal of Political and Military Sociology* 22(1), vii; Melson, 'Provocation or Nationalism', 80; 1915. Report by German consul Roessler from Aleppo, no. 120, 27 July, in Y. Ternon (ed.), *The Armenian Genocide: Facts and Documents*, New York: Diocese of the Armenian Apostolic Church of America, 34; H. Fein. 1978. 'A Formula for Genocide: Comparison of the Turkish Genocide (1915) and the German Holocaust (1939–1945)', *Comparative Studies in Sociology* 1, 279 (Fein also quoted Bryce and Toynbee, *The Treatment of Armenians*, 633); V. Dadrian. 1994. 'A Review of the Main Features of the Genocide', *Journal of Political and Military Sociology* 22(1), 3 (Dadrian also quoted Morgenthau and Talaat expressing the same view); 1915. Gage to Morgenthau, December, R. G. 59,867.4016/253/encl., quoted in A. Hairapetian. 1984. '"Race Problems" and the Armenian Genocide: The State Department File', *Armenian Review* 37(1), 57.
191. Dadrian, *Warrant for Genocide*, 113.
192. Ibid., 160.
193. Miller and Miller, *Survivors*, 49.
194. Bryce and Toynbee, *The Treatment of Armenians*, 633, quoted in Fein, 'A Formula for Genocide', 279.
195. Dadrian, 'The Armenian Genocide', 62.
196. Dadrian, *Warrant for Genocide*, 93–99; Dadrian, *The History of the Armenian Genocide*, 179–80.
197. Dadrian, *Warrant for Genocide*, 94–101.
198. Ternon, *History of a Genocide*, 197. Ternon qualified this statement by noting: 'Lacking the minutes of the Central Committee's deliberations, one can only offer up hypotheses.'
199. R. Suny. 1983. *Armenia in the Twentieth Century*, Chico, CA: Scholars Press, 18.
200. Morgenthau, *Ambassador Morgenthau's Story*, 227.
201. Dadrian, *Warrant for Genocide*, 118–19.
202. Miller and Miller, *Survivors*, 41.
203. Morgenthau, *Ambassador Morgenthau's Story*, 302–3.
204. Ternon, *History of a Genocide*, 195.
205. Ibid.
206. Ibid., 195–96; Bloxham, *The Great Game*, 71.
207. Ternon, *History of a Genocide*, 209–10; Dadrian, *Warrant for Genocide*, 152.
208. Mazian, *Why Genocide?*, 88.
209. Ternon, *History of a Genocide*, 211.
210. Mazian, *Why Genocide?*, 88.
211. Ternon, *History of a Genocide*, 214.
212. Morgenthau, *Ambassador Morgenthau's Story*, 198.
213. Ibid., 199; Dadrian, *Warrant for Genocide*, 116–17; Ternon, *History of a Genocide*, 214–16.
214. R. de Nogales. 1926. *Four Years Beneath the Crescent*, trans. Muna Lee, New York: Scribner's, 76, quoted in Dadrian, *Warrant for Genocide*, 117.
215. Ternon, *History of a Genocide*, 215.
216. Dadrian, *Warrant for Genocide*, 116.
217. Ternon, *History of a Genocide*, 216.
218. Ibid.
219. Bryce and Toynbee, *The Treatment of Armenians*, 637–38.
220. Ibid., 641–42.
221. 1915. Report from Reverend F.H. Leslie (missionary from Ourfa), quoted by American consul Jackson in report to American ambassador at Constantinople Henry Morgenthau, from

Aleppo, 28 June, R.G. 59, 867.4016/92, no. 303, in 1984, in 'Documents: The State Department File', *Armenian Review* 37(1), 89.

222. Miller and Miller, *Survivors*, 82.

223. Ibid.

224. Ibid., 83.

225. Ibid.

226. Ibid., 83–84.

227. 1915. Report on persecution of Armenians, by an American citizen and an eyewitness, 'A Brief Statement of the Present Situation of the Armenian Exiles in this Region, June 20, 1915', R. G. 59, 867.4016/97, no. 1130, in 1984, in 'Documents: The State Department File', 93.

228. 1915. Communication from US consul at Aleppo J.B. Jackson to Ambassador Morgenthau, 12 May, R. G. 59, 867.4016/72, quoted in Graber, *Caravans to Oblivion*, 114.

229. Dadrian, 'The Armenian Genocide', 83.

230. Bryce and Toynbee, *The Treatment of Armenians*, 649.

231. Miller and Miller, *Survivors*, 43. There were tens of thousands of Special Organization members used for this task, and they reported directly to senior government officials and members of the CUP; see V. Dadrian. 1986. 'The Naim-Andonian Documents on the World War I Destruction of Ottoman Armenians: The Anatomy of a Genocide', *International Journal of Middle East Studies* 18(3), 342; Libaridian, 'The Ultimate Repression', 205.

232. Miller and Miller, *Survivors*, 44.

233. Morgenthau, *Ambassador Morgenthau's Story*, 209.

234. Mazian, *Why Genocide?*, 70, 72. 'Department II' of the Turkish War Office operated a secret propaganda campaign; see Dadrian, *The History of the Armenian Genocide*, 220.

235. Mazian, *Why Genocide?*, 73–75.

236. Dadrian, *Warrant for Genocide*, 145.

237. Dadrian, 'The Armenian Genocide', 84.

238. Miller and Miller, *Survivors*, 72.

239. Ibid., 74–75.

240. Document 22, *Blue Book*, quoted in B. Papazian. 1918. *The Tragedy of Armenia: A Brief Study and Interpretation*, Boston: Pilgrim Press, 118–19.

241. Graber, *Caravans to Oblivion*, 109; Libaridian, 'The Ultimate Repression', 205.

242. Ibid.; 1917. *Germany, Turkey and Armenia: A Selection of Documentary Evidence Relating to the Armenian Atrocities from German and Other Sources*, London: J.J. Keliher, 126.

243. Libaridian, 'The Ultimate Repression', 205.

244. 1915. Report of Consul Leslie A. Davis to Ambassador Morgenthau, 11 July, quoted in Ternon, *The Armenian Genocide*, 33.

245. Bryce and Toynbee, *The Treatment of Armenians*, 638.

246. Ibid., 641.

247. Ibid.

248. Ibid., 640.

249. Ternon, *History of a Genocide*, 218.

250. Morgenthau, *Ambassador Morgenthau's Story*, 224.

251. Graber, *Caravans to Oblivion*, 104.

252. A. Andonian (ed.). 1920. *Documents officiels concernant les massacres Arméniens*, Paris: Imprimerie Tourabian, 148, quoted in Ternon, *History of a Genocide*, 252.

253. Ternon, *History of a Genocide*, 252.

254. Ibid., 252–53.

255. Ibid., 335.

256. Ibid., 254. Portion in quotation marks from Dr. M. Niepage, 'Quelques documents sur le sort des Arméniens', 149, as quoted in Ternon, *History of a Genocide*.

257. Miller and Miller, *Survivors*, 84.
258. Ternon, *History of a Genocide*, 256.
259. Bryce and Toynbee, *The Treatment of Armenians*, 647.
260. Dadrian, 'The Naim-Andonian Documents', 342. This figure excluded Armenian soldiers executed by Turkish forces and other subgroups.
261. Melson, 'Provocation or Nationalism', 66; Walker, *Armenia*, 230.
262. Libaridian, 'The Ultimate Repression', 206; Ternon, *History of a Genocide*, 260.
263. Miller and Miller, *Survivors*, 44.
264. Bryce and Toynbee, *The Treatment of Armenians*, 634.
265. Melson, *Revolution and Genocide*, 44.
266. Fein, 'A Formula for Genocide', 282.
267. Dadrian, *Warrant for Genocide*, 155–58.
268. Ibid., 158.
269. Dadrian, 'The Armenian Genocide', 53.
270. V. Dadrian. 1998. 'The Armenian Genocide and the Legal and Political Issues in the Failure to Prevent or to Punish the Crime', *University of West Los Angeles Law Review* 29, 48.
271. Dadrian, *Warrant for Genocide*, 125.
272. Quoted in Smith, 'Introduction', viii.

Part II

THE RWANDAN GENOCIDE

Chapter 4

'A EUROPEAN UNDER BLACK SKIN'
Precolonial and Colonial Rwanda

'The grave is only half-full. Who will help us fill it?' blared Rwandan radio station Radio Télévision Libre des Mille Collines (RTLM) in April 1994.[1] Hundreds of thousands of Hutu answered the call, murdering their Tutsi and even Hutu compatriots in a frenzied orgy of bloodlust. At a speed that even Hitler could only have dreamt of, close to one million Tutsi and moderate Hutu were killed between April and July 1994, in a genocide distinguished by both its unprecedented intensity and extraordinary level of popular participation.[2] Despite the Convention on the Prevention and Punishment of the Crime of Genocide, despite the presence of a United Nations force in Rwanda when the genocide erupted and despite all the technological and communications facilities at the world's disposal by the 1990s, the international community did little more than avert its gaze.

In the years that have elapsed since the Rwandan genocide, scholars have endeavoured to gain an understanding of the events that transpired. Many of the facts of the genocide have been established; scholars have also examined preceding events and possible causes for the apocalypse. Yet there are many questions that remain unanswered. Why, for example, did the genocide erupt in 1994, and not in the early 1960s, when there was enormous ethnic tension associated with the decolonization process? Why, indeed, did genocide erupt after three decades of relatively peaceable coexistence of Hutu and Tutsi in Rwanda? And how did such complete polarization between the groups emerge so rapidly, when just a few years prior to the slaughter regionalism was the principal point of fracture in Rwandan society, ethnicity was not the dominant force in political debates and some Rwandans even scoffed at the concept of 'ethnic politics'?[3] In order to explore these questions, this chapter and the following chapters will examine the evolution of Hutu-Tutsi relations in Rwandan society, from the precolonial period to the outbreak of the genocide. They will chart the emergence of the Tutsi as an outgroup, and consider how the vulnerability of the Tutsi minority developed over time. The temporal model will provide a framework through which to analyse the cycles of risk escalation and retreat and long periods of stability and relatively low risk that characterize Rwanda's history. The model also provides a useful framework through which to analyse the very rapid process of risk escalation that occurred in the years immediately preceding the genocide. Through an examination of the long history of Hutu-Tutsi relations in Rwanda, a cogent picture of the factors that led to the Rwandan genocide, and how they developed over time, emerges.

'Every "serious" study of Rwanda . . . begins by giving the ethnic composition of the population (84 per cent Hutu, 15 per cent Tutsi and 1 per cent Twa)' quipped a United Nations commissioner in 1962, and more than fifty years later this still remains the case.[4] The key role of Hutu and Tutsi identities and interrelations in understanding Rwandan history is undisputed. Amazingly, however, this is where agreement ends regarding the nature and significance of subgroup identity within Rwanda. Researchers of various kinds—historians, anthropologists, political scientists—seem to have spent an inordinate amount of time discussing the Hutu and Tutsi identities, their commonalities, differences and the nature of relations between as well as within the groups.[5] Yet many have reached strikingly different conclusions. The distinction between the Hutu majority and Tutsi minority subgroups has been varyingly described as one of race, tribe, caste, class, domination and subjugation, ethnicity, and political identity. Each descriptor appears to have more than a kernel of truth, but also elements of distortion and inaccuracy. Moreover, the nature of these identities is not a static one, as they have changed over time and in response to both internal and external influences.

The Tutsi can probably only truly be described as an 'outgroup'—that is, as relatively powerless, subject to legal discrimination and 'outside the universe of obligation of the dominant group'—from around the time of Rwandan independence.[6] Yet the cleavages between Hutu and Tutsi were a feature of Rwandan society long before this period. Indeed, in contrast to the Armenians in the Ottoman Empire—who can in many respects be identified as an outgroup well prior to the politicization of Armeno-Turkish relations—Hutu-Tutsi relations were politicized well before the Tutsi can be identified as an outgroup. It was in the precolonial and colonial periods that many of the forces that would ultimately lead to the genocide emerged and were manipulated in ways that would put Rwanda at risk—forces such as the polarization of the Hutu and Tutsi subgroups, the emergence of the racial paradigm through which intergroup relations were interpreted and the impact of regional differences on Rwandan politics. This chapter, therefore, will commence by examining the emergence of racial cleavages in the precolonial period. It will then explore how German and then Belgian colonialism impacted upon Rwandan society, ultimately leaving it vulnerable to genocide.

Precolonial Rwanda

Rwanda, as a nation, appears to have evolved over several centuries. The Nyiginya Tutsi clan achieved political dominance in central Rwanda, and this dominance slowly expanded to cover most of the present-day nation.[7] As they did so, they incorporated many of the customs of the surrounding populations and assimilated their leaders.[8] By the nineteenth century, the Rwandan kingdom was a complex and highly organized structure. The *mwami*, or king, was the sacred ruler of the nation. The *mwami* appointed three types of chiefs for each district—ensuring no particular chief became too powerful.[9] The chiefs of the land ruled over the attribution of land and agricultural production, including its taxation. The military chiefs were in charge of recruiting soldiers for the king's armies, managing the royal cattle and had some judicial functions.[10] The chiefs of the pastures/cattle ruled over the grazing lands and pastoralists. Below this level were hill chiefs, who were responsible for landholdings, taxation and grazing rights for each hill (large sections of Rwanda feature rolling hills).[11]

In some parts of Rwanda at least, Tutsi, Hutu and Twa subgroups appear to have existed for as long as anyone can remember. As the Rwandan kingdom solidified its rule, however, subgroup identification became linked with the stratification of the society.[12] Cattle, owned and managed by Tutsi pastoralists, became the central symbol of wealth and status within the society.[13] Tutsi also dominated positions of political power.[14] Hutu were generally agriculturalists, and considered to be of a lower status than Tutsi. Twa were either hunter-gatherers or potters, and were apparently despised by both Hutu and Tutsi, although the occasional Twa held an administrative post. Hutu and Tutsi relations were characterized by patron-client relationships, the most prominent of which was *ubuhake*. Under this system, a patron—usually a Tutsi—loaned a client one or more cows, and offered a form of protection. In return, the client—typically Hutu—was expected to provide agricultural products to the patron, and sometimes also perform agricultural or other work for the patron.[15] The relationship could be 'moderately reciprocal', particularly given the high status given cows within traditional Rwandan society, but was more often one of unequal power, with considerable potential for exploitation.[16]

The hierarchical occupational pattern of the subgroups in precolonial Rwanda has led scholars such as Mary Atterbury to consider the groups 'castes'.[17] However, there was probably a racial distinction, at least originally, between the groups as well. The distinct physical characteristics of Hutu and Tutsi suggest a separate racial origin, although neither oral tradition nor studies of phenotype and genotype can confirm or discount this hypothesis.[18] The anthropologist Mahmood Mamdani posited that while the Tutsi 'may have existed as an ethnic identity before the establishment of the state of Rwanda', the Hutu identity emerged as 'a transethnic identity of subjects'.[19] That is, Hutu emerged only in opposition to the

Tutsi, as an identity of those subjected by the Tutsi. Moreover, Mamdani asserted, as Tutsi rulers absorbed the leaders of the newly subjected groups into their own ranks, the Tutsi identity itself became increasingly transethnic.[20] Hutu and Tutsi were very clearly distinct identities, although perhaps ones that defy easy categorization. They were passed on via patrilineal descent. Intermarriage between the groups was not forbidden, and varied from being common in some areas to rare in others. In the case of intermarriage, the family adopted the group identity of the father. There were no Rwandans who identified as being 'half-Hutu, half-Tutsi'. A notable aspect of precolonial Rwanda is that group identity was not necessarily fixed. It was possible, although by all accounts rare, for a prosperous Hutu to 'become' Tutsi in a process called *kwihutura*. Similarly, downtrodden Tutsi would occasionally become Hutu.

The relationship between Hutu, Tutsi and Twa was not the sole, or even necessarily predominant, characterization of precolonial Rwandan society, however. In central Rwanda, the *inzu* (house), a group of relations crossing several generations, was an important social grouping.[21] Lineage groups were given paramount importance in northern Rwanda and held control over the land.[22] Catharine Newbury's anthropological study of the region of Kinyaga in southwestern Rwanda found the dominant social system there to be based upon kinship and residential location, at least until the close of the nineteenth century.[23] In addition, there was a clan system throughout Rwandan society. There were fourteen major and numerous minor clans, and their membership cut across Hutu, Tutsi and Twa group identities. It has been argued that until the middle of the nineteenth century, at least, 'these clan identities were in fact more primordial than the Twa-Hutu-Tutsi categorization'.[24] Finally, the national identity, that of the *Banyarwanda*, or the people of Rwanda, must also be considered. The kingdom of Rwanda was very clearly a precolonial state. The *Banyarwanda*, despite their multiple identities, shared a language, religion, culture and customs.

There were significant variations in the level of control the kingdom exerted in the central regions compared to the periphery, and regional differences have played a very important role in Rwandan history. The central region, comprising the districts of Nyanza, Kigali and Astrida, was most firmly under the *mwami's* control. In central Rwanda, subgroup identity was a predominant feature of the society, and the institution of *ubuhake* was most established there. A sense of social cohesion was prominent, and the disadvantages to the Hutu as a lower-status group were at least partially offset by a number of compensations.[25] For example, a Hutu could request his patron assist him in relations with administrative authorities; the multiplicity of authorities curbed the ability of any one of them to be overly excessive; and Hutu were occasionally land chiefs and commonly hill chiefs—giving them at least some opportunity for social mobility.[26] The ability for the occasional Hutu to become Tutsi has also been credited as preventing the emergence of a Hutu counterelite. In the northern and northwestern districts, clientship was not imposed successfully by the Tutsi until the beginning of the twentieth century.[27] Several Hutu principalities, such as Kiberi, Bushiru and Bukonya, were only incorporated into Rwanda after the arrival of the Europeans and with European assistance.[28] Northern Hutu were unused to the institution of *ubuhake*, possessed their own distinct culture and had not previously experienced the social stratification of central Rwanda.[29] Tutsi rule was maintained and expanded through oppression rather than cooperation, and the forcible imposition of the Tutsi system of *igikingi* land rights.[30] Under *igikingi*, all land was owned by the *mwami*, who granted access to it through administrative chiefs. Other peripheral zones of Rwanda had been conquered during the nineteenth century, but were again less well controlled than central Rwanda and had more particularist systems in place.[31]

The reign of *Mwami* Rwabugiri (1860–95) saw the 'final and the most spectacular expansion of the boundaries of the Rwandan state'.[32] The state structure and its power were further centralized. A system of forced labour, *ubuletwa*, was introduced during this period, and became the most unequal form of clientship. Under this system, Hutu were required to perform manual labour for the local hill chief, as 'payment' for occupation of the land.[33] This was specifically imposed only on the Hutu, 'thereby polarizing the social difference between Hutu and Tutsi'.[34] It also removed the previous power of the lineage head as land chief, weakening the importance of lineages. But while this system confirmed the unequal power relations between Hutu and Tutsi, and the increasing importance of these subgroup identities, a number of mitigating factors—such as the fluidity of identity, and the continued Hutu presence in lower administrative positions—continued to exist.

German Colonial Rule

In 1894, German Count Gustav Adolf von Götzen was the first European recorded as arriving in Rwanda. Von Götzen became governor of German East Africa, which included Rwanda, and which had been allocated to Germany by the European powers at the Berlin Conference in 1885. The Germans were welcomed cordially by the *mwami*. Interestingly, Count von Götzen recorded that the Hutu made a great impression upon him, welcoming his explorative expedition as their liberators—a sentiment quickly repressed by the Tutsi.[35] Later, the first Resident of Rwanda (Residents were appointed government officials that resided in a colony), Richard Kandt, would comment on his 'poignant shame at the undignified role the Hutu of Central Rwanda were condemned to'.[36] Van Götzen and Kandt's initial impressions of Rwanda provide a rare glimpse into the nature of Rwandan society at this time, their thoughts perhaps less cloaked by the pressures of their colonial roles at this early stage. Kandt appeared to have genuine humanitarian concerns, and wrote of 'humanitarian precepts which call for the suppression of abuses of power and of the arbitrariness with respect to the subdued population'.[37]

This suggests that not only were there significant divisions within Rwandan society operating at this point, but also elements of exploitation rather than reciprocity, and a desire by at least some Hutu for change. Nevertheless, Kandt managed to reconcile his concerns with German plans for indirect rule, as he concluded: 'Our political and colonial interests require that we should support the king and maintain the Tutsi domination which involves a strong dependence on the part of the masses of Rwanda.'[38]

There was a very light German presence in Rwanda throughout Germany's colonial tenure. Initially, only twenty-four military officers and six administrators were maintained in Rwanda; even by 1914 the total number of Europeans in the country was ninety-six, including missionaries.[39] The treatment of the German colonial period is generally very brief in the scholarship—their short tenure, system of indirect rule and low numbers of officials in Rwanda meant they 'could not really modify Rwandese society in depth'.[40] Nevertheless, there were three significant outcomes of German colonial rule. The first was the reinforcement of the *mwami* system and of the power of the Tutsi aristocracy. *Mwami* Musinga had recently ascended to the throne in a coup d'état, and used German support to help shore up his position and suppress revolts against his power; he also guided the Germans towards policies that benefited his government.[41] The second important outcome was that during their occupation the Germans assisted in securing the boundaries of Rwanda, annexing Hutu principalities and solidifying Tutsi control in areas in the north and east of the country with military actions.[42] Third, alongside German rule came the first Christian missions in Rwanda. Indeed, the Catholic White Fathers were actually the first Europeans to reside in Rwanda, settling even prior to the first German officials.[43] The White Fathers introduced the 'hitherto unknown and highly revolutionary doctrine for Rwanda of the fundamental equality of all Christians in the eyes of Christ'.[44]

Belgian Colonial Rule under the League of Nations Mandate

Belgian forces occupied Rwanda and Burundi in 1916, in the course of the First World War. The legitimacy of this occupation was subsequently confirmed when Ruanda-Urundi was formally placed under a League of Nations mandate in 1923. Belgium became responsible 'for peace, good order, and good administration' in Ruanda-Urundi.[45] Despite Ruanda-Urundi being placed under a single mandate, Belgium recognized the two nations' distinct histories and identities, and administered each country separately at most levels. The changes imposed by Belgian colonial rule had a profound impact on Rwanda, ultimately leading to the Tutsi becoming an 'outgroup', and leaving the country vulnerable to upheaval upon decolonization. In this respect, understanding the impact of Belgian colonial rule upon Rwanda is crucial to understanding the roots of the subsequent violence.

Broadly speaking, the Belgian impact on Rwanda during the period until 1947, when Ruanda-Urundi was transferred from the League of Nations mandate to become a United Nations trust territory under Belgian trusteeship, can be grouped into four main spheres of influence. First, and of greatest impact, was the Belgian racialization of the Hutu-Tutsi distinction. Second, the changes to Rwandan governmental and societal structures imposed by Belgium were of great influence. A third major factor was the provision of education, and particularly the differential access to education offered to each subgroup. Finally, the church and missionary activity in Rwanda had a large impact on the society. The following section will examine each of these factors in turn, with a view to exploring how Belgian colonial policies influenced subgroup identities and relations, and the structure of Rwandan society, in ways that would ultimately leave it at risk of genocide.

The first years of Belgian rule were devoted to assessing the situation in Rwanda and deciding upon the nature of future development programs. As the Belgians made their inventory, they were profoundly affected by the racial paradigm through which Rwandan society had been interpreted thus far. The first explorers to reach Rwanda had been quick to notice and comment upon the three subgroups that comprised the population—the Hutu, Tutsi and Twa. The distinction between the groups was immediately interpreted as a racial one, and much study was conducted into the 'significant differences in their physical characteristics'.[46] Tables were produced showing the difference between average weight and height in each of the three groups, along with other comparative measurements such as arm length and even nose width. Anthropologists also solidified and augmented the hierarchical rankings of each group within the society. The Twa were confirmed as being of the lowest order. Described in 1925 as a 'worn out and quickly disappearing race', a typical male Twa was 'very hairy . . . with a monkey-like flat face and a huge nose, he is quite similar to the apes whom he chases in the forest'.[47] The colonizers quickly came to regard the Hutu as only slightly more noticeable, describing them as: 'generally short and thick-set with a big head, a jovial expression, a wide nose and enormous lips. They are extroverts who like to laugh and lead a simple life.'[48] True praise was reserved almost exclusively for the Tutsi:

> The Mututsi of good race has nothing of the Negro, apart from his colour . . . his features are very fine: a high brow, thin nose and fine lips framing beautiful shining teeth . . . gifted with a vivacious intelligence, the Tutsi displays a refinement of feelings which is rare among primitive people. He is a natural-born leader, capable of extreme self-control and of calculated goodwill.[49]

But the racially obsessed Europeans went much further than simple hierarchical rankings of each 'race'. The idea that a 'negroid race' could be of sufficient intelligence and development to organize a kingdom such as that of Rwanda was apparently inconceivable. Thus the 'Hamitic hypothesis' was invoked. First proposed by explorer John Speke, this theory supposed that superior, ruling groups within Africa (this category eventually to include the Tutsi) were actually migrant descendants of Noah's son Ham. They were thus not truly 'Negro', but the lowest rung on the Caucasian ladder.[50] The notion behind this concept, which had multiple variations, was that as descendants of Noah they remained part of humanity, with their organizational faculties attributed to these origins.[51] As descendants of Noah's cursed son Ham, however, they were (comfortably) inferior to Europeans.[52] Some variations, however, went so far as to suggest the Tutsi was 'a European under black skin'.[53] Where, precisely, the Tutsi came from was the source of much conjecture. Southern Ethiopia and ancient Egypt were commonly proposed, although some of the more bizarre theories suggested India, Tibet, the lost continent of Atlantis and even the Garden of Eden.[54] Of more importance were the three concepts at the heart of the theory: that the Tutsi were a distinct race, that they were racially superior to the Hutu and Twa and that they were subjugators of foreign origin. These ideas, according to Prunier, 'can be traced as the major cause of the violence Rwanda has experienced at recurrent intervals since 1959'.[55] Similarly, Professors Jean Ndayambaje and Mutabaruka from the National University of Rwanda conclude that 'in no small way' the Hamitic hypothesis 'was the first step toward genocide'.[56] Mamdani goes beyond even these analyses, suggesting that it was not the Hamitic hypothesis as such but the Belgian institutionalization of the racialized concept of Tutsi identity that led to the enduring legacy of this theory.[57] Indeed, Belgian policies on ruling Rwanda were predicated upon this paradigm.

Belgian authorities initially decided to continue the indirect system of rule over Rwanda bequeathed from the German colonialists. Indirect administration enabled Belgium to rule over the nation despite having very few officials there—in 1923, there were a total of sixty-four Belgian colonial officials for the entirety of Ruanda-Urundi.[58] The model of indirect rule was modified, however, to meet the Belgian goal of 'a humanitarian, paternalistic reformism aimed at introducing the rulers to Western bureaucratic standards of probity and efficiency and securing for the majority of the population personal liberty from the rulers' abuse'.[59] To this end, Belgian authorities enacted some very substantial changes. The *mwami's* powers were significantly curbed; when *Mwami* Musinga refused to support the spread of Christianity, he was simply deposed and replaced by his more pliable eighteen-year-old son, who became *Mwami* Mutara. Belgian authorities reorganized the chieftaincy structure. The traditional triple hierarchy of the chiefs—involving the chief of the land, the chief of the pastures and the military chiefs—was streamlined and redefined between 1926 and 1931, to leave a single chief per area. The reorganization served to make chiefs accountable to the Belgian administration rather than authorities within the indigenous hierarchy, and allowed for the bureaucratization of the role.[60] The reforms also resulted in the 'Tutsification of the chiefship as an institution'.[61] Previously, the chief of the land had sometimes been a Hutu, although the other chieftaincies were usually held by Tutsi. The racial policies of the Belgians, however, led to the role of chief becoming almost exclusively a Tutsi one. According to René Lemarchand, probably the foremost author on Rwanda and Burundi during this period:

> The impact of indirect rule has been, first of all, to destroy the old balance of forces between cattle chiefs, land chiefs and army chiefs, which in previous times had served to protect the Hutu peasantry against undue exactions. The concentration of power in the hands of a single chief, exercising unfettered control over his people, was bound to lead to abuses: not only did it deprive the Hutu of opportunities to play one chief off against another, but it also eliminated the channels of appeal offered by the previous arrangement . . . social injustice became a corollary of indirect rule.[62]

The Belgian government sought to make a number of modernizing economic changes to Rwanda, including the development of a road and infrastructure network, measures to prevent famine, the introduction of cash crops and antierosion measures. In order to obtain funding to enact these changes, taxes introduced by the Germans were confirmed and expanded, and became individual rather than communal.[63] In a nonmonetary economy, however, taxes could provide only very limited funding. The primary method the Belgian administration employed to reach its goals was the system of *corvée*, or forced labour. The *ubuletwa* form of clientship was thus expanded both in scope and region to meet the needs of the Belgian colonists, while still maintaining the system of indirect rule. Thus, chiefs became responsible for such tasks as maintenance of roads, which they met by increasing *ubuletwa* from the traditional one day in every five (and previously only operable in central Rwanda) to two or even three days in every six.[64] Whereas formerly *corvée* had been a communal obligation of a lineage (who, for example, could dictate one man to fulfil the obligation for the lineage), it became an individual obligation for all men, and occasionally women.[65] It is important to note that *ubuletwa* was only imposed on Hutu. Mamdani has remarked: 'More than any other, it testified to the existence of Tutsi privilege in colonial Rwanda and highlighted the social separation between the *petit* Tutsi [ordinary Tutsi, not associated with power] and the average Hutu.'[66] Additionally, while increasing the importance of Hutu and Tutsi subgroup identities, this measure decreased the significance of lineage groupings as *corvée* was no longer organized communally. A further modernizing change was the introduction of compulsory crops. Each farming family was required by law to cultivate a certain area with famine-resistant crops, usually cassava or sweet potatoes, in order to prevent seasonal food shortages and famine.[67] In some areas, the cultivation of coffee crops also became compulsory, as Belgium tried to introduce an exportable crop and a cash economy to Rwanda.

There were two primary results of the Belgian taxation and *corvée* policies. The first was that Hutu were burdened more than ever to meet these requirements. In 1932, one missionary commented that 'the authorities had requisitioned his parishioners so often they scarcely had time to grow food, and famine threatened'.[68] He calculated that over half the male villagers in his area were requisitioned every day.[69] The second outcome of these policies was that Tutsi chiefs became primarily agents of the Belgian colonial authorities, being required to implement unpopular Belgian policies (albeit not without benefit to themselves), but no longer offering the same personal connections or protections that previously characterized the *ubuhake* relationship. *Ubuhake* had not only spread to new regions and in a new form; it also had became more bureaucratized, more oppressive and offered less advantage to the client.[70] Moreover, the 'Tutsification' of the chieftainship, and the spread of *ubuletwa*, to which only the Hutu were subject, increased polarization along ethnic lines. The positive results designed to arise from these economic changes were very slow to emerge, and not yet understood or appreciated by the labouring Hutu. Many scholars have at least partly blamed the forced labour system for the 1943 famine, citing the exploitation of labour as denying that same labour to the food production sector.[71] While Belgian famine prevention policies would eventually be effective, their benefits were not yet felt. Similarly, while the introduction of the coffee cash crop would come to have a significant impact, as yet the benefits were only potential, and not understood by those forced to cultivate the crop. Perhaps Lemarchand summarized the situation in this period best: 'The general impression conveyed by the record is that the lot of the Hutu masses was unquestionably worse under Belgian rule than at any other time in the past.'[72]

A number of the policies imposed by Belgium, such as the 'Tutsification' of the chieftainship, were a reflection of the racialized Belgian interpretation of the Hutu-Tutsi distinction in Rwandan society. Full implementation of this racialized perspective, however, required a system whereby subgroup identity could be readily confirmed. To this end, in 1933–34 colonial authorities conducted an official census. Every Rwandan was classified as either Hutu, Tutsi or Twa, and issued with an identity card that listed the bearer's subgroup identity. The methods by which colonialists identified the subgroup to which an individual belonged have become a source of contention within the scholarship, a point in the now highly politicized debate over the origins of the Hutu-Tutsi distinction. Numerous sources have made claims along the following lines:

> As they had little other basis upon which to make a distinction, the Belgians used the arbitrary economic criteria of cattle ownership to determine an individual's ethnic group. A person who owned more than 10 cattle was classified as Tutsi, one who owned fewer was classified as Hutu. The Twa were classified according to their occupation as potters and hunters.[73]

Yet there simply were not enough cows in Rwanda for this to be the case.[74] It appears that there were multiple ways in which identity could be established: ownership of herds of cattle, physical measurements and information provided by the church.[75] In particular, local missionaries knew their communities well, and this knowledge included that of subgroup identity. Following the census, identity remained hereditary, passing from a father to his children, but the previous fluidity, whereby the occasional Hutu could become Tutsi or vice versa, was eradicated under the identity card system.

The education system established by the colonial authorities in Rwanda strongly reflected the colonial belief in the racial superiority of the Tutsi. The Tutsi elite were given preferential access to educational opportunities, and almost exclusive access to postprimary education.[76] Even at the primary level discrimination was institutionalized, with Tutsi receiving their education in a separate stream in French, while Hutu received instruction in Kiswahili.[77] Overall, the education system established in Rwanda was elementary and rudimentary, reflecting the genuine Belgian fear that educating subordinate classes could threaten the stability of the nation. Primary schools, run almost exclusively by the missionaries (albeit some with government subsidies), provided only a very basic education, with an emphasis on agriculture and pastoralism.[78] Most students attended only 'first degree primary', receiving two years of education and a minimal level of literacy.[79] Entry to education above this level was severely restricted, with further primary education available to only small numbers of students. Until 1948, the only postprimary school in Rwanda was Groupe Scholaire d'Astrida, which focussed upon vocational training and was almost exclusively reserved for Tutsi.[80] There were no provisions for secondary, liberal or higher education. Perhaps the 1924 *Report on the Administration of Ruanda-Urundi* by the Belgian Ministry for Colonies best revealed the Belgian attitude towards this issue:

> Education ought to convey only knowledge which the natives will find useful in the social role which each of them is called to play. To act contrary to this rule, is to risk creating a class of ill-adapted and uprooted persons who cannot avoid being a disruptive element.[81]

It was thus a source of pride for the Belgians that almost all the Rwandans in school that year were Tutsi.[82] Such practices, however, meant that education thus further accentuated the divisions between Hutu and Tutsi.

The significant involvement of the church in education was not coincidental, as the church and its missionaries played a major role in the development of Rwanda during the entire colonial period. Whilst the White Fathers missionaries had often been at odds with German colonial policies, they quickly established a close collaborative relationship with the Belgian colonial authorities. Thus, in accordance with Belgian policy, the White Fathers came to enthusiastically support Tutsi rule—despite its seeming incompatibility with Christian teachings. The Hamitic hypothesis came to be heavily internalized and institutionalized within the Rwandan church. For example, in an interview in 1935, Vicar Apostolic Monseigneur Léon Classe commented: 'Evidently, the Watutusi are not ordinary natives. Superior race, race of chiefs, they constituted an area more propitious than the others for the germination of good seeds.'[83] While Protestant missionaries did make small inroads, the White Fathers' Catholic influence nevertheless maintained a strong dominance throughout the colonial period.

The missionaries achieved a remarkable level of success in Rwanda during the decades of colonial rule. When the newly installed *Mwami* Mutara duly converted to Christianity, a period of mass conversion of the Tutsi aristocracy and Hutu masses followed. Compared to less than fifty thousand converts in 1930, there were over two hundred thousand Catholics in Rwanda in 1935—10 per cent of the population.[84] By 1947, the vast majority of Tutsi chiefs and subchiefs were Catholic, and almost all were Christian.[85] The period of mass conversion between 1930 and 1935, which came to be known as *La Tornade* (The Tornado), appeared not to be purely based on religious fervour.[86] As historian Ian Linden has noted, 'Under Belgian rule education became the portal which gave access to political power, but . . . it was also "the portal of the Church".'[87] Conversion offered Tutsi practical advantages. Interestingly, many converts retained their traditional beliefs simultaneously with their Christian religious practices, seeing little contradiction in following two religious systems.[88] Yet despite the church's support for Tutsi rule and focus upon Tutsi conversion, its achievements during this period could not be described as exclusively reinforcing the caste system. The revolutionary Christian doctrine of 'All men as equal before God'—even if now only meant in a broad, abstract sense rather than a political one—had a significant impact on the Hutu. The education offered the Hutu, while basic, 'was undoubtedly a major contributor to the Hutu awakening in the fifties'.[89] Finally, while seminaries offered preferential entry to Tutsi (at least until after the Second World War), they also offered places for Hutu, providing almost the only opportunity for them to receive anything beyond an elementary schooling.[90] Hutu graduates of the seminaries would come to play a pivotal role in Rwanda from the 1950s onwards.

To summarize, the period between the advent of colonialism and the end of the Second World War, and in particular the first thirty years of Belgian colonial rule, led to a number of major changes in Rwandan society. These changes had a massive impact upon the Hutu and Tutsi subgroups and their relations. Under colonial rule, the borders of Rwanda were formalized, and the system of Tutsi domination standardized throughout the country. In the north and northwest, and in other peripheral regions of Rwanda, this imposition was strongly resented. While the colonialists maintained they were implementing a system of indirect rule, they made fundamental changes to the nature of that rule. The power of the *mwami* was significantly reduced, while the chieftaincy system was altered: it was 'streamlined', 'Tutsified', and the chiefs were required to do the work of and answer to the Belgian authorities rather than the *mwami*. The nature of *ubuhake* was fundamentally altered, and it was imposed in areas where it had not previously been operable. While it was held up as a traditional system and used as justification for Tutsi domination, Prunier has described *ubuhake* during the colonial period as actually being a 'noxious synthetic product . . . that . . . was strongly resented'.[91] The racialization of the Hutu-Tutsi distinction and the institutionalization of this racialized conception led to a Hutu-Tutsi polarization that had not previously existed. Continued Tutsi domination of Rwandan society was now predicated on the Hamitic hypothesis that identified Tutsi as racially superior; as a result, this hypothesis, including the corollary of Tutsi as foreign subjugator, was heavily internalized. Many of the Belgian imposed changes also decreased or removed some of the mitigating factors associated with Tutsi domination, along with a number of elements that promoted social cohesion, albeit often inadvertently. The unpopular *ubuletwa* forced labour system was imposed only on the Hutu—a substantial source of polarization. Opportunities for Hutu wishing for social mobility, while previously uncommon, were almost completely eliminated. Subgroup identity was augmented, at the expense of focus upon the national, unitary identity of *Banyarwanda*. Belgian intent was benign; it was working towards improving infrastructure, health, education and productivity in Rwanda, and making slow but steady progress. Unfortunately, however, it was the changes listed above, and their inadvertent consequences, that would be the most significant outcomes of this part of the colonial period.

Belgian Colonial Rule under the United Nations Trusteeship

The progress and development of Rwanda during the first thirty years of Belgian colonial rule was significant, but according to one author, 'in comparison with the 1948–58 period of the Belgian administration, the previous thirty years were like the turtle compared to the hare'.[92] The cause for the rapid change of pace was the transfer of Belgium's colonial authority over Rwanda from a League of Nations mandate to a United Nations (UN) trusteeship. On 13 December 1946, the Agreement for the Territory of Ruanda-Urundi was approved by the General Assembly of the United Nations. In some respects, the UN trusteeship agreement was broadly similar to the now-defunct League of Nations mandate, and the general responsibilities of good governance remained.[93] Yet there were major new requirements, such as taking 'all proper measures to assure the political evolution of the peoples of Ruanda-Urundi', and ensuring progression towards independence.[94] Furthermore, as part of the agreement there would be triennial UN visiting missions to the territory. Barely had the ink dried on the agreement when the first such mission touched down on Rwandan soil in 1948. Their report, and the subsequent UN critique of Belgian rule, ushered in a period of great change and development in Rwanda. For the next decade, the Rwandan political environment was dominated by the recommendations of the triennial visiting missions, and Belgium's attempts to integrate them with its own philosophy regarding the future of Rwanda.

The report of the 1948 visiting mission praised Belgium's economic, educational and social achievements in Rwanda, along with its concern to preserve the indigenous political structure and institutions.[95] It expressed concern, however, with the slow pace of change, and the paternalistic Belgian attitude.[96] The report made four major recommendations. The first was that education, of both the masses and the elite, should be expanded, with an emphasis particularly on higher education.[97] The second was for increased indigenous responsibility in the administration, and specifically with matters that affected 'the country as a whole and not Africans exclusively'.[98] The third recommendation of the mission was that '[t]he administration should seek further to democratize the whole political structure as far as possible'.[99] Finally, it recommended the abolition of *ubuletwa*.

The Belgian government grumbled but acquiesced in the major recommendations. In response to the mission's recommendations that electoral institutions be established and that indigenous authorities be given greater responsibility, Belgian authorities announced a major overhaul of the conciliar system.[100] The indigenous political structure was reformed to create advisory councils for each level of the chiefdom. Councils would be partially elected, through an indirect system whereby a portion of the membership of each council was selected by the subordinate council.[101] (At the lowest level, the subchiefdom councils were composed of members chosen by an electoral college.) These councils would advise and be consulted on all matters of importance to that level of administration—for example, the chiefdom councils had to be consulted regarding all major decisions of the chief.[102] Additionally, the Belgian government began work on a ten-year plan for the development of Ruanda-Urundi. The plan primarily focussed upon economic development, with substantial funding for roads, transportation and industrial expansion.[103] Public health, agriculture and education also received significant financial support. *Ubuletwa* was abolished and replaced with a monetary tax, although numerous Hutu reported to the anthropologist Catharine Newbury that they in fact continued to be required to perform this labour until the late 1950s.[104]

The first elections for the councils did not take place until 1953. While they resulted in some Hutu representation at the lowest levels, at the level of the Territorial and Superior Councils, over 90 per cent of members came from the Tutsi minority.[105] The failure of the reforms to provide Hutu representation was a significant one. The tiny but rapidly growing number of politically aware Hutu, having heard of the forthcoming democratization since 1948, but realizing that nothing akin to democratization had eventuated, began to realize the need for more radical change—and the central role that challenging Tutsi hegemony would play in that struggle.[106] Nevertheless, the elections marked some very important political developments. As Rawson has noted:

> The conciliar system provided within the indigenous political system the idea of
> elections, the concept of conciliar deliberation, and a broad base of participation

in the processes of government. The power of the kings and chiefs was at last made subject to the control of representative councils.[107]

The 1951 UN visiting mission had recommended the dissolution of the *ubuhake* system; in 1954, the Rwandan Superior Council (*Conseil Supérieur*) announced that it would comply with this recommendation, despite Belgian concerns. *Ubuhake* had been described by the Belgians as 'the essential symbol of loyalty for the masses to their rulers', and one of the three pillars upon which the authority of the Tutsi was based.[108] (The second of the pillars, the Tutsi role as protector of the Hutu, had been eroded since the advent of the Belgian administration and was no longer a significant factor.[109]) Yet there was no doubt that *ubuhake* was inhibiting the development of the country. Growing numbers of cattle may have been a symbol of wealth, but they were also overcrowding pasturelands and limiting the land available to grow agricultural crops.[110] Moreover, the 'spirit of *ubuhake*', a spirit of subservience, was inhibiting Hutu incentive and initiative.[111] As the Tutsi ceded control over cattle, however, they tightened their control over the land.[112] The third pillar of Tutsi domination, that of land tenure, had not been addressed within the reforms to dissolve *ubuhake*. Thus, Tutsi continued to possess rights over the grazing land (on behalf of the *mwami* under the *igikingi* system), and could continue to demand payment—in money, services or cows—for grazing rights.[113] As Rawson commented, 'The Batutsi lost little in the division of the cattle, while the Bahutu, who had to pay for grazing rights, barely profited from the maintenance of their cattle.'[114] The issue of land tenure became a major source of division between Hutu and Tutsi subgroups.

By the mid-1950s, the first results of Belgium's ten-year plan for Rwanda were apparent. There had been no serious famine since that of 1943–44. Whilst the Belgians still considered there to be some risk of famine in Rwanda, a range of strategies had been put in place to both prevent and mitigate the impact of such an event.[115] These included improvements in agricultural yield, increased food storage, and a capacity to import and transport food and aid if required. Previous famines had disproportionately affected Hutu, whose ties to the land and the seasons left them with little ability to combat drought, but this vulnerability was now lessened by these colonial measures.[116] In other ways, too, subgroup identity was decreasing in importance as a factor determining important aspects of life.[117] Whereas in precolonial times the cost of traditional healers for medical problems had been prohibitive for many Hutu, under the Belgian administration medical care became widely available, effective and affordable—independent of subgroup identity.[118] Living standards, too, were becoming more equitable—at least if one excluded wealthy Tutsi from the comparison.[119]

The educational component of the ten-year plan was also beginning to have an impact. By 1954, some 750,000 Rwandan children were attending school, although the vast majority continued to receive only a rudimentary one- or two-year primary education.[120] Postprimary education was slowly expanding—by 1954 there were 1,400 trainee teachers, and by 1956, 2,500 students received secondary education across Ruanda-Urundi.[121] This still represented only a tiny fraction of the population, however, which drew increasing criticism from the UN Trusteeship Council.[122] Moreover, the Tutsi minority continued to dominate the secondary schools.[123] Indeed, the UN visiting mission for 1957 noted that less than 10 per cent of students in secondary schools in Rwanda were Hutu.[124] The Belgian administration retained its misgivings about almost any sort of higher education, and particularly for Hutu children. Researcher Mary Duarte remarked:

> By 1960—indeed, after four decades under Belgian control—Ruanda-Urundi had neither a viable education system nor an educated elite prepared to govern. Fewer than 100 natives of Ruanda-Urundi had received post-secondary education, and no literate population had emerged.[125]

The African studies specialist Jnanabrota Bhattacharyya, however, has commented:

> On the other hand, the spread of primary education to about three fourths of the population is not without political and social consequences even when this is not followed up for most pupils by higher education. Literacy, even low literacy, furnishes an equipment for better communication and thereby for better political mobilization ... In the Hutu's political awakening in the fifties, the role of extensive primary education must be duly recognized. Education awakened a sense of resentment and bitterness among the masses, which was politically explosive.[126]

By the 1950s over half the Rwandan population had converted to Catholicism, and the church was in a position of having great influence.[127] After training a generation of Tutsi clergy, in the aftermath of the Second World War the church underwent a period of profound change. The upper-class, conservative Belgian priests who had constituted the first generation of missionaries were increasingly replaced by Belgian Fathers of more disparate and humble social origins, who identified more naturally with the oppressed Hutu.[128] Moreover, in the aftermath of Nazism, the new priests were 'strongly influenced by antiracist ideological currents'.[129] As Atterbury has noted: 'The new conditions made it possible for Hutu to emphasize the tenet of Catholic doctrine that all men are equal before God, as they began their campaign for a manifestation of this equality in the political, social, and cultural structure of the society.'[130] It was not an uncontested process—Tutsi priests sought to defend their traditional privilege from the same pulpits, and there was considerable friction at multiple levels within the church.[131] Nevertheless, 'it was through the Church that the Hutu first gained access to education, as well as opportunities for status and authority.'[132] The church provided employment for the first group of Hutu seminarians and educated Hutu that emerged from the secular schools when they were shunned by all other potential employers.[133] And as they assumed control over church publications, the first murmurings of Hutu resentment began to be heard.[134]

In addition to the new routes opening up through education and the church, the economic focus of the ten-year plan began to offer alternative routes through which Hutu could seek prestige and prosperity within Rwandan society. Under *ubuhake*, the economy had revolved around cows, inextricably linked with the patron-client bonds and the inferior status of the Hutu. As the economy increasingly became a monetary one, however, Hutu began to realize the advantages and opportunities associated with commerce. The number of African-owned shops in Rwanda exploded in the late forties and early fifties.[135] Hutu also found employment as teachers, tradesmen, truck drivers, miners and in the growing private sector.[136] By far the greatest influence, however, was the cash crop of coffee:

> The introduction of coffee was revolutionary . . . since it freed the Hutu, now become a coffee-planter, from his exclusive dependence on the 'cow economy'. Coffee was thus an instrument of emancipation and gave the Hutu the self-confidence and the economic basis he needed to break his bonds.[137]

Yet the land tenure problem had not been resolved, and a large portion of the coffee had to be paid for use of the land.[138] This was a further source of Hutu resentment of the system governing their nation.

In 1956 the Belgian government further reformed the conciliar system in response to the recommendations of the 1954 UN visiting mission. Adult male suffrage was introduced into the election process. Notables responsible for electing the subchiefdom councils—that is, the lowest level of councils—would themselves now be elected rather than nominated. (Each council would subsequently vote on the membership of the superordinate council, as previously done.) Overall, the Tutsi faced a 20 per cent loss in representation at the subchiefdom electoral college level.[139] The results varied quite dramatically by region, with the greatest Tutsi losses in northwest Rwanda and Tutsi gains in central Rwanda, where Tutsi influence had been operable for centuries and *ubuhake* was most entrenched.[140] In some areas, at least, 'a caste-wise polarization was emerging'.[141] Once again, however, at each ascending level of the councils, Hutu representation diminished. At the highest level of the Superior Council, the Tutsi increased their majority to 97 per cent of the membership. Even so, for the Tutsi elite these elections 'rang the first warning bell for the local authorities that the emerging consciousness among the Hutu masses posed a serious challenge to them'.[142] For the Hutu, the elections had exposed their demographic dominance, and the potential of Hutu power; yet in the end, they had 'changed nothing at all'.[143]

The advent of the UN trusteeship thus fundamentally changed the nature of Belgian colonial rule, and the outcomes of the first decade of Belgian governance under the auspices of the UN contrast quite significantly with those from the period of the League of Nations mandate. The first three decades of Belgian

colonialism led to the solidification of Tutsi rule, the consolidation of Tutsi privilege, the internalization of the Hamitic hypothesis within Rwandan society and
an increased focus upon Hutu and Tutsi identities at the expense of other identities—including an increased polarization between those identities. By contrast,
the policies implemented in Rwanda in the late forties and early fifties came to
be—often unintentionally–opportunities for Hutu. Expanded education gave
Hutu a thirst for knowledge; the first forays into a democratic system led to a
dawning awareness of the possible power of the Hutu majority. The abolition of
ubuhake, and the more varied opportunities in the new money economy, opened
potential routes to prestige for Hutu; a new generation of priests preached about
the equality of all men before God. Some of the worst of the depredations eased,
including the abolition of *corvée* and *ubuhake*. The standard of living of Hutu and
(at least some) Tutsi even converged to some extent. Yet in all these areas, Hutu
remained substantially disadvantaged. The limited opportunities were countered
by an increased awareness of the constraints. The prevailing system of power relations could no longer go unchallenged.

Notes

1. M. Mamdani. 2001. *When Victims Become Killers: Colonialism, Nativism, and the Genocide in Rwanda*, Princeton, NJ: Princeton University Press, 212.
2. A more detailed discussion of the number of victims is presented in chapter 6.
3. Mamdani, *When Victims Become Killers*, 154–55.
4. United Nations. 1962. *Question of the Future of Ruanda-Urundi: Statement made by Mr. Majid Rahnema, United Nations Commissioner for Ruanda-Urundi, at the 1265th meeting of the Fourth Committee*, A/C.4/525, 23 January, 4.
5. A note on the terminology used in chapters 4–6. Kinyarwanda is a language that uses prefixes extensively, but in conformance with general practice in academic writing on Rwanda, the terms 'Hutu', 'Tutsi' and 'Twa' will be used, without prefixes, to denote both singular and plural. In Kinyarwanda the prefix 'mu-' denotes singular, and 'ba-' plural. Where quotes include these prefixes, they have not been altered. Rwanda will be spelled as such whenever referred to in the singular, despite the misspelling of 'Ruanda' during the colonial period. Where the colony of 'Ruanda-Urundi' is mentioned, the original spelling has been used; additionally, the spelling in quotes is the original. Finally, it must be noted that the terms used to denote the Hutu/Tutsi distinction, such as race, ethnicity, caste, etc., have themselves come to have political meaning, and been interpreted by some to indicate an author's 'pro-Hutu' or 'pro-Tutsi' stance. For this reason, wherever possible the author has attempted to use apolitical terms to describe the subgroups. When a particular term has been used, the author has endeavoured to use the term most common to the historical period under discussion.
6. H. Fein. 1979. *Accounting for Genocide: National Responses and Jewish Victimization during the Holocaust*, New York: Free Press, 9.
7. African Rights. 1995. *Rwanda: Death, Despair and Defiance*, rev. ed., London: African Rights, 2.
8. Ibid., 3.

9. M. D'Hertefelt. 1965. 'The Rwanda of Rwanda', in J.L. Gibbs, Jr. (ed.), *Peoples of Africa*, New York: Holt, Rinehart and Winston, 425–26.

10. Ibid., 428.

11. L. Melvern. 2000. *A People Betrayed: The Role of the West in Rwanda's Genocide*, London: Zed Books, 9.

12. M. Atterbury, 1970. *Revolution in Rwanda*, Occasional Paper 2, Madison: African Studies Program, University of Wisconsin, 10.

13. Ibid.

14. Ibid., 11.

15. Ibid., 12; D'Hertefelt, 'The Rwanda of Rwanda', 423.

16. African Rights, *Rwanda*, 4; Atterbury, *Revolution in Rwanda*, 12.

17. Atterbury, *Revolution in Rwanda*, 11.

18. Mamdani, *When Victims Become Killers*, 41–75.

19. Ibid., 74.

20. Ibid.

21. D'Hertefelt, 'The Rwanda of Rwanda', 415.

22. Ibid., 414; Mamdani, *When Victims Become Killers*, 65–66.

23. L.R. Bäck. 1981. 'Traditional Rwanda: Deconsecrating a Sacred Kingdom', in H.J.M. Claessen and P. Skalník (eds), *The Study of the State*, The Hague: Mouton Publishers, 26; C. Newbury. 1988. *The Cohesion of Oppression: Clientship and Ethnicity in Rwanda, 1860–1960*, New York: Columbia University Press.

24. African Rights, *Rwanda*, 3.

25. Atterbury, *Revolution in Rwanda*, 18.

26. Mamdani, *When Victims Become Killers*, 69; J. Maquet. 1954. *Le Système des relations sociales dans le Ruanda ancien*, Tervuren, Belgium: Annales du Musée Royal du Congo Belge, 127, cited in H. Codere. 1962. 'Power in Ruanda', *Anthropologica* 4, 60; Atterbury, *Revolution in Rwanda*, 17.

27. D'Hertefelt, 'The Rwanda of Rwanda', 424.

28. G. Prunier. 1995. *The Rwanda Crisis: History of a Genocide*, New York: Columbia University Press, 19.

29. Atterbury, *Revolution in Rwanda*, 18.

30. Prunier, *The Rwanda Crisis*, 20–21.

31. Ibid., 21.

32. Mamdani, *When Victims Become Killers*, 69.

33. Ibid., 66.

34. Ibid.

35. G. von Goetzen. 1899. *Durch Afrika von Ost nach West*, Berlin: n.p., 155, cited in M. D'Hertefelt, 'Myth and Political Acculturation in Rwanda (U.N. Trust Territory)', in A. Dubb. (ed.), *Myth in Modern Africa: The Fourteenth Conference Proceedings of the Rhodes-Livingstone Institute for Social Research*, Lusaka, Northern Rhodesia: The Rhodes-Livingstone Institute, 1960, 119.

36. R. Kandt. 1921. *Caput Nili*, 5th ed., Berlin: n.p., 305, cited in D'Hertefelt, 'Myth and Political Acculturation', 119.

37. Kandt, *Caput Nili*, 462–63, quoted in D'Hertefelt, 'Myth and Political Acculturation', 120.

38. Ibid.

39. Melvern, *A People Betrayed*, 7; Prunier, *The Rwanda Crisis*, 25.

40. Prunier, *The Rwanda Crisis*, 25.

41. Atterbury, *Revolution in Rwanda*, 19; H. Codere. 1973. *The Biography of an African Society, Rwanda 1900–1960: Based on Forty-Eight Rwandan Autobiographies*, Tervuren, Belgium: Koninklijk Museum Voor Midden-Afrika, 326.

42. Codere, *Biography of an African Society*, 326; D'Hertefelt, 'Myth and Political Acculturation', 120; Prunier, *The Rwanda Crisis*, 25.

43. J. Bhattacharyya. 1967. 'Belgian Administration in Ruanda during the Trusteeship Period with Special Reference to the Tutsi-Hutu Relationship', Ph.D. diss., University of Delhi, 46.

44. A. Segal. 1964. *Massacre in Rwanda*, Fabian Research Series 240, London: Fabian Society, 6.

45. F. Wagoner. 1968. 'Nation Building in Africa: A Description and Analysis of the Development of Rwanda', Ph.D. diss., American University, 57.

46. D'Hertefelt, 'The Rwanda of Rwanda', 407.

47. 1925. *Rapport Annuel du Territoire de Nyanza*, quoted in Prunier, *The Rwanda Crisis*, 6.

48. Belgium, Ministère des Colonies. *Rapport sur l'administration belge du Ruanda-Urundi, 1925*, 34, quoted in Prunier, *The Rwanda Crisis*, 6.

49. Ibid.

50. Mamdani, *When Victims Become Killers*, 82, 84.

51. Ibid., 81.

52. Ibid., 80–87.

53. F. Menard. 'Les Barundi', Archives des Père Blancs, Rome, quoted in Mamdani, *When Victims Become Killers*, 88.

54. Prunier, *The Rwanda Crisis*, 7–8.

55. Ibid., 37.

56. J.D. Ndayambaje and J. Mutabaruka. 1999. 'Colonialism and the Churches as Agents of Ethnic Division', in J.A. Berry and C.P. Berry (eds), *Genocide in Rwanda: A Collective Memory*, Washington, D.C.: Howard University Press, 31.

57. Mamdani, *When Victims Become Killers*, 87.

58. Belgium, Ministère des Colonies. *Rapport sur l'administration belge du Ruanda-Urundi, 1923*, 5, quoted in Wagoner, 'Nation Building in Africa', 63–64.

59. D'Hertefelt, 'The Rwanda of Rwanda', 435.

60. Mamdani, *When Victims Become Killers*, 90.

61. Ibid., 91.

62. R. Lemarchand. 1970. *Rwanda and Burundi*, New York: Praeger Publishers, 119–20.

63. Mamdani, *When Victims Become Killers*, 94.

64. Ibid., 95, 97.

65. Prunier, *The Rwanda Crisis*, 27.

66. Mamdani, *When Victims Become Killers*, 98.

67. Ibid., 95–96.

68. C. Watson. 1991. *Exile from Rwanda: Background to an Invasion*, Issue Paper, Washington, D.C.: U.S. Committee for Refugees, 4, quoted in Mamdani, *When Victims Become Killers*, 95.

69. Ibid.

70. Prunier, *The Rwanda Crisis*, 29–30.

71. D. Kamukama. 1997. *Rwanda Conflict: Its Roots and Regional Implications*, 2nd ed., Kampala, Uganda: Fountain Publishers, 24.

72. Lemarchand, *Rwanda and Burundi*, 123.

73. Ndayambaje and Mutabaruka, 'Colonialism and the Churches', 33. A similar example can be found in African Rights, *Rwanda*, 8–9.

74. Mamdani, *When Victims Become Killers*, 98.

75. T. Gatwa. 1998. 'The Churches and Ethnic Ideology in the Rwandan Crises (1900–1994)', Ph.D. diss., University of Edinburgh, 84, cited in Mamdani, *When Victims Become Killers*, 99.

76. Atterbury, *Revolution in Rwanda*, 20; H. Adeney. 1963. *Only One Weapon: Facing Difficulty and Danger with Christ in Troubled Rwanda*, London: Ruanda Mission, C.M.S., 8; Bhattacharyya, 'Belgian Administration', 58–59.

77. Mamdani, *When Victims Become Killers*, 89–90.

78. Bhattacharyya, 'Belgian Administration', 59.

79. Ibid., 59–60.
80. Ibid., 58–59.
81. Belgium, Ministère des Colonies. *Rapport sur l'administration belge du Ruanda-Urundi, 1924,* 29, quoted in Atterbury, *Revolution in Rwanda,* 29.
82. Belgium, Ministère des Colonies. *Rapport sur l'administration belge du Ruanda-Urundi, 1924,* 29, quoted in Atterbury, *Revolution in Rwanda,* 21.
83. P. Neuray. 1935. 'Quelques heures avec Mgr. Classe', 'Tornade', *Grands Lacs,* 1 March, 215–16, quoted in Bhattacharyya, 'Belgian Administration', 54.
84. Bhattacharyya, 'Belgian Administration', 50–51; Société des Nations. *Rapport présenté par le gouvernement Belge au Conseil de la Société des Nations au sujet de l'administration du Ruanda-Urundi, 1935,* 88, cited in A. Des Forges. 1969. 'Kings Without Crowns: The White Fathers in Ruanda', in D. McCall, N. Bennett and J. Butler (eds), *Eastern African History,* Boston University Papers on Africa 3, New York: Frederick A. Praeger, 196.
85. Bhattacharyya, 'Belgian Administration', 51.
86. I. Linden. 1977. *Church and Revolution in Rwanda,* New York: Manchester University Press, 152.
87. Ibid.
88. R. Nyrop et al. 1969. *Area Handbook for Rwanda,* Washington, D.C.: U.S. Government Printing Office, 1969, 54, 64.
89. Bhattacharyya, 'Belgian Administration', 55.
90. Ibid., 61.
91. Prunier, *The Rwanda Crisis,* 30.
92. Wagoner, 'Nation Building in Africa', 106.
93. Ibid., 107.
94. P. Leroy. 1949. *Législation du Ruanda-Urundi,* Usumbura, Burundi: Les Presses Lavigeria, 12–13, quoted in Wagoner, 'Nation Building in Africa', 108–9.
95. D. Rawson. 1966. 'The Role of the United Nations in the Political Development of Ruanda-Urundi, 1947–1962', Ph.D. diss., American University, 51–52.
96. United Nations. *Visiting Mission 1948,* T/217, 16, 20, quoted in Rawson, 'The Role of the United Nations', 34, 51.
97. Rawson, 'The Role of the United Nations', 37.
98. United Nations, *Visiting Mission 1948,* 17–18, quoted in Rawson, 'The Role of the United Nations', 38.
99. United Nations, *Visiting Mission 1948,* 19, quoted in Rawson, 'The Role of the United Nations', 36.
100. Rawson, 'The Role of the United Nations', 64.
101. Ibid., 93.
102. Ibid.
103. Ibid., 88.
104. Newbury, *The Cohesion of Oppression,* 146.
105. United Nations. 1960. *Visiting Mission to Trust Territories in East Africa, 1960: Report on Ruanda-Urundi,* T/1538, 3 June, 37.
106. Ibid.; Mamdani, *When Victims Become Killers,* 115.
107. Rawson, 'The Role of the United Nations', 163.
108. Ibid., 173–74; Bhattacharyya, 'Belgian Administration', 168–69.
109. Rawson, 'The Role of the United Nations', 174.
110. Wagoner, 'Nation Building in Africa', 147.
111. Ibid., 147–48.
112. Ibid., 148.
113. Rawson, 'The Role of the United Nations', 177.

114. Ibid.

115. Codere, *Biography of an African Society*, 320. It must be noted that while there had been significant improvements to roads and infrastructure, by world standards these remained extremely poor. For example, Health Officer Frank Lambrecht, who spent considerable time in Rwanda between 1945 and 1959, recounted in his memoirs numerous stories of the difficulties of travelling through Rwanda. Frank Lambrecht. 1991. *In the Shade of an Acacia Tree*, Philadelphia: American Philosophical Society.

116. Codere, *Biography of an African Society*, 320–22.

117. Ibid., 322.

118. Ibid., 323.

119. P. Leurquin. 1960. *Le Niveau de vie des populations rurales du Ruanda-Urundi*, Louvain: Éditions Nauwelaerts, 203.

120. Bhattacharyya, 'Belgian Administration', 72.

121. Ibid.; M. Duarte. 1994. 'Education in Ruanda-Urundi, 1946–61', *The Historian* 57(2), 280.

122. United Nations. 1952. *United Nations Trusteeship Council Official Records*, 11th Session, 427th Meeting, 24 June, 28; United Nations. 1954. *United Nations Trusteeship Council Official Records*, 13th Session, 28 January–25 March, 8, both cited in Duarte, 'Education', 280.

123. M.G. Cyimana. 1959. 'Plaidoyer pour le menu people au Rwanda-Burundi', *Revue Nouvelle*, 15 March, reproduced in F. Nkundabagenzi (ed.). 1961. *Rwanda Politique: 1958–1960*, Brussels: Centre de Recherche et d'Information Socio-Politiques, 63.

124. United Nations. 1957. *United Nations Visiting Mission to Trust Territories in East Africa, 1957, Report on Ruanda-Urundi*, T/1346, paragraph 268, cited in Atterbury, *Revolution in Rwanda*, 31.

125. Duarte, 'Education', 284.

126. Bhattacharyya, 'Belgian Administration', 77.

127. Atterbury, *Revolution in Rwanda*, 32.

128. Prunier, *The Rwanda Crisis*, 44; Linden, *Church and Revolution*, 223.

129. Mamdani, *When Victims Become Killers*, 113.

130. Atterbury, *Revolution in Rwanda*, 32.

131. Mamdani, *When Victims Become Killers*, 113; Linden, *Church and Revolution*, 223–26.

132. A. Segal. 1964. 'Rwanda: The Underlying Causes', *Africa Report* 9(4), 3.

133. Mamdani, *When Victims Become Killers*, 114.

134. Bhattacharyya, 'Belgian Administration', 55.

135. Linden, *Church and Revolution*, 226.

136. Ibid., 227; A.L. Latham-Koenig. 1962. 'Ruanda-Urundi on the Threshold of Independence', *The World Today* 18(7), 289.

137. Ibid., 289–90.

138. Rawson, 'The Role of the United Nations', 178.

139. D'Hertefelt, 'Myth and Political Acculturation', 123.

140. Bhattacharyya, 'Belgian Administration', 177; J. Webster. 1966. *The Political Development of Rwanda and Burundi*, Occasional Paper 16, Syracuse, NY: Syracuse University Maxwell Graduate School of Citizenship and Public Affairs, 31.

141. Bhattacharyya, 'Belgian Administration', 177.

142. Ibid., 188.

143. Webster, *The Political Development*, 34; Atterbury, *Revolution in Rwanda*, 37.

Chapter 5

'A MASSIVE REJECTION OF THE TUTSI AS FELLOW NATIONALS'

Race, Violence and Independence

The 1954 UN visiting mission to Rwanda would be the last to observe that '[t] here appeared to be very little development of general or even local public opinion' in the country.[1] By the mid-1950s, the rapid changes of the previous years led to the emergence of a Hutu consciousness, or what has been dubbed the 'Hutu awakening'. This awareness originated amongst the new Hutu intelligentsia, as the first generation of Hutu seminarians came of age. Initially, at least, '[t]he masses seemed unaware of the changes taking place in their world'.[2] The emergent counterelite contrasted the democratic notions of equal rights, equal opportunities and majority rule with the systemic injustices to which Hutu were subject, and felt keenly the frustrations of Hutu powerlessness.[3]

In March 1957, the *Bahutu Manifesto* was published, signed by nine members of the Hutu counterelite, including future Rwandan president Grégoire Kayibanda. It has been described as 'probably the most important document in modern Rwandan political development', in part because 'it presented . . . the realization that there was an organized Hutu opposition'.[4] The *Bahutu Manifesto* challenged every facet of Rwandan society:

> Some people have asked whether this is a social or a racial conflict . . . In reality and in the minds of men it is both. It can, however, be narrowed down for it is primarily a question of a political monopoly held by one race, the Mututsi, and, in view of the social situation as a whole, it has become an economic and social monopoly. In view, also, of the *de facto* selection in education, this political, economic and social monopoly has also become a cultural monopoly, to the great despair of the Bahutu, who see themselves condemned forever to the role of subordinate manual workers,

and this, worse still, after achieving an independence which they will have unwittingly helped to obtain.[5]

The *Manifesto* proposed a wide-ranging series of actions to address the situation. Its greatest impact, however, was in the 'psychological climate it created among the Hutu masses. The issues raised in the *Manifesto* became a staple news item in the local press and a prime subject of discussion on the hills'.[6] Slowly the message of the Hutu counterelite began diffusing throughout Rwanda.

According to Kuper, 'The Manifesto may seem to an external observer quite conciliatory in tone: it was menacing, nevertheless, to many Tutsi elite as a challenge to Tutsi privilege by a nascent Hutu political movement'.[7] That the Tutsi elite had already perceived this threat, and had formulated an approach to managing it, was evident from the *Mise au Point* (Statement of Views). Published, like the *Manifesto*, to influence the 1957 UN visiting mission, the focus of the *Mise au Point* 'was on preparing Rwanda for quick independence through proper utilization, preparation, and recognition of the elite'.[8] The *Mise au Point* called for further education of the elite and greater participation of the elite in the governing of the country, with the clear goal of a rapid transition to self-government.[9] But equally significant was that which was omitted from the document.[10] Nowhere was there any reference whatsoever to the deep cleavages between the Hutu and Tutsi subgroups. Instead, faced with a challenge to their previous hegemony, the Superior Council 'set up a characteristically mythical reinterpretation of the ancient socio-political structure of Rwanda'.[11] The Hamitic myth was replaced with a focus upon the cooperation between Hutu, Tutsi and Twa, and the essential feature of Rwandan society was recast as 'its homogeneity as a people and a nation'.[12] The Hutu-Tutsi-Twa distinctions were to be radically deemphasized in a bid for the elite to retain its power. Both the *Bahutu Manifesto* and the *Mise au Point* were key documents in that they 'provided the ideological basis for much of the political action which followed'.[13]

The report of the 1954 visiting mission to Ruanda-Urundi had completely failed to mention the problem of subgroup identity in Rwanda, and it was left to the Belgians to point this out in their response: 'The Visiting Mission . . . makes no reference to the deep cleavages which divide the Batutsi, the Bahutu, the Batwa and the Waswahili. Those cleavages are obvious . . . and they dominate the whole of social life'.[14] In 1957, the *Mise au Point* and *Bahutu Manifesto* awaiting the visiting mission ensured that these issues could not help but be noticed. Yet the only solution the 1957 mission recommended, with 'almost ridiculous optimism', was further education.[15] Rawson noted that the failure of the UN Trusteeship Council to realize 'the disintegrative potential of the traditional social stratification . . . was a crucial factor in the developmental process'.[16] In the same vein, the 1957 mission would fail to deal with the land tenure problem, despite its 'economic, social and ultimately political ramifications' being 'most acute'.[17] Yet at this stage, as many authors have acknowledged, the political ideals of the Hutu and Tutsi were being expressed in a moderate fashion, and 'the way was still open for peaceful change and compromise in Rwanda'.[18] It is unfortunate that the UN Trusteeship Council, the Belgian administration and the indigenous authorities all failed to take decisive action in response to the *Mise au Point*, the *Bahutu Manifesto* or the rising tide of ferment within Rwanda. The *mwami* further inflamed the situation, adopting a partisan pro-Tutsi stance, which was particularly damaging in light of the *mwami's* traditional role as the ultimate arbiter in Rwandan society.[19] Thus, it was in a climate of increasing tension and polarization that the first Rwandan political parties were formed.

There were four political parties that emerged in Rwanda in the late 1950s. The Parti du Mouvement et de l'Émancipation Hutu (PARMEHUTU; later the prefix Movement Démocratique Rwandais was added to form MDR-PARMEHUTU) was led by Kayibanda. It 'insisted on a genuine democratization of all existing institutions before the granting of independence'.[20] The party drew support from the Hutu counterelite, and from central and northern Rwanda.[21] Its program was developed on the basis of the *Bahutu Manifesto*, and it announced its goal as 'a true union of all the Rwandan people without any race dominating another as is the case today'.[22] L'Association pour la Promotion Sociale de la Masse, or APRO-SOMA, was led by Joseph Habyarimana Gitera. APROSOMA sought 'to unite Hutu and Tutsi poor against Tutsi privilege', and primarily drew support from the southern regions of Rwanda.[23] According to Kuper, however, 'It developed in prac-tice as a Hutu party'.[24] In opposition to PARMEHUTU and APROSOMA stood Union Nationale Rwandaise, or UNAR. Created by conservative Tutsi (although nominally led by Hutu François Rukeba), it espoused the 'traditionalist' view of Rwandan society.[25] Strongly monarchist and anti-Belgian, it advocated immediate independence.[26] Bhattacharyya commented:

> Although the Tutsi authorities constituted the hard core of the party, loyalty to UNAR was by no means confined to the Tutsis. It had a large number of adherents among the Hutus, explained partly by the feudal prestige and influence the Tutsi authorities still enjoyed among the masses and partly by the threats and pressure they used.[27]

The final political party was Rassemblement Démocratique Ruandais (RADER), a moderate Tutsi party advocating reconciliation and democracy, but which only ever attracted a marginal following.[28]

'Rwanda in 1959 . . . was a land of tensions, rumours, and troubles', wrote anthropologist Helen Codere, reflecting on her time in the country.[29] Tension increased dramatically when the Belgian administration announced on 13 January a plan for the decolonization of the Congo, in the wake of the Leopoldville riots.[30] The new policy had arisen from the report of the working group that had recently visited the Congo; a similar group visited Ruanda-Urundi in April. Intergroup frictions escalated as organizations representing each subgroup sought to convince the working group of their proposals for Rwanda's future. The Superior Council petitioned the working group for autonomy and indigenous government.[31] Hutu leaders, by contrast, feared a rapid decolonization plan for Ruanda-Urundi would lead to independence 'before the Hutu were politically mature'.[32] Observer M.A. Munyangaju noted the atmosphere as these developments unfolded:

> The situation is very tense between Bahutu and Batutsi. A small quarrel would be enough for starting off a ranged battle. The Batutsi realize that after this, everything is finished for them and are preparing for the last chance. The Bahutu also see that a trial of strength is in the making and do not wish to give up.[33]

Tensions rose still further with the unexpected death of *Mwami* Mutara III on 25 July 1959. Almost immediately, wild rumours began circulating as to the cause of death—the partisan nature of these rumours revealing the deep cleavages in Rwandan society at this time. One rumour, apparently widely believed by Tutsi, claimed that the Belgians had poisoned the *mwami* in concert with the Hutu political movements and/or the Catholic missions.[34] Another rumour, believed by many Hutu, posited that he was killed by Tutsi conservatives because in the month prior to his death he had shown a more conciliatory attitude towards the Hutu.[35] With no clear succession plan in place, the atmosphere was extremely tense. At Mutara's funeral, a representative of the *abiru*—the *mwami's* inner court and the guardians of tradition—announced that Jean Baptiste Ndahindurwa, son of former *mwami* Musinga and half-brother of Mutara, would reign as *Mwami* Kigeli V.[36] The Belgian administration was taken by complete surprise, but given the atmosphere of extreme tension and the large numbers of traditionally armed Rwandans at the funeral, had little choice but to agree.[37] The choice of Ndahindurwa was not necessarily a poor one, and it also resolved what could have been a protracted and difficult succession process.[38] The way in which the events unfolded, however, led to a significant loss of prestige by the Belgian administration. As the *Report of the Commission of Enquiry* noted: 'The population got the impression that the Trusteeship Authority was placed before a *fait accompli* and that it had to agree. Some thought, and rumours were not wanting, that the European authority had suffered a defeat.'[39] As Atterbury remarked, 'Both Hutu and Tutsi revolutionaries gained the impression that resort to violence could be undertaken with hope of success.'[40] Additionally, the manner in which Kigeli's ascension was organised and announced by the *abiru* meant Kigeli was inextricably associated with Tutsi conservatism. This precluded him from adopting the neutral role of supreme arbiter traditional of a *mwami* and undermined the *mwami's* traditional role as a force for national unity.[41]

The Rwandan Revolution

Rwanda has been described as a 'simmering cauldron' during the period of August to October 1959.[42] Elections were due at the end of the year; however, the form they would take had not been finalized.[43] The report of the working group was anticipated, with potentially enormous ramifications for the future of the country. Rumours abounded, creating 'extraordinary pressure and tension'.[44] The political parties commenced a period of frenetic activity. UNAR's approach, in particular, involved violence and a campaign of intimidation against opposition leaders and supporters.[45] By 1 November, it took only a spark to ignite the Rwandan revolution. An altercation in which a band of 'young UNAR militants' attacked a PARMEHUTU leader led to a Hutu retaliation that escalated into revolution.[46] Hutu-led violence and the burning of Tutsi huts rapidly spread. On the night of 3–4 November this violence first erupted in Ndiza, where the PARMEHUTU leader had been attacked; by the following day it had spread throughout the Gitaramana district.[47] Incidents of incendiarism then spread throughout the country: to Ruhengeri and Gisenyi districts in the north on 5 and 6 November, then districts in the northeast and western central areas the following day. By 8 November the fires had spread to the extreme north of the country; the central districts of Nyanza and Kigali, where Tutsi influence was most predominant, were targeted on 9 and 10 November.[48] Only three districts, Astrida, Cyangugu and Kibungu, escaped significant uprisings.[49]

As the subsequent visiting mission report noted:

> The operations were generally carried out by a fairly similar process. Incendiaries would set off in bands of some tens of persons. Armed with matches and paraffin, which the indigenous inhabitants used in large quantities for their lamps, they pillaged the Tutsi houses they passed on their way and set fire to them. On their way they would enlist other incendiaries to follow in the procession while the first recruits, too exhausted to continue, would give up and return home. Thus day after day fires spread from hill to hill. Generally speaking the incendiaries, who were often unarmed, did not attack the inhabitants of the huts and were content with pillaging and setting fire to them.[50]

It is notable that, by and large, there were few fatalities associated with these attacks. Nevertheless, serious damage was done, as thousands and thousands of huts were pillaged and burnt, plantations plundered and livestock killed.[51] In some parts of the north, not a single Tutsi hut was left standing.[52]

The Tutsi reaction to the uprising was swift and far more organized than the largely spontaneous Hutu incendiarism.[53] UNAR leaders, working from the *mwami*'s palace, quickly organized commando units, and dispatched them to arrest or kill specific Hutu leaders.[54] According to the UN visiting mission report:

> Each commando party amounted to some hundreds of persons or more, and included a majority of Hutu, but the leaders were generally Tutsi or Twa. The group would set off on its mission with very definite instructions. In other cases, emissaries were sent out from Nyanza with verbal orders instructing them to bring back or kill certain persons . . . It seems to be an established fact, moreover, that in

many cases a commando group set out with orders only to arrest a person, but in effect killed him, either because he resisted arrest or because some attackers had the instinct to kill.[55]

Well over a dozen prominent Hutu were killed in this way, including two leaders of APROSOMA. The president of APROSOMA, Gitera, was also targeted, but successfully protected by the Belgian administration.[56] As Lemarchand remarked, 'The Tutsi repression was not only better organized but more specifically related to political aims.'[57] UNAR appeared to be trying to eliminate the Hutu leadership, and thus its opposition.

The Belgian administration, despite anticipating the disturbance, took more than a week to bring the situation under control.[58] It was not until 14 November that quiet was fully restored. At least two hundred people were dead, and several hundred more were wounded.[59] On 10 November, at the height of the disturbances, the Belgian government had published a major policy statement on the future of Rwanda. Based upon the findings of the working group that had visited Rwanda in April and May—and whose report the Belgian government had possessed since 2 September but had not published—the statement announced a number of 'radical political and administrative reforms in the Territory'.[60] The guiding principle of the reforms was that '[t]he Belgian Government would first establish . . . a system of government . . . which would be given a progressive measure of autonomy subject to the general control of Belgium'.[61] To this end, the previous structure of subchiefdoms, chiefdoms and councils would be completely overhauled. Communes were to be created, with councillors for each commune to be elected through universal male suffrage.[62] Councillors would then elect a burgomaster. A new state council would be elected by the commune councils, which together with the *mwami* would progressively be granted legislative powers.[63] The *mwami* himself, however, while remaining the constitutional head of state, would largely become a figurehead. Despite the failure of their announcement to calm the violence and tensions between the Hutu and Tutsi, the Belgian administration moved extraordinarily quickly to implement the policy changes.[64]

The uprising of November 1959 has commonly been called a revolution, yet as Wagoner has noted, 'nothing was really overthrown', 'there was no violent upheaval of political institutions . . . no attacks were directed against the *Mwami's* palace or against Administration centres or officials'.[65] According to Wagoner, what was truly revolutionary was 'the changes in thought and attitude. Suddenly the Hutu in the hills learned that if he banded together he would find the courage to stand against his Tutsi overlord . . . Suddenly he was proud to be Hutu, to be short and sturdy instead of long and spindly.'[66] Given that the Hutu remained relatively powerless at this stage, perhaps what was more important was the similar change in attitude in the Belgian administration. In the course of the uprising, hundreds of Tutsi chiefs and subchiefs had fled, been killed, been forced to resign due to Hutu opposition or had been involved in the Tutsi counterattacks and subsequently arrested or removed from office.[67] The Belgian administration filled these vacant posts predominantly with Hutu. Thus, by 1 March the number of Hutu chiefs went from 0 to 22, out of a total of 45 chiefdoms, and the number of Hutu sub-chiefs rose from 10 to 297, out of a total of 531.[68] Furthermore, in the wake of the violence, on 5 December Belgium appointed Colonel Logiest as the 'Special Civilian Resident', to ensure the maintenance of peace and order and implement the major policy changes. Colonel Logiest had 'a known leaning toward the Hutu cause', and expressed this very early in his residency:[69]

> What is our goal? It is to accelerate the politicization of Rwanda . . . Not only do we want elections but we want everybody to be aware of this. People must go to the polls in full freedom and in full political awareness. Thus we must undertake an action in favour of the Hutu, who live in a state of ignorance and under oppressive influences. By virtue of the situation we are obliged to take sides. We cannot stay neutral.[70]

Rawson has suggested that 'given the circumstances, the Administration was almost forced into a position prejudicial to the Batutsi, favouring the Bahutu'; others have posited that the administration made a more active choice to take a pro-Hutu stance at this stage.[71] Either way, as Wagoner has commented, four months after the revolution, it 'had suddenly become a smashing Hutu success'.[72]

The atmosphere remained charged in the wake of the revolution in Rwanda. Sporadic outbreaks of violence destabilized the nation throughout 1960. In March Hutu burnt Tutsi huts in Gisenyi (northwest) and Biumba (northern central), while in April similar incidents occurred in Astrida in the south.[73] Between 16 and 18 May, more than five hundred huts were set alight in the Budaha region; a local incident in Gikongoro escalated to result in over one thousand huts being burnt in the area in early June.[74] Violence was reported in Kigali in June, Gisenyi and Rubengera in July and August. In October, the Shangugu district 'went up in flame[s]'.[75] The northwest of Rwanda was subject to the harshest violence—despite its small Tutsi population, its history of relatively recent Tutsi infiltration with colonial assistance had left strong anti-Tutsi sentiments.

Such violence contributed to the growing refugee problem in Rwanda. Immediately following the November uprising, the administration reported around seven thousand refugees, with the vast majority being from Ruhengeri in the northwest. The authorities attempted to resettle some in their original districts, while others were relocated to new areas.[76] Yet each wave of violence increased the refugee problem and by 19 April, the Belgian administration reported some twenty-two thousand refugees. Lemarchand, however, has noted:

> True, a sizeable number of refugees left their homelands to escape the violence unleashed by the November riots, but the overwhelming majority began their exodus

well after the rioting, when they suddenly found themselves confronted with Hutu chiefs and subchiefs, all appointed by the administration . . . the sheer arbitrariness, indeed the ruthlessness, with which many of these chiefs used their authority resulted in a further exodus of Tutsi families.[77]

The Belgian administration made concerted efforts to provide care for and resettle the refugees. It was hampered, however, by UNAR leaders continually politicizing the refugees' problems, and UNAR's hostile attitude towards the administration.[78] The administration reported to the visiting mission that 'it was absolutely certain that if the Tutsi leaders and the *Mwami* changed their attitude the great majority of refugee cases would be closed without delay'.[79] As Lemarchand has noted, however, 'Before long the refugees were converted into ardent supporters of UNAR.'[80] During 1960, some 14,500 of the Rwandan refugees sought asylum outside the country.[81] But this was only a fraction of the numbers that would follow.

Accompanying the violence during this period was even further polarization of the cleavages along racial lines.[82] UNAR's campaign specifically targeted Tutsi with a progressive agenda, undermining the possibility of more unifying platforms gaining currency.[83] In the wake of the revolution, there was also an 'intense politicization of the racial cleavages by PARMEHUTU'.[84] The Hamitic hypothesis was reinterpreted, and, according to Lemarchand: 'The Tutsi are [now] seen as the Hamitic foreigners who imposed their rule on the unsuspecting Bantu populations by cunning and cruelty, using their cows and beautiful women to bait the Hutu into submission.'[85] Lemarchand has posited that, while the revolution was initially motivated by the egalitarian notions of progressive Hutu, 'only through the exploitation of ethnic cleavages, that is through the politicization of clientship, could they hope to rally the support of the peasantry'.[86] According to Bhattacharyya, these processes were inexorably leading to 'a massive rejection of the Tutsis as fellow nationals' by Hutu.[87] Indeed, the first indication of this can be found in the immediate aftermath of the revolution. As the peace was restored, future Rwandan president Kayibanda published a statement in late November 1959 calling for nothing less than the segregation of Hutu and Tutsi into separate living zones.[88]

The UN visiting mission that arrived in Rwanda in March 1960 did little to aid the situation. Relations between the UN and the Belgian administration were strained, as each perceived a different route to Rwandan independence. The UN sought 'national reconciliation' in Rwanda, a general amnesty 'with regard to the events of November since it is convinced that without them national reconciliation will be difficult' and 'reintegrating the UNAR leaders into the normal political life of the country'.[89] The administration countered that the idea of an amnesty was itself not politically neutral, noting that the Tutsi had gone far beyond the Hutu in the scope of their crimes, which included assassination, torture and imprisonment.[90] Moreover, given the UNAR leadership's involvement in such crimes:

In the present circumstances, there was reason to fear that an amnesty might be construed as an endorsement of assassinations and violence as accepted political tactics. The political ideas of the UNAR were not involved . . . If certain persons had sought refuge outside the country it was not because of their political opinions but as a result of ordinary offences under the general law.[91]

The visiting mission also examined the issue of land tenure, and made numerous other recommendations. But as Rawson observed, 'Its observations came too late to be useful in changing the political situation.'[92]

Despite the atmosphere of tension and intermittent violence, the administration proceeded with the communal elections set for June 1960. The political scene had changed considerably since the previous November. PARMEHUTU, APROSOMA and RADER adopted a '*Front Commun*' in late April, resolving to cooperate and work together towards democratization and to support the Belgian administration.[93] UNAR was increasingly isolated. Many of its leaders were imprisoned or in exile and it had lost significant political power with the replacement of many of the Tutsi chiefs and subchiefs with Hutu. The results of the elections propelled PARMEHUTU to power, with some 75 per cent of the vote.[94] The subsequent transfer of power to Hutu leaders was fraught with difficulties, however. Rather than a transition to a truly democratic local government, Lemarchand has dubbed the process as one of 'the transference of political clientelism to the Hutu stratum.'[95] First RADER, then APROSOMA deserted the *Front Commun*, and by November 1960 had formed a new *Front Commun* with UNAR. They jointly declared:

> The dictatorial regime PARMEHUTU that we are living under and we deplore, is a power held by a political party that is racial, racist and antidemocratic, finding pleasure in deliberately crushing all the other parties by methods either of corruption or intimidation. Here the bad (the Tutsi feudality) is replaced by a worse (the PARMEHUTU dictatorship).[96]

Meanwhile, groups of Tutsi refugees in the border zones of Uganda and the Congo—who came to be known as *inyenzi* (cockroaches)—instigated cross-border raids into a number of Rwandan communes. This terrorism 'at first strengthened caste solidarity among the Hutu, but in time the sheer arbitrariness of retaliative measures caused considerable disaffection among the Hutu peasantry'.[97] The power wielding of the burgomasters also led to growing popular resentment.[98] Despite these factors, the administration continued to strengthen the Hutu position of power still further. A new provisional council and provisional government were established, headed by Kayibanda and led by a strong majority of PARMEHUTU ministers.[99] *Mwami* Kigeli, who had left the country in July when it was apparent the communal elections were not going well, was prevented from returning by the administration.[100] The *mwami* and UNAR petitioned the UN repeatedly, where they found a sympathetic General Assembly. On 20 December 1960, the General Assembly thus recommended that legislative elections planned for 15 January be postponed, to a date to be determined by a UN commission that would visit Ruanda-Urundi in late January; that an amnesty be granted; and that further work be undertaken towards 'national harmony'. PARMEHUTU responded furiously, concerned that such actions would advantage their opponents.[101] It was in this context that the Gitarama coup d'état occurred.

The Belgian government had reluctantly agreed to the UN's recommendation to delay legislative elections; however, when the Ostend conference in early January— recommended by the UN as an attempt towards national reconciliation—failed to produce a result, the administration proceeded to grant internal autonomy to the provisional government on 25 January, much to the UN's chagrin.[102] As Bhattacharyya has noted, 'The Hutu parties received the hint.'[103] Three days later, on the same day that the UN commission arrived in Usumbura (Burundi), the Rwandan interior minister called all the burgomasters and communal councillors to a meeting at Gitarama. There, in front of a crowd of thousands of people, Rwanda was pronounced a republic, a president and legislative assembly were elected, and Prime Minister Grégoire Kayibanda was charged with the responsibility of forming a government.[104] Belgium promptly recognized the powers of the Kayibanda government.[105] The United Nations was incensed, despite strenuous Belgian denials of any foreknowledge or complicity in the coup.[106] Nevertheless, a stern General Assembly resolution in April 1961 'warned Belgium that it alone was responsible for the administration of the Territory', recommended legislative elections be held in August with United Nations surveillance, demanded a referendum on the institution of the monarchy and repeated its demands for an amnesty.[107]

Following the coup, PARMEHUTU effectively took control of running the nation. Belgian administrators remained in the background, managing accounts, preserving law and order, and advising Hutu ministers.[108] Belgium also sought to follow at least some of the UN recommendations, including the enactment of a general amnesty for the period from 1 October 1959 to 1 April 1960, with the exception of certain very serious crimes.[109] The legislative elections were set for 25 September, and had two components. Not only would the forty-four seats of the legislative assembly be elected, but it would simultaneously be a referendum on the future of the monarchy as an institution, and the person of Kigeli V as the *mwami*.

The two months prior to the elections were characterized by repeated outbreaks of violence, incendiarism and a large rise in the number of refugees. In Butare (southwest of Kigali) alone, forty-four people were killed, twenty-three hundred huts were burnt and twenty-two thousand refugees wandered.[110] In Kibungo (in the southeast), an attempt was made on the life of a burgomaster, a PARME-HUTU official was assassinated, sixty-seven people were killed in the violence and a further eight thousand became refugees.[111] Belgian security forces struggled to prevent the situation from spiralling out of control. As the UN reported:

Serious disturbances took place in several regions of the country, including the Districts of Myanza, Astrida, Gitarama, and Kiungu and some communes in Kigali and Kibuye. As a result of the incidents there, tens of thousands of new disaster victims and refugees had to leave their homes and seek refuge.[112]

Certainly both sides initiated and participated in the violence.[113] UN Commissioner Gassou clearly believed, although only implicitly stated to the General Assembly, that most of the violence was instigated by PARMEHUTU cadres.[114] He noted that:

> Curiously enough, the victims were nearly always active or passive supporters of the opposition parties, both Bahutu and Batusti . . . the areas affected were always ones in which the opposition appeared to have great influence . . . the final result of the disorders was always the violent elimination of the opposition in the areas concerned.[115]

Gassou also noted the conflict apparent in the role of the burgomasters as both authorities responsible for the maintenance of law and order, and members of political parties campaigning for electoral victory. By contrast, Colonel Logiest believed 'that it was the extremists of the Opposition who stood to benefit by provoking disturbances'.[116] According to Logiest, it was the opposition 'who always struck the sparks which provoked the mass reaction of the Hutu, a violent and blundering reaction which it was then impossible to control'.[117] The violence did not cease until 18 September, a week prior to the elections.

There was an overwhelming turnout of 95 per cent of registered voters for the election. PARMEHUTU received 77.7 per cent of the votes, UNAR 16.8 per cent, APROSOMA 3.5 per cent and RADER less than 1 per cent. This led to PARMEHUTU dominating the legislative assembly with thirty-five of the forty-four seats, UNAR receiving seven and APROSOMA two.[118] Atterbury commented upon the results: 'The Legislative Assembly thus had an ethnic composition of 84% Hutu and 16% Tutsi—corresponding closely to the proportion of Hutu and of Tutsi in the population.'[119] About 80 per cent of voters also declared a preference for the abolition of the monarchy. After much debate and vacillation, the United Nations eventually agreed to accept the results of the elections as free and fair. The final preparations for independence commenced.

Following the elections, Rwanda continued to be beset by sporadic violence and a large refugee problem. If the preelection violence had been instigated by both PARMEHUTU and opposition forces, the preindependence violence consisted largely of bands of Tutsi *inyenzi* conducting cross-border raids from bases in neighbouring countries. According to Rwandan government sources, there were no fewer than twenty-seven incidences of such violence between October 1961 and May 1962.[120] There were many acts of murder (including of Belgians), huts being set alight and pillage. Biumba in northern Rwanda was particularly targeted, and attackers were often armed with machine guns or revolvers, as well as more traditional weapons. Biumba was also the location of a particularly harsh reprisal by the authorities, when following two raids there was a massacre of local Tutsi, further burning of huts and considerable pillage.[121] The highest estimates put the death toll at between one and two thousand.[122] The UN reported, 'The situation . . . appeared alarming to all experienced observers.'[123] Commissioner Rahnema, speaking to the UN in January 1962, went even further, accusing PARMEHUTU of 'adopting a social policy apparently designed to eliminate the opposition and the Tutsi minority'.[124] In Rwandan society he saw 'the symptoms of an explosive situation', and believed the 'social and political tension' there 'may result either in the gradual extermination of the majority of the Tutsi population, or it may at any moment degenerate into violence and, possibly, civil war'.[125]

The refugee situation was particularly problematic, difficult to quantify let alone resolve. Partially, this was due to the fluid nature of the problem. By mid-1961, a UN report noted, 'the great majority' of refugees from the November 1959 revolution and subsequent violence that continued into October 1960 had returned to their native districts and 'been reintegrated', or had resettled within Rwanda.[126] For those who had left Rwanda, the largest numbers were in the Congo and Uganda, but it was 'very difficult to obtain exact figures'.[127] The disturbances in August and September 1961, prior to the legislative elections, had created 'tens of thousands' of new refugees.[128] In November 1961, it was estimated that there were 40,000 refugees spread throughout Rwanda, while another 32,500 had escaped to Burundi.[129] A final commission had been sent to Ruanda-Urundi in early 1962, in part to address the refugee problem. Nevertheless, at independence approximately 100,000 Rwandan refugees were scattered between Uganda, Tanzania, Burundi and the Congo.[130] The inability of either Belgium or the United Nations to manage the violence of decolonization that created these refugees, or to adequately resolve the refugee problem, left a legacy that would play a key role in leading to Rwanda's genocide.

The inability to resolve the refugee problem, however, did not stop the preparations for independence. Finally, after a maze of administrative matters and technicalities were sorted out, and the UN's continual push for a Rwanda-Burundi federation was quashed, on 1 July 1962 the Republic of Rwanda achieved independence.

Assessing the Risk of Genocide

It is at this juncture that the Tutsi minority can, for the first time, be properly described as an 'outgroup'. For the first time, Tutsi were now a relatively powerless minority within Rwanda. Furthermore, as a result of the influence of the Hamitic hypothesis, they were perceived as foreigners 'outside the universe of obligation of the dominant group'.[131] Hutu-Tutsi relations had become highly politicized during the decolonization process, with lasting consequences for the Tutsi position within the new nation. The first precondition for genocide was thus met, marking Rwanda as a society at risk of massive violence. And, already, this risk had been recognized. UN Commissioner Rahnema was perhaps the first expert observer to recognize the potential for the Tutsi to be targeted in genocidal violence. His warning of the risk of the 'extermination of the majority of the Tutsi population' seems eerily prescient from a postgenocide perspective.[132]

Yet the position of the Tutsi at the time of independence was far from immediately dire. In examining the development of the preconditions for genocide in Rwanda, it is important to distinguish between pre- and postindependence violence. Prior to independence, the Tutsi were far less vulnerable than subsequently. The violence that occurred during the decolonization process had a significant element of reciprocity. Both Hutu and Tutsi instigated attacks at political and communal levels, and both groups also had sufficient capacity to coordinate reprisals in response to the other's attacks. Moreover, both groups were aware of the Belgian presence in Rwanda, and UN oversight, in conducting their actions. In the immediate wake of independence, it is significant that the Tutsi minority retained at least some political voice. Under agreements reached with the United Nations, UNAR had secured two ministerial posts in the government and some additional senior postings, which along with its seven elected seats in the legislative assembly ensured a viable opposition.[133] As Lemarchand has noted:

> What is more, UNAR was allowed to set up its own local headquarters (in Kigali), to print its own newspaper (*Unité*), and to criticize the government at will. Clearly, to use 'racial dictatorship' to describe this state of affairs [as the March 1961 report of the UN commission had] would be patently inaccurate.[134]

Whilst only the first precondition for genocide emerged directly from the decolonization process in Rwanda, almost all of the tactics of the genocidal regime of the 1990s—and most of the ideological bases upon which it would be conducted—were powerfully foreshadowed in this earlier period. At the rhetorical level alone, the similarity is profound. Thus, as UNAR leader Rukeba roared in 1959, 'He who does not belong to this party will be regarded as the people's enemy, the Mwami's enemy, Rwanda's enemy', so too would Hutu extremists in the 1990s equate support for anyone other than themselves with supporting Rwanda's enemies.[135] The *mwami* had responded to the demands of the Hutu counterelite by labelling them 'a bad tree' with 'evil fruits of discord' to be 'cut, uprooted, and burned'.[136] In the 1994 genocide, killing Tutsi would be 'tree felling' and 'bush clearing', and the killing of children 'pulling out the roots of the bad weeds'.[137] The rhetoric is a reflection of broader similarities. Rwanda's first attempt at democratization, during decolonization, was marred by the intimidation of political opponents, violent election campaigns, assassinations of political leaders and vicious attacks upon political groups with a progressive agenda. Exactly the same can be said of the democratization process in the early 1990s. The twin themes of using violence to achieve political goals, and the desperate struggles of political groups for outright victory rather than an accommodating solution, first emerged during this period. Similarly, the reinterpretation of the Hamitic hypothesis by PARMEHUTU, and the racial paradigm within which subgroup divisions were perceived in the late 1950s, foreshadowed the propaganda of the 1990s. In each period, the extensive use of rumour featured markedly.

Perhaps most importantly, it was during Rwanda's decolonization that the political powers first perceived the impotence of international forces. Arguably, Belgium's perceived lack of control over the succession of *Mwami* Kigeli V contributed to the violence later in 1959. Belgium's response to the violence—granting Hutu more power within the following four months than they had been able to access through years of peaceable campaigning—can be viewed as a realistic response to a changing political climate, but also as rewarding violent, rather than peaceful, methods. The inability of either Belgian forces or the United Nations to arrest the ongoing intergroup violence set a precedent for violent transition within the society, which had never previously existed on such a scale. Perhaps most significant, however, was the impact of the United Nations' sustained push for an amnesty for the November revolution. That the United Nations sought amnesty for all of the crimes committed during the course of the revolution, including very serious crimes, and that it eventually obtained amnesty for all but the most serious, cannot be underestimated. Here was the international 'supreme arbiter' advocating impunity, and reintegration into the political scene, for those who had sought to achieve political goals through the most violent means. When Hutu extremists thus insisted in January 1994 that it would be perfectly possible to engage in massive violence despite the presence of a United Nations peacekeeping force, they could make this statement not only in the knowledge of a legacy of ineffective peacekeeping forces worldwide, but of the legacy of impunity left by the United Nations in their own country.[138]

The first risk factor for genocide in Rwanda—the existence of an 'outgroup'— resulted directly from the Belgian colonialist experience. Belgian colonialism also left Rwanda very vulnerable to the development of what many models consider the second precondition of genocide—that of 'internal strife'. Belgium's colonial legacy had bequeathed Rwanda with a massive refugee problem, both within the country and around its borders; an extremely limited ability for self-defence; a severe lack of infrastructure essential for rapid economic development; and the lack of an elite with the appropriate education and experience for governing the nation. In many respects, therefore, the relative peace in the immediate aftermath of Rwandan independence was surprising.

Rwanda at Independence

On 1 July 1962 the Republic of Rwanda celebrated its official independence. Yet it was beset with grave challenges from almost the first day. Two *inyenzi* incursions into Rwanda on 4 and 17 July—challenging the nation as it drew its very first breath—were unsuccessful, as the authorities had received advance intelligence warning of both.[139] Following these attacks, the situation settled, and Rwanda began the process of nation building. A number of development projects were commenced in conjunction with other nations, Rwanda sought foreign aid from numerous sources and an austerity campaign began, which included the raising of taxes.[140] A program commenced to 'democratize' education, which meant radically altering the ethnic composition of the student body to more accurately reflect that of the nation.[141] The number of students and the diversity of education available also increased rapidly. The problems of land tenure had been addressed in the Constitution of the Republic of Rwanda, in which Article VI proclaimed: 'Private property is inviolable. Private property cannot be expropriated if it is not for public use and in return for fair and predetermined compensation in accordance with the law.'[142] A final redistribution of cattle and land erased the last remnants of the feudal system, although not without some discord.[143] The maintenance of ant-ierosion measures and coffee cultivation suffered, however, as the Belgians were no longer present to enforce these unpopular but vital measures.[144] Coffee cultivation, as Rwanda's largest export product, was essential to provide the nation with cash income. Overall, however, and despite the dire predictions of some foreign officials and reporters, the first year and a half of Rwandan independence was surprisingly calm, and surprisingly successful.

The relative peace in the immediate aftermath of Rwanda's independence was not indicative of UNAR and/or Tutsi acceptance of the new situation, but rather representative of UNAR's disorganization and factionalism.[145] A UNAR 'government in exile' underwent multiple shake-ups, and was further paralysed by a lack of fixed residence, the geographical isolation of UNAR leaders in different refugee communities and controversy over funds.[146] The *inyenzi*, while led by UNAR leaders, were never tightly organized or managed and their power to act was dependent upon their situation as refugees. Following Rwandan independence, in Uganda and Tanganyika government efforts were made to curb the *inyenzi*.[147] In the Congo, refugees became enmeshed in the ongoing civil war there, and concerns over local conditions precluded a focus upon *inyenzi* activity.[148] In Burundi, by contrast, there was some sympathy for the refugee cause. The forty-five thousand refugees were mostly located in close proximity to the Rwandan border, and administrative control was poor.[149] UNAR propaganda and activity encouraged refugees to join the *inyenzi*, although many were already predisposed to the counterrevolutionary platform.[150] As Lemarchand has noted, 'In no other country were conditions so eminently favourable to the conduct of counter-revolutionary activities.'[151] Thus, it was from Burundi that the *inyenzi* would launch its most successful attack on Rwanda. Rwanda's risk of genocide was about to rise sharply.

The Bugesera Invasion and December 1963–January 1964 Massacres

There are conflicting reports as to the precipitants for the Bugesera invasion. The August 1963 communal elections may have inflamed the situation. In these first elections since independence, tactics such as intimidation of UNAR candidates resumed, and there were several killings.[152] UNAR responded by boycotting the elections, which only had the effect of PARMEHUTU receiving 98 per cent of the votes cast and almost total governmental power.[153] At the same time, UNAR had obtained funding from various sources, and had acquired some weaponry. Rukeba had been able to facilitate at least some organization and coordination amongst the *inyenzi*.[154]

On the night of 20 December, a major *inyenzi* attack was launched. Around three hundred refugees, armed 'with bows, arrows and home-made rifles', crossed the border from Burundi into Rwanda at Nemba, and moved into the Bugesera region.[155] They attacked and surprised a small Rwandan military camp, killing four soldiers and seizing two jeeps, some light arms and ammunition.[156] En route to Kigali, they next stopped at a Tutsi refugee camp in Nyamata, where they were reinforced by hundreds of local Tutsi.[157] It was not until the group—now numbering well over one thousand—was within a dozen miles of Kigali that it met any resistance. At the Kanzenze Bridge on the Nyabarongo River, they encountered a company of the Rwandan National Guard, and a brief battle ensued.[158] The company, under the command of a Belgian military advisor, easily repelled the invaders, and several hundred Tutsi were killed.[159] The remainder 'withdrew in full flight', and some were pursued by the National Guard all the way back to the border.[160] Accompanying this main invasion were a series of raids from other refugee centres. On 21 and 22 December a number of small-scale raids launched from the Congo were repelled by the army; on 25 December Ugandan authorities intercepted another group of *inyenzi* before they could reach the Rwandan border; a second group from Uganda, about six hundred men, managed to cross the border on 27 December but were quickly routed by the now fully mobilized Rwandan army.[161]

The reaction of the Kayibanda government was one of shock and panic. The National Guard was put on full alert, but as an army of only one thousand men, with only basic equipment and not even enough trucks to mobilize in one effort or enough radios to supply each platoon, there was little confidence in the security that the army could provide.[162] Three further actions were thus taken in response to the invasion. First, telegrams were sent to the United Nations and the Organization of African Unity. As Wagoner noted, however, 'Rwanda soon learned that despite all the ideals written into charters and protocols, if her borders were to be secure she would have to secure them herself.'[163] Second, the government sought to neutralize the threat that could be posed by Tutsi leaders within the country—potential collaborators with the external forces. A document had been found on the body of one of the invaders listing the names of Tutsi leaders and a plan for their role as officials in a new Tutsi-led government, supposedly to be installed on Christmas Day.[164] These leaders were quickly arrested, along with other prominent Tutsi. Twenty-three were summarily executed on 23 December, including leading members of UNAR and RADER; others were released after being severely beaten.[165]

But it was the third action taken by the government in response to the invasion that would have the most devastating effect. Government officials were dispatched to each prefecture to organize 'civilian defence forces' to aid the army.[166] As Lemarchand has noted:

> These arrangements were made within a few hours, in an atmosphere of panic, and therefore with little attention to procedural details or co-ordination. Meanwhile, Kigali Radio repeatedly beamed emergency warnings, asking the population to be 'constantly on the alert' for Tutsi terrorists. In this atmosphere of intense fear, saturated with rumour and suspicion, the worst was bound to happen.[167]

'The worst' began in the prefecture of Gikongoro on 23 December. In this area, with a high Tutsi population and encompassing Nyanza—the former seat of Tutsi domination—rumours circulated that Kigali had fallen, the *mwami* had been returned to power and further *inyenzi* attacks were imminent.[168] The prefect of Gikongoro responded to the government call for self-defence with a plan of attack: 'We are expected to defend ourselves. The only way to go about it is to paralyse the Tutsi. How? They must be killed.'[169] According to Lemarchand: 'This was the signal for the slaughter. Armed with clubs, pangas [a long knife used for cutting grass] and spears, the Hutu methodically began to exterminate all Tutsi in sight—men, women and children.'[170]

The violence was brutal, and the widespread use of traditional arms and farming implements led to incidents of shocking atrocities. Gikongoro was the centre of the massacres, but the violence quickly spread to other areas. It is generally accepted, however, that there was no central organization to these events.[171] Rather, 'Panic combined with local circumstances to produce mass slaughter.'[172] Indeed, fear appears to have been the primary motivator for the attacks. European observers in the nation during December 1963 and January 1964 reported an atmosphere of 'near panic throughout Rwanda'.[173] The report of the United Nations commission that investigated the massacres concluded that they were a result of Hutu 'fear and panic' following the *inyenzi* incursion.[174] Even in Kibungo prefecture, the fear was palpable. There, the Catholic White Fathers and communal leaders worked together to maintain some sense of calm, and they successfully prevented the outbreak of violence.[175] Nevertheless, as the East African specialist Aaron Segal concluded, 'The degree of fear was such that the White Fathers were convinced that the burning of a single Tutsi hut would have prompted the entire Tutsi population of the prefecture to take refuge.'[176]

Lemarchand has commented that '[p]opular participation in violence created a kind of collective catharsis through which years of pent-up hatred suddenly seemed to find an outlet'.[177] Without central organization, however, the massacres abated relatively quickly, and had ceased by mid-January.[178] Estimates of the numbers killed vary widely. Both Lemarchand and Segal, in Rwanda in early 1964, estimated between 10,000 and 14,000 were killed, including some Hutu.[179] The Rwandan government's estimate of 870 casualties is described by Lemarchand as 'patently inaccurate'.[180] The United Nations estimate of casualties between 1,000 and 3,000 was significantly lower than that of both Lemarchand and Segal, although the difficulty of obtaining an accurate estimate was emphasized in the report in question.[181] Aside from a few sensationalist media reports in the immediate wake of the violence, there was no suggestion that this was genocide. Indeed, UN Commissioner Max Dorsinville, in Rwanda both as the massacres unfolded in late December to early January and again in February after their cessation, reported, 'There is no question of a systematic elimination or extermination of the Batutsi, or of what some sources have hastened to call genocide.'[182] Once the violence had ceased, it did not recommence, despite further *inyenzi* raids in late January and early February.[183] And whilst a number of Tutsi leaders were killed, nearly half of Rwanda's administration continued to be staffed by Tutsi, and they continued to form the majority of teachers at secondary schools.[184] Nevertheless, in the wake of the violence thousands more Tutsi chose to leave Rwanda as refugees. Estimates of Rwandan refugees in 1964 put over 200,000 in Burundi, 78,000 in Uganda, 36,000 in Tanzania and 22,000 in the Congo—a total of over 336,000.[185]

Both the international and internal responses to the massacres failed to mete out any serious consequences to those involved in the violence. The United Nations had been apprised of the situation very quickly, and a commissioner was despatched to investigate. Commissioner Dorsinville refrained from any harsh criticism of the Rwandan government or even from demanding the cessation of the violence, accepting the 'formal assurances' given by Kayibanda on 31 December that 'the local authorities had been instructed to do their utmost to avoid abuses and calm the population', and further assurances that 'those responsible for these excesses will be ruthlessly punished'.[186] Internationally, the response was delayed substantially by the lack of media in Rwanda, and the events were not widely reported until after their cessation. Of the numerous countries providing aid to Rwanda, only the Swiss demanded an investigation into the massacres, and Burundi was the only nation to officially protest the events.[187] Internally, the role of the government in stopping the violence remains unclear. At least one source reported that, contrary to the UN report, orders to stop the killing were not given until

12 January.[188] The atmosphere of fear of an *inyenzi* takeover must be taken into consideration, however. Nevertheless, Kayibanda's reaction to the first commission of enquiry into the events revealed a deep ambivalence. When this commission, set up at the request of the Swiss government, found two government ministers and a number of prefects, burgomasters and other local officials to be incriminated in the events, Kayibanda rejected its findings and ordered a second investigation.[189] The second investigation, not surprisingly, implicated far fewer individuals, most of whom received only light prison sentences. The massacres also left the UNAR leadership heavily decimated, and the UNAR newspaper *Unité* was no longer published. The UN report into the events described them as resulting 'in the silencing of the opposition'.[190] Yet Rwanda's survival in the face of invasion also served to become a source of national solidarity and pride for the Hutu majority. The crisis brought a sense of cohesion to the Kayibanda government that had not previously existed, and a resurgence of popular support.[191]

The December 1963–January 1964 Massacres and the Temporal Model

The temporal model provides a useful framework through which to analyse the Bugesera invasion and the subsequent outbreak of massacres. The *inyenzi* incursion, as an invasion attempt, simultaneously fulfilled the preconditions of 'internal strife' and 'the perception of the outgroup as posing an existential threat to the dominant power'. The invasion was clearly viewed by the Kayibanda government as posing a real threat to its survival, triggering the risk escalation process. The immediacy and severity of this threat provoked a response that was also both immediate and severe. While in international terms a massacre with a death toll of three thousand or even ten thousand may not be regarded as especially grave, it must be emphasized that in Rwanda this was an unprecedented level of violence. Both the *inyenzi* attacks in the lead-up to Rwandan independence and those immediately after independence had not provoked such a response, as they were not perceived as posing an existential threat to the nation. Prior to independence the presence of Belgium and the oversight of the United Nations offered a form of protection; the two attacks following independence were easily repelled, despite Rwanda's extreme vulnerability. Similarly, *inyenzi* attacks in late January and early February 1964—in the immediate wake of the massacres—were also relatively insignificant, thereby failing to offer sufficient threat to provoke further violence.[192]

The *inyenzi* attacks singularly met the precondition of 'internal strife' and the association of the outgroup with an existential threat to the nation, sufficient to provoke the massacres. Very quickly after the incursion, however, it began to be apparent that the threat was not an ongoing one. As this threat was perceived as having been overcome, therefore, the preconditions of internal strife and the perception of the Tutsi as posing an existential threat to the nation were no longer operable. There was effectively a process of risk regression—a retreat on the continuum leading to genocide. Rwanda returned to a position of only meeting the precondition of the existence of an 'outgroup'. This was reflected in the climate of relative tolerance and moderation that quickly returned to the nation. By mid-1964 the Kayibanda government was again expressing its desires for peace and tolerance: 'Today more than ever, after the hard lesson inflicted on the terrorists, Rwanda wants to be a tolerant and peaceful nation. This is the will of all the people, and this is the will of all its leaders.'[193] While admittedly this tract was prepared for an international audience, the government clearly differentiated between the *petits* Tutsi refugees, whom they explicitly stated were not responsible for the 'terrorist attack', and the 'great feudal criminals' who were.[194] The Tutsi, while outsiders, were not homogenized and vilified as a group. Furthermore, there was no ongoing violence or persecution of Tutsi within Rwanda. Nevertheless, the massacres did result in an increased perception of the Tutsi as an 'outgroup'. In particular, while Tutsi continued in numerous administrative roles, the massacres led to the almost complete absence of Tutsi from political participation in the nation, a situation that would remain for the duration of Kayibanda's presidency.

There were two further outcomes of the massacres that are significant with respect to the subsequent genocide. Once again, the concept of impunity featured prominently in the wake of the massacres. The United Nations had not been heavily critical of the Kayibanda government during the massacres, nor did it insist upon the perpetrators being brought to justice in their wake. International development aid to Rwanda continued uninterrupted, even following Kayibanda's decision to disregard the findings of the first commission of enquiry. No one appeared to mind that the second was a whitewash. Indeed, beyond impunity, the massacres actually had a very positive outcome for Kayibanda's regime. Hutu pride and solidarity increased, and the government experienced a resurgence in popular support. For the second time in five years, anti-Tutsi violence had led to a desired political outcome.

Finally, it is worth examining why the massacres did not escalate into a genocide. In Rwanda in 1964, there was a very powerful restraint in operation. That is, the Kayibanda government simply did not have anything like the entrenched power required for such a course of action. With a poorly equipped army of just one thousand men, it had only halted a disorderly invasion of lightly armed refugees less than twenty kilometres from its capital. In the absence of any conceivable means to initiate a genocide, such a course of action could not even be contemplated. While there is some evidence of 'destructive communication', a further precondition for genocide, it was not at a level sufficient to meet the precondition. Chiefly, such communication consisted of panicky Kigali Radio reports of the threat of *inyenzi* attacks, and wild rumours that circulated throughout the country.

All Tutsi were not linked with the *inyenzi* in these communications, and Tutsi were not dehumanized. Yet it is interesting to note that when the first reports of the massacres reached the Western world, they were freely described as genocide. With limited and wildly inaccurate information, press reports did not hesitate to allege that a genocide was underway. Vatican Radio, with little information, even accused Rwanda in February 1964 of 'the most terrible and systematic genocide since the genocide of the Jews by Hitler'.[195] While such reports were grossly inaccurate, as later confirmed by the United Nations commission investigating the massacres, that they were made at all is still of significance. Rwanda's potential for genocide was widely and easily recognizable.

The parallels between the Hamidian massacres in Ottoman Armenia and the 1963–64 massacres of Tutsi offer significant insight into how risk of genocide develops over time. While the massacres were very different in severity, level of central organization and duration, in both cases there is strong evidence of a cyclic process of escalation and retreat underway. The process of risk escalation prior to the Armenian massacres was a long one; in Rwanda it was much more rapid, although the colonial legacy that left Rwanda extremely vulnerable to such a process has already been noted. In each instance, a triggering event led to the outgroup being closely associated with an existential threat to the ruling powers; in each instance, this provoked violent massacres of the outgroup in response. In each case, however, there were powerful constraints impinging on any possible further escalation of the violence. The Ottoman government was ever mindful of the threat of European intervention; the Rwandan government lacked the power even to contemplate more systematic violence. In both cases, therefore, there was a process of retreat following the massacres. In Rwanda in particular, this retreat to a more accommodating approach is quite marked. This highlights that the processes that lead to genocide are not necessarily linear, but rather marked by cycles of escalation and retreat.

Notes

1. United Nations. 1954. *United Nations Visiting Mission to Trust Territories in East Africa, 1954, Report on Ruanda-Urundi*, T/1168, 2, quoted in D. Rawson. 1966. 'The Role of the United Nations in the Political Development of Ruanda-Urundi, 1947–1962', Ph.D. diss., American University, 98.
2. Rawson, 'The Role of the United Nations', 225–26.
3. R. Lemarchand. 1966. 'Political Instability in Africa: The Case of Rwanda and Burundi', *Civilisations* 16(3), 318; A. Segal. 1964. *Massacre in Rwanda*, Fabian Research Series 240, London: Fabian Society, 8.
4. F. Wagoner. 1968. 'Nation Building in Africa: A Description and Analysis of the Development of Rwanda', Ph.D. diss., American University, 158.

5. M. Niyonzima et al. 1957. *Manifesto of the Bahutu: Note on the Social Aspect of the Indigenous Racial Problem in Ruanda*, in United Nations. 1957. *United Nations Visiting Mission to Trust Territories in East Africa, 1957, Report on Ruanda-Urundi*, T/1346, Annex I, 3.

6. R. Lemarchand. 1970. *Rwanda and Burundi*, New York: Praeger Publishers, 152.

7. L. Kuper. 1977. *The Pity of It All: Polarisation of Racial and Ethnic Relations*, London: Duckworth, 176.

8. Wagoner, 'Nation Building in Africa', 155.

9. High Council of State (Ruanda). 1957. *Mise au Point* [Statement of views], in United Nations, *Visiting Mission 1957*, Annex II, 12.

10. M. Atterbury. 1970. *Revolution in Rwanda*, Occasional Paper 2, Madison: African Studies Program, University of Wisconsin, 45.

11. M. D'Hertefelt. 1960. 'Myth and Political Acculturation in Rwanda (U.N. Trust Territory)', in A. Dubb (ed.), *Myth in Modern Africa: The Fourteenth Conference Proceedings of the Rhodes-Livingstone Institute for Social Research*, Lusaka, Northern Rhodesia: The Rhodes-Livingstone Institute, 122.

12. Ibid.; Atterbury, *Revolution in Rwanda*, 58.

13. J. Webster. 1966. *The Political Development of Rwanda and Burundi*, Occasional Paper 16, Syracuse, NY: Syracuse University Maxwell Graduate School of Citizenship and Public Affairs, 39.

14. United Nations. 1955. *Observations of the Administering Authority on the Report of the Visiting Mission*, T/1164, 47, quoted in Rawson, 'The Role of the United Nations', 173.

15. Wagoner, 'Nation Building in Africa', 161.

16. Rawson, 'The Role of the United Nations', 219.

17. Ibid., 179.

18. Wagoner, 'Nation Building in Africa', 162.

19. J. Maquet. 1961. *The Premise of Inequality in Ruanda: A Study of Political Relations in a Central African Kingdom*, London: Oxford University Press, 124.

20. Lemarchand, *Rwanda and Burundi*, 160.

21. J. Bhattacharyya. 1967. 'Belgian Administration in Ruanda during the Trusteeship Period with Special Reference to the Tutsi-Hutu Relationship', Ph.D. diss., University of Delhi, 243; D'Hertefelt, 'Myth and Political Acculturation', 125.

22. 1959. 'Manifeste-Programme du Parmehutu', 18 October 1959, in F. Nkundabagenzi (ed.), *Rwanda Politique: 1958–1960*, Brussels: Centre de Recherche et d'Information Socio-Politiques, 1961, 113.

23. M. Mamdani. 2001. *When Victims Become Killers: Colonialism, Nativism, and the Genocide in Rwanda*, Princeton, NJ: Princeton University Press, 123; Kuper, *The Pity of It All*, 177; D'Hertefelt, 'Myth and Political Acculturation', 125.

24. Kuper, *The Pity of It All*, 177.

25. Mamdani, *When Victims Become Killers*, 120.

26. G. Prunier. 1995. *The Rwanda Crisis: History of a Genocide*, New York: Columbia University Press, 47.

27. Bhattacharyya, 'Belgian Administration', 246.

28. RADER, *Statuts*, I, quoted in Lemarchand, *Rwanda and Burundi*, 160; Kuper, *The Pity of It All*, 177.

29. H. Codere. 1986. 'Fieldwork in Rwanda, 1959–1960', in P. Golde (ed.), *Women in the Field: Anthropological Experiences*, 2nd ed., Berkeley: University of California Press, 162.

30. Atterbury, *Revolution in Rwanda*, 48.

31. Conseil Supérieur. 1959. 'Rapport soumis au Groupe de Travail par le Conseil Supérieur du Pays', April, in Nkundabagenzi, *Rwanda Politique*, 76–86.

32. United Nations. 1960. *Visiting Mission to Trust Territories in East Africa, 1960: Report on Ruanda-Urundi*, T/1538, 3 June, 18–21, cited in Webster, *The Political Development*, 44.

33. M.A. Munyangaju. 1959. 'Aspects des problèmes importants au Rwanda-Burundi', 30 January, quoted in Bhattacharyya, 'Belgian Administration', 218.

34. Bhattacharyya, 'Belgian Administration', 235; Kuper, *The Pity of It All*, 182.
35. Wagoner, 'Nation Building in Africa', 178; Atterbury, *Revolution in Rwanda*, 54.
36. United Nations, *Visiting Mission 1960*, 56.
37. Ibid.; Bhattacharyya, 'Belgian Administration', 238; Wagoner, 'Nation Building in Africa', 180.
38. United Nations, *Visiting Mission 1960*, 58; Wagoner, 'Nation Building in Africa', 180.
39. *Rapport de la Commission d'enquête*, 27–28, quoted in Bhattacharyya, 'Belgian Administration', 240.
40. Atterbury, *Revolution in Rwanda*, 56.
41. Kuper, *The Pity of It All*, 189.
42. Atterbury, *Revolution in Rwanda*, 64.
43. Ibid.
44. Codere, 'Fieldwork in Rwanda', 163.
45. Bhattacharyya, 'Belgian Administration', 255–56.
46. Lemarchand, *Rwanda and Burundi*, 162.
47. United Nations, *Visiting Mission 1960*, 73.
48. Ibid.; Atterbury, *Revolution in Rwanda*, 70; J. Hubert. 1965. *La Toussaint Rwandaise et sa répression*, Brussels: Academie Royale des Sciences D'Outre-mer, 31–32.
49. Hubert, *La Toussaint Rwandaise*, 32.
50. United Nations, *Visiting Mission 1960*, 73.
51. Lemarchand, *Rwanda and Burundi*, 167.
52. United Nations, *Visiting Mission 1960*, 73.
53. United Nations, *Visiting Mission 1960*, 75, 77; R. Lemarchand. 1970. 'The Coup in Rwanda', in R. Rotberg and A. Mazrui (eds), *Protest and Power in Black Africa*, New York: Oxford University Press, 904.
54. United Nations, *Visiting Mission 1960*, 75, 77.
55. Ibid., 77.
56. Atterbury, *Revolution in Rwanda*, 71.
57. Lemarchand, *Rwanda and Burundi*, 164; Lemarchand, 'The Coup in Rwanda', 905.
58. United Nations, *Visiting Mission 1960*, 73, 78; Bhattacharyya, 'Belgian Administration', 262.
59. According to the United Nations estimate, *Visiting Mission 1960*, 82. Hubert estimated that between 1 November 1959 and 31 May 1961, only seventy-four persons were known to have been killed (Hubert, *La Toussaint Rwandaise*, 40); Bhattacharyya estimated a total of around three hundred persons were killed during the fortnight (Bhattacharyya, 'Belgian Administration', 270).
60. United Nations, *Visiting Mission 1960*, 88.
61. Ibid.
62. Webster, *The Political Development*, 61.
63. United Nations, *Visiting Mission 1960*, 89.
64. Ibid., 94.
65. Wagoner, 'Nation Building in Africa', 190, 193.
66. Ibid., 193.
67. Ibid., 196; Lemarchand, *Rwanda and Burundi*, 173; United Nations, *Visiting Mission 1960*, 85.
68. United Nations, *Visiting Mission 1960*, 85–86.
69. Wagoner, 'Nation Building in Africa', 198.
70. Lemarchand, *Rwanda and Burundi*, 175.
71. Rawson, 'The Role of the United Nations', 234; Wagoner, 'Nation Building in Africa', 198; Lemarchand, *Rwanda and Burundi*, 175; Bhattacharyya, 'Belgian Administration', 273; P. Tabara. 1992. *Afrique: La face cachée*, Paris: La Pensée universelle, 179–85.
72. Wagoner, 'Nation Building in Africa', 197.
73. United Nations, *Visiting Mission 1960*, 84.

74. Lemarchand, *Rwanda and Burundi*, 174, 179.

75. Bhattacharyya, 'Belgian Administration', 272.

76. United Nations, *Visiting Mission 1960*, 83–84; Belgium, Service de l'information du Ruanda-Urundi. 1960. *Rwanda: Le problème des réfugiés et sinistrés après les troubles de 1959–1960*, Brussels: Service de l'information du Ruanda-Urundi, 100.

77. Lemarchand, *Rwanda and Burundi*, 173.

78. Ibid.; United Nations, *Visiting Mission 1960*, 84.

79. United Nations, *Visiting Mission 1960*, 84–85.

80. Lemarchand, *Rwanda and Burundi*, 173.

81. Belgium, *Le problème des réfugiés*, 97; United Nations. 1960. *Question of the Future of Ruanda-Urundi: Statement Made by the Representative of Belgium at the 1077th Meeting of Fourth Committee*, A/C.4/462, 15 December, 2.

82. L. Kuper. 1975. *Race, Class, and Power: Ideology and Revolutionary Change in Plural Societies*, Chicago: Aldine Publishing Company, 195; Bhattacharyya, 'Belgian Administration', 313.

83. Kuper, *The Pity of It All*, 189.

84. Bhattacharyya, 'Belgian Administration', 314.

85. R. Lemarchand. 2003. 'Comparing the Killing Fields', in S. Jensen (ed.), *Genocide: Cases, Comparisons and Contemporary Debates*, Copenhagen: Danish Centre for Holocaust and Genocide Studies, 158.

86. Lemarchand, 'Political Instability in Africa', 318.

87. Bhattacharyya, 'Belgian Administration', 271.

88. Lemarchand, *Rwanda and Burundi*, 169.

89. United Nations, *Visiting Mission 1960*, 166–68.

90. Rawson, 'The Role of the United Nations', 234.

91. United Nations. 1960. *Statement of Mr. Claeys Bouuaert, Twenty-sixth Session*, T/SR.1112, 414, quoted in Rawson, 'The Role of the United Nations', 235.

92. Rawson, 'The Role of the United Nations', 275.

93. Atterbury, *Revolution in Rwanda*, 73–74.

94. Service d'Information du Rwanda-Burundi (ed.). 1960. 'Les élections communales au Rwanda', in Nkundabagenzi, *Rwanda Politique*, 272.

95. Lemarchand, *Rwanda and Burundi*, 187.

96. J.H. Gitera et al. 1960. 'Relation des travaux du Comité d'étude des problèmes Twa—Hutu—Tutsi et Zungu au Rwanda (Réunion tenue à Kigali les 24, 25 et 26 novembre 1960)', in Nkundabagenzi, *Rwanda Politique*, 347.

97. Lemarchand, *Rwanda and Burundi*, 189.

98. Ibid.

99. Bhattacharyya, 'Belgian Administration', 297.

100. United Nations. 1960. *Question of the Future of Ruanda-Urundi: Written Statement by Kigeri V. Mwami of Rwanda*, A/C.4/467, 19 December, 5; Wagoner, 'Nation Building in Africa', 204.

101. United Nations. 1961. *Question of the Future of Ruanda-Urundi: Note from the Aprosoma and Parmehutu Parties Concerning the Coup d'État at Gitarama on 28 January 1961*, A/C.4/477, 4 April, 2–3.

102. United Nations. 1961. *Lettre du Ministre des Affaires Etrangères au Président de la Commission*, Pierre Wigny, 25 January, A/4706/Add 1, in Nkundabagenzi, *Rwanda Politique*, 381–82; Bhattacharyya, 'Belgian Administration', 302–4.

103. Bhattacharyya, 'Belgian Administration', 305.

104. United Nations, *Note from the Aprosoma*, 5–6.

105. Belgian government. 1961. *Rapport sur l'administration belge du Ruanda-Urundi pendant l'année 1960*, Brussels: Fr. Van Muysewinkel, 44–45; United Nations. 1961. *Communiqué officiel du gouvernement belge définissant son attitude envers les événements de Gitarama*, A/4706/Add 1, 1 February, in Nkundabagenzi, *Rwanda Politique*, 397–98.

106. United Nations, *Note from the Aprosoma*, 4; United Nations. 1961. *Question of the Future of Ruanda-Urundi: Statement Made by the Representative of Belgium at the 1108th Meeting of the Fourth Committee on 20 March 1961*, A/C.4/473, 6.
107. Bhattacharyya, 'Belgian Administration', 306–7.
108. Wagoner, 'Nation Building in Africa', 215.
109. Ibid., 224.
110. Ibid., 231.
111. United Nations. *Report of the United Nations Commission*, A/4994 and A/4994/Add. 1, 28–29, quoted in Wagoner, 'Nation Building in Africa', 231.
112. United Nations, *Report of the United Nations Commission*, A/4994, 60.
113. Lemarchand, *Rwanda and Burundi*, 195.
114. United Nations. 1962. *Question of the Future of Ruanda-Urundi: Statement Made by Mr. E. Gassou, United Nations Commissioner for Ruanda-Urundi, at the 1264th Meeting of the Fourth Committee*, A/C.4/524, 19 January, 2–3.
115. Ibid.
116. United Nations. 1962. *Question of the Future of Ruanda-Urundi: Statement Made by Mr. Majid Rahnema, United Nations Commissioner for Ruanda-Urundi, at the 1265th Meeting of the Fourth Committee*, A/C.4/525, 23 January, 13.
117. Ibid., 13–14.
118. Wagoner, 'Nation Building in Africa', 234.
119. Atterbury, *Revolution in Rwanda*, 77.
120. Rwanda, Ministère des Affaires Étrangères. 1964. *Toute la vérité sur le terrorisme "Inyenzi" au Rwanda: Une mise au point du Ministère des Affaires Étrangères du Rwanda*, Kigali: Services d'information, 11–12.
121. Mamdani, *When Victims Become Killers*, 129.
122. United Nations. 1962. *Question of the Future of Ruanda-Urundi: Report of the United Nations Commission for Ruanda-Urundi Established under General Assembly Resolution 1743 (XVI)*, A/5126, 30 May, 45.
123. Ibid., 45.
124. United Nations, *Statement Made by Mr. Majid Rahnema*, 17.
125. Ibid., 17–18.
126. United Nations, *Report of the United Nations Commission*, A/4994, 58. See also Belgium, *Le problème des réfugiés*, 100.
127. United Nations, *Report of the United Nations Commission*, A/4994, 59.
128. Ibid., 60.
129. Ibid., 132.
130. Webster, *The Political Development*, 84. Wagoner gives a figure of 130,000, 'Nation Building in Africa', 252.
131. H. Fein. 1979. *Accounting for Genocide: National Responses and Jewish Victimization during the Holocaust*, New York: Free Press, 9.
132. United Nations, *Statement Made by Mr. Majid Rahnema*, 17–18.
133. Lemarchand, *Rwanda and Burundi*, 197.
134. Ibid.
135. This quote is cited in *Mémoire sur la révolution Rwandaise de Novembre 1959 présenté à la mission de visite de l'ONU par la délégation Hutu au Conseil Provisoire du Rwanda*, Kigali: n.p., 1960, 15, quoted in Lemarchand, *Rwanda and Burundi*, 159.
136. 'Position du Conseil supérieur et du Mwami', quoted in Wagoner, 'Nation Building in Africa', 166.
137. H. Hintjens. 1999. 'Explaining the 1994 Genocide in Rwanda', *The Journal of Modern African Studies* 37(2), 268; Prunier, *The Rwanda Crisis*, 142.
138. H. Ngeze. 1994. 'Who Will Survive the War of March?' *Kangura*, January 1994, quoted in African Rights. 1995. *Rwanda: Death, Despair and Defiance*, rev. ed., London: African Rights, 73.

139. 'Indépendance du Rwanda: Un an et demi de paix et de concorde nationale', in Rwanda, Ministère des Affaires Étrangères, *Toute la vérité*, 13–14.

140. Webster, *The Political Development*, 83.

141. Ibid.

142. 'Constitution de la République Rwandaise', in Nkundabagenzi, *Rwanda Politique*, 392.

143. Webster, *The Political Development*, 84; Lemarchand, *Rwanda and Burundi*, 230–33.

144. Webster, *The Political Development*, 84.

145. Lemarchand, *Rwanda and Burundi*, 197–227.

146. Ibid., 203–6.

147. Ibid., 207–10.

148. Ibid., 210–15.

149. Ibid., 215–16.

150. Ibid., 216–17. It is important to note that not all refugees supported the *inyenzi*, and some were opposed to their methods and objectives.

151. Ibid., 215.

152. Wagoner, 'Nation Building in Africa', 256.

153. Ibid., 256–57.

154. Lemarchand, *Rwanda and Burundi*, 219–20.

155. Segal, *Massacre in Rwanda*, 13.

156. Ibid.

157. Lemarchand, *Rwanda and Burundi*, 223.

158. Wagoner, 'Nation Building in Africa', 258.

159. Ibid.; Lemarchand, *Rwanda and Burundi*, 223.

160. Wagoner, 'Nation Building in Africa', 258.

161. Lemarchand, *Rwanda and Burundi*, 222.

162. Wagoner, 'Nation Building in Africa', 298.

163. Ibid., 265.

164. Ibid., 259.

165. Ibid.; Segal, *Massacre in Rwanda*, 14; Lemarchand, *Rwanda and Burundi*, 223.

166. Segal, *Massacre in Rwanda*, 14; Wagoner, 'Nation Building in Africa', 259.

167. Lemarchand, *Rwanda and Burundi*, 223.

168. Segal, *Massacre in Rwanda*, 15.

169. Lemarchand, *Rwanda and Burundi*, 223–24.

170. Ibid., 224.

171. The UN report on the massacres concluded: 'These brutal acts were in no sense dictated by the government in Kigali.' United Nations, Press Services Office of Public Information. 1964. 'The Situation in Rwanda and Burundi', SG/SM/24, 3 March, in E. Coppieters (ed.). 1963. *Chronique de politique étrangère* 16(4–6), 705.

172. Segal, *Massacre in Rwanda*, 15.

173. Wagoner, 'Nation Building in Africa', 264.

174. United Nations, 'The Situation in Rwanda and Burundi', 705.

175. Segal, *Massacre in Rwanda*, 14.

176. Ibid., 14–15.

177. Lemarchand, *Rwanda and Burundi*, 224.

178. Segal, *Massacre in Rwanda*, 17.

179. Ibid., 15; Lemarchand, *Rwanda and Burundi*, 225.

180. Lemarchand, *Rwanda and Burundi*, 224.

181. United Nations, 'The Situation in Rwanda and Burundi', 705; 1964. 'Rwanda.—Raids by Watutsi Refugees on Rwanda—Mass "Reprisal" Killings of Resident Watutsi—U.N. Investigation in Massacres', *Keesling's Contemporary Archives*, 23–30 May, 20086.

182. United Nations, 'The Situation in Rwanda and Burundi', 705.

183. Ibid.

184. Ibid.

185. J. Sayinzoga. 1982. 'Les Réfugiés Rwandais: Quelques repères historiques et réflexions socio-politiques', *Journal of the Swiss Society of African Studies* 20(1), 51.

186. United Nations, 'The Situation in Rwanda and Burundi', 705.

187. Lemarchand, *Rwanda and Burundi*, 226–27.

188. 'Rwanda.—Raids by Watutsi Refugees', 20086.

189. Lemarchand, *Rwanda and Burundi*, 226.

190. United Nations, 'The Situation in Rwanda and Burundi', 705.

191. Lemarchand, *Rwanda and Burundi*, 227.

192. 'The Situation in Rwanda and Burundi', 705.

193. Rwanda, Ministère des Affaires Étrangères, *Toute la vérité*, 13.

194. Ibid., 20.

195. 'Brève réponse à quelques grossières calomnies que l'on a lancées contre le Rwanda', (mimeo., n.p., n.d.), quoted in Lemarchand, *Rwanda and Burundi*, 224.

Chapter 6

'A COCKROACH GIVES BIRTH TO ANOTHER COCKROACH'

From Coexistence to Extermination

The Kayibanda government ruled for a further nine years following the conflagrations of December 1963–January 1964. Kayibanda's Rwanda had always been a Hutu nation; following the massacres, however, this was even more pronounced.[1] The government became and remained an entirely Hutu affair.[2] Obstructions to the achievement of political goals were at times blamed on 'cockroachism'.[3] The view of the Hutu/Tutsi divide remained a racial one, with the colonial ancillary to the Hamitic hypothesis—that the Tutsi were foreigners—remaining salient within the society.[4] In this context, little was done to address the refugee problem. Tutsi could and did, however, continue to participate in civil society.[5] A quota system limited Tutsi access to education to ostensibly their numerical proportion within society, but was loosely enforced. In February 1966, a further *inyenzi* attack, perceived to pose a fairly serious threat, was easily repelled by the National Guard; despite the situation remaining threatening well into April, there were no reprisals, no panic amongst the population and the situation was managed by the government, without a response targeting Rwandan Tutsi.[6] Thus, in 1969, a handbook prepared to provide American officials with information about Rwanda stated, 'The position of the Tutsi in the republican society in 1969 was still undefined.'[7]

Of course, the Kayibanda government had other pressing concerns beyond the issue of race. Rwanda at independence had the dubious distinction of having one of the smallest capital cities in the world—a reflection of its lack of development generally. Addressing the nation's developmental needs was a strong priority. In May 1964, Kayibanda established Rwanda's first university—the National University of Rwanda at Butare, which by 1966 had 127 students enrolled.[8] The Hutu *Coopérative Travail, Fidelité, Progrès* (TRAFIPRO) was expanded to become a national commercial cooperative with the aid of Swiss funding, buying and exporting cash crops, and in return importing and selling essential goods (such as soap, salt, matches, lamps and toothpaste) at minimal markup in its own commercial stores.[9] At independence the Kigali airport consisted of a dirt strip with four tin huts, but with Belgian assistance an international airport was constructed. French and then German assistance established Radio Rwanda, the first radio station for the nation. But Rwanda faced some formidable barriers to development. Some 50 per cent of the population was under fifteen years of age, and the population growth rate was very high, at 3.6 per cent.[10] Even with the austerity program instituted by Kayibanda, in the first full year of independence Rwanda's expenses for normal operations reached almost 11 million dollars, while its income amounted to only just over 6.5 million.[11] Thus, it was immediately in significant deficit from normal operations, leaving no money whatsoever for desperately needed development projects. Coffee production—the primary source of Rwanda's income—fell by over two-thirds following independence.[12] Economic problems were compounded following the *inyenzi* attacks at the close of 1963. In response to the attacks, the government doubled the size of the National Guard, and by 1966, the budget for national defence had soared to 27 per cent of total expenditure.[13]

These problems were made worse by a severe lack of adequately trained and experienced government leaders and administrative personnel.[14] Even if programs were articulated in Kigali, local administrators did not have the expertise to implement them.[15] Furthermore, Kayibanda's austerity program began to slip. Even Kayibanda himself abandoned his Volvo and single well-worn suit (in which he had appeared at all official occasions) for a Mercedes Benz and a new wardrobe.[16] Corruption crept in at many levels, and went completely unpunished.[17] By late 1965, despite grants and long-term loans from Belgium to aid with the deficit, Rwanda was in serious financial difficulties. Following the elections that year (in which Kayibanda ran unopposed and received over 90 per cent of the votes), the president had little choice but to accept a devaluation of the Rwandan franc as a condition of a loan from the International Monetary Fund (IMF)—the only alternative being complete bankruptcy.[18] A five-year plan was launched for 1966–70, which led to some improvements. In particular, coffee production rose considerably, and the mining sector boomed, both providing much-needed foreign exchange earnings.[19] Rwanda, however, still had one of the lowest gross domestic products (GDP) in the world. As one commentator noted, 'Although Rwanda's government pursues a development policy, the resource base is too thin.'[20] Whilst the achievement of a Hutu-led government had been enough to ensure Kayibanda's popularity immediately postindependence, by the late sixties the first rumblings of discontent could be heard.

The Coup d'État

In 1970 René Lemarchand identified one of the key objectives of the Kay-ibanda government as being 'to build up support from within'.[21] A particular danger was the increasing number of 'unemployed intellectuals', Hutu students and graduates for whom the economy could provide few opportunities.[22] The unrest amongst this group had a strong racial overtone, as Tutsi still dominated the highest levels of education, and their disproportionate presence in both the civil service and private business provoked resentment. There was also dissension within the government, and during the 1969 elections a number of prominent Hutu were expelled from PARMEHUTU.[23] There were reports of unrest in the army in both 1969 and 1971, and in 1972 there was a major shake-up of personnel in government ministries; additionally, nine out of ten provincial governors were replaced.[24]

Thus, the atmosphere was already uneasy when, in neighbouring Burundi, large-scale massacres of Hutu (by the mostly Tutsi army) broke out. The violence spilled over to provoke renewed ethnic hostility in Rwanda, although, as one author noted, the hostilities were also 'a symptom of the country's economic difficul-ties'.[25] In the university and colleges, lists of Tutsi students were posted by Hutu students, along with a demand for their removal.[26] The turbulence spread to the civil services and even private businesses, although Prunier has suggested that those responsible for provoking it were often those with the most to benefit.[27] According to Prunier, rural people showed little interest; Filip Reyntjens, professor of Afri-can law and politics, by contrast, observed in 1973 that in Gitarama and Kibuye prefectures some Tutsi on the hills were 'asked' to leave and their houses burnt.[28] Hostility erupted into violence, but it remained at a fairly contained level. There were local incidents of racially motivated murder, with estimates of those killed ranging from the official government figure of six to press reports claiming up to five hundred victims.[29] The government's response to the violence was sluggish and lacklustre.[30] Several authors have suggested that Kayibanda allowed the hostilities to continue, or actively fermented them, in an attempt to deflect criticism of his government's performance in other areas.[31] Kayibanda's official call for ethnic tol-erance and calm, particularly within the restive education sector, was ineffective.[32] The violence began to spread to attacks based on personal grievances rather than ethnicity; class and regional issues were also apparent.[33] Meanwhile, a further wave of Tutsi emigration had been triggered.[34]

It was in this atmosphere that Major-General Juvénal Habyarimana, commander of the National Guard, took power in a bloodless coup on 5 July 1973. The Hab-yarimana coup was a very popular one.[35] The new president quickly restored peace to the country and guaranteed the security of the Tutsi minority.[36] In a 'Message to the Nation' the day after seizing power, Habyarimana stated:

The National Guard intervened when the country had been thrown into the abyss. It has just saved peace. This peace we want to be enduring, and a bearer of progress in national development. You all have the duty to strive for the re-establishment of peace and national unity . . . love your countrymen without distinction of ethnic or regional origin.[37]

The atmosphere in Rwanda following the coup was one of 'widespread popular relief', and, as it became apparent that the new regime 'appeared pretty mild', calm and stability returned to the nation.[38]

The Seizure of Power and the Temporal Model

While Rwanda returned to an atmosphere of peacefulness very quickly following the coup d'état, it is useful to analyse this episode utilizing the temporal model. Conditions of internal strife had been building within Rwanda since the late 1960s. Principally these were the difficult economic conditions, along with the disaffection of the young generation of Hutu intellectuals, although other contributing factors included the increased corruption and internal political dissension within the government. Throughout his presidency, Kayibanda had continued to facilitate the concept of Tutsi as 'outsiders' within Rwandan society. Thus, predictably, the unrest crystallized into being primarily expressed along intergroup cleavages, although it must be noted that the previous educational advantages offered to Tutsi and ongoing Tutsi overrepresentation in the higher levels of the educational system gave some cause for grievance.

Again, however, it was not until the internal strife posed some kind of existential threat to the ruling power that hostility erupted into violence. In this case, the threat came from Burundi, where the largely Tutsi army began massacres of Hutu, and particularly educated Hutu. This served to remind Hutu in Rwanda of their fear of a return to Tutsi domination. Nevertheless, the threat remained 'once removed', in Burundi rather than Rwanda itself, and this accounts for the very limited violence in Rwanda at this time. Indeed, had Kayibanda offered more effective leadership, it could likely have been avoided altogether. But Kayibanda, having twice seen anti-Tutsi violence lead to positive outcomes for his Hutu political platform, did no such thing. Yet it is interesting to observe that, by and large, Rwandan society did not embrace anti-Tutsi violence in 1973, and was relieved when Habyarimana curtailed the unrest and proposed an agenda of reconciliation. While intergroup cleavages remained, polarization at this point was only partial. Perhaps remembering the upheavals of the early 1960s, few Rwandans viewed a return to violence as a solution to Rwanda's problems. And, as Habyarimana's coup resolved the internal strife, Rwanda once again quickly returned to meeting just the first precondition for genocide, that of the existence of an outgroup. Once again, this represents a cycle of risk escalation, followed by a period of retreat. In this case, the process was a much less intense one, reflective of the much more distant existential threat operable. Yet it highlights that, as was the case prior to the Armenian genocide, there were multiple instances of risk escalation and retreat in Rwanda. This is indicative of the cyclic process that ultimately facilitates a final escalation towards genocide.

Development and Stability in Rwanda

After seizing power, Habyarimana initially outlawed all political parties. In 1975, however, he formally instituted a system of single-party rule. He established the Mouvement Révolutionnaire National pour le Développement (MRND) as the single party, and every Rwandan citizen was required to be a member. Elections were held, although Habyarimana was repeatedly the only presidential candidate. Legislative, executive and judicial powers were all highly centralized,[39] and a new constitution adopted in 1978 increased the centralization of power still further. The country was divided into ten prefectures, each headed by a prefect, and 143 communes, each led by a burgomaster. Communes were further divided into hills, sectors and cells, leading to an extraordinary level of administrative organization and control. Prefects and burgomasters were no longer elected, but appointed from above, and had wide-ranging powers at the local level.[40] Politically, the regime suffered some internal struggles, and in 1980, a former security chief was accused of plotting a coup d'état.[41] It is worth noting that both this leader and his faction were anti-Tutsi, and strongly opposed to Habyarimana's efforts towards reconciliation.[42] Beyond this, however, the regime enjoyed a relatively high level of political stability for the first fifteen years of its rule.

Political stability during this period was accompanied by steady economic development, and improvements in a wide range of developmental indicators. In 1962, per capita income in Rwanda had been the third lowest in the world. By 1976 it was seventh from the bottom, and by 1985 a very respectable eighteenth—outperforming all other economies in the region.[43] Moreover, by 1987 this achievement was accompanied by the lowest inflation rate, the lowest debt level, and the highest rate of growth in its gross national product (GNP) within the region, and a per capita income comparable with that of China.[44] The economy had diversified from its former overwhelming dependence on subsistence agriculture; at the same time, agriculture remained in equilibrium, food production was increasing and erosion was relatively well managed.[45] Medical care was improving, and the mortality rate decreasing.[46] The percentage of children in primary school had increased from 49.5 per cent in 1978 to 61.8 per cent in 1986, notwithstanding the complications presented by the high growth rate of the population.[47] Despite the rural nature of Rwanda's population, 'By the early 1990s, 70 per cent of the population had access to clean drinking water, there was a good road network in all regions, and local clinics and schools operated in the main towns of each district.[48] The provision of electricity had also reached impressive levels. One author, arriving in Rwanda after living in Tanzania and Kenya and visiting Burundi and Angola, wrote: 'By comparison, Rwanda in the mid-1980s gave an impression of extreme orderliness; this was the "Switzerland of Africa" . . . Rwandans were relatively well provided for, even compared with wealthier neighbouring countries.'[49]

Rwanda's development did not come without substantial costs, however. For the ordinary Rwandan, the most arduous of these was *umuganda*, unpaid cooperative communal labour. The program was instituted by President Habyarimana in February 1974, and required all Rwandans to work for the state one day per week, usually a Saturday. While technically voluntary, even Habyarimana himself spoke of it as 'a necessary obligation for all the inhabitants of the country'.[50] The program was justified as the reestablishment of a customary precolonial institution, as necessary for the development of the nation and as a reaction to the colonial monetarization of the Rwandan economy.[51] The *umuganda* program gave the state an enormous amount of unpaid labour at its disposal, which became economically very important. *Umuganda* labour built schools, roads, health centres and bridges, along with enabling reforestation projects and antierosion works. Yet, as Verwimp has noted, 'the political and ideological functions of *umuganda* were even more important than its economic benefits to the state'.[52] Ideologically, the policy 'was explicitly designed to make sure that all Rwandans would do manual labour'.[53] Habyarimana repeatedly idealized peasant labour in his speeches and pronouncements, and indeed defined the ideal Rwandan as one who enthusiastically embraced manual labour—a definition not without a racial component.[54]

Umuganda was a powerful political tool. Local officials were responsible for the organization of *umuganda*, and, 'not surprisingly, the cronies and friends of the regime escaped *umuganda*'.[55] According to Verwimp, the policy was also used to humiliate Rwandan intellectuals and academics.[56] Furthermore, '*Umuganda* also gave the local party and state officials knowledge and experience in the mobilization of the peasant population. A skill that was to prove deadly during the genocide.'[57] *Umuganda*, however, was just one practice that reflected the very tight government control of the population and the potential for corruption within Habyarimana's Rwanda. Not only was the entire population called on to perform *umuganda*, but it was also placed into administrative units down to the level of the cell, with each cell comprising fifty families. All citizens had identity cards listing their address and ethnic identity. Permission had to be sought to change residence, and would only be granted if there was a valid reason, such as getting a job in a different area.[58] For most people, there were few choices in life. In 1986–87, only 7 per cent of Rwandan children progressed to secondary school, with the attendant possibility of subsequently finding a nonagricultural job.[59] For the remainder, moving to cities was forbidden, and farming very often the only available option. Thus, some 93 per cent of the population remained in rural areas, and 92.8 per cent of the labour force worked in agriculture.[60] Even for the few in the cities, control remained tight. Thus, Aimable Twagilimana, a Rwandan university lecturer, reported in her book *The Debris of Ham* of being required to attend 'animation' sessions every Wednesday afternoon, in which the president and his policies had to be repeatedly praised.[61]

The political and administrative structure of the nation bred corruption and policies of regional favouritism that emanated from the very top. At the lower levels, contacts and influential friends could get one anything from exemption from *umuganda*, to permission to move, to a passport.[62] Prefects and burgomasters in Rwanda were 'local authorities whose powers were literally unlimited and unaccountable to any but their superiors', a circumstance particularly conducive to corruption.[63] At the higher levels, Rwanda's good level of organization, well-managed economy, commitment to rural development and relative lack of corruption compared to its neighbours saw it become a favourite of foreign aid donors.[64] The creaming off of foreign aid became a principle source of enrichment for the elite.[65] As a result, 'the ruling families grew extremely rich at the expense of the Rwandese exchequer. In addition, President Habyarimana, his wife, and particularly his wife's family, siphoned off a substantial percentage of foreign aid.'[66]

Rwanda faced some very significant demographic and environmental pressures, which numerous scholars have posited were substantial contributing factors to the genocide. In the late 1980s, Rwanda's annual population growth rate of 3.3 per cent was the fourth highest amongst nations with low development, and Rwandan women had the highest birthrate in the world.[67] Combined with an average life expectancy of only forty-eight to forty-nine years, this meant that by 1991, some 57.5 per cent of the population was less than twenty years old.[68] Prunier has suggested that 'part of the violence of the genocide can be traced to the fact that by the late 1980s large numbers of disaffected unemployed youths had drifted to Kigali and to a lesser extent to smaller towns'.[69] The strength of Catholicism within Rwanda has been cited as an explanation for the lack of family planning; Habyarimana himself also appeared opposed to the concept.[70] Rwanda's Population Bureau 'was a sham', and the Ministry of the Interior approved when 'radical Catholic pro-life commandos raided pharmacies to destroy condoms'.[71] As African Rights has pointed out, however, 'there is in fact no hard evidence to link either population density or rate of population growth with hunger'; additionally, 'no theoretically significant or certain [causal] effect between population growth and depletion of national resources, growth of GNP, savings and investment or hunger has yet been proven'.[72]

In the case of Rwanda, for most of the twentieth century at least, African Rights' assertions appear to have been borne out. As the political scientist Peter Uvin has elucidated:

According to some estimates, Rwanda experienced 17 years of famine between 1900 and 1950. Yet the population during this time period was only between 1 and 2 million. However, by the middle of the 1980s, Rwanda had a population in excess of 8 million, most of whom were better nourished and had been free of famine for more than 30 years.[73]

In the first two decades of Rwandan independence, food and agricultural production per capita actually increased—with Rwanda being one of only three sub-Saharan countries to achieve this.[74] Yet, as Uvin himself acknowledged, there were significant land pressures, and some of the ways in which they had been addressed were unsustainable in the long term. There was a large expansion of crop area during the sixties and seventies. Hundreds of thousands of hectares of pasture were converted into more productive cropland.[75] Much of this was land in eastern Rwanda and had formerly belonged to Tutsi, who had fled the country as refugees.[76] Additionally, hundreds of swampy valleys were drained and used to grow crops. Furthermore, the land was used more intensely, and left fallow less often.[77] By the late 1980s, 'there was hardly any land left for crop expansion'.[78] No technological innovation had been introduced to improve productivity, and the importation of fertilizer—which could have significantly improved food production—was reserved for the vast tea plantations that provided valuable export dollars.[79] Furthermore, the rigid system of administrative control made the transfer of farmland from parents to the rising generation of young men very difficult.[80] As the 1980s drew to a close, the previous equilibrium in food production began to slide.

An examination of Habyarimana's attitude towards the issue of Hutu and Tutsi identities during the first fifteen years of his rule presents a complex and at times contradictory picture. When Habyarimana first seized power he immediately guaranteed the safety of the Tutsi, and he was popularly considered 'the protector of the Tutsi' for much of the period of his rule.[81] Indeed, Habyarimana justified his seizure of power on the grounds that ethnic divisions had to be closed.[82] René Lemarchand, in an analysis of the Habyarimana regime in 1975, commented: 'If power in Rwanda is still the monopoly of a specific ethnic segment, identified with the Hutu subculture, the prospects of a Hutu-Tutsi *rapprochement*, both within and outside Rwanda, have never been brighter since independence.'[83] Habyarimana formally committed to a policy of 'reconciliation' after taking power, and, 'took several concrete steps' in this direction.[84] There was some reintegration of Tutsi into political life. There was a Tutsi cabinet member from 1974 to 1979, for example, and numerous Tutsi senior civil servants. Even as late as 1990 there was more than token Tutsi political participation, with one Tutsi minister, one Tutsi ambassador, two Tutsi in the legislative assembly, and two Tutsi in the central committee of the MRND.[85] Furthermore, while at times friction within the MRND centred around Habyarimana's pro-Tutsi stance, he remained committed to his position despite the challenges involved.[86] Indeed, according to Twagilimana, a common theme of the 'animation' sessions that Rwandans were required to regularly attend was 'the unity between the Hutu, the Tutsi, and the Twa'.[87]

Yet there is as much to question Habyarimana's perceived pro-Tutsi stance as there is to confirm it. Alongside the policy of reconciliation was a policy of 'ethnic and regional balance'. This policy supposedly aimed at redressing past injustices, providing fairness in opportunity and fostering unity, but instead 'was a clear legitimization and institutionalization of ethnicity and regionalism at the expense of merit'.[88] This policy was intricately linked with that of the quota system. Under this system, the number of Tutsi in primary schools, secondary schools, higher education and public employment was not to exceed 9 per cent, that being judged as their proportion of the population. Sources disagree as to how strictly the policy was enforced.[89] Effectively, however, the policy functioned as a form of legal discrimination against Tutsi in education and the public service. Tutsi were able to prosper in other spheres, however, such as the church, the private sector and in business. Tutsi refugees outside of Rwanda were not welcomed back into the country as indigenous citizens. And while there was undoubtedly some Tutsi participation in politics, Twagilimana has asserted that the overwhelming message to Tutsi was to 'avoid politics', and Tutsi were thus treated as 'strangers in their own country'.[90] Tutsi participation in politics was 'limited to a scope said to befit their minority status', and 'Tutsi were carefully kept away from the organs of power: the army and the local state'.[91]

A further outcome of these policies was that they 'created great ethnic and regional awareness', ensuring that subgroup identity remained a salient feature of the society.[92] That is, ethnicity clearly remained a political issue, and the Tutsi clearly remained an outgroup. If one takes that a step further and considers it in conjunction with Habyarimana's veneration of peasant society and the value of manual labour, and particularly within the paradigm of the indirect and allusive communication style typical of the Rwandan elite, one can perceive an underlying racialism at work. Verwimp has gone even further, suggesting that a clear anti-Tutsi rationale existed at the very heart of the regime.[93] Verwimp has noted a speech given by Habyarimana shortly after taking power in 1973 in which he defined the single goal of the coup as 'to ban once and for all the spirit of intrigue and feudal mentality'—'feudal mentality' clearly referring to the Tutsi subgroup.[94] 'What we want', Habyarimana continued, 'is to give back labour and individual yield its real value.'[95] According to Verwimp, 'Habyarimana is saying that only the Hutu peasant, the one tilling the land, is productive and good for society.'[96]

A factor that further complicates any analysis of Habyarimana's complex and contradictory approach to ethnicity is the intimate relationship through the 1970s and 1980s between ethnic and regional issues. So powerful was regionalism under the Habyarimana regime that Twagilimana has spoken of the 1973 coup as one 'that put a region at the helms of the country'.[97] Habyarimana was from Gisenyi prefecture in the northwest, and over the course of his rule Gisenyi and neighbouring Ruhengeri, and Hutu from these regions, came to be strongly overrepresented in resource allocation, positions of leadership and power, and access to goods and services. By the mid-1980s, nearly one-third of the most important posts in Rwanda were filled by individuals from Gisenyi alone.[98] Students from Gisenyi received over one-third of all grants to study overseas in 1987–88.[99] In the early 1990s, a survey revealed almost half of public institutions were headed by individuals from Gisenyi or Ruhengeri, despite these areas containing only one-fifth of the population of Rwanda.[100] Almost all the senior army and security posts were filled by those from the northwest, and the ranks of the security forces were dominated by men from this area.[101] Additionally, Gisenyi and Ruhengeri were significantly and chronically overrepresented in the government budget for regional government and development.[102] This regional favouritism was itself not without an ethnic component, given the lower proportion of Tutsi in the northwest than elsewhere in Rwanda.

While regionalism and ethnicity were intimately related due to the policy of 'ethnic and regional balance', it was regionalism, rather than ethnicity, that was the dominant point of fracture in Rwandan society for most of the period of Habyarimana's rule.[103] Twagilimana has commented that the Habyarimana regime 'overwhelmingly favoured the "région sacrée" at the expense of Tutsi and southern Hutu. This policy created great ethnic and regionalist awareness, especially in the 1980s, but regional animosity was by far a more acute political problem in that period.'[104] So dominant was regionalism that:

[t]here was a very short period at the end of the 1970s when it was commonly said in the south that a Tutsi from Gisenyi and Ruhengeri was better treated than a Hutu from the South. This proposition does not necessarily mean that the few Tutsi living in those two prefectures were treated well.[105]

Twagilimana has gone so far as to suggest that Habyarimana 'created a new ethnic subgroup, the Hutu of the south, who were marginalized just like the Tutsi', and that 'if Rwanda was a Hutu nation . . . after July 1973, the Hutu of Gisenyi and Ruhengeri (north) were "more equal" than the Hutu of the south.'[106] Mamdani, too, noted that, even as late as 1991, 'the regional question was far more politically volatile than was the "ethnic" question'.[107] In the turmoil of the early 1990s, however, when the Habyarimana government suddenly found itself needing to rapidly resolve regional divisions, ethnicity would be used as the political tool to do so. This process would directly contribute to the genocide.[108]

While Habyarimana was willing to accord Rwandan Tutsi at least a limited place within Rwandan society, this sentiment did not extend to the Tutsi refugees who had fled Rwanda during the conflagrations of 1959–64 and 1972–73. The Rwandan government refused any right of return, ostensibly because Rwanda was 'overpopulated' and could not reabsorb them.[109] There had been approximately

336,000 official refugees in 1964. By 1990, natural population growth had led to about 500,000–600,000 refugees and their children who still identified themselves as such.[110] Their fortunes varied considerably, from those who were able to make new lives in Europe and North America and those in Tanzania who benefited from well-run refugee camps and an offer of citizenship, to the majority who faced varying levels of disadvantage and discrimination in Burundi, Zaire and Uganda. But it was the fate of the refugees in Uganda that would ultimately impact forcefully upon the Habyarimana regime. In Uganda, the large refugee population had endeavoured to integrate, and had often successfully established new homes, accessed education and even joined the Ugandan administration and armed forces.[111] Yet they continued to be the victims of persistent discrimination.[112]

In the early 1980s, the Obote government in Uganda targeted the *Banyarwanda* (as the Tutsi population in Uganda was called) in a series of persecutions. Prunier has noted the enormous psychological impact this had on the refugees:

> Many of the young men . . . had felt that Rwanda was an old story, their parents' story, and that they were now Ugandans. And then they suddenly discovered that people among whom they had lived for thirty years were treating them as hated and despised foreigners. The shock was tremendous.[113]

In response, many joined Museveni's National Resistance Army (NRA), which overthrew the Obote regime and set up a government in 1986. Yet the Museveni government also failed to offer the *Banyarwanda* the integration they had sought and been led to expect, and discrimination continued.[114] As a result, many Tutsi refugees in Rwanda began to consider the possibility of a return to Rwanda. In 1987, at the seventh congress of the Rwandese Alliance for National Unity in Kampala (which had originally formed amongst refugees as a welfare organization in 1979), a decision was made to transform the organization into the Rwandese Patriotic Front (RPF), 'an offensive political organization dedicated to the return of exiles to Rwanda, by force if necessary'.[115] At the same time, the world diaspora of Rwandan refugees became increasingly focussed upon Rwanda. In 1988 at a world congress of Rwandan refugees, the lack of a 'right of return' was a dominant issue.[116] As Mamdani has noted, 'The Second [Habyarimana] Republic's greatest single failure was that it was unable to even pose the question of how to integrate the Tutsi diaspora within the postcolonial polity.'[117] The cost of this failure was about to become apparent.

A Series of Challenges

By the late 1980s, the stability and growth Habyarimana had been able to maintain in Rwanda for the previous fifteen years began to unravel. A series of shocks befell Rwanda, which together would recreate conditions of internal strife in the nation.

The first such shock was economic. The price of coffee on the international markets—Rwanda's main export and accounting for over three-quarters of its export earnings—had been in decline since 1986, and in 1989 it dropped precipitously, to about 50 per cent of its previous value. Coffee exports, worth US$144 million in 1985, declined to US$30 million by 1993.[118] Additionally, tin, another significant export, had also lost value during the 1980s, and Rwanda's only tin mining company had closed as a result.[119] In 1989 alone, Rwanda's GDP declined by 6 per cent.[120] Initially, the Habyarimana government managed the situation through increasing external debt, but it quickly found itself unable to meet its balance of payment requirements.[121] Under strong pressure from the IMF and the World Bank, in 1990 Rwanda agreed to a package of structural adjustment measures.[122] In November of that year, the Rwandan franc was devalued by 67 per cent, and a second devaluation of 15 per cent was carried out in June 1992.

The Rwandan population immediately felt the impact of the economic decay. Living standards dropped, inflation rose and the prices of food and basic commodities increased.[123] Education and health care budgets were slashed, leading to a sharp rise in maternal and infant mortality levels.[124] Those employed in the civil service and parastatals grew increasingly concerned about their job security; new job opportunities for those seeking employment all but disappeared.[125] In rural areas, the collapse in coffee prices disrupted rural credit systems, which resulted in a decrease in food production.[126] Many families began to experience severe economic hardship.[127] Meanwhile, at the government level, the economic contraction led to an increase in corruption. The government initially blamed the country's economic woes on 'a conspiracy of traders, merchants and intellectuals'.[128] As the political scientist Helen Hintjens has noted, this rhetoric was not without a racial overtone, as these were professions in which Tutsi tended to dominate.[129]

During the course of its rule, the Habyarimana regime had become increasingly reliant on foreign aid. Foreign aid accounted for less than 5 per cent of Rwanda's GNP in 1973; by 1986 that had increased to 11 per cent, and by 1991 it represented a massive 22 per cent of GNP.[130] This dependence, and the economic crisis of the late eighties and early nineties, meant Rwanda was very vulnerable to the increasing Western pressure for democratization that emerged at this time.[131] With the end of the Cold War, a growing internal critique of the Habyarimana regime found a sympathetic audience amongst the international donor community.[132] When French president François Mitterrand announced in June 1990 that future economic aid to African states would be linked to multiparty democracy, Habyarimana—given Rwanda's disastrous finances and the fact that France was the second-largest donor of foreign aid to Rwanda—had little choice but to adopt reform.[133] Thus, in July 1990, Habyarimana 'suddenly declared that he supported a multiparty system'.[134] A commission was established to make recommendations regarding a new democratic national charter—although the long period it was given in which to make its recommendations is indicative of the government's reluctant stance. At the same time, the Rwandan government began to moderate its position on the 'right of return' for Tutsi refugees, possibly in response to international concern over human rights issues. A special commission created to examine the issue proposed a limited repatriation exercise involving refugees from Uganda, which was due to take place in November 1990.[135] For the RPF, now quietly preparing to invade Rwanda, these changes provided a strong incentive to act. As the political scientist Wm. Cyrus Reed noted, 'By legalizing political activities domestically and softening its stand on the right of return for refugees, the regime in Kigali was taking a major initiative on the two central demands of the RPF, without their participation.'[136] If refugees could be repatriated peacefully, and if the RPF could no longer claim to be fighting a totalitarian dictatorship, it was in danger of losing its rationale and support base.[137] Furthermore, RPF intelligence appeared to indicate the Habyarimana regime could be easily toppled.[138] Thus, preparations for an invasion were accelerated.

The RPF Invasion

On 1 October 1990, approximately four thousand RPF soldiers crossed the border into Rwanda from southern Uganda, and began to fight to take control of the country. *Banyarwanda* soldiers in Museveni's National Revolutionary Army had formed secret cells and infiltrated key areas of the NRA for the past two years in order to meet their revolutionary goals. On the night of 30 September they secretly abandoned their barracks, taking arms, communications equipment and vehicles with them, and hoping to crush the Rwandan Armed Forces (FAR).[139] Initially, they had some quick successes, proceeding sixty kilometres into Rwanda and capturing the northern city of Gabiro (including a large military depot and barracks there) and a second city, Nyagatare.[140] Once the FAR mobilized, however, the fighting was fierce, and the RPF advance stalled. Habyarimana quickly sought international assistance, and French and Zairean troops arrived to help the Rwandan army.[141] Bizarrely, the government faked an RPF attack on Kigali during the night of 4–5 October, both to increase international military assistance for the regime and to serve as a pretext for mass arrests in urban areas.[142] As Prunier has commented:

> It soon became obvious that these arrests did not target supporters of the RPF (there were very few and even these few were not all known to the police) but indiscriminately swept up educated Tutsi, opposition-minded Hutu, [and] anyone who was in the bad books of the power elite.[143]

Meanwhile, the RPF commander had been killed on the second day of the invasion; two other senior commanders were killed shortly thereafter. RPF forces, short on equipment and supplies, were forced to withdraw, and the Habyarimana regime had claimed victory by the end of the month.

Yet for the RPF, this was the beginning rather than the end. After regrouping under the command of Major Paul Kagame, a second attack was launched on 23 January 1991. The RPF captured Ruhengeri—a favoured region seen as the heartland of the regime—and sent the country into an immediate panic.[144] Whilst in Ruhengeri the RPF managed to obtain a significant amount of military equipment before unilaterally withdrawing after one day and before FAR reinforcements could arrive.[145] Such guerrilla operations became the standard tactics of the RPF, and the FAR seemed powerless to prevent them. In response, the government embarked upon what Prunier has described as a 'frantic recruitment drive' for the armed forces: 'The FAR, which had numbered 5,200 on 1 October 1990, had grown to 15,000 by mid-1991, 30,000 by the end of that year, and 50,000 by . . . mid-1992.'[146] French support helped train and arm the new recruits.

The invasion led to renewed massacres targeting the Tutsi minority. The first occurred during the initial RPF assault. Between 11 and 13 October in Kibilira commune in Rwanda's northwest, approximately 348 Tutsi civilians were killed.[147] While it appears to have been incited by local authorities—and included significant burning of houses, as in previous massacres—the Rwandan government did little to discourage such crimes.[148] A second massacre occurred shortly after the RPF capture of Ruhengeri. According to Twagilimana, Habyarimana himself was present at the meeting to plan this massacre.[149] In this massacre of Bagogwe, a distinct subgroup of Tutsi that lived in the mountainous forest regions of Gisenyi and Ruhengeri, at least one thousand civilians were killed.[150]

The outbreak of massacres highlights the rapid escalation of risk of genocide underway. The RPF invasion was perceived by the Habyarimana regime as a serious existential threat, contributing to the outbreak of ethnic violence. The internal strife that beset Rwanda at the close of the 1980s, including the economic crisis and the international demands for major political reform, had produced only low-level anti-Tutsi rumblings. While very serious challenges, neither posed an existential threat to the regime at that stage, although the demands for political reform had the potential to do so in the future. Furthermore, the dual cleavages operable in Rwandan society at this point—regionalism and ethnicity—precluded a singular focus on subgroup identity that could have led to greater discrimination. By this time, the Tutsi had been an outgroup in Rwanda for almost three decades. During this period, there had been two cycles of risk escalation followed by periods of retreat. For the vast majority of the time, however, only the first precondition for genocide—that of the presence of the Tutsi as an outgroup—was operable in Rwandan society. This was not sufficient to check the ability of the society to exist stably. Discrimination was relatively mild, as was the politicization of ethnicity for much of the period. Once again, it took the association of the outgroup with an existential threat to the dominant power to trigger the risk escalation process. The RPF invasion of Rwanda was perceived as posing a serious existential threat to the Habyarimana regime, and as a result precipitated significant anti-Tutsi violence.

Paradoxically, a government movement towards further democratization and even ethnic reconciliation unfolded alongside the increasing repression. In the wake of the mass arrests in Kigali that had followed the RPF invasion, the internal opposition pushed for rapid political change to prevent such oppressiveness from becoming commonplace.[151] In response, Habyarimana accelerated government progress towards a multiparty system significantly. The freedom of the press increased notably at the beginning of 1991.[152] Opposition political parties were permitted to form from March of that year, and by June a new constitution allowing for multiple political parties had been approved via referendum and come into force.[153] Four main parties quickly emerged. The Mouvement Démocratique Républicain (MDR) was effectively the offspring of MDR-PARMEHUTU from the Kayibanda era, and drew its support base from the central and southern regions—in clear opposition to the MRND hegemony in the northwest.[154] The Parti Social-Démocrate (PSD) developed its base in the southern prefectures of Butare and Gikongoro, but had a following throughout the south. It was dubbed 'the party of intellectuals', and attracted both Hutu and Tutsi supporters.[155] The Parti Libéral (PL) recruited mainly in the cities, appealing to many Tutsi but also to Hutu, and particularly to 'those of "mixed" parentage who openly scoffed at "ethnic" politics'.[156] The least significant party was the Parti Démocrate-Chrétien (PDC), which had some difficulty attracting supporters given the Catholic Church's long and very close relationship with the MRND.[157] According to Mamdani:

> The opposition organized along two different lines: regional and ideological. The regional dimension highlighted the demand that power be anchored in a base broader than simply the northwest of the country. Ideologically, the opposition seemed to call for a more liberal arrangement, in both politics and economics. Neither the power nor the opposition was organized along 'ethnic' lines. While one of the opposition parties, the *Parti Libéral*, had a mainly Tutsi leadership, it was not a Tutsi party. By the time of the 1990–91 reform, even in the first year that followed the RPF invasion, the regional question was far more politically volatile than was the 'ethnic' question.[158]

Mamdani's statement is further confirmed by the Habyarimana government's seeming attempts to promote further ethnic reconciliation at some levels—although admittedly these were half-hearted and in direct contradiction with other actions. Yet in a speech given in November 1990, in the immediate aftermath of the RPF invasion, Habyarimana promised that ethnic identity would be removed from all future identity cards and official papers.[159] (Two weeks later, the minister of the interior announced on Radio Rwanda that the plan had been cancelled.) He also acknowledged the right of return for refugees.[160] And as late as mid-1992, a coalition cabinet approved the abolishment of the 'ethnic and regional balance' policy within the education system, replacing it with merit-based entrance to further education.[161] It was the peace process with the RPF, and its entanglement with the democratization process, however, that would truly challenge the nature of the Habyarimana government.

Following the RPF attacks, the government entered into negotiations for a cease-fire. An initial cease-fire agreement, reached in March 1991 at N'Sele in Zaire, collapsed almost immediately, and low-intensity fighting continued unabated for several more months.[162] By September a second cease-fire agreement had been negotiated; however, it too was observed 'largely in the breach'.[163] At the same time as it was negotiating cease-fire agreements with the RPF, the Habyarimana government was also negotiating the transition to democracy within Rwanda. An attempt by Habyarimana to form a 'coalition' government that in fact contained only one member from the opposition parties led to strong opposition protests.[164] Meanwhile, the MRND itself attempted to reform, changing its name to the National Republican Movement for Democracy and Development (its initials remained the same), although little else changed.[165] In early 1992 the government reluctantly agreed to a more genuine coalition arrangement, which took office in April. Habyarimana retained the presidency, and the MRND nine of the nineteen cabinet posts, 'including the key ministries of defense and interior'.[166] MDR, the largest opposition party, accepted the prime ministership and two cabinet posts, the PL and the PSD each received three posts, and the smaller PDC obtained one.[167] Importantly, the MRND retained an almost exclusive hold on authority at the local level, retaining MRND prefects, burgomasters and administrative officials. It took considerable time before the opposition parties were able to infiltrate this machinery of the state.[168] In the meantime, the new coalition government pressured the MRND into serious negotiations with the RPF for a comprehensive peace agreement.[169] The quest for peace and the quest for democratization became irrevocably intertwined.

The Path to Genocide

Anti-Tutsi murmurs within the government were heard only days after the RPF invasion. The Rwandan minister of justice 'declared that the Tutsi were *ibyitso,* "accomplices" of the invaders. He continued that "to prepare an attack of that scale required trusted people [on the inside]. Rwandans of the same ethnic group offered that possibility better than did others"'.[170] The virulently anti-Tutsi newspaper *Kangura* also published bitter attacks on the RPF and Tutsi shortly after the invasion.[171] For Habyarimana and the *akuzu*—a small elite group centred around Habyarimana's wife that 'had come to dominate the most strategic positions both in central ministries and in regional government'—resurrecting the 'ethnic' issue appeared to offer some distinct political advantages.[172] Both the civil war and the democratization process now seriously threatened the power of Habyarimana and the hegemony of this small group based in the northwest. Habyarimana's regionalist policies meant he had lost many of his earlier supporters from central and southern Rwanda, which would be costly in a future election. By recasting the political climate around ethnicity, Habyarimana sought to reclaim these lost supporters.[173] For the *akuzu*, any power-sharing arrangement could only decrease their power, and it was in their interest to disrupt it. Reviving ethnic fear and hatred was the political tool chosen by the elite to accomplish this goal.[174] The RPF, in planning their invasion, apparently had not anticipated such a consequence. As Lemarchand has noted, the RPF failed to:

> foresee the catalytic effect of the invasion on Hutu solidarities, and the growing determination of hardliners within the government to manipulate ethnic hatreds for political advantage. The perceptions that the RPF leaders had of themselves—that of liberators dedicated to the overthrow of a thoroughly corrupt and oppressive dictatorship—turned out to be sadly out of sync with the image that a great many Hutu had of their would-be 'liberators'.[175]

As the power of Habyarimana and the *akuzu* became increasingly challenged in early 1992—through the establishment of the coalition government and an agreement with the RPF to commence negotiations for a peace settlement in July—ethnicity came to dominate the Rwandan political climate. A new political party was formed, the Coalition pour la Défense de la République (CDR). The CDR was 'composed of ultra-extremist Hutu predominantly from Gisenyi and Ruhengeri, who called the Hutu of the other parties traitors', and was 'grounded in extreme ethnic and regional ideology'.[176] But as Twagilimana has noted, 'In many cases it functioned as the extreme, northern wing of MRND . . . CDR carried the banner of Hutu extremism and did the dirty work that MRND could not afford to do in the open because of its claim to be a national party and the positioning for possible elections in the future.'[177] The CDR 'called for the total defeat of the Rwandan Patriotic Front, the extermination of Tutsi and the Hutu who had embraced the political opposition to MRND, and the reinforcement of a Hutu state in Rwanda'.[178] Its militia, *Impuzamugambi* ('those with the same goal'), worked closely with the MRND militia *Interahamwe* ('those who stand together'), which had been created the previous year, and both would play a leading role in the pregenocidal violence and the genocide itself.[179]

Alongside the CDR, a 'Hutu Power' ideology emerged from the fringes to become mainstream during the early 1990s.[180] Hutu Power focussed on the concept of Tutsi as an alien race (rather than an indigenous ethnicity), and was closely linked to the *akuzu*, the Habyarimana government and the CDR. It was in this context that the Bugesera massacres erupted in March 1992. Between 4 and 9 March, approximately 277 people were killed; additionally, houses were set alight, goods looted, and cattle stolen and eaten.[181] The MRND *Interahamwe*, the CDR *Impuzamugambi*, and civil and military authorities were all involved in organizing and perpetrating the massacres.[182] The Bugesera massacres were significant as the first massacres to occur outside of the northwest centre of power; according to Twagilimana, at least one of the purposes of the massacres was 'to verify the feasibility of massacres in the political south'.[183] The Bugesera massacres also marked the beginning of terrorist-style activities by the MRND and CDR militias, including bombings in major southern cities.[184]

By mid-1992, a clear process of risk escalation was underway. The first precondition for genocide, the existence of an outgroup, had been operable for some three decades. Since the late 1980s the Habyarimana regime had also been subject to significant internal strife, with major economic and political challenges. The RPF incursion of October 1990, and the subsequent civil war, had triggered a perception of the Tutsi as posing an existential threat to the hegemony of the Hutu regime. Local precipitants and constraints had subsequently determined the outbreaks of several massacres. There had been three massacres of Tutsi, the massacre in Kibilira commune in October 1990, the Bagogwe massacre in early 1991 and the Bugesera massacre in March 1992. Each had occurred with at least some level of official sanction, and the latter two are notable for the role of Rwandan authorities in their organization and execution. The timing of the first two massacres appears related to RPF offensives. There were also a number of societal changes reflecting Rwanda's increasing risk of genocide. The issue of ethnicity had come to dominate the political climate, and other societal cleavages (such as regional issues) had been deemphasized. Moreover, Rwanda now began to proceed along the 'continuum of destruction' towards genocide further than ever before. The first application of 'destructive uses of communication' had been seen in the immediate wake of the RPF invasion (such as the comments made by the Rwandan minister of justice and the anti-Tutsi newspaper *Kangura*). In 1992, the formation of the CDR and the emergence of the 'Hutu Power' ideology into mainstream politics saw extremist Hutu ideology become a powerful force in determining Rwanda's future. This time, the cyclic process of risk escalation would not be countered by a subsequent retreat—this time, the escalation process would take the nation to the brink of genocide.

In July 1992, the negotiations that would lead to the Arusha Accords commenced between the Habyarimana coalition government and the RPF. Beginning with a cease-fire agreement, they progressed to agreement on the rule of law, democracy, respect for human rights and national unity, 'a concept that explicitly rejected religious and ethnic discrimination, and included a commitment to ending the refugee problem'.[185] By early 1993, a protocol for a 'broad-based transitional government' (BBTG) had been finalized, which split positions of power between the MRND, the RPF and the opposition parties.[186] The BBTG would assume power for eighteen months following the finalization of the accords, at which point elections would be held. But negotiations then stalled over the creation of new armed forces, and Rwanda quickly descended into a further round of violence and civil war. Ironically, immediately following the departure of an international commission that had been in the country to monitor human rights abuses, massacres erupted in the northwest.[187] In Gisenyi, three hundred Tutsi were killed between 21 and 26 January in a rampage by extremist Hutu militia.[188] Partially in response, on 8 February RPF forces broke the cease-fire agreement and mounted an offensive. Previous guerrilla operations meant that the RPF already controlled land around Biumba in northern Rwanda; they also held Gatuna, and had effectively closed down the road leading from Rwanda to Uganda.[189] (This was of strategic and economic significance, as it meant exports and imports had to take a longer route through Tanzania.[190]) The February offensive was successful. Within two weeks, the RPF had doubled the area under their control, and, leaving the Rwandan Armed Forces in disarray, had proceeded to within thirty kilometres of Kigali.[191] Rather than marching upon the capital, however, and potentially facing French troops and massive civilian opposition to a takeover, the RPF unilaterally declared a cease-fire.[192] In subsequent negotiations, it agreed to return to its earlier position.[193] Yet the success of the attack had placed the Habyarimana regime under hugely increased pressure.

During the course of the Arusha negotiations, the *akuzu* and other power holders within Rwanda had come to realize the magnitude of the threat to their hegemony. Extremist Hutu ideology offered a means to counteract this threat, 'a means for the ruling *Akuzu* to retain power by mobilizing much of the Hutu populace and suppressing their opposition'.[194] And, as African Rights has elucidated, whereas in many societies extremists are to be found on the fringes, in Rwanda 'the extremist ideology developed right at the heart of government, and from the outset the extremists had all the instruments of state power at their disposal'.[195] As the Arusha negotiations proceeded apace in the second half of 1992, some of the Hutu extremists also began to conceive of this ideology as justifying a 'final solution' to the problems in Rwanda—through the elimination of the Tutsi and Hutu opposition, and the creation of a pure Hutu republic.[196] According to Prunier:

> It now seems likely that the genocide plan was first put together in outline at that time [late 1992]. Certainly nothing had yet reached an organized stage, and such plans were probably limited to the most hot-headed CDR and *Interahamwe* extremists. But it is probably during those late months of 1992 that the general notion of 'solving' the power-sharing question by a large-scale slaughter of most Tutsi and of all the known Hutu opposition supporters, began to look to the hardline *akuzu* circles like both an attractive and a feasible proposition (Prunier, *The Rwanda Crisis*, 168–169).

Others have placed the emergence of a genocidal ideology as occurring slightly earlier, between late 1991 and early 1992.[197] For example, one document that had reached Belgium's attention by March 1992 referred to 'a secret military staff charged with the extermination of the Tutsi of Rwanda in order to solve forever, in their way, the ethnic problem in Rwanda and to destroy the domestic Hutu opposition'.[198] Whatever the precise timetable of the emergence of a genocidal ideology, most scholarship accepts that Habyarimana and even the *akuzu* had not seriously considered genocide prior to 1991; by the close of 1992, however, the possibility of genocide was becoming very real.

The emergence of an extremist Hutu ideology within the central corridors of power in Rwanda meant that ideologues had full opportunity to propagate their views through massive and ongoing propaganda. Following the October 1990 RPF invasion, anti-Tutsi propaganda had quickly become increasingly virulent. The infamous 'Hutu Ten Commandments', first published in December 1990, proscribed business or even sexual relations between Hutu and Tutsi, accused Tutsi of only working 'for the supremacy of their ethnic group' and referred to the Tutsi as the 'Tutsi enemy', for which the Hutu 'must cease to have pity'.[199] As the historian Alison Des Forges has elucidated, many Rwandans—Hutu and Tutsi—were frightened by the RPF invasion:

> Tutsi recalled the reprisal killings at the time of invasions by refugee groups in the 1960s and feared they would be targeted again. Hutu remembered the slaughter of tens of thousands of Hutu by Tutsi in neighbouring Burundi in 1972, 1988, and in 1991 and dreaded killings on a similar scale by the RPF. Authorities at the highest level knew that the RPF had been reduced by losses during the first months to a number less than half that of the Rwandan army and that their own army was backed by several hundred highly trained and well-armed French troops. Well aware of the fears of their own subordinates and of ordinary citizens, they could have put the danger in perspective and calmed the population. Instead Habyarimana and his advisors exaggerated the risk in hopes of increasing support for themselves.[200]

As the dual threats of democratization and the RPF increasingly challenged the power of Habyarimana and the ruling clique, their response was a propaganda campaign of astonishing proportions and sophistication. The RPF and Tutsi were pitted as foreign and feudal oppressors, seeking to 'return' Rwanda to a state of Tutsi dominance and Hutu oppression.[201] Tutsi living within Rwanda were linked both to the RPF and to Tutsi who had exploited the Hutu in previous generations.[202] The *akuzu* revived and elaborated a conspiracy theory known as the Bahima conspiracy, through which they claimed there existed a Tutsi plan to slaughter (or at the very least enslave) the Hutu, and that drastic measures must be taken to prevent such events from occurring.[203] Extensive propaganda linking any opposition to the MRND with support for the RPF was also undertaken. Thus, a huge pro-democracy rally in Kigali in January 1992 was labelled as having being organized by the RPF; opposition parties were accused of having 'plotted with the enemy' to undermine Rwanda.[204] Most of the newly 'independent' press was in fact supported by either the MRND, *akuzu* or opposition parties, and journalists presenting opposition views 'were often harassed, arrested and persecuted by the government.'[205] Thus, the messages most often received by ordinary Rwandans were those supported by the MRND or the *akuzu*, in whose papers 'overt hate speech against the Tutsi became so systematic as to seem the norm'.[206] From September 1993, the extremist press was augmented by the notorious Radio-Télévision Libre des Mille Collines (RTLM), a radio station that 'played a key role in inciting violence against Tutsis and moderate Hutus'.[207] Accurate news reports were extremely difficult to obtain.[208] Meanwhile, the extremist media 'nurtured a culture of fear, suspicion, and terror among the Rwandan population'.[209]

Habyarimana's close ties with Hutu extremism were clearly evident, even as he participated in the Arusha process. In November 1992, for example, MRND vice-president of Gisenyi section and Hutu extremist Léon Mugesera gave a speech in Gisenyi that concluded: 'The fatal error we made in 1959 was to let them [the Tutsi] leave the country. Their home is Ethiopia, and we are going to find them a shortcut, namely the Nyabarongo River. I must insist on this point. We must act forcefully! Get rid of them!'[210] Twagilimana, in quoting this speech, has noted that 'Mugesera said that he was speaking for the President, who did not deny the fact. Nor did the President condemn the heinous speech.'[211] And indeed, when the genocide did take place, tens of thousands of Rwandans' dead bodies were dumped in the Nyaborongo River.[212] Habyarimana also revealed his disdain for the Arusha peace process directly on a number of occasions, at one stage even calling the July 1992 cease-fire agreement 'a piece of trash . . . which the government is not obliged to respect'.[213] Nevertheless, in March 1993, he had little choice but to return to the negotiating table. The civil war and increased militarization had left the Rwandan economy in a shambles. Military expenses accounted for a massive 70 per cent of the operating expenses of the state, and even resources allocated for nonmilitary purposes were being co-opted.[214] There had already been considerable internal displacement as a result of the civil war between 1990 and 1992, but the 1993 RPF offensive saw approximately one million Rwandans flee from the northern parts of the country.[215] Most of these displaced persons ended up in camps, where 'serious malnutrition and disease' quickly became prevalent.[216] Furthermore, these internal refugees were from the country's main food-producing region. As a result, agricultural production plummeted by 15 per cent in 1993.[217] Even in the less affected southern regions of Rwanda, there was acute hunger in many areas.[218] Finally, and perhaps most importantly, the RPF had proven its military superiority over the FAR.

Thus, when both parties returned to the negotiating table in Arusha on 16 March 1993, the disparity in bargaining positions was such that the RPF could finish the negotiations with what Bruce Jones has described as a 'victor's deal'.[219] Two key issues were negotiated in Arusha in this way. The first was the composition of an integrated Rwandan Armed Forces, which would combine the FAR and RPF forces into a new, smaller and unified army, and replace the Presidential

Guard with a smaller and integrated Republican Guard. The government delegation originally proposed for the RPF to be given 15 per cent of positions in
the FAR; the RPF, by contrast, sought a 50-50 split.[220] The RPF refused any
significant compromise, and eventually obtained agreement to a 60-40 split of the
armed forces in the government's favour, and a 50-50 split of all senior command
positions.[221] Implementation of such an agreement, combined with the RPF having been ceded the charge of the Ministry of the Interior earlier in negotiations,
would have given the RPF 'decisive control over forces of coercion in the new
state'—and removed most of the *akuzu* from power.[222] According to Jones, 'this
element in particular was impossible to implement in Kigali'.[223]

The second issue was that of the position of the CDR. The RPF refused
to accept any inclusion of the extremist CDR in the peace process, preventing
it being allocated any positions of power, even in the transitional government.
Nor, however, was there any feasible means of containing the extremists, or curb-
ing their power to prevent attempts to undermine the agreement.[224] As Jones has
commented:

> Conflict resolution theory would suggest two options in dealing with such oppo-
> sition—give those who lose in political transformation a stake in the new arrange-
> ments in order to minimize their destructiveness . . . or keep them out of new
> arrangements but find ways to ensure that they are unable to undermine the transi-
> tion bargain.[225]

Such was the RPF's position of strength, however, that they resisted advice from
several mediators to include the CDR in the accords.[226] Following the finalization
of these negotiations, Habyarimana sought to delay signing the completed agreement. International pressure, however, and finally a threat that international funds
would be withheld from the almost bankrupt government, meant that Habyarimana joined the other parties in formally signing the Arusha Accords on 4 August
1993.[227]

Crowds of Rwandans celebrated in the streets of Kigali following the signing of
the Arusha Accords.[228] As African Rights has noted, 'They promised what most
Rwandese desperately wanted: peace, justice, democracy and reconciliation.'[229] Yet:
'This also spelled an end to the rule of the clique around Habyarimana. They
introduced what the extremists dreaded: power-sharing, an end to privileges and
the principle of accountability.'[230] Habyarimana himself, while having participated
in the negotiations and signed the final accords, was in no way a proponent of
their implementation. Throughout the negotiation process, he had worked steadily
and quite successfully to both distance himself from the negotiations and split
the opposition. Such was the political climate that he could present the government delegation that had participated in the negotiations as being really a delegation from the internal opposition within the government.[231] (This despite the
fact that the second phase of negotiations was led by the minister of national

defence, a member of the MRND.) The internal opposition was thus depicted as internal Hutu accomplices of the RPF, and complicit in the RPF campaign to return Rwanda to a feudal oligarchy replete with Hutu oppression.[232] Through this and other such machinations, Habyarimana was successful in splitting most of the opposition parties into 'Hutu Power' and 'moderate' factions. As the process of implementing the broad-based transitional government (BBTG) commenced, factions and individuals within each party began to compete for power and the allocated seats within the proposed parliament.[233] As part of the Arusha Accords, the United Nations had been requested to provide a peacekeeping force, to be deployed in Rwanda thirty-seven days after the signing of the accords in order to secure the transitional government. Such an unrealistic timetable could not be met, and it was not until 21 October that the lead party of the United Nations Assistance Mission for Rwanda (UNAMIR) arrived in the country.[234] In this way, the first deadline associated with the Arusha Accords, the establishment of the BBTG within thirty-seven days, was missed. It would be the first of many.

As delays continued over the implementation of Arusha, Hutu extremists pursued their campaign with a frenzied intensity. The extremist message 'was repeated over and over on the national radio and on the RTLM and in extremist newspapers and in the many political rallies that took place'.[235] According to Lemarchand:

> What emerges from [extremist propaganda] is an image of the Tutsi as both alien and clever—not unlike the image of the Jews in Nazi propaganda. His alienness disqualifies him as a member of the national community; his cleverness turns him into a permanent threat to the unsuspecting Hutu. Nothing short of physical liquidation can properly deal with such danger.[236]

Indeed, comparisons between extremist Hutu and Nazi propaganda are common throughout the genocide scholarship on Rwanda. In a similar vein to the Jews of Europe, Tutsi 'were even attributed magical and demonic qualities.'[237] Such was the extent of the dehumanization of Tutsi that 'many peasants were shocked when they actually saw RPF soldiers because they literally expected them to have "horns, a tail and eyes which glow in the dark, just as the radio programmes had described them"'.[238] As journalist and author McCullum commented:

> After a while, the endless repetition of lies to an illiterate and poverty-stricken population looking for someone on whom to blame all their woes and with no alternative way of assessing reality becomes a truth of a sort, capable of inciting an uncontrollable bloodlust.[239]

Consolidating Hutu solidarity was also an essential component of the process of preparing for genocide. The ideology of 'Hutu Power' was utilized to transcend intraethnic divisions such as party allegiances and regional issues.[240] Thus, at one rally in Kigali on October 23, MDR second vice-president and Hutu Power advocate Froduald Karamira concluded his extremist and virulent speech with: 'Hutu

Power! MRND Power! CDR Power! Interahamwe Power! JDR Power! All Hutu are One Power!'[241] President Habyarimana's position with respect to Hutu Power had become ambiguous, however, and Karamira and others now openly criticized him as being too accommodating of the RPF.[242]

Rapid Escalation of Risk

The period of the early 1990s can thus be characterized as one in which an extremely rapid process of risk escalation was underway in Rwanda. The situation escalated beyond the stage of the outbreak of massacres to that of the emergence of an extremist ideology that advocated genocide. Unlike the Kayibanda regime of the 1960s, when the Habyarimana regime was forced to respond to a refugee incursion into the nation, it had sufficient power to contemplate such a radical solution to the threat the Tutsi were perceived to pose. Once the extremist ideology emerged, it was very quickly spread throughout the nation by a massive propaganda campaign. By the close of 1992 the propaganda was fulfilling both of the requirements usually associated with this precondition for genocide: asserting the singular rights of the dominant group, and ideologically legitimizing a genocidal ideology. During this period a second group of 'outsiders' was defined by the perpetrators, and similarly targeted in extremist propaganda. This group, commonly labelled 'moderate Hutu', included any Hutu that opposed the extremism, sought a more moderate agenda for Rwanda, was willing to negotiate with the RPF, or even simply did not embrace the extremist ideology with sufficient fervour. Throughout 1993, as the genocidal ideology was translated into concrete plans and preparations, the nation was saturated with propaganda of astonishing virulence, vilifying both Tutsi and moderate Hutu. Thus, like in the period of 1910–15 in Ottoman Turkey, the period between 1990 and 1994 in Rwanda can be identified as one of extremely rapid risk escalation. Yet, also similarly, in the absence of precipitants, and the presence of constraints, genocide did not yet erupt in Rwanda.

Initially, an operable constraint against the outbreak of genocide may have simply been organizational, as the extremists needed to arrange sufficient arms, militia, local leadership, communications networks and the like to be able to enact the planned apocalypse. To some extent, Rwanda's tight central organization facilitated this process, but much work was still required. The recruitment and training of militia was accelerated, death lists were prepared and circulated, and large volumes of arms of various kinds were imported and distributed.[243] Some 581,000 kilograms of machetes were imported into Rwanda between January 1993 and March 1994—estimated as being enough for one in every three Hutu males in the country.[244] The role of France in 'arming Rwanda' with more modern weapons has been particularly criticized in the wake of the genocide.[245]

A further goal of the extremists was to 'routinize' violence and confirm their ability to act with impunity.[246] The massacres of the early nineties had served not only to accustom Rwandans to violence, but to also confirm an international attitude of indifference, and—crucially—continued French support for the regime. Prunier remarked on this period:

> The French sent troops to protect the Hutu government [in response to the October 1990 RPF invasion] and gave all the wrong messages to this monoethnic, embattled, scared dictatorship. They gave them the message that they would back their security, that they would stand by them. Of course, the Hutu government tested this French commitment. They did a bit of massacring in October 1990, then again in 1991—small massacres of about 300 people at a time, nothing much compared to what would happen later. Each time, they watched to see how the French were going to react. The Hutu were pleased by France's tolerance and understanding, and they began to raise the level of violence. Had the French made it clear that they did not support this extremism, the situation might not have deteriorated so badly.[247]

On 21 October 1993, with the climate in Rwanda tense and the implementation of Arusha still delayed, the president of Burundi, Melchior Ndadaye, was assassinated. The situation in Rwanda immediately and dramatically deteriorated.[248] As Mamdani has put it, Rwandans viewed Burundi 'as some sort of an accursed Siamese twin'.[249] Despite a similar ethnic composition, the Tutsi minority in Burundi had retained power postindependence, and indeed until genuine democracy had been introduced earlier that year. Previous waves of anti-Hutu violence in Burundi, perpetrated by the Tutsi government and army, had caused agitation and unrest in Rwanda. Ndadaye, however, was the first Hutu president and had been elected democratically. Thus, his assassination by elements in the almost exclusively Tutsi Burundian army 'was taken as a prophetic lesson that the only alternative for the Hutu was between power and servitude, that there could be no power sharing between Hutu and Tutsi'.[250] As the news of Ndadaye's assassination spread, there were sporadic outbursts of violence against Tutsi and moderate Hutu, with over one hundred people killed in the following days.[251] Extremists took advantage of the psychological impact of Ndadaye's murder to convince those still hesitant of their cause.[252] Hundreds of thousands of Hutu refugees began to stream over Rwanda's borders, fleeing massacres perpetrated by the Burundian army, and arriving with tales of terror.[253] Violently anti-Tutsi, they 'were now available for political mobilization precisely where they were most needed—in the southern central regions, seen by the *akuzu* as the least "reliable"'.[254] These refugees would come to be known as some of the cruellest of the perpetrators of the Rwandan genocide.

Meanwhile, as UNAMIR troops continued to arrive, Habyarimana—only partially in control of the situation—sought to delay further the implementation of the Arusha Accords.[255] By 28 December, UNAMIR had reached sufficient strength to allow for the agreed contingent of RPF troops to be stationed in Kigali, and for RPF civilian leaders to arrive.[256] There was no longer any reason to postpone the installation of the BBTG. Yet Habyarimana encouraged factional struggles between opposition figures, sought to change the composition of the agreed-upon transitional parliament and generally manoeuvred to delay the implementation of the Arusha Accords as much as possible.[257] The proposed date for the installation of the transitional government was postponed repeatedly, from January to February, February to March and March to April. In late February a string of political assassinations—in which members of the leadership of the PSD, the CDR and the RPF were all killed—led to rioting in Kigali that 'approached civil war intensity'.[258] There was no doubt that the situation was extremely grave. The International Federation for Human Rights, the UN Special Rapporteur for Rwanda, and UNAMIR commander General Dallaire all expressed serious concerns about the situation.[259] As Alison Des Forges has noted: 'The warnings of catastrophe were many and convincing; although international decision makers did not know everything, they knew enough to have understood that disaster lay ahead.'[260] Tutsi themselves were aware of the rumoured forthcoming 'apocalypse', but as Hintjens has commented:

> Such dangers may have seemed unbelievable to ordinary Rwandan Batutsi, who were probably more concerned with daily survival than with questions of political ideology ... Unintentionally, there may have been so many warnings that they became rumours, tending to disarm the intended victims of the genocide rather than prepare them for self-defence; perhaps the Batutsi had already heard the little boy cry 'wolf' so many times that they no longer listened. By April 1994 it was too late.[261]

The response of the international community was to place intense pressure on President Habyarimana to implement the Arusha Accords. Rwanda's exceptionally precarious financial position and threats of a 'donor's boycott' meant that by the end of March, Habyarimana was 'down to his last few shots'.[262] And then, on the evening of 6 April, as Habyarimana's plane descended into the Kigali airport, it was shot down, killing the president and all on board, including the new president of Burundi.

Genocide

By the time of Habyarimana's assassination, all of the preconditions for genocide had been operable in Rwanda for a significant amount of time. Local precipitants and constraints appear to have finally determined the outbreak of genocide. These included the organization of the genocide, testing of possible international reactions and the assassination of the Burundian president in October 1993. In early 1994, it appeared Hutu extremists were actively grappling with the question of whether or not UNAMIR would intervene in the event of genocide. The extremist newspaper *Kangura*, whose editors were particularly well connected (to the point of predicting many events in Rwanda in this period, including Habyarimana's death), ran an article in January that dealt with this specific issue, and appeared to conclude that it would be possible to proceed with genocide despite the presence of UNAMIR.[263] The Hutu extremists themselves engineered further precipitants, with a string of political assassinations.

The last stumbling block became the Arusha Accords. In many respects, the Arusha Accords had functioned as a restraint during this period, particularly with regard to the international attention they focussed upon the country. But for the extremists, implementing Arusha was a zero-sum game, and one they were about to lose. As the implementation of Arusha became truly imminent, this restraint became a precipitant. The subsequent assassination of Habyarimana threw the accords into disarray. The time to act had arrived.

That the shooting down of President Habyarimana's plane was a pretext upon which to commence the Rwandan genocide, rather than a proximate cause, is evidenced by the fact that the genocide commenced within moments of the crash.[264] Precisely who shot down the plane has never been conclusively established. Nevertheless, a recent expert investigation has provided overwhelming evidence that Hutu extremists were responsible for the attack.[265] Within an hour of its occurrence, roadblocks had been erected in Kigali and members of the Presidential Guard had been dispatched to commence killing opposition figures—the lists having previously been prepared.[266] Prime Minister Agathe Uwilingiyimana was killed on 7 April, along with ten Belgian UNAMIR soldiers who were tasked with protecting her. In response, Belgium withdrew its UNAMIR contingent and other countries quickly joined the desertion, despite UNAMIR commander General Dallaire's protests.[267] As the Presidential Guard, the *Interahamwe* and the *Impuzamugambi* worked through their 'death lists' in the first days of the genocide, behind the scenes Colonel Bagosora—probably the leader of the genocidal campaign—worked to 'install a regime of extremists masquerading as a legitimate government'.[268] Meanwhile, in response to the violence the RPF contingent in Kigali had left its barracks, and commenced fighting the extremists. Kigali became a city of horror, with the RPF fighting the government troops, militia killing thousands of Tutsi and moderate Hutu according to their 'death lists', and Tutsi presenting at roadblocks in an effort to escape being 'shot or hacked to death'.[269] As early as 7 April, the carnage began to spread throughout the country; meanwhile, RPF forces had mobilized and commenced fighting in the north by 12 April.[270]

The genocide spread throughout Rwanda with a shocking intensity. 'Army and militia forces went street to street, block by block, and house to house, in Kigali and every major city save Butare in the south . . . Tutsi were dragged out of homes and hiding places and murdered, often after torture and rape.'[271] Roadblocks were everywhere, and anyone carrying an identification card that labelled them Tutsi— or at times even if they simply 'looked' Tutsi, had married a Tutsi or even simply befriended one—was stopped and killed. Indeed, investigators have estimated that 1.8 per cent of the victims of the genocide were Hutu who fit into one of the above categories.[272] Thousands upon thousands of Tutsi either fled or were driven from their homes and congregated in churches, schools and stadiums. Seeking sanctuary in these public places, and particularly in places of worship, they were instead massacred en masse. 'Parish churches, along with schools and similar facilities, were soon piled thigh-high with the shot, hacked and savaged corpses of the victims.'[273] At best, church authorities were complicit bystanders, at worst direct participants and accomplices.[274] As the month of April progressed, the extremist government consolidated their control over Rwanda, and it became clear that international forces would not intervene to stop the killing.[275] The genocide reached new peaks of intensity. As Prunier described:

> The hurricane of death had crushed 80 per cent of its victims in about six weeks between the second week of April and the third week of May. If we consider that probably around 800,000 people were slaughtered during that short period . . . the daily killing rate was at least five times that of the Nazi death camps.[276]

The Hutu extremist provisional government organized and coordinated the genocide through the regular organs of government.[277] Orders were passed down through and enacted by prefects, burgomasters and local administrative officials. The Presidential Guard, the Rwandan Armed Forces, police and militias organized much of the killing. They themselves executed those on the 'death lists', perpetrated many of the large-scale massacres, manned the roadblocks and led the killings in each area. It was ordinary Hutu peasants, however, who were the main perpetrators of the genocide: 'Without massacres by machete-wielding civilian mobs, in the hundreds and thousands, there would have been no genocide.'[278] Many, subjected to years of extremist propaganda and the murderous urgings of RTLM as the genocide unfolded, were willing and even enthusiastic participants. The prospect of loot—and even the eventual prospect of gaining control over Tutsi land—was a sufficient motivator for some.[279] Others were more reluctant, but were swept along by the 'masquerade of legitimacy' of acting under government orders.[280] The work of the genocide was presented as a 'special work *umuganda*', machetes were distributed in the same way tools were usually distributed for *umuganda* and killing was referred to by euphemisms such as 'tree felling,' 'bush clearing' and—for the killing of women and children—'pulling out the roots of the bad weeds'.[281] In some areas, killing even started at designated hours, paused for a lunch break, and finished for the day at 5.00 P.M.[282] The high level of centralized authority, and a culture of obedience to authority, also played a role. Coercion was also used to compel many to participate in the genocide, and 'those who refused to kill were almost always killed themselves'.[283] The nature of the killing was horrific. While the authorities were armed with machine guns and the like, Hutu peasants most commonly killed with a machete: 'The use of machetes often resulted in a long and painful agony and many people, when they had some money, paid their killers to be finished off quickly with a bullet rather than being slowly hacked to death.[284] Torture and mutilation were common, and often included a sexual element such as the cutting off of sexual organs. Tens of thousands of Tutsi women and girls were raped. The perpetrators 'raped as part of their attempt to exterminate Tutsi'.[285] Propaganda in the lead-up to the genocide depicted Tutsi women as arrogant, devious and scornful of Hutu men, inciting sexual violence.

There were few opportunities to resist the 'hurricane' of the genocide as it swept through the nation. In the province of Butare, the Tutsi prefect (the only one in the country) refused to follow the orders to kill at the outbreak of the genocide. Within two weeks, he and his family had been murdered, a Hutu extremist prefect installed and members of the Presidential Guard flown in to commence the killing.[286] In Kibuye there was initially a display of great communal solidarity, with the entire community fending off the *Interahamwe* that arrived to instigate massacres.[287] A combination of threats and promises by the *Interahamwe*, however, left the Tutsi isolated and forced to flee into some hills in the area. Despite desperate attempts at resistance, most were eventually killed.[288] Other Tutsi attempting to flee found themselves caught at the roadblocks. Many attempted to hide—'in the ceilings of houses, in holes in the ground, in the forest, in the swamps'.[289] A few, often with the assistance of compassionate Hutu providing them with food and water, managed to survive.

Yet the organizations that could possibly have curbed the genocide, and saved many thousands of lives, were conspicuously absent. The dismal response of the United Nations and the international community is well documented. As the genocide studies scholar Adam Jones has commented: 'The UN and the international community was fully aware, within a few days of Habyarimana's death on April 6, that killing on a genocidal scale was occurring in Rwanda. They did nothing.'[290] Nothing, that is, except organize a rapid evacuation of their own diplomats, peacekeepers and nationals. Some peacekeepers were even ordered to abandon thousands of Tutsi whom they were protecting, in order to assist with the evacuation; others literally stood and watched the killings as they obeyed their orders not to intervene.[291] According to investigative journalist and author Linda Melvern:

> The officers of UNAMIR believe to this day that had the European troops that came to rescue the expats stayed on in Rwanda, the killing could have been stopped there and then. Colonel Luc Marchal is convinced of this. Together with the moderates in the Rwandan army and with the peacekeepers there would have been ample troops to restore calm.[292]

Whether these forces could have halted the genocide has been a subject of debate in the scholarship; that the UN and international community did not even attempt intervention has been universally condemned. On 20 April, the UN Security Council voted to all but withdraw UNAMIR. 'Indeed, Security Council members—notably France and the US—both cautioned against and actually ridiculed the use of the word "genocide".[293] By mid-May, however, 'the reports of genocide in Rwanda, and images particularly of bloated victims floating downriver into Lake Victoria, had generated such a public outcry worldwide that the UN was forced to reconsider its decision'.[294] Such was the reluctance, political manoeuvrings and ineptitude amongst the Security Council, however, that UNAMIR II did not arrive until after the genocide was over.[295]

The astonishing intensity of the genocide—so severe that in Kigali garbage trucks had to be used to collect some sixty thousand bodies before they rotted on the streets—could not be sustained indefinitely.[296] By late April, killings in Gisenyi and the western part of Ruhengeri stopped simply because almost every Tutsi had already been killed.[297] By mid-May, the vast majority of victims had already been killed, and authorities began to focus upon finding and killing 'the last surviving Tutsi'.[298] Meanwhile, the Hutu extremist government, distracted by the work of genocide, had not been able to prevent the RPF from advancing into the country. The RPF had gained control of much of northern Rwanda in a careful campaign, and by mid-June 'had decisively defeated Rwandan government forces, which were pushed into a limited zone in the southwest of the country'.[299] At the same time, France sought UN approval for 'Operation Turquoise', a French military operation to establish a 'safe zone' in southwestern Rwanda. On 4 July the RPF finally gained full control over Kigali; the next day the French forces established their safe zone. Yet as Adam Jones has noted:

> Foreign forces finally staged a decisive intervention—but one that primarily benefited the *génocidaires* . . . The French intervention succeeded in saving the lives of thousands of Tutsis, but that was not its main motivation. Rather the intervention was a continuation of the long-standing French support for the Hutu Power government. It permitted the orderly evacuation of nearly *two million* Hutus, including tens of thousands of *génocidaires*, to refugee camps in neighbouring Zaire.[300]

By 18 July it was all over. The remaining government strongholds had been captured by the RPF, which declared victory and a unilateral cease-fire.[301] For approximately one million Tutsi and moderate Hutu, however, victory had come too late.[302]

One of the most striking aspects of the Rwandan genocide, upon which there has been frequent comment, was the extraordinary pace at which it unfolded. Yet in stark contrast to the intensity of the genocide is the long period of latent risk that preceded it. Rwandan society was already possessed of intergroup tensions between Hutu and Tutsi prior to European infiltration. During the period of colonial rule, the hierarchical system that characterized the central dominions of precolonial Rwanda was hugely expanded, augmented and given a new ideological justification. The polarization of intergroup relations that marked the decolonization process was of sufficient severity to elicit the first international warnings of risk of genocide in Rwanda. Yet there were a further thirty-two—mostly peaceful—years prior to that risk being realized. Indeed, while Rwanda might have experienced decades of low-level risk of genocide, the rapidity of the risk escalation process that took the nation to the brink of disaster is almost as striking as the pace of the genocide itself. This highlights that there are both very long-term and quite short-term processes of major influence to the timing of genocide. A broadly similar pattern in the timing of the emergence of risk factors for genocide can be discerned between the Armenian and Rwandan case studies. Despite the differing continents, time periods and protagonists involved, each case was characterized by the presence of one or two risk factors for genocide over long periods of time, by cycles of risk escalation followed by retreat, and ultimately by a rapid cluster of subsequent risk factors, culminating in the outbreak of genocide itself. The significance of these findings for the temporal model of the risk of genocide will be discussed in the following chapter.

Notes

1. M. Mamdani. 2001. *When Victims Become Killers: Colonialism, Nativism, and the Genocide in Rwanda*, Princeton, NJ: Princeton University Press, 134.
2. R. Lemarchand. 1970. *Rwanda and Burundi*, New York: Praeger Publishers, 197.
3. Fred Wagoner. 1968. 'Nation Building in Africa: A Description and Analysis of the Development of Rwanda', Ph.D. diss., American University, 292.
4. Mamdani, *When Victims Become Killers*, 134–35, 138.
5. Ibid., 135.
6. Wagoner, 'Nation Building in Africa', 266–67.
7. R. Nyrop et al. 1969. *Area Handbook for Rwanda*, Washington, D.C.: U.S. Government Printing Office, 75.
8. Wagoner, 'Nation Building in Africa', 307–8. It is interesting to note that the students were 'almost equally divided between Hutu and Tutsi', which Wagoner interpreted as 'a credit to Kayibanda's spirit of tolerance'.
9. Ibid., 305; Lemarchand, *Rwanda and Burundi*, 252.
10. Wagoner, 'Nation Building in Africa', 271.
11. Ibid., 295.
12. A.L. Latham-Koenig. 1964. 'Attempted Genocide in Ruanda', *The World Today* 20, 100.
13. Wagoner, 'Nation Building in Africa', 319–22.
14. Ibid., 273.
15. Ibid., 334.
16. Ibid., 274; Lemarchand, *Rwanda and Burundi*, 239.
17. Wagoner, 'Nation Building in Africa', 345, 349.
18. Ibid., 349–53.
19. W. Weinstein. 1974. 'Ruanda-Urundi (Rwanda-Burundi)', in G. Henderson, R. Lebow and J. Stoessinger (eds), *Divided Nations in a Divided World*, New York: David McKay Company, 371.
20. Ibid., 359.
21. Lemarchand, *Rwanda and Burundi*, 198.

22. Ibid., 239.
23. Weinstein, 'Ruanda-Urundi', 359.
24. Ibid.
25. Ibid.
26. J.D. Ndayambaje and J. Mutabaruka. 1999. 'Colonialism and the Churches as Agents of Ethnic Division', in J.A. Berry and C.P. Berry (eds), *Genocide in Rwanda: A Collective Memory*, Washington, D.C.: Howard University Press, 41.
27. G. Prunier. 1995. *The Rwanda Crisis: History of a Genocide*, New York: Columbia University Press, 60.
28. Ibid., 61; F. Reyntjens. 1985. *Pouvoir et droit au Rwanda: Droit public et evolution politique, 1916–1973*, Tervuren, Belgium: Musée Royal de l'Afrique Centrale, 503, cited in J. Burnet. 1998. 'The Search for a Middle Ground in a Country Divided: The Production of Ethnic Identity and Violence in the Rwandan Genocide', MA thesis, University of North Carolina at Chapel Hill, 31.
29. Prunier, *The Rwanda Crisis*, 61; J. Greenland. 1976. 'Ethnic Discrimination in Rwanda and Burundi', in W. Veenhoven et al. (eds), *Case Studies on Human Rights and Fundamental Freedoms: A World Survey*, 5 vols, The Hague: Martinus Nijhoff, vol. 4, 115.
30. Mamdani, *When Victims Become Killers*, 137.
31. For example, Prunier, *The Rwanda Crisis*, 60–61; Greenland, 'Ethnic Discrimination', 115; L. Melvern. 2006. *Conspiracy to Murder: The Rwandan Genocide*, rev. ed., London: Verso, 20.
32. G. Kayibanda. 1973. 'Message presidential de pacification', Kigali, 22 March, in *Remarques Africaines* 419 (1–15 April), 7–8.
33. Prunier, *The Rwanda Crisis*, 61.
34. Ibid.
35. Burnet, 'The Search for a Middle Ground', 31.
36. Ibid.; Prunier, *The Rwanda Crisis*, 61.
37. J. Habyarimana. 1973. 'Message to the Nation', 6 July, in J. Habyarimana. 1981. *Discours, Messages et Entretiens: 5 juillet 1973—décembre 1974*, Kigali: ORINFOR, 17.
38. Prunier, *The Rwanda Crisis*, 61, 75.
39. Mamdani, *When Victims Become Killers*, 143.
40. Ibid., 144.
41. Ibid., 141.
42. Ibid.
43. Prunier, *The Rwanda Crisis*, 78. Prunier cited World Bank Yearly Developments Reports, compiled by F. Reyntjens. 1994. *L'Afrique des Grands Lacs en crise*, Paris: Karthala, 35, for his data.
44. Prunier, *The Rwanda Crisis*, 78; Mamdani, *When Victims Become Killers*, 144.
45. Prunier, *The Rwanda Crisis*, 78; Mamdani, *When Victims Become Killers*, 145; P. Uvin. 1996. 'Tragedy in Rwanda: The Political Ecology of Conflict', *Environment* 38(3), 11.
46. Prunier, *The Rwanda Crisis*, 78.
47. Ibid., 78–79.
48. H. Hintjens. 1999. 'Explaining the 1994 Genocide in Rwanda', *The Journal of Modern African Studies* 37(2), 256.
49. Ibid., 244.
50. P. Verwimp. 1999. *Development Ideology, the Peasantry and Genocide: Rwanda represented in Habyarimana's Speeches*, Working Paper 13, New Haven, CT: Yale University Genocide Studies Program, 26. Verwimp quoted a speech given by Habyarimana at a seminar for burgomasters in August 1975.
51. Ibid., 26.
52. Ibid., 27.
53. Ibid.
54. Ibid., 27; Mamdani, *When Victims Become Killers*, 146.

55. Verwimp, *Development Ideology*, 27.
56. Ibid., 29.
57. Ibid., 28.
58. Prunier, *The Rwanda Crisis*, 77.
59. United Nations Development Program. 1990. *Human Development Reports* and United Nations Development Program. 1994. *Human Development Reports*, both cited in Verwimp, *Development Ideology*, 10–11.
60. Ibid., 10.
61. A. Twagilimana. 2003. *The Debris of Ham: Ethnicity, Regionalism, and the 1994 Rwandan Genocide*, Lanham, MD: University Press of America, 79–80.
62. Ibid., 81; Prunier, *The Rwanda Crisis*, 77.
63. Mamdani, *When Victims Become Killers*, 152.
64. African Rights. 1995. *Rwanda: Death, Despair and Defiance*, rev. ed., London: African Rights, 23.
65. Prunier, *The Rwanda Crisis*, 84.
66. African Rights, *Rwanda*, 23.
67. Verwimp, *Development Ideology*, 10, 24.
68. Ibid., 10; Prunier, *The Rwanda Crisis*, 79.
69. Prunier, *The Rwanda Crisis*, 79.
70. Verwimp, *Development Ideology*, 25.
71. Ibid., 24; Prunier, *The Rwanda Crisis*, 89.
72. African Rights, *Rwanda*, 16; the second quote is cited by African Rights as from P. Uvin. 1994. *The International Organization of Hunger*, London: Kegan Paul International, 195.
73. Uvin, 'Tragedy in Rwanda', 10.
74. Ibid., 12; Mamdani, *When Victims Become Killers*, 145.
75. Uvin, 'Tragedy in Rwanda', 10.
76. Ibid.
77. Ibid., 11.
78. Mamdani, *When Victims Become Killers*, 146.
79. Verwimp, *Development Ideology*, 16.
80. African Rights, *Rwanda*, 18.
81. Mamdani, *When Victims Become Killers*, 142.
82. 'Interview Accordée par le Président de la République rwandaise, le militant Géneral-Major Juvénal Habyarimana, au journaliste Yuki Sato, Reporter au "Mai Ni Chi Shimbun" (Japon), qui venait de passer 12 jours au Rwanda, en compagnie d'un photographe du même organe de presse japonais, M. Taro Nakamura (12 juillet 1980)', in J. Habyarimana, *Discours, Messages et Entretiens: Édition 1980*, Kigali: ORINFOR, 238.
83. R. Lemarchand. 1975. 'Recent History' in section on 'Rwanda', in *Africa South of the Sahara, 1974*, London: Europa Publications, 660, quoted in Mamdani, *When Victims Become Killers*, 140.
84. Mamdani, *When Victims Become Killers*, 140.
85. Ibid., 140–41.
86. Ibid., 141.
87. Twagilimana, *The Debris of Ham*, 80.
88. Ibid., 79.
89. For example, see Mamdani, *When Victims Become Killers*, 139; Prunier, *The Rwanda Crisis*, 75; Twagilimana, *The Debris of Ham*, 76.
90. Twagilimana, *The Debris of Ham*, 77.
91. Mamdani, *When Victims Become Killers*, 138, 141.
92. Twagilimana, *The Debris of Ham*, 78.
93. Verwimp, *Development Ideology*, 14.

94. J. Habyarimana. 1973. 'Speech at the Occasion of the Opening of the Academic Year in Butare, October 14, 1973', *Discours et Entretiens 1973,* 44, quoted in Verwimp, *Development Ideology,* 14.

95. Ibid.

96. Verwimp, *Development Ideology,* 14.

97. Twagilimana, *The Debris of Ham,* 85.

98. Mamdani, *When Victims Become Killers,* 152.

99. African Rights, *Rwanda,* 22–23.

100. Mamdani, *When Victims Become Killers,* 151.

101. Ibid., 152; African Rights, *Rwanda,* 22; Twagilimana, *The Debris of Ham,* 76; B. Jones. 1999. 'Civil War, the Peace Process, and Genocide in Rwanda', in T. Ali and R. Matthews (eds), *Civil Wars in Africa: Roots and Resolution,* Montreal: McGill-Queen's University Press, 60.

102. African Rights, *Rwanda,* 23.

103. Jones, 'Civil War', 60.

104. Twagilimana, *The Debris of Ham,* 78.

105. Ibid.

106. Ibid., 82–83.

107. Mamdani, *When Victims Become Killers,* 155.

108. Twagilimana, *The Debris of Ham,* 85.

109. African Rights, *Rwanda,* 27.

110. Prunier, *The Rwanda Crisis,* 63; Mamdani, *When Victims Become Killers,* 161.

111. African Rights, *Rwanda,* 26.

112. Ibid.

113. Prunier, *The Rwanda Crisis,* 70.

114. Ibid., 71–73; African Rights, *Rwanda,* 28.

115. Prunier, *The Rwanda Crisis,* 72–73, 67.

116. Ibid., 74.

117. Mamdani, *When Victims Become Killers,* 155.

118. Uvin, 'Tragedy in Rwanda', 11.

119. Twagilimana, *The Debris of Ham,* 91.

120. *World Bank Annual Report, 1990,* cited in D. Kamukama. 1997. *Rwanda Conflict: Its Roots and Regional Implications,* 2nd ed., Kampala, Uganda: Fountain Publishers, 2.

121. Hintjens, 'Explaining the 1994 Genocide', 256; Jones, 'Civil War', 56.

122. Hintjens, 'Explaining the 1994 Genocide', 257.

123. African Rights, *Rwanda,* 20; Twagilimana, *The Debris of Ham,* 91; Uvin, 'Tragedy in Rwanda', 11.

124. Hintjens, 'Explaining the 1994 Genocide', 257.

125. African Rights, *Rwanda,* 20; Uvin, 'Tragedy in Rwanda', 11.

126. African Rights, *Rwanda,* 20.

127. Uvin, 'Tragedy in Rwanda', 14.

128. Hintjens, 'Explaining the 1994 Genocide', 256.

129. Ibid., 256–57.

130. Prunier, *The Rwanda Crisis,* 79. Prunier noted that he was citing OECD figures.

131. Jones, 'Civil War', 60.

132. Mamdani, *When Victims Become Killers,* 152–53; Uvin, 'Tragedy in Rwanda', 12.

133. Prunier, *The Rwanda Crisis,* 89; Twagilimana, *The Debris of Ham,* 92. Belgium was the largest foreign aid donor to Rwanda.

134. Prunier, *The Rwanda Crisis,* 90.

135. Ibid., 90–91.

136. W.C. Reed. 1996. 'Exile, Reform, and the Rise of the Rwandan Patriotic Front', *The Journal of Modern African Studies* 34(3), 487.

137. Prunier, *The Rwanda Crisis*, 91.
138. R. Lemarchand. 1995. 'Rwanda: The Rationality of Genocide', in O. Igwara (ed.), *Ethnic Hatred: Genocide in Rwanda*, London: ASEN Publications, 61.
139. Prunier, *The Rwanda Crisis*, 91–94; Mamdani, *When Victims Become Killers*, 186.
140. Reed, 'Exile, Reform', 488.
141. Kamukama, *Rwanda Conflict*, 48.
142. Prunier, *The Rwanda Crisis*, 102, 108; Melvern, *Conspiracy to Murder*, 15.
143. Prunier, *The Rwanda Crisis*, 109.
144. Ibid., 119–20.
145. Ibid., 120.
146. Ibid., 113.
147. Ibid., 109–10; Melvern, *Conspiracy to Murder*, 16.
148. Prunier, *The Rwanda Crisis*, 110; African Rights, *Rwanda*, 51.
149. Twagilimana, *The Debris of Ham*, 108.
150. Ibid., 107–9; Mamdani, *When Victims Become Killers*, 192.
151. Prunier, *The Rwanda Crisis*, 121.
152. Mamdani, *When Victims Become Killers*, 153–54.
153. Ibid.
154. Ibid., 154.
155. Twagilimana, *The Debris of Ham*, 103.
156. Mamdani, *When Victims Become Killers*, 154.
157. Twagilimana, *The Debris of Ham*, 103.
158. Mamdani, *When Victims Become Killers*, 154–55.
159. Prunier, *The Rwanda Crisis*, 122.
160. Mamdani, *When Victims Become Killers*, 153.
161. Prunier, *The Rwanda Crisis*, 145–46.
162. Jones, 'Civil War', 62–63.
163. Ibid., 63.
164. African Rights, *Rwanda*, 31.
165. Ibid.
166. A. Des Forges. 1999. *"Leave None to Tell the Story": Genocide in Rwanda*, New York: Human Rights Watch, 53.
167. Ibid.
168. Ibid., 54.
169. Ibid., 60.
170. Reyntjens, *L'Afrique des Grands Lacs*, 94, quoted in Des Forges, *Genocide in Rwanda*, 50.
171. Des Forges, *Genocide in Rwanda*, 66.
172. Hintjens, 'Explaining the 1994 Genocide', 259.
173. Twagilimana, *The Debris of Ham*, 105.
174. Uvin, 'Tragedy in Rwanda', 12–13.
175. Lemarchand, 'Rwanda: The Rationality of Genocide', 61.
176. Twagilimana, *The Debris of Ham*, 103.
177. Ibid., 103–4.
178. Ibid., 104.
179. Ibid., 104–7.
180. Mamdani, *When Victims Become Killers*, 189.
181. Twagilimana, *The Debris of Ham*, 111.
182. Ibid., 110.
183. Ibid., 112–13.
184. Ibid., 113.

185. Reed, 'Exile, Reform', 492–93.
186. Ibid., 493–94.
187. Prunier, *The Rwanda Crisis*, 173–74.
188. Ibid., 174; Mamdani, *When Victims Become Killers*, 192.
189. Prunier, *The Rwanda Crisis*, 135.
190. Ibid.
191. Reed, 'Exile, Reform', 494.
192. Prunier, *The Rwanda Crisis*, 177–78.
193. Jones, 'Civil War', 70.
194. African Rights, *Rwanda*, 45.
195. Ibid., 44.
196. Ibid., 45.
197. Verwimp, *Development Ideology*, 4.
198. Belgian Senate. 1997. *Report of Rwanda Commission of Inquiry*, 6 December, 493–94, quoted in Verwimp, *Development Ideology*, 4.
199. Twagilimana, *The Debris of Ham*, 99–100.
200. Des Forges, *Genocide in Rwanda*, 65.
201. Ibid., 73.
202. Ibid.
203. Twagilimana, *The Debris of Ham*, 263.
204. Hintjens, 'Explaining the 1994 Genocide', 261; Prunier, *The Rwanda Crisis*, 171; T. Longman. 1997. 'Rwanda: Democratization and Disorder: Political Transformation and Social Deterioration', in J. Clark and D. Gardinier (eds), *Political Reform in Francophone Africa*, Boulder, CO: Westview Press, 298.
205. Burnet, 'The Search for a Middle Ground', 51.
206. Article 19. 1996. *Broadcasting Genocide: Censorship, Propaganda and State-Sponsored Violence in Rwanda 1990–1994*, London: Article 19, quoted in Burnet, 'The Search for a Middle Ground', 51.
207. African Rights, *Rwanda*, 78.
208. Burnet, 'The Search for a Middle Ground', 53.
209. Ibid.
210. Speech given by Léon Mugesera in Kabaya (Gisenyi), 22 November 1992, quoted in Twagilimana, *The Debris of Ham*, 106.
211. Twagilimana, *The Debris of Ham*, 106.
212. Hintjens, 'Explaining the 1994 Genocide', 255.
213. Prunier, *The Rwanda Crisis*, 170.
214. Des Forges, *Genocide in Rwanda*, 122–23.
215. Mamdani, *When Victims Become Killers*, 204.
216. United Nations Information Centre. 1993. 'United Nations Observer Mission Uganda-Rwanda', *Africa News Service*, 23 August, quoted in Mamdani, *When Victims Become Killers*, 204.
217. Des Forges, *Genocide in Rwanda*, 122. Adverse weather conditions also contributed to the decrease.
218. African Rights, *Rwanda*, 20.
219. Jones, 'Civil War', 69.
220. Ibid.
221. Ibid.
222. Mamdani, *When Victims Become Killers*, 211.
223. Jones, 'Civil War', 69.
224. Ibid., 71.
225. Ibid., 79.
226. Ibid., 70–71.
227. Des Forges, *Genocide in Rwanda*, 124.

228. Ibid., 125.
229. African Rights, *Rwanda*, 36.
230. Ibid.
231. Mamdani, *When Victims Become Killers*, 210.
232. Ibid.
233. Jones, 'Civil War', 72.
234. Ibid., 72–73.
235. Twagilimana, *The Debris of Ham*, 141.
236. Lemarchand, 'Rwanda: The Rationality of Genocide', 62.
237. Hintjens, 'Explaining the 1994 Genocide', 267.
238. A. Destexhe. 1995. *Rwanda and Genocide in the Twentieth Century*, New York: New York University Press, quoted in Burnet, 'The Search for a Middle Ground', 53.
239. H. McCullum. 1995. *The Angels Have Left Us: The Rwanda Tragedy and the Churches*, Geneva: WCC Publications, 18. McCullum cited a rural illiteracy rate of 70 per cent.
240. Des Forges, *Genocide in Rwanda*, 139.
241. Recording of RTLM broadcasts, 17–31 October 1993 (tape provided by Radio Rwanda), quoted in Des Forges, *Genocide in Rwanda*, 138–39.
242. Des Forges, *Genocide in Rwanda*, 139; Prunier, *The Rwanda Crisis*, 166, 182.
243. Des Forges, *Genocide in Rwanda*, 128; McCullum, *The Angels*, 15–19.
244. Des Forges, *Genocide in Rwanda*, 127.
245. See, e.g., ibid., 116–22; 'Arming Genocide in Rwanda', *Foreign Affairs* 73(5), 1994, 86; McCullum, *The Angels*, 14–15; Prunier, *The Rwanda Crisis*, 113–14, 164–65; African Rights, *Rwanda*, 49, 67–68.
246. Uvin, 'Tragedy in Rwanda', 13.
247. G. Prunier. 2001. 'Genocide in Rwanda' in D. Chirot and M. Seligman (eds), *Ethnopolitical Warfare: Causes, Consequences, and Possible Solutions*, Washington, D.C.: American Psychological Association, 115.
248. Des Forges, *Genocide in Rwanda*, 135.
249. Mamdani, *When Victims Become Killers*, 215.
250. Ibid.
251. Des Forges, *Genocide in Rwanda*, 137.
252. Prunier, *The Rwanda Crisis*, 200.
253. Ibid.
254. Lemarchand, 'Rwanda: The Rationality of Genocide', 66.
255. Twagilimana, *The Debris of Ham*, 122.
256. Des Forges, *Genocide in Rwanda*, 141.
257. Ibid.; Prunier, *The Rwanda Crisis*, 203–4.
258. Prunier, *The Rwanda Crisis*, 206–7.
259. Hintjens, 'Explaining the 1994 Genocide', 270.
260. Des Forges, *Genocide in Rwanda*, 142.
261. Hintjens, 'Explaining the 1994 Genocide', 270.
262. Prunier, *The Rwanda Crisis*, 209.
263. African Rights, *Rwanda*, 71–73.
264. Lemarchand, 'Rwanda: The Rationality of Genocide', 67.
265. L. Melvern. 2012. 'Rwanda: At Last We Know the Truth', *The Guardian*, 10 January 2012. Retrieved 12 February 2012 from http://www.guardian.co.uk/commentisfree/2012/jan/10/rwanda-at-last-we-know-truth?INTCMP=SRCH
266. Lemarchand, 'Rwanda: The Rationality of Genocide', 67; Prunier, *The Rwanda Crisis*, 223; Twagilimana, *The Debris of Ham*, 122.

267. M. Barnett. 1997. 'The UN Security Council, Indifference, and Genocide in Rwanda', *Cultural Anthropology* 12(4), 559–60.
268. Des Forges, *Genocide in Rwanda*, 6; Prunier, *The Rwanda Crisis*, 240.
269. A. Jones. 2006. *Genocide: A Comprehensive Introduction*, London: Routledge, 238.
270. Prunier, *The Rwanda Crisis*, 236.
271. Jones, *Genocide*, 238.
272. Ibid., 245.
273. Ibid., 239.
274. Prunier, *The Rwanda Crisis*, 250; Mamdani, *When Victims Become Killers*, 226.
275. Des Forges, *Genocide in Rwanda*, 6–8.
276. Prunier, *The Rwanda Crisis*, 261.
277. Ibid., 244.
278. Mamdani, *When Victims Become Killers*, 225.
279. Prunier, *The Rwanda Crisis*, 248.
280. Des Forges, *Genocide in Rwanda*, 12.
281. Hintjens, 'Explaining the 1994 Genocide', 268; Prunier, *The Rwanda Crisis*, 142.
282. Jones, *Genocide*, 243; Mamdani, *When Victims Become Killers*, 220.
283. Hintjens, 'Explaining the 1994 Genocide', 269.
284. Prunier, *The Rwanda Crisis*, 255–56.
285. Des Forges, *Genocide in Rwanda*, 215.
286. Prunier, *The Rwanda Crisis*, 244.
287. Mamdani, *When Victims Become Killers*, 220.
288. Ibid., 221.
289. Des Forges, *Genocide in Rwanda*, 12.
290. Jones, *Genocide*, 239.
291. Ibid., 238; Melvern, *Conspiracy to Murder*, 188.
292. Melvern, *Conspiracy to Murder*, 191.
293. Jones, *Genocide*, 239.
294. Jones, 'Civil War', 78.
295. Ibid.; Des Forges, *Genocide in Rwanda*, 23.
296. Prunier, *The Rwanda Crisis*, 255.
297. Ibid., 261.
298. Des Forges, *Genocide in Rwanda*, 10.
299. Jones, *Genocide*, 244.
300. Ibid.
301. Jones, 'Civil War', 76.
302. Melvern, *Conspiracy to Murder*, 252–53. Estimates of the total death toll vary. The nature of the violence precludes the establishment of a definitive figure.

Part III

THE PATH TO GENOCIDE

Chapter 7

'DRIVEN BY ETHNIC EXCLUSIVISM'
On the Timing of Genocide

It is a paradox that the eruption of genocide is unpredictable, yet never seems to occur without prior warning. In 1880, for example, two different observers of the Armenians in Turkey asserted them to be subject to a governmental 'policy of extermination'; in 1895, a third observer declared 'the extermination of the Armenians' imminent.[1] In 1962, UN Commissioner Rahnema accused the ruling party in Rwanda of 'a social policy apparently designed to eliminate . . . the Tutsi minority'; according to this commissioner, the Tutsi were at serious risk of extermination.[2] All these observers were ultimately correct, as the Armenian and Rwandan genocides of 1915 and 1994 testify. Yet their dire predictions were wrong in one crucial aspect: the timing of when genocide would occur. In both cases, the predictions were not wrong by weeks or months, but decades. Such examples highlight the difficulty of attempts to map the path that leads to genocide. Despite widespread acknowledgement that societies at risk of genocide can be recognized as such, there remains an inability to predict accurately when the risk of genocide is likely to be realized. Yet understanding why genocide occurs *when* it does is a crucial component of understanding the nature of this crime. Furthermore, attempts to prevent genocide are at least partially contingent upon the ability to accurately predict its onset.

The temporal model of the preconditions for genocide offers new insights into the timing of genocide.[3] Whilst previous models of the preconditions can identify the necessary prerequisites, they offer little or no insight as to their chronological development. As the preceding chapters demonstrate, however, the events preceding the Armenian and Rwandan genocides suggest that risk factors develop in a particular and somewhat predictable pattern. Eight key stages have been identified and elucidated in the temporal model:

1. The presence of an outgroup. This can be defined as a relatively powerless minority, with whom relations are politicized, and which is subject to legal discrimination.
2. Significant internal strife. Significant, ongoing destabilization that affects the dominant group and the outgroup, and for which there is no clear solution.
3. The perception of the outgroup as posing some kind of existential threat to the dominant power.
4. Local precipitants and constraints determine the nature and time of the dominant group's response. A violent response is typical, with the onset of massacres quite likely.
5. A process of retreat from the intensity of the circumstance, or further escalation. While the process is commonly one of retreat, repeated cycles of escalation through the preceding stages followed by retreat ultimately facilitates further escalation.
6. The emergence of a genocidal ideology within the dominant power, typically accompanied by concerted efforts by the dominant group to further augment their power, and a deepening perception of the outgroup as posing an existential threat.
7. An extensive propaganda campaign, a key component of which features attempts to present the victim group as a grave threat to the dominant power.
8. Case-specific precipitants and constraints determine the precise timing of an outbreak of genocide.

This chapter will examine each of the stages of the temporal model more closely. It will utilize the stages of the model to explore how the risk of genocide develops over time and is ultimately realized in at-risk societies. It identifies at which stages societies at risk of genocide may nevertheless be quite stable, which factors are likely to trigger instability and increased risk, and which factors are likely to cluster together closely in a dramatic risk escalation process. It also explores how societies can experience a nonlinear progression, with long-standing reductions in risk levels. Finally, it considers how the temporal model can offer greater predictive capacity than previous models, while acknowledging the inherent limitations of predicting genocide.

The Early Stages

The first precondition of genocide in the temporal model is identified as the presence of an 'outgroup' within the society. This is common to several models, including those of Fein and Mazian.[4] According to Fein, such a group is defined as 'outside the universe of obligation of the dominant group'.[5] As Kuper has noted, outgroups are typically discriminated against in multiple sectors of society, often including the political structure, the economy, opportunities for education and so forth.[6] There are three clear markers that define a distinct group as an 'outgroup' for the purposes of this model. First, the group will be relatively powerless, particularly in the political sphere. For example, both the Armenians in the Ottoman Empire and the Tutsi in Rwanda were excluded from participation in the political organs of power. Second, relations between the dominant group(s) and the outgroup will be politicized, to at least some extent. At times this may be a marked feature of the society, whilst at other times it may be more latent. But at all times it will remain available as a political tool, able to be utilized at will by the dominant group. For example, one can consider Hutu-Tutsi relations during the late 1970s and early 1980s in Rwanda, discussed in chapter 6. At this time, intergroup relations were not a dominant issue, and indeed were officially denoted by the policy of 'ethnic and regional balance'—one ostensibly designed to reduce intergroup tension. Yet this policy effectively retained ethnicity as a political issue. The internal struggles within the ruling party during this period—in part over Habyarimana's pro-reconciliation stance towards the Tutsi—are indicative of the continued salience of intergroup tension as a political issue. The third marker of an 'outgroup' is legalized discrimination against it. In Ottoman Turkey, with Armenians officially *giaours*, this was quite pronounced; in Rwanda, such discrimination was relatively mild. Nevertheless, the presence of any form of legal discrimination is indicative of this precondition.

The case studies of both the Armenian and Rwandan genocides reveal that, in the absence of other preconditions for genocide, societies can exist stably for decades with the presence of an outgroup. That is, a society that meets the first precondition for genocide, but no others, can be quite stable for extended periods. The Armenians, for example, can be classified as an outgroup in the Ottoman Empire for decades, if not a century or more, prior to the Armenian genocide; the Jews, too, were an outgroup in Europe for centuries prior to the Holocaust. Other groups, like the Tutsi, can be identified as long-standing distinct groups, but ones that became an 'outgroup' only after relatively recent political upheaval—in the Tutsi case, after decolonization. In the Holocaust, whilst the Jews were a long-standing outgroup, other groups only came to be targeted as such in the period immediately prior to the calamities—such as the disabled and the mentally ill. This suggests that while outgroups typically are of long standing, it is also possible for perpetrators to identify and create an outgroup very quickly prior to a genocide. In the Cambodian genocide, for example, the identification and targeting of 'educated' Cambodians as an outgroup was a very rapid process. Generally, however, outgroups can and do exist for long periods stably within societies.

The second precondition for genocide, to further pursue the models of both Fein and Mazian, is 'significant internal strife'. The case studies of both Armenia and Rwanda indicate major disruption within each society. In Rwanda in the late 1980s, for example, such internal strife included both an economic and a political crisis. For the Young Turks between 1910 and 1914, as elucidated earlier, such strife included losing a war, losing vast tracts of Ottoman territory and severe financial pressure, amongst other elements. The precondition of internal strife thus is defined by significant, ongoing destabilization that affects both the dominant group(s) and the outgroup, and for which there is no clear solution. Whereas a society can exist stably in the presence of an outgroup, that is, whilst meeting the first necessary but not sufficient precondition for genocide, a society in which the first two preconditions for genocide are present is considerably less stable. By nature, a society facing significant internal strife is unsustainable in the long term: a solution of some kind must be found for the nation's woes.

The internal strife may not be related in any way to the presence of the outgroup, and may not initially lead to any increased discrimination against the outgroup, or to deterioration in conditions specifically affecting it. Yet the outgroup, relatively powerless and already subject to discrimination, is extremely vulnerable to being targeted at such a time of national stress. At the very least, members of the outgroup are likely to be increasingly victim to harassment and discrimination. In Rwanda in the early 1970s, for example, this is precisely what happened. Similarly, as the Ottoman Empire declined throughout the nineteenth century, so too did the security and safety of the Armenian minority. But the longevity of the presence of the first two preconditions for genocide in the Ottoman Empire, without the situation escalating further, is probably atypical. The Armenians were only one of a number of outgroups within the empire, and several others were targeted more severely than the Armenians at different times of peak internal strife prior to 1878. Historical accounts of minorities in societies that exhibit the first two preconditions for genocide indicate they have a much greater awareness of their vulnerability, and the potential danger of their circumstances, than accounts of minorities in societies where only the first precondition is present. There is a clear perception of an escalation of risk.

The Risk Escalation Process

It is at this point that the temporal model differs significantly from previous models of the preconditions for genocide. The examination of the case studies of the Armenian and Rwandan genocides, with particular regard to how risk factors for these genocides developed over time, suggests that there is a distinct factor likely to become operative at this juncture, destabilizing the already precarious situation and dramatically increasing the risk profile of the outgroup. That is, the outgroup comes to be perceived as posing, or at the very least associated with, an existential threat to the dominant group. Such a perception, it is important to note, is always a construction of the dominant power. (Were the outgroup as a whole genuinely to pose an existential threat to the dominant power, the outgroup itself would be possessed of sufficient power that it could not be properly considered as such.) There may be a real and serious threat to the dominant power or the mainstream society; however, the link between such a threat and the outgroup as a whole is typically tenuous, and manipulated by political power brokers. More often, such a threat may have some factual basis, but is distorted, exaggerated or otherwise manipulated by the relevant powers, if not wholly manufactured. Indeed, the role of the dominant power in the characterization of the outgroup as an existential threat is crucial. Intellectuals and politicians in a society with an outgroup may often view this group as a threat; however, it is only when the power brokers of the nation embrace such a view that it becomes dangerously toxic. The presence of significant internal strife often facilitates such circumstances, as powers seek a convenient scapegoat for the nation's troubles.

Some examples from the Rwandan case study provide further clarity. In Rwanda, there were multiple instances when the Tutsi as a whole group—for varying reasons—came to be perceived as an existential threat. The Bugesera invasion in Rwanda in December 1963, for example, when a few hundred Tutsi refugees crossed into Rwanda and were joined by several hundred more internally displaced Tutsi, led to *all* Tutsi being perceived as threatening to the survival of Rwanda as a Hutu nation. In 1972–73, again Rwandan Tutsi were perceived as an existential threat, this time in response to the massacres of Hutu by (mostly) Tutsi soldiers in neighbouring Burundi. The Rwandan Patriotic Front (RPF) invasion by second-generation Ugandan Tutsi refugees in October 1990 also led to further perceptions of Rwandan Tutsi as posing an existential threat to the nation. Thus, according to the infamous 'Hutu Ten Commandments' published in December 1990, '*all* the Tutsi . . . only work for the supremacy of their ethnic group'.[7] In each of these cases, there was a sizeable leap from the actual threat to the resulting manipulation and distortion of the circumstances in order to characterize the Tutsi outgroup as a whole as posing an existential threat. That signifies a considerable and dangerous escalation of the risk of violence, and a dramatic destabilization of conditions.

At this stage, the roles of precipitants and constraints become crucial. By nature, an existential threat to the dominant group is one that requires a concerted response if that group is to maintain its position of power. The case studies suggest that the result will typically be violent, with the onset of massacres quite likely. Several factors can influence the strength and timing of the dominant group's response: the potency and immediacy of the existential threat, and how directly the threat is or can be linked to the outgroup. At this juncture, however, on the precipice of violence, precipitants and constraints specific to the local circumstance are likely to be the most important determinants. The diversity of accelerants that can be operable, combined with any constraint needing to override the strong motivation of the dominant power to deal with the perceived or proclaimed threat, makes endeavours to prevent violent outbreaks at this point fraught with difficulty.

Consideration of the circumstances surrounding the outbreaks of violence in Ottoman Turkey in both 1894 and 1895, for example, aids in understanding the central role of precipitants and constraints. As discussed in chapter 2, by 1894 Sultan Abdul Hamid II had long characterized the Armenians as an existential threat to his crumbling empire. In 1878 he had been forced to accept the Treaty of Berlin, which proclaimed the civic equality of the Armenian minority—inimical to the *millet* system that formed the foundation of the empire.[8] The severe constraints against violent retaliation towards the Armenian population operable then—including the weakness of the empire after its wartime defeat, and the very real threat of further European intervention—had prevented major violence. But as these constraints weakened by the early 1890s, the stipulations of the Treaty of Berlin remained valid, but never realized, and the perceived existential threat of the Armenians remained. The government, seemingly looking for a pretext, allowed a number of minor incidents in Sassoun to trigger a retaliatory massacre out of all proportion to any actual threat. In response, the European Powers renewed many of the demands of the Treaty of Berlin in a new memorandum—effectively reigniting Ottoman perceptions of the Armenians as an existential threat. In response to international pressure to sign the memorandum, another minor incident—this time a protest march—was used as a convenient trigger to launch a much more intense and widespread burst of massacres. In each case, once the predisposing factors were in place, it was precipitants and constraints specific to the particular circumstance that influenced the onset of a violent response to resolve the perceived existential threat.

The above example also serves to highlight the next stage of the temporal model: that of a process requiring either retreat or escalation. More commonly, the process is one of retreat—retreat, that is, to a lower risk profile. Two separate drivers can determine a path of retreat. First, a level of resolution of the existential threat that is deemed acceptable to the dominant power may remove the need for continued violence—a factor that can often coincide with a desire to restore some stability to the nation through the restoration of peace. Alternatively, the process of retreat may be driven by the authority's relative lack of power, that is, an inability to realistically contemplate escalation. Very often, some combination of the two factors will influence the outcome in a given circumstance. If we consider once again the example of the Hamidian massacres in the 1890s, this process can be seen clearly. The massacres of 1895, for example, were precipitated by both international pressure to give the Armenian minority more rights and security, and by the Armenian rally protesting the failure of a concerted response to the Sassoun massacre a year earlier. To a considerable extent, the massacres from October to December 1895 can be regarded as functionally effective in dealing with these threats to the empire. The Armenians were terrified into submission—at least temporarily. The bluff of the international powers was called and found wanting—weakening their position and credibility. At the same time, however, it was not clear that the international powers would not intervene in the event of a more global or deadly campaign against the Armenian minority. In 1896, for example, when violence broke out in Constantinople—before the eyes of European diplomats—for a short time at least there appeared to be a real threat of international intervention. Undoubtedly, that threat was an influential factor determining the cessation of not only the massacre in Constantinople, but also the large-scale massacres of that period generally. Ultimately, the Ottoman sultan chose a process of retreat rather than escalation. The solution was a limited one: the existential threat posed by the Armenians had been resolved to the maximum extent possible given the relative powerlessness of the sultan with respect to the international powers.

Depending upon the particular circumstance, there can be a retreat to any one of the preceding stages of the temporal model. The earlier the stage to which there is a retreat, however, the more stable that retreat will be, and, interestingly, the more the dominant power will have an investment in that retreat. Consider, for example, the anti-Tutsi massacres in Rwanda in December 1963–January 1964, in the wake of the Bugesera invasion. Quite rapidly following these events it became clear that there would not be a Tutsi-led coup attempt in Rwanda. Accordingly, the risk profile for genocide retreated to just the continuing presence of an outgroup, the first risk factor in the temporal model. As this occurred, Rwandan president Kayibanda actively called for tolerance, differentiating between a terrorist element and ordinary Tutsi refugees, whom the government explicitly stated were not responsible for the invasion.[9] President Kayibanda did not homogenize, dehumanize or vilify the Tutsi outgroup, and actively sought at least some level of rapprochement.

Such overtures are more common than might be expected in societies at risk of genocide. In 1973, when President Habyarimana seized power in Rwanda in a bloodless coup, a similar process unfolded. As discussed earlier, at the time of Habyarimana's coup Rwanda was beset by internal strife, and there was again some perception of the Tutsi as an existential threat, as a result of the 1972 killings in neighbouring Burundi. Though he would later lead Rwanda to the brink of genocide, at this stage Habyarimana led Rwanda to greater stability—including by actively seeking reconciliation with the Tutsi outgroup. If the retreat is more limited, however, with two or more risk factors remaining operable, such reconciliation is less likely to be sought, and the situation is inherently less stable. Thus, conditions for Armenians in the Ottoman Empire, where significant internal strife continued after the Hamidian massacres, remained far more hostile and less stable. Nevertheless, in the immediate aftermath of the Young Turk seizure of power, there was at least a brief attempt at reconciliation.

A vital element in understanding the development of the risk of genocide over time is to consider the cyclic pattern that emerges at this stage of retreat/escalation. In both the Armenian and Rwandan case studies, one can plot the risk profile reaching this stage multiple times and then retreating to an earlier stage, in a cyclic process that lasted (in each case) for a period of decades if not generations. In

Rwanda, for example, the risk profile escalated to this stage in 1963–64, 1972–73 and 1990. The repeated cycles of progression and then retreat in both case studies suggest the importance of the entrenchment of this process prior to further escalation. As discussed in the introduction, psychologist Ervin Staub has explored the role of a 'continuum of destruction', whereby initially limited acts of harm psychologically facilitate subsequent, more destructive actions. Gradually, feelings of responsibility for others' welfare and inhibitions against killing break down.[10] The cyclic process that preceded both the Armenian and Rwandan genocides seems to have greatly facilitated the normalization of ethnic violence within Ottoman and Rwandan societies, and the dehumanization of the outgroup as the vilified 'other'. It appears that over time a lasting suspicion or distrust of the outgroup comes to permeate the society, even in the absence of a specific cause for distrust at a particular point. These suspicions can later be of great significance as would-be perpetrators seek to impose their own interpretation of the history of majority-outgroup relations onto a society. In particular, they can be manipulated by authorities to link the outgroup to an existential threat. During times of internal strife or crisis, vilification of the outgroup is thus a readily available strategy for the political elite. The longer the period over which these cycles occur, and the more often they do, the more available and 'normal' such a strategy becomes.

Later Stages of High Risk

Three profound effects of the cycle of escalation and retreat facilitate further escalation to eventual genocide. The first is that the strategy of utilizing the outgroup as a convenient scapegoat in times of national crisis can be quite effective at rallying the majority in the desired political direction, while decreasing the focus on any more awkward issues for the political elite. As the strategy is used repeatedly at times of internal strife, the outgroup can become inextricably linked to the nation's difficulties. It can appear that the authorities are always trying to resolve the 'same' issue—for which the outgroup is held responsible. In such circumstances, the temptation for 'final' escalating violence is clear. The second effect of this cycle is that the risk to which the outgroup is exposed is not limited to the tenure of any particular ruling power. The repeated politicization of ethnic issues, the repeated scapegoating of the outgroup and the distrust and suspicion towards this minority become embedded features of the society. The outgroup remains vulnerable to political manipulation by successive regimes. Thus, the Hamidian massacres of the 1890s took place under the rule of Sultan Abdul Hamid II, whilst the genocide was engineered by the Young Turks, who overthrew him. The third effect of this cycle is what Vahakn Dadrian has termed the 'legacy of impunity'.[11] That is, as ruling powers discover that they can provoke ethnic violence, and even massacres, with little consequence, they are emboldened to act increasingly recklessly. For example, the lack of a concerted international response to the Sassoun massacre of Armenians in 1894 facilitated the subsequent massacres; similarly, the lack of an international outcry at the limited anti-Tutsi massacres in Rwanda in the early 1990s encouraged further violent outbreaks.

Such outcomes may influence regimes to contemplate further escalation, rather than retreat, at this critical juncture. In the Armenian and Rwandan case studies, each ruling group ultimately preferred a process of escalation at this stage—placing the nation at grave risk of genocide. The next stage, that of the emergence of an ideology that can be used to legitimize genocide—or at least its emergence from the radical fringes—came to be a feature of each society. The presence of this ideology is conducive to the formation of a genocidal plan; and, once such a plan develops, the ideology will in turn become increasingly radical and more specifically about justifying genocidal goals. As discussed in chapter 3, in Ottoman Turkey this ideology was that of pan-Turkism, which excluded the Armenian minority. A nation, according to Turkish ideologue Ziya Gökalp, was 'a society . . . of people who speak the same language . . . and are united in their religious and aesthetic ideals'.[12] What emerged as an ideology that excluded the Armenian minority led quite rapidly to the emergence of a plan for genocide. In a dialectical process, as the plan was formulated, justifying it required further ideological radicalization. The Armenian minority was no longer simply excluded, but seen as actively and dangerously threatening. In just six short years, Enver Pasha went from declaring the Armenians 'brothers' to declaring 'they will have to be destroyed'.[13]

Key to escalation at this juncture are the dual drivers of the entrenched power of the dominant authority, and deepening perceptions of the outgroup as an existential threat to the nation. Evidence from the Armenian and Rwandan case studies has indicated that a regime without sufficient power to realistically contemplate genocide will not attempt or threaten to do so. For example, consider Rwanda in 1963–64. In many respects, this society appears to be at far greater risk of genocide than Rwanda in the late 1980s. Hutu leaders had not only just secured independence for the nation, but in the process also managed to secure almost all organs of power under their own leadership. Victory had resulted from a fierce, racially driven campaign, which portrayed Tutsi as foreign invaders and oppressors 'who imposed their rule . . . by cunning and cruelty'.[14] Then, after eighteen months of quite peaceful nation building, the Bugesera invasion shook the country deeply. Superficially at least, the risk of the emergence of a genocidal ideology at this point seems great. The Kayibanda government, however, simply did not have the power to contemplate such a course of action. Its army was woefully inadequate; its leadership was only just grasping the rudiments of running a country. Thus, the rhetoric very quickly returned to themes of unity and cooperation. 'Rwanda wants to be a tolerant and peaceful nation', declared Kayibanda.[15] A quarter of a century later, by contrast, Habyarimana and the *akuzu* had a far tighter grip on the nation as they contemplated genocide.

The second driver of the emergence of an ideology that facilitates genocide is a deepening perception of the outgroup as posing an existential threat to mainstream society and/or the nation. Such perceptions are themselves at least partially manipulated by the dominant power. Usually the threat is presented as intractable—somehow justifying the escalated approach being contemplated. 'Who could tell the difference between the *inyenzi* who attacked in October 1990 and those of the 1960s?' asked Hutu propagandists in 1993.[16] Indeed, characterizing the outgroup in this way is crucial for the potential success of genocidal plans. Regime leaders possessed of a genocidal ideology appear to grasp that a particularly effective approach to reducing the natural inhibitions of humankind towards the mass murder of other humans is to present such actions as necessary self-defence. In order for this to be feasible, however, the outgroup must therefore be regarded as being dangerously threatening to the dominant group. For example, as elucidated earlier, in the wake of the RPF invasion of Rwanda in October 1990, Habyarimana exaggerated the ongoing risk posed by the RPF rather than publicizing its very serious losses.[17] As the 1990s progressed, official propaganda presented the RPF as posing a grave existential threat to Rwanda, refusing to acknowledge a more balanced view that would recognize their willingness to share power under the auspices of the broad-based transitional government and to participate in democratic elections. The reality of the situation mattered less than the potential for such threats to be considered real, grave and pressing by the population.

The emergence of an ideology that facilitates genocide, usually shortly followed by the outlines of a genocidal plan, is further characterized by a huge drive for power by the potential perpetrators. This can take multiple and very diverse forms, but each with the central goal of ensuring sufficient power and means to conduct the genocide being contemplated. Thus, in the Committee of Union and Progress (CUP) in Ottoman Turkey, it took the form of factional jousting for seats on the central committee. Later, as the genocide grew imminent, tactics included the disarming of all Armenians, separation of men from their families and specific strategies to deal with areas of previous resistance. In Rwanda, too, pro-genocidal parties manoeuvred within government circles for sufficient power to enact their plans; massive imports of arms were ordered; and there was a massive buildup of troops. Characteristic, too, of a society in which this precondition is operable is a number of 'tests' of the power of the dominant group. Typically, these tests will be to gauge the support of the population, and/or test the international reaction to the proposed course of action—that of both allies and enemies. For example, as the genocidal ideology took root in Rwanda in the early 1990s, a number of massacres occurred. According to Twagilimana, at least one of the purposes of the Bugesera massacres in March 1992, in which approximately 277 people were killed, was 'to verify the feasibility of massacres in the political south'.[18] Similarly, Prunier has remarked upon the Hutu government's close attention to the reaction of their French ally to the massacres of the early 1990s. According to Prunier, after each massacre, the Habyarimana government:

> watched to see how the French were going to react. The Hutu were pleased by France's tolerance and understanding, and they began to raise the level of violence. Had the French made it clear that they did not support this extremism, the situation might not have deteriorated so badly.[19]

Finally, it must be noted that once a country's risk profile for genocide reaches this stage, the situation is inherently grave and precarious. The final three risk factors that lead to genocide, of which the emergence of a genocidal ideology is the first, clustered together very closely in both the Armenian and Rwandan case studies. Even early estimates of the emergence of a genocidal ideology within the CUP in Ottoman Turkey, such as Dadrian's estimate of 'the outlines of a genocidal scheme' being in place by the close of 1910, suggest a very short period between the emergence of this ideology and the onset of genocide.[20] In the Rwandan case study, the time periods under consideration are even shorter. Again, taking a relatively early estimate of the emergence of a genocidal ideology in late 1991 would still leave a period of only two and a half years until the onset of genocide—and, as discussed previously, there are competent arguments to suggest that date might be closer to late 1992. Potentially, the time period between the emergence of a genocidal ideology and the onset of genocide could be as short as eighteen months. Even the longest estimate suggested by the Armenian and Rwandan genocides would be under five years. This suggests that once this stage is reached, the society is at extreme risk of genocide, and the situation is inherently unstable.

The emergence of a genocidal ideology is very quickly followed by the next stage, that of an extensive propaganda campaign. As discussed in the introduction, the importance of this has already been elucidated by a number of scholars of the preconditions for genocide. Kuper identified ideological legitimation as a necessary precondition for genocide to occur; Fein referred to the necessity of the elite adopting a political formula that justifies the nation's domination and idealizes the singular rights of the dominant group.[21] Mazian's model most clearly highlights the vital communicative aspect of this precondition. Termed 'destructive uses of communication', Mazian's precondition refers to both communications that support the superiority of the dominant group, and those that reduce the inhibitions of the masses and justify the genocidal goals.[22] Melson, too, has commented upon the tendency of the dominant group to link the victim group with enemies of the larger society and state.[23]

The preceding study of the Armenian and Rwandan genocides confirms a number of crucial aspects to this precondition. For the dominant power, now espousing a genocidal ideology, the goal at this stage is to create the societal conditions under which this ideology can be realized. Key to that is a propaganda campaign that vilifies the outgroup. Extensive efforts are made to dehumanize the outgroup, which may be labelled as dogs, cockroaches, devils or any other derogatory classification. Thus, Hutu propaganda declared, 'A cockroach gives birth to another cockroach . . . a Tutsi stays always exactly the same.'[24] As mentioned above, also critical to the success of any potential genocide is the disintegration of the ordinarily operable inhibitions towards the killing of other humans. The strategy of presenting the genocide as an act of self-defence against an outgroup that poses a grave existential threat to the nation is essential to neutralizing moral inhibitions. Thus, a crucial component of the propaganda campaign will focus on the threat of the outgroup, and the necessity of a response in self-defence. Such campaigns are particularly effective when they run over some time, allowing the messages to be absorbed by wide segments of the population, and additionally when the dominant group is able to prevent the dissemination of any opposing perspectives; however, any extensive propaganda campaign that vilifies and presents the outgroup as an existential threat to the nation is a very strong sign of the likely imminent onset of genocide.

A nation that has experienced the preceding seven preconditions for genocide is a nation on the brink of disaster. The risk factors that predispose a nation to genocide are all present. As in stage four of this model, case-specific precipitants and constraints now come to govern events. A striking feature of this stage in both the Armenian and Rwandan case studies is how an important accelerant was closely tied with a sharply heightened perception of the outgroup as posing an existential threat. In the Rwandan case, for example, the military superiority displayed by the RPF in early 1993, and their ability to return to the subsequent Arusha negotiations in a position of strength, was interpreted by the Hutu extremists to mean that the Tutsi were an ever more real and severe threat to Rwanda. By mid-1993, for example, Hutu propagandists asserted, 'We know that they have attacked us with the intention of massacring and exterminating 4.5 million Hutu and especially those who have gone to school.'[25] A similar picture had emerged in Turkey by 1914. There, Russian intervention had led to Turkey signing a new Armenian Reform Agreement under duress, which the Young Turks regarded as an attack on Ottoman sovereignty.[26] As the Russian minister for foreign affairs, Serge Sazonov, recalled, the Turkish attitude to the reforms was one of 'undisguised ill-will', as the Young Turks perceived them as 'an attempt on Turkish independence'.[27] The Armenians themselves were thus seen as highly threatening to the integrity of the Ottoman Empire. In both cases, these events heightened the existential threat these outgroups were perceived to pose. In both cases, this spike occurred almost exactly fourteen months prior to the onset of the subsequent genocides. This suggests the important role of the perception of the outgroup as posing an existential threat in this final stage before the outbreak of genocide.

Beyond the key role of the identification and dissemination of the existential threat in facilitating the onset of genocide, precipitants and constraints appear to be locally driven. They can vary widely. In Rwanda, for example, the prospect of there being no further way to delay the implementation of the Arusha Accords—that is, the seeming imminence with which the Hutu power brokers would have had to cede their hegemony over the nation—played a precipitating role in the onset of the genocide. Concerning Ottoman Turkey, as outlined in chapter 3, numerous scholars have commented upon the crucial role of the start of the First World War in removing a powerful constraint against genocide—that of the threat of international intervention. By this stage of the process, ruling elites have invested heavily in the genocidal process. They are not simply reacting to circumstances as they arise, but actively attempting to manipulate those circumstances to their own advantage. Thus, they may be attempting to create triggers or remove constraints in order to facilitate the onset of genocide. For example, Dadrian has suggested that the desire to annihilate the Armenians may have played a role in influencing Turkey's decision to enter the war.[28] Similarly, there is strong evidence that Hutu extremist members of President Habyarimana's own entourage were responsible for the shooting down of the presidential plane. The sheer variability of what can function as a precipitant or constraint at this stage, combined with the dominant authority's heavy investment in a genocidal strategy and desire to manipulate circumstances to its own advantage, make this stage inherently grossly unstable and unpredictable. The only possible caveat to the above is to note that, even for a regime that has invested heavily in a genocidal strategy, and that may conceive it as the only route possible for the nation, making the decision to actually commence genocide appears to be a significant hurdle. In both the Armenian and Rwandan cases, the situation remained poised on the brink of genocide for several months before the final leap was taken.

The Progression of Risk over Time

Having laid out the temporal model above, it is important to clarify how this model improves our understanding of the progression of the risk of genocide. As outlined in the introduction, previous models have identified the necessary and sufficient preconditions for genocide, but, beyond placing them in an approximate order, offered very little information regarding the time periods over which they were likely to develop. This model offers greater insight. First, it confirms the generally long-term nature of these processes. Second, each stage of the model has been rigorously defined, and assessed for its risk level and relative stability. This enables researchers to readily identify a society at any particular stage, even as that stage unfolds. The relative stability of that stage can be assessed, and observers can be on the alert for the specific markers of the subsequent stage of the model—indicating destabilization and risk escalation processes are underway. For example, consider a nation in which there is an outgroup, where outgroup-majority relations are politicized and in which there is legal discrimination in place against the out-group. In the absence of other risk factors, such a society could be described as meeting only the first precondition for genocide. It would be at some risk, but not grave or imminent risk, of genocide, and would be quite likely to be stable over relatively long periods. The history of the nation, and whether the outgroup had been previously targeted in violent processes from which there had then been a process of retreat, would also be relevant in considering the risk profile. Monitoring the nation for signs of significant internal strife would enable identification of any possible escalation of the risk profile for genocide.

Stage five of the model, a cyclic process of retreat or escalation, is key to under-standing how the risk of genocide develops over time. Rulers at this stage must choose between a process of escalation, potentially leading to future genocide, or a process of retreat. The model offers some clues as to which choice is more likely in a given circumstance. First, a nation that has reached this juncture previously and retreated to an earlier stage in the model—and particular a nation that has cycled through this process multiple times—may be more likely to consider escalation as a serious option. This is particularly so if previous cycles of more limited violence, as occur at stage four of the model, have been conducted with impunity. Fur-ther escalation may also be more likely if the outgroup has repeatedly been made a scapegoat in times of national crisis. Alternatively, a group without sufficient power to conduct more massive violence will almost certainly prefer a process of retreat. This decision will also be influenced by the strength and intractability of the perceived existential threat posed by the outgroup, or linked to the outgroup. Paradoxically, this can be a somewhat dialectical process, as the dominant power at least partially manipulates this perception of threat, but then acts to counter it seemingly without consideration of its own role in the process.

Interestingly, whilst this stage of a cyclic process of retreat or escalation has never previously been formally elucidated in a model of the preconditions of genocide, it has instinctively been recognized by observers of specific instances of genocide. In an at-risk society, it is at this stage that genocide will often first be predicted. Observers of this stage can sense a very real risk of genocide, sufficient to express it officially in high-level warnings. Thus, to recall the paragraph with which this chapter commenced, when the observers of the Armenians in Otto-man Turkey in 1880 and 1895, and of Rwanda in 1962, spoke of the threat of the extermination of the Armenian and Tutsi minorities, respectively, they unwit-tingly identified points where each nation was contemplating escalation or retreat. Indeed, this highlights one of the difficulties of attempting to track the path that leads to genocide—this is a critical juncture, but an early one that more often will lead to a process of retreat rather than escalation.

The cyclic nature of the way in which risk factors for genocide develop over time effectively limits any model of these factors from acquiring a predictive capac-ity until after the critical juncture of stage five has been passed. This cyclic pattern highlights the inherent difficulty of trying to predict how the risk profile of a society will develop over time. The most common process at stage five of the temporal model is a process of retreat—meaning nations can exhibit some risk factors for genocide over long periods, before further escalation. Alternatively, however, if a regime opts for a process of further escalation at this stage, there can be quite a short time period between early stages and late stages of the model. For example, as elucidated in the preceding chapters, in Rwanda between the late 1980s and 1994 there was a very rapid and dramatic process of risk escalation. Such variability has contributed to a generally poor understanding of the development of risk of genocide over time. The temporal model, however, provides a logical lens through which to interpret such variability.

It is a sign of the strength of the temporal model that immediately after stage five it begins to offer a very real timeline for the onset of genocide. The Armenian and Rwandan case studies suggest that stages six to eight of the model typically cluster together very closely. The emergence of a genocidal ideology is very quickly followed by an extensive propaganda campaign. Once both have been established, the situation becomes governed by case-specific precipitants and constraints. Quite specifically, the Armenian and Rwandan cases suggest a severe risk of genocide occurring between eighteen months and five years from the onset of stage six. The model becomes even more specific at the final stage, suggesting a marked jump in the perceived existential threat posed by the outgroup around a year before the onset of genocide. It also acknowledges, however, the likelihood of a nation remaining poised on the brink of genocide for some months before its outbreak.

Finally, variations in the strength of the perception of the outgroup as an existential threat provide a further means of assessing the development of risk of genocide over time, as well as once again highlighting the importance of this critical factor in the process. This single factor is closely linked to several key escalations in the risk of genocide. The emergence of a perception of the outgroup as an existential threat to the dominant power precedes the limited violence against the outgroup usually associated with stage four of the model. As a society might cycle through this stage several times, each time the violence will be preceded by an increase in the perception of the group as a threat. Indeed, the process of escalation at stage five, leading to the emergence of a genocidal ideology, is closely linked to a growing perception of the outgroup as an intractable threat for which there is no other recourse. A central goal of the propaganda campaign is to legitimize the genocidal ideology, using the supposed existential threat to do so. And in the final stage prior to the outbreak of genocide, there is a further spike to the perceived threat of the outgroup—with propaganda presenting it as a grave and imminent threat, and the proposed course of action as necessary self-defence. Thus, monitoring the strength of this perception within a society offers a parallel approach to assessing the development of risk factors for genocide over time.

Beyond offering an improved understanding of how risk factors for genocide develop over time, the temporal model also provides a new perspective on inhibitory factors that may delay or prevent the onset of genocide. These will be explored in further detail in the following chapter.

Notes

Sections of this chapter originally appeared in Deborah Mayersen. 2010. 'On the Timing of Genocide', *Genocide Studies and Prevention* 5(1), 20–38, and are reprinted with permission from University of Toronto Press. © 2010 *Genocide Studies and Prevention*. doi: 10.3138/gsp.5.1.20

1. O. Gaidzakian. 1898. *Illustrated Armenia and the Armenians*, Boston: n.p., 205; M.G. Rolin-Jaequemyns. 1891. *Armenia, The Armenians, and the Treaties*, London: John Heywood, 70; M. Mac-Coll. 1895. *England's Responsibility Towards Armenia*, London: Longmans, Green, iii.

2. United Nations. 1962. *Question of the Future of Ruanda-Urundi: Statement Made by Mr. Majid Rahnema, United Nations Commissioner for Ruanda-Urundi, at the 1265th Meeting of the Fourth Committee*, A/C.4/525, 23 January, 17.

3. D. Mayersen. 2010. 'On the Timing of Genocide', *Genocide Studies and Prevention* 5(1), 20–38.

4. H. Fein. 1979. *Accounting for Genocide: National Responses and Jewish Victimization during the Holocaust*, New York: Free Press, 9; F. Mazian. 1990. *Why Genocide? The Armenian and Jewish Experiences in Perspective*, Ames: Iowa State University Press, ix–x.

5. Fein, *Accounting for Genocide*, 9.

6. L. Kuper. 1981. *Genocide: Its Political Use in the Twentieth Century*, New Haven, CT: Yale University Press, 57–58.

7. A. Twagilimana. 2003. *The Debris of Ham: Ethnicity, Regionalism, and the 1994 Rwandan Genocide*, Lanham, MD: University Press of America, 99.

8. R. Melson. 1992. *Revolution and Genocide: On the Origins of the Armenian Genocide and the Holocaust*, Chicago: University of Chicago Press, 65; J. Bryce. 1896. *Transcaucasia and Ararat: Being Notes of a Vacation Tour in the Autumn of 1876*, rev. 4th ed., London: Macmillan, 458; F. Greene. 1896. *Armenian Massacres or The Sword of Mohammed*, n.p.: American Oxford, 435.

9. Rwanda, Ministère des Affaires Étrangères. 1964. *Toute la vérité sur le terrorisme "Inyenzi" au Rwanda: Une mise au point du Ministère des Affaires Étrangères du Rwanda*, Kigali: Services d'information, 13, 20.

10. E. Staub. 1989. *The Roots of Evil: The Origins of Genocide and Other Group Violence*, Cambridge: Cambridge University Press, 17.

11. V. Dadrian. 1998. 'The Armenian Genocide and the Legal and Political Issues in the Failure to Prevent or to Punish the Crime', *University of West Los Angeles Law Review* 29, 48.

12. Melson, *Revolution and Genocide*, 166.

13. G.S. Graber. 1996. *Caravans to Oblivion: The Armenian Genocide 1915*, New York: J. Wiley, 45; H. Morgenthau. 2000. *Ambassador Morgenthau's Story*, Ann Arbor, MI: Gomidas Institute, 229 (originally published 1918).

14. R. Lemarchand. 2003. 'Comparing the Killing Fields', in S. Jensen (ed.), *Genocide: Cases, Comparisons and Contemporary Debates*, Copenhagen: Danish Centre for Holocaust and Genocide Studies, 158.

15. Rwanda, Ministère des Affaires Étrangères, *Toute la vérité*, 13.

16. A. Des Forges. 1999. *"Leave None to Tell the Story": Genocide in Rwanda*, New York: Human Rights Watch, 73.

17. Ibid., 65.

18. Twagilimana, *The Debris of Ham*, 112–13.
19. G. Prunier. 2001. 'Genocide in Rwanda', in D. Chirot and M. Seligman (eds), *Ethnopolitical Warfare: Causes, Consequences, and Possible Solutions*, Washington, D.C.: American Psychological Association, 115.
20. V. Dadrian. 1998. *Warrant for Genocide: Key Elements of Turko-Armenian Conflict*, New Brunswick, NJ: Transaction Publishers, 93–99.
21. Kuper, *Genocide*, 84; Fein, *Accounting for Genocide*, 9.
22. Mazian, *Why Genocide?*, ix.
23. Melson, *Revolution and Genocide*, 162.
24. Des Forges, *Genocide in Rwanda*, 73.
25. Ibid., 78.
26. Y. Ternon. 1981. *The Armenians: History of a Genocide*, Delmar, NY: Caravan Books, 178.
27. S. Sazonov. 1928. *Fateful Years: 1909–1916 The Reminiscences of Serge Sazonov*, London: Jonathan Cape, 136, 145.
28. V. Dadrian. 2003. 'The Armenian Genocide: An Interpretation', in J. Winter (ed.), *America and the Armenian Genocide of 1915*, Cambridge: Cambridge University Press, 62.

Chapter 8

'OUR ONLY HOPE, THEREFORE, RESTS ON THE OBSTACLE'

Constraints against Genocide

Genocide is a relatively rare phenomenon. Whilst the large numbers of victims of genocide in the past century highlight the catastrophic impact of every outbreak, nevertheless it is far less common than both intrastate and international warfare. Most wars do not lead to genocidal attacks upon the 'enemy', and most states do not seek to eliminate their minorities, even in the presence of long-standing divisions. This highlights that only in very specific circumstances will genocide erupt. As we have seen, such circumstances have typically been described and analysed through the prism of models of the preconditions of genocide. These models have substantial strengths in explaining the escalatory factors that lead to extreme violence, but are considerably weaker with respect to factors that may mitigate such risk. At best, some models may identify one or two mitigating factors, or highlight that partial fulfilment of preconditions is insufficient for genocide onset. Yet it is only through a much more direct focus on constraints that their critical role is apparent. Through explicitly highlighting the role of constraints, the temporal model offers a more comprehensive understanding of the timing of genocide, and of factors that may prevent or delay its onset. This chapter will explore the vital role of constraints. It will consider constraints as they have most commonly been conceptualized within current models, that is, as nonfulfilment or partial fulfilment of preconditions. Utilizing the temporal model, it will then analyse how a direct focus on the role of constraints can offer an improved understanding of the timing of the Armenian and Rwandan genocides, and a more compelling explanation as to why the pregenocidal massacres in each case did not escalate into genocide. It is only through incorporating a direct and explicit focus on constraints that a more comprehensive picture emerges.

Constraints or Nonfulfilment of Preconditions?

The most common way in which factors that mitigate genocide have been considered is as the nonfulfilment, or partial fulfilment, of preconditions. This conceptualization can be valuable in understanding why some high-risk situations do not escalate into genocide. For example, the Hamidian massacres only partially fulfilled some of the most widely accepted preconditions for genocide presented within various models. Certainly the Armenian minority was perceived as an outgroup, and the Ottoman Empire experienced substantial internal strife prior to the 1894–96 massacres. The further precondition of 'destructive uses of communication' (alternatively conceptualized as the use of propaganda, or incitement), however, was probably not fulfilled to the extent necessary for genocide (F. Mazian. 1990. *The Armenian and Jewish Experiences in Perspective*, AMES: Iowa State University Press, ix–x). This precondition may include components that assert the singular rights of the dominant group, and those that ideologically legitimize the genocide through dehumanizing the targeted group and justifying the genocide goals. It is clear that this precondition was partially fulfilled, prior to and during the Hamidian massacres, with several different types of destructive uses of communication in use. The most obvious is the use of propaganda. For example, Turkish and Moslem officials commonly described Armenians as 'dogs', which served as a tactic of dehumanization.[1] The perceived Armenian superiority in financial matters was attributed to a vicious and cunning Armenian character, increasing the dissociation by the Turks and thereby lessening the barriers to the massacres.[2] Immediately before the massacres, reports were circulated in some areas—often by Moslem clerics—that the Armenians were preparing an uprising, and would probably be supported by the European governments.[3] This, combined with the religious underpinning of the society, provided a justification for massacre.

There is particularly strong evidence of destructive uses of communication in the months preceding the 1895 massacres. Ottoman provincial officials misrepresented the Scheme of Armenian Reforms, which contained almost nothing not previously granted, and used it to create even further enmity between Moslems and Christians.[4] In Aleppo, the reforms were misrepresented to the extent that the Armenians believed that new privileges would be conferred upon them, while the Moslems believed they would be placed in a position of inferiority to the Christians.[5] In Ourfa, the news of the acceptance of the reforms was reported to the Turkish population as the granting of autonomy to the Armenians—an interpretation that Lepsius charged as originating from government officials.[6] This had 'a disastrous effect' on Moslem-Armenian relations, and was combined with rumours that the Armenians were attacking mosques and using dynamite in other Anatolian towns.[7] The British ambassador repeatedly pressed the sultan to publish the Scheme of Armenian Reforms and thereby clear up the misunderstandings; however, the sultan refused to do so.[8] Thus, destructive uses of communication that dehumanized the Armenians and attempted to justify the massacres can clearly be identified. Yet in comparison with the types and volume of destructive communication prior to and during instances of genocide, the propaganda of this period was generally less intense and less extreme. This suggests that this precondition was only partially fulfilled, and not to the extent necessary for genocide.

The approach of considering constraints as partial or nonfulfilment of preconditions goes some way towards explaining why the Hamidian massacres did not escalate into an attempt to eliminate the Armenian minority. Arguably, however, it precludes a focus on factors that were of more direct impact, and that can be more clearly analysed through an explicit focus on constraints, as the following section demonstrates.

The Role of Constraints

Directly focussing on the role of constraints alongside that of escalatory factors offers a more comprehensive and compelling understanding of the path that leads to genocide than the current dominant focus on preconditions. Constraints play a crucial role in determining both whether and when genocide will occur in an at-risk nation. The temporal model highlights three particularly important stages in which the role of constraints is vital. First, at stage four of the model, in which the nation is experiencing significant internal strife and perceives an outgroup as posing an existential threat, local precipitants and constraints will determine the nature and severity of the response to that perceived threat. Similarly, at stage seven of the model, when a nation is poised on the brink of genocide, case-specific precipitants and constraints will determine its timing. Perhaps most important, however, is the role of constraints at stage five, when either a process of retreat or escalation will be considered following a limited outbreak of violence. It is during this unstable stage, when leaders are considering how to manage their minority populations in circumstances of intergroup violence, internal strife and perceived threat, that the presence or absence of constraints plays a key role in determining whether a process of retreat or escalation will be pursued. In the cases of the Armenian and Rwandan genocides, and the pregenocidal massacres that preceded them, constraints played a crucial role in determining the events that transpired. Three particular constraints can be identified as of particular importance: international factors, capacity to conduct genocide and ideological factors. Each of these will be explored in turn. Only by actively considering the role of constraints can a model of the preconditions of genocide offer a comprehensive analysis of when and if genocide is likely to occur in an at-risk nation.

International Factors

The prospect of international intervention appears to be a leading constraint that inhibits genocide. In the case of the Hamidian massacres, it is clear that this was a substantial inhibitory factor. The threat of European intervention—even if unrealized—effectively limited any escalation of the massacres into genocide. This threat had been present since the very genesis of the 'Armenian question'. As outlined earlier, there is strong evidence that the Ottoman government perceived the Armenian minority as an existential threat from the late 1870s, but was constrained from targeting them for fear of European intervention on their behalf. The recent history of the Russo-Turkish war meant that the Ottoman government viewed such intervention as a very real possibility. By the time of the Hamidian massacres, the Ottoman government had growing confidence that it could act with impunity, but only to a limited extent. When the massacre in Constantinople in 1896 led to a heightened perception of the risk of European intervention, not only did it quickly abate, but there were no further outbreaks of large-scale violence. This is in stark contrast to the rapid spread of massacres throughout Anatolia in 1895, when the Great Powers failed to respond concertedly.

Arguably, the threat of European intervention significantly shaped the onset and severity of most of the anti-Armenian violence between the 1880s and the 1915 genocide. It is hard to overestimate the significance of the removal of this constraint. The American traveller to Ottoman Armenia George Hepworth remarked in 1898:

> The hand of Turkey has been restrained for reasons of expediency, but it is the same hand, and it has not lost its cunning. If 'the Turk' could have his own way, unhampered by the public opinion of Europe, there would neither be an Armenian nor a missionary in Anatolia at the end of twenty years, for both are equally obnoxious.[9]

He then went on to make a prescient observation:

> When the lapse of time brings inevitable forgetfulness of past horrors, when the Powers have too much business on hand to give attention to Turkish affairs, the sword will once again be unsheathed. I am neither a prophet nor the son of a prophet, but when an avalanche has started, and is stopped halfway by some obstacle, it is logical to declare that the avalanche will continue its destructive journey whenever the obstacle is removed. The desire to destroy remains in the avalanche all the time, and our only hope, therefore, rests on the obstacle.[10]

There is no doubt that the outbreak of the First World War was crucial to the onset of the Armenian genocide. The war removed the threat of international intervention, the key constraint that had limited the scope and extent of anti-Armenian violence since the inception of the 'Armenian question'. It is only through considering the role of international factors as a key constraint that a comprehensive understanding of the causes and timing of the Hamidian massacres and Armenian genocide emerges.

International factors were also a significant constraint in the case of the massacres in Rwanda in December 1963–January 1964. The Rwandan government was keenly aware of the observation of the international community in this immediate postindependence period. It was also particularly cognizant of UNAR's easy recourse to international protest, and particularly to the United Nations. In the immediate wake of the Bugesera invasion, Rwanda appealed for international assistance in defending itself. Telegrams were sent to the United Nations and the Organization of African Unity, although it soon became apparent that assistance would not be forthcoming. Investigation, however, would be. UN Commissioner Max Dorsinville arrived with astonishing speed after the outbreak of the massacres; he was in Rwanda from late December to early January as the massacres were underway, and again in February following their cessation. The Kayibanda government appears to have had some degree of fear that UNAR's noisy international appeals regarding the violence—even after its cessation—were an attempt to delegitimize its sovereignty and trigger international intervention. In an impassioned speech on 28 January 1964, President Kayibanda accused the 'neo-colonialists' of pursuing false accusations of genocide to provoke installation of UN forces and the return of foreign military forces in Rwanda.[11] This highlights that the government perceived that any continuation or escalation of the violence could place its sovereignty at risk—a most compelling constraint indeed.

The role of international factors prior to the 1994 genocide stands in stark contrast to that during the 1963–64 massacres. There is widespread recognition that the international community could, and should, have acted to prevent or curb this genocide, but failed to do so. The report commissioned by the Organization of African Unity in the aftermath of the genocide was entitled 'Rwanda: The Preventable Genocide', and highlights over several chapters the many actions that might have been taken.[12] Similarly, the independent enquiry into the actions of the United Nations during the genocide noted:

> The failure by the United Nations to prevent, and subsequently, to stop the genocide in Rwanda was a failure by the United Nations system as a whole. The fundamental failure was the lack of resources and political commitment devoted to developments in Rwanda and to the United Nations presence there. There was a persistent lack of political will by Member States to act, or to act with enough assertiveness.[13]

There were many warnings of impending genocide, and many opportunities for a stronger international response. As outlined earlier, Hutu extremists even appeared to test the international response to anti-Tutsi violence in the early 1990s, with several small-scale massacres prior to the genocide. Many nongovernmental orga-nization (NGO) and even UN reports gave advance warning of the potential for genocide, but were largely ignored. A January 1994 article in the extremist Rwandan newspaper *Kangura*—whose well-connected editors often predicted key events in the country—even appears to have directly considered the prospect of international intervention in the event of genocide, and concluded that it would be possible to proceed with genocide despite the presence of UNAMIR forces.[14] The 1994 genocide was notable for the complete failure of international actors to act as a constraint.

Capacity to Conduct Genocide

The lack of capacity of a regime to conduct genocide can be a compelling con-straint. The massive scale of genocide requires the potential perpetrators to have a high degree of control over the government, a high level of centralization of power, army or militia forces of sufficient power to conduct genocide, the ability to disseminate large volumes of propaganda to justify the genocide and a raft of other organizational requirements. Essentially, a regime has to consider whether it has sufficient power to have a realistic chance of successfully pursuing a genocidal policy. A regime lacking sufficient capacity to conduct genocide will likely refrain from contemplating doing so.

The case studies of the pregenocidal massacres in the Ottoman Empire and Rwanda highlight the inhibitory role of a lack of capacity to conduct genocide. At the time of the Hamidian massacres, for example, the Ottoman Empire was finan-cially destitute, had lost significant territory and was subject to the oversight of the Great Powers of Europe. The potential costs to the empire of exterminating the Armenians—such as European intervention leading to Russian occupation of the Armenian provinces (which it lacked the capacity to defend) were extremely high. The Ottoman government did not have the capacity to both conduct genocide and be sure of retaining its sovereignty. As a result, it could not pursue a genocidal campaign. Similarly, the Rwandan government in 1963 did not have anything like the entrenched power required to contemplate genocide. With a poorly equipped army of just one thousand men, it had been deeply shocked and threatened by the very small and even less equipped force that comprised the Bugesera invasion. In the absence of any conceivable means to initiate a genocide, such a course of action could not even be contemplated.

In contrast to the weakness of the late Ottoman Empire and newly independent Rwanda, both the Young Turks and the Habyarimana regime were able to prepare for genocide from positions of much greater strength. The extremist faction of the Young Turks had firm control of the country by 1914, and was able to obviate the threat of European intervention through entering into the First World War. Furthermore, military mobilization enabled the government to separate Armenian men of military age from their families, to disarm them and ultimately to kill them with minimal resistance. Similarly, the civil war in Rwanda in the early 1990s enabled the Habyarimana regime to massively expand its armed forces, import large numbers of weapons and spread anti-Tutsi propaganda throughout the country. The high levels of centralization of power in Rwanda and the hegemony of the *akuzu* also facilitated the genocide.

It is also worth noting that Rummel's extensive quantitative work on the role of democracy in inhibiting genocide appears to be related to the requirement that nations possess sufficient power to seriously contemplate a genocidal strategy.[15] Genuine democracies, by nature, permit the dissemination of opposing viewpoints, and voting processes can remove a leadership from its position of power. Thus, democratic leaders (unless possessed of sufficient power and intention to overthrow the democratic system in their country) have insufficient power to contemplate genocide. According to Rummel and others, therefore, there has never been a genocide in a functioning democracy, or at least not against an enfranchised population therein.[16] This offers an explanation for the strongly protective role of democracy in mitigating the risk of genocide.

Ideological Factors

The third factor that emerged as a constraint in the Armenian and Rwandan cases is the role of ideology. Ideological factors are typically conceptualized as an escalatory factor in models of the preconditions of genocide, and indeed they often function as such. On closer inspection, however, the role of ideological factors can be more complex. The absence of a genocidal ideology may function not only as a passive constraint—that is, as the lack of fulfilment of a precondition—but as a factor that actively inhibits escalation and promotes retreat to lower levels of risk. Additionally, ideological factors can act as an intermediary variable, facilitating or inhibiting other processes on the path to genocide. Moreover, there can be a dialectic relationship between ideological and other factors that together combine to result in an escalation or reduction of risk of genocide. Some examples will elucidate the complex and sometimes inhibitory role of ideological factors further.

During the Hamidian massacres, for example, the ideology that legitimized the massacres was not a genocidal ideology, and contributed to preventing the escalation of the massacres into a wider attempt to eliminate the Armenian minority as a whole. As has been previously elucidated, the ideology of the *millet* system was inherently dangerous for the Armenians, allocating them only the status and rights of second-class citizens. Under this ideology, when they were perceived to have usurped their rightful place within the system, they lost the right to life and property. Thus, in the context of the Armenian renaissance, European intervention in Ottoman affairs and the increasing religiosity of the empire under Sultan Abdul Hamid II, the ideology legitimized the massacres. Yet this ideology did not actively exclude the Armenians, or singularly assert the rights of the dominant Moslem population. That is, there remained a legitimate place for the Armenians to exist within the *millet* system. The ideology justified massacre, but only under certain conditions. The massacres themselves changed those conditions. For example, by reducing the numbers of Armenians the massacres effectively resolved the issue of proportionate representation within the Scheme of Armenian Reforms; plunder reduced the Armenians to financial inferiority; and the European inaction effectively rendered meaningless any promises of civic equality. Once these conditions were changed, the ideology no longer justified further massacre as a strategy. The ideology that had proved so dangerous for the Armenians thus ultimately also functioned as a protective factor.

Ideological factors also played an inhibitory role in the 1963–64 massacres in Rwanda. Over decades of colonial rule, the Hamitic hypothesis had been widely promulgated and internalized within Rwanda. As previously discussed, the hypothesis posited the Tutsi to be racially distinct, racially superior and subjugators of foreign origin. While the profound changes in Rwanda during the decolonization process went some way towards challenging this hypothesis, nevertheless the legacy of its long internalization within Rwandan society continued. This legacy had the potential to facilitate genocide, as it subsequently did prior to the 1994 genocide; however, in the immediate postindependence period it also functioned as a constraint. In a society in which Tutsi privilege had been long entrenched and was still being dismantled, it was arguably inconceivable to posit a Rwanda in which Tutsi did not have the right to live. For Hutu, the concept of a Rwanda in which they had equal rights, equal access to resources and democratic representation was itself a radical ideological change. Taking that further to exclude Tutsi completely was unthinkable at that time.

Ideology can also play a more complex role than might be expected, even when that ideology is one that promulgates genocide. Evidence from the Armenian and Rwandan case studies suggests that a genocidal ideology emerges (or moves from the fringes to mainstream society) relatively close to the time of the outbreak of genocide. This suggests that, to some extent at least, ideology only becomes a driving factor after stage five of the temporal model, when a process of escalation is already underway. That is, ideological factors can function as an intermediary variable. If a nation is constrained at this stage from pursuing a path towards genocide, such an ideology is unlikely to emerge. When, however, it does emerge, typically the ideology both justifies and drives escalatory processes. The relationship between ideology and other escalatory factors is thus a dialectical one. It may also become increasingly radical and specifically 'genocidal' over time. For example, the doctrine of extreme Turkish nationalism radicalized following its emergence, and propaganda increasingly posed the Armenians as primed to rebel, treasonous and a grave threat to the Moslem population. This was a substantial change from earlier pan-Turkish ideology, which excluded the Armenians as non-Turkish, but did not directly attempt to justify targeting them in a genocidal campaign. Ideological factors, therefore, need to be recognized as factors that can not only drive escalatory processes, but also play an intermediary and even inhibitory role in certain circumstances.

As this chapter has demonstrated, understanding the important role of constraints is critical to understanding the timing of genocide. It also explains factors that may prevent the outbreak of genocide in at-risk nations. Models of the preconditions for genocide have typically focussed overwhelmingly or exclusively on escalatory factors. While these have provided great insight into the path that leads to genocide, they provide an incomplete understanding of these processes. Elucidating the role of constraints provides much greater insight into the often nonlinear progression of the risk of genocide, and the factors that may prevent its onset even in circumstances of grave risk. These may include international factors, issues surrounding capacity or ideological factors. They may also be factors unique to a particular society. The temporal model, through incorporating constraints as an integral component, offers a more comprehensive understanding of the risk of genocide.

Notes

1. F. Greene. 1896. *Armenian Massacres or The Sword of Mohammed*, n.p.: American Oxford, 423; E. Bliss. 1896. *Turkey and The Armenian Atrocities*, Boston: H.L. Hastings, 555.
2. S. Astourian. 1992. 'Genocidal Process: Reflections on the Armeno-Turkish Polarization', in R. Hovannisian (ed.), *The Armenian Genocide: History, Politics, Ethics*, New York: St. Martin's Press, 59–60.
3. Bliss, *Turkey and the Armenian Atrocities*, 556; J. Bryce. 1896. *Transcaucasia and Ararat: Being Notes of a Vacation Tour in the Autumn of 1876*, rev. 4th ed., London: Macmillan, 506.
4. Ibid.
5. Ibid.
6. J. Lepsius. 1897. *Armenia and Europe: An Indictment*, London: Hodder and Stoughton, 158.
7. Ibid.
8. Bryce, *Transcaucasia and Ararat*, 506.
9. G. Hepworth. 1898. *Through Armenia on Horseback*, New York: E.P. Dutton, 340.
10. Ibid., 341.
11. Rwanda, Ministère des Affaires Étrangères. 1964. *Toute la vérité sur le terrorisme "Inyenzi" au Rwanda: Une mise au point du Ministère des Affaires Étrangères du Rwanda*, Kigali: Services d'information, annex 4.
12. Organization of African Unity, *Rwanda: The Preventable Genocide*, July 2000. Retrieved 12 April 2013 from http://www.africaunion.org/official_documents/reports/report_rowanda_genocide.pdf
13. United Nations Security Council. 1999. *Report of the Independent Inquiry into the Actions of the United Nations during the 1994 Genocide in Rwanda*, S/1999/1257, 16 December. Retrieved 12 February 2012 from http://daccess-dds-ny.un.org/doc/UNDOC/GEN/N99/395/47/IMG/N9939547.pdf?OpenElement

14. African Rights. 1995. *Rwanda: Death, Despair and Defiance,* rev. ed., London: African Rights, 71–73.

15. R.J. Rummel. 1995. 'Democracy, Power, Genocide and Mass Murder', *Journal of Conflict Resolution* 39(1), 3–26.

16. G. Stanton. 2005. 'Early Warning', in D. Shelton (ed.), *Encyclopedia of Genocide and Crimes Against Humanity,* Detroit, Mich.: Macmillan Reference, 271–73. Retrieved 4 October 2007 from http://www.genocidewatch.org/aboutus/stantonearlywarningarticle.htm; N. Riemer. 1998. 'Protection Against Genocide: Towards a Global Human Rights Regime', in S. Feinstein, K. Schierman and M. Littell (eds), *Confronting the Holocaust: A Mandate for the 21st Century—Part Two,* Lanham, MD: University Press of America, 300.

Chapter 9

'A PATTERN . . . REPEATED NUMEROUS TIMES'
The Wider Applicability of the Temporal Model

A key question concerning the usefulness of the temporal model in understanding how risk factors for genocide develop over time is that of its broader applicability beyond the Armenian and Rwandan cases. There are compelling reasons to suggest it may have such broader applicability. First, several risk factors within the model have parallels within other models of the preconditions for genocide, which themselves have been developed through comparative analysis of a wide range of case studies. These include the Holocaust, the Cambodian genocide and the mass killings in Argentina. Second, the dissimilarities between the Armenian and Rwandan case studies utilized to develop the temporal model suggest the findings are likely to be robust across other diverse examples as well. These genocides (and the events preceding them) contrast on several key variables, including the basis of exclusion (that is, religious or ethnic difference), the occurrence of genocide within the context of global war, the level of pregenocidal propaganda, and geographic and temporal location. To some extent, it is an inherent limitation of models that they present 'ideal types' rather than reflecting the complex and fluid dynamics of specific situations—and particularly so for circumstances as extreme as those involving genocide. Nevertheless, assessing the wider applicability of the temporal model is critical to determining its value. In this chapter, therefore, the model will be briefly tested against two additional contemporary case studies: the genocide in Darfur and the nongenocidal but at-risk example of the position of ethnic Haitians in the Dominican Republic. From these examples, it is possible to make further conclusions on the wider applicability of the temporal model of the preconditions for genocide.

Darfur

The first example is that of Darfur. As a contemporary case of genocide, this provides a potentially challenging test for the temporal model. Yet, as Prunier has remarked, 'It is a cliché that Sudan is a complex country, and the problem with clichés is the element of truth which gave rise to them in the first place.'[1] Moreover, whilst the majority of scholars of genocide recognize the events in Darfur as such, this is often done with some qualification. Prunier has termed it 'the ambiguous genocide' and 'quasi-genocide'—genocide according to the definition in the 1948 Genocide Convention but not his own definition.[2] Alex de Waal and others have suggested the crisis is more complex than the genocide label would suggest—de Waal goes so far as to remark that while it was genocide strictly according to the UN definition, it does not fit the spirit of the Genocide Convention.[3] Darfur is a case of genocide, it seems, but an atypical one. Cognizant of this conjecture, and the complex nature of this example, a brief analysis will nevertheless be presented.

Darfur is a vast region in western Sudan, spanning approximately 250,000 square kilometres and home to around six million people. Whilst most of the inhabitants are Moslem, there is a multiplicity of ethnic groups. Groups such as the Fur, Masalit and many others have traditionally been the sedentary agriculturalists in the region, referred to as 'African' groups. Pastoralist, nomadic and seminomadic tribes, including the Beni Hussein, northern Rizeigat and others, are generally of Arab descent, and are referred to as 'Arab' tribes. Many aspects of these identities, however, are ideological constructions of the twentieth century rather than reflective of any visible racial difference.[4]

In seeking to identify an outgroup in historical Darfur, as the first precondition for genocide, it is tempting to classify all Darfurians as such. The region was consistently neglected under British colonial rule; little changed following Sudan's independence in 1956. A succession of Sudanese governments in Khartoum continued to marginalize and neglect Darfur, while it was repeatedly rocked by the encroachment of neighbouring wars.[5] Ultimately, however, it was the African tribes that became an outgroup in Darfur. Ethnic tensions between Arab and African groups spiked in the mid-1980s as a result of three factors. A severe drought and famine in 1984–85 led to clashes between the pastoralists and agriculturalists for the scarce resources available. At the same time, the region was flooded with arms from Libya. The traditional system of law and justice was overwhelmed by the influx of weapons, and an epidemic of crime followed.[6] Meanwhile, an Arab supremacist ideology had taken root and begun to be an important political influence.[7] By the latter part of the 1980s, these factors led to a civil war erupting between the Arab and African groups in Darfur. By 1989, some three thousand people had been killed—predominantly African Fur—and 'each side accused the other of being driven by ethnic exclusivism'.[8] It was not really until the 1990s, however, when the Sudanese government began stripping the Fur and other African groups of their access to power, whilst at the same time augmenting that of the Arab tribes, that the African groups took on all the features of a true outgroup.

There were many sources of internal strife operative in both Darfur and Sudan as a whole, which rapidly served to escalate the situation further. These included the long-running Sudanese civil war, ongoing from 1983; the continual spillover of the Chadian-Libyan war; and further drought in the region. Events were also strongly influenced by Khartoum. As Human Rights Watch has elucidated:

> In a pattern that was to be repeated numerous times throughout the 1990s, rather than working to defuse tensions and implement peace agreements, the Khartoum government inflamed tensions by arming the Arab tribes and neglecting the core issues underlying the conflict over resources: the need for rule of law and socio-economic development in the region.[9]

Following the Arab-Fur civil war, there was a decrease in the level of violence in the first part of the 1990s. Nevertheless, the risk profile for genocide increased, as the African tribes came to be increasingly perceived as posing an existential threat to an Arabist Sudan. Darfur became the object of a fierce ideological campaign. In what Flint and de Waal have described as an ambitious project of social transformation, designed to create a new Islamist constituency, 'a raft of programmes aimed at building an Islamic Republic was launched'.[10] This included efforts to create heightened Islamic consciousness, down to the level of every village.[11] The spread of this ideology combined with the relative strength of the African tribes as an outgroup—including their strength in violent clashes—to increase perceptions of the 'Africans' as an existential threat. Recurring droughts, and the resulting clashes over scarce resources, exacerbated the situation.[12] As Prunier has noted:

> The fact that the pace of the violence slowed down somewhat during the 1990s did not change that basic outlook. The state of ethnic relations resulting from the frantic ideological manipulation of that period remained a permanent threat to non-Arabs in the province.[13]

Meanwhile, administrative reforms in Darfur significantly reduced the power of both the Fur and Masalit tribes at official levels, whilst new administrative posts were given to Arabs.[14] With these risk factors operable in Darfur (an outgroup, significant internal strife and perceptions of the outgroup as posing an existential threat), precipitants and restraints governed repeated outbreaks of violence of varying intensity. Indeed, as Prunier has acknowledged, 'Since 1985 Darfur had been a time-bomb waiting for a fuse.'[15]

By the late 1990s, the conflict was steadily worsening. As Daly remarked, 'the Fur, Zaghawa, and Masalit . . . [were] the focus of ever-increasing violence from Arab militias, and pleas for government protection fell on deaf ears or were even punished'.[16] Hundreds of Masalit villages were burnt and by the end of 1998, over one hundred thousand Masalit had fled to Chad.[17] Self-defence groups had emerged in response to the ongoing conflict, and in 2001–2 they organized themselves as the Sudan Liberation Movement/Army (SLM/A) and the Justice and Equality Movement (JEM). Both stood in opposition to the Khartoum government's socioeconomic and political marginalization of Darfur.[18] The rebel movements began attacking government targets in late 2002. In April 2003, the Sudanese government was shocked by the rebel attack in Eli Fashir, the capital of North Darfur, in which rebels destroyed five military aircraft and occupied the airport. According to Prunier, 'In an atmosphere charged with racism an armed rebellion by the "inferior" group is fraught with enormous danger for the civilians of that group.'[19] Suddenly, the rebels were perceived as a serious existential threat to Sudan. According to a 2004 Human Rights Watch report: 'Civilian as well as military authorities in the current government are said to consider the Darfur rebellion as a "regime threat". The rebels pose . . . [a] menace to their hold on office.'[20] Moreover, with the rank and file of the Sudanese military composed largely of Darfurians, who could not be fully trusted in this circumstance (at least until carefully screened), although officers were mostly Arab, there was no obvious military solution.[21] This perceived existential threat contributed to the escalation of the conflict to genocidal proportions.[22]

Things intensified very quickly. In May 2003, the Sudanese president assembled a Special Task Force on Darfur to respond to the crisis. The task force decided upon a quasi-genocidal strategy, co-opting the ideology of Arab supremacy. The Arab supremacist ideology developed into an ideology of advocating exclusive Arab rights to the land of Darfur. According to one communiqué later issued by the *Janjaweed* (Arab militia), the Sudanese president had issued directives 'to change the demography of Darfur and empty it of African tribes'.[23] Neither the ideology nor the goal can be described as completely genocidal, with elements of both ethnic cleansing—that is, forced collective displacement—and genocide present.[24] Following the elucidation of this ideology, the government sought the power to enact it. A major strategy was to formalize its relationship with the already existing *Janjaweed* militias. The *Janjaweed*, rough bands of Arab militia who had previously enjoyed some support from the Sudanese government due to their pro-Arab position, were now given arms, training, regular army uniforms and regular salaries, including large numbers of new recruits.[25] Later, they began to operate in cooperation with the regular army, as various units were screened for trustworthiness. [26]

The next stage predicted by the temporal model is that of a massive propaganda campaign. Whilst there is not a lot of easily obtainable information on the use of propaganda in Darfur during this period, there is strong evidence from survivor accounts that the army and *Janjaweed* had received and internalized crucial statements legitimizing their actions. For example, as one survivor recounted:

The *Janjaweed* were accompanied by soldiers. They attacked the people, saying: 'You are opponents to the regime, we must crush you. As you are Black, you are like slaves. Then the entire Darfur region will be in the hands of the Arabs. The government is on our side. The government plane is on our side, it gives us food and ammunition.'[27]

What official propaganda there was, however, confirmed the claim of the situation in Darfur as posing an existential threat. Thus, a pro-government Sudanese newspaper declared in January 2004: 'The unity of the Sudan is in danger because London and Washington want to reproduce in Darfur the peace agreement signed with the South which schedules power- and wealth-sharing, self-determination and an international monitoring system.'[28] Like the perpetrators of the Rwandan and Armenian genocides, the Sudanese government attempted to present their genocidal campaign as self-defence, 'branding the [rebel] insurgency as an African attempt to rid Darfur of the "Arab race"'.[29]

The violence exploded in July 2003.[30] It was not just counterinsurgency against the rebel movements: civilians were a central target. Villages were bombed from the air, surrounded by *Janjaweed* and sometimes regular soldiers as well, then looted and often burnt to the ground. Sometimes men and boys would be executed; at other times, anyone who could not run away was killed.[31] Women were frequently raped.[32] By 2005, over eight hundred villages had been damaged or destroyed.[33] Very quickly, refugee camps sprang up, and became overcrowded with survivors from such attacks. As the violence has waxed and waned since mid-2003, a further strategy of the government of Sudan has become 'genocide by attrition'—fostering huge mortality in the camps through preventing food and medical aid from reaching the refugees.[34] By the end of 2004, a UN official estimated that '10,000 people per month were dying in the camps'.[35] Recent estimates suggest at least three hundred thousand Darfurians have been killed in the conflict.[36] Yet, as Prunier has noted, while genocidal elements were present, 'it was not an attempt to kill everybody; rather it was a matter of large-scale attacks and massacres aimed at terrorising and displacing the population'.[37] Nevertheless, both the massive death toll and the indictment of Sudanese president Omar al-Bashir on the charge of genocide by the International Criminal Court highlight the severity of events in Darfur.

The brief analysis presented above suggests that the temporal model of the risk factors for genocide is applicable to the case of Darfur. The key elements of the model can all be identified. Particularly noticeable is the central role of perceptions of the outgroup as posing an existential threat in driving the escalation of the crisis. That is, it was only when Sudanese government authorities came to view the Darfur rebellion as a 'regime threat' that their response escalated to genocidal proportions.[38] Ideological and propaganda elements are also present. Whilst they are not quite as strongly ubiquitous as prior to the Rwandan genocide, for example, this appears to be reflective of the less ideologically extreme nature of the situation. That is, while there have clearly been genocidal acts committed in Darfur, the central thrust of the campaign appears to be more one of ethnic cleansing than genocide. This might also explain the relatively rapid escalation of the situation in 2003. The less ideologically extreme nature of ethnic cleansing may meet fewer psychological barriers in its path, enabling more rapid progression through the escalation process. Other factors, such as the perceived immediacy of the existential threat and the extreme isolation of Darfur (reducing the likelihood of a public outcry) may have also played a role. Broadly speaking, however, and within the limits of the very brief analysis of this complex situation that has been conducted, it is reasonable to conclude that the temporal model is applicable to the crisis in Darfur.

The Dominican Republic

The second example chosen to assess the broader applicability of the temporal model is that of a nongenocidal but at-risk society, the Dominican Republic. The Dominican Republic, in the Caribbean, shares the island of Hispaniola with its much poorer neighbour, Haiti. Of the Dominican Republic's estimated nine million inhabitants, up to one million are Haitian or of Haitian descent.[39] Yet the position of Haitians in the Dominican Republic is so politicized that these figures are controversial. According to Michele Wucker:

> The Dominican politicians say there are a million—many, many more than the 300,000 to 500,000 Haitians that more judicious scholars have estimated. The more Haitians there seem to be, the more righteous a senatorial or mayorial candidate sounds when he pledges to protect Dominicans from the black hordes.[40]

Whatever their number, they can be regarded as an 'outgroup'. Indeed, in the Dominican Republic today, this group exhibits all the features of an outgroup as defined by the temporal model. Many ethnic Haitians born in the Dominican Republic are legally discriminated against and denied citizenship, despite the Dominican Constitution's declaration of their citizenship rights. Ethnic Haitian children are denied education in the Dominican Republic's education system, or denied opportunities for advancement to secondary or tertiary education. All ethnic Haitians—and even Dominicans who are regarded as having a 'black' Haitian appearance—are at constant risk of being deported without any kind of due process—even if they do possess Dominican citizenship documents. This outgroup is also regularly used as a political tool by Dominican politicians for party political ends. The group remains exceptionally powerless. Without official Dominican documents, ethnic Haitians cannot vote, gain access to any but the most poorly paid jobs or even obtain a driver's licence. The issue of documentation is a critical one: whilst some ethnic Haitians are illegal immigrants, many are systematically denied citizenship documents and rights despite being born in the Dominican Republic and legally entitled to citizenship.

There is a long, deeply rooted history of anti-Haitian sentiment in the Dominican Republic.[41] The nation repelled a twenty-two-year occupation by Haiti, from 1822 to 1844, to claim independence—a history still manipulated by the elite to present Haitians as invaders and a potentially dangerous threat to Dominican society.[42] In the late 1800s, Haitian migration to the Dominican Republic commenced to provide labour for the sugar industry. Even at this early stage, Haitian culture was presented as backwards and as an obstacle to Dominican attempts at modernization.[43] Haitians in the Dominican Republic can thus be defined as an outgroup from the time of their first arrival. By the 1920s, some Dominican intellectuals were portraying Haitian migration to the frontier regions of the Dominican Republic as a 'pacific invasion' threatening the nation.[44] This presaged the first escalation of risk for Haitians, leading to the 1937 massacre—the severest anti-Haitian violence of the twentieth century.

The 1930s, after dictator Rafael Trujillo seized power in 1930, saw the northern frontier region become the locus of significant internal strife. There were ongoing border disputes with Haiti, not finally resolved until 1936. Dominican efforts to impose border controls, curb illicit trade, and impose tariffs and taxes to protect and grow the Dominican economy during the economic depression of the 1930s were all repeatedly frustrated.[45] The frontier region, with its ethnically mixed population far from the centre of political control, also presented serious challenges to attempts at nation building.[46] Finally, 'Trujillo was also deeply concerned that revolutionary exiles might launch an invasion across the Haitian-Dominican border and that the area would provide easy passage for illegal arms coming into the Dominican Republic.'[47] There was no doubt that the northern frontier region was a barrier to the success of the regime.

There is a long record of Dominican perceptions of Haiti and Haitians as an existential threat. The Trujillo regime contained a number of virulently anti-Haitian politicians, but, perhaps surprisingly, Trujillo was not initially amongst them.[48] It was only when Trujillo himself, as the key power holder, came to view ethnic Haitians as posing an existential threat to the Dominican Republic that the situation escalated to dangerous levels. The precipitant to this escalation appears to have been a tour of the frontier region undertaken by Trujillo in August and September of 1937.[49] In the wake of this tour, Trujillo unleashed an unprecedented massacre. Between 2 and 8 October 1937, somewhere between fifteen thousand and twenty thousand ethnic Haitians along the northern frontier of the Dominican Republic were rounded up and slaughtered.[50] Hundreds of Dominican troops perpetrated the massacre, primarily with machetes. At first, Haitians were allowed to escape across the border, but by 5 October, official checkpoints were closed, and the military slaughtered all those it caught trying to flee.[51] By the time Trujillo finally halted the massacre on 8 October, the region had been all but completely emptied of Haitians.[52] Later, he justified the massacre to the United States, Mexican and Cuban governments 'as a nationalist defense against the putative "pacific invasion" of Haitians', and as a response to 'the only threat that hovers over the future of our children'.[53] A further campaign in the first half of 1938 led to hundreds more Haitians being killed in the southern frontier region, and thousands forcibly deported.[54]

In many respects, the massacre was functionally successful from a Dominican perspective. It largely resolved the perceived existential threat posed by the border population, as it removed Haitians from the frontier and led to its 'Dominicanization'.[55] Additionally, the expected Haitian military response never materialized, nor was there any serious condemnation from the United States.[56] Trujillo enjoyed complete impunity in the wake of the massacre. While the situation retreated to a much lower risk level, with primarily only the first risk factor present, it ushered in decades of anti-Haitianism in both Dominican government and society.

The Dominican Republic has not experienced further outbreaks of anti-Haitian violence on the scale of the 1937 massacre. Arguably, this is because it has not faced any serious existential threats with which the Haitians could be closely linked during this time. An alternative explanation might consider the protective role of the affine government and population in neighbouring Haiti, which, as discussed in the introduction, Midlarsky has identified as a factor reducing victim vulnerability.[57] Nevertheless, the Dominican Republic has been clearly identified as a nation at ongoing risk of ethnic cleansing and/or genocide by Minorities at Risk.[58] The presence of an outgroup is well defined. Within Dominican public discourse, there is a recurring theme that presents ethnic Haitians as an existential threat—an ominous portent for future escalation. Joaquín Balaguer, Dominican president from 1966 to 1978 and again from 1986 to 1996, spoke of the threat of 'Haitian imperialism' and 'peaceful invasion', referring to contact with Haitians as leading to 'ethnic corruption' and 'ethnic decay'.[59] Even more remarkably, when 1994 presidential candidate Peña Gómez was alleged to have Haitian ancestry, some 31 per cent of Dominican respondents to an election campaign poll 'believed that national sovereignty could be at risk if Peña Gómez became president'.[60]

Several times in the past two decades there have been periods of internal strife, and each has been marked by an increased perception of ethnic Haitians as a threat and increased targeting of them. According to David Howard, 'During the 1990s, racism and nationalism became the basis for a racist agenda in internal Dominican politics.'[61] In this period, the targeting of Haitians typically took the format of mass deportations without due process. Human Rights Watch has chronicled the triggers for a number of mass expulsions in the 1990s:

> The infamous 1991 wave of mass expulsions was triggered by international pressure on the Dominican government to improve its treatment of Haitian cane cutters,

and in particular to stop the practice of forced labor . . . Presidential elections held in May 1996 sparked a smaller burst of deportations, as politicians manipulated anti-Haitian sentiment to sway voters . . . Mass deportations began in January [1997], apparently in response to an angry public debate that had erupted over government plans to recruit additional Haitian cane cutters . . . A massive deportation campaign took place in November 1999, again in an apparent backlash against international pressure.[62]

Similar cycles of escalation and retreat have continued. Furthermore, organizations such as Human Rights Watch and Minorities at Risk have highlighted the potential for further escalation of the situation into ethnic cleansing or genocide.[63] The temporal model of the risk factors for genocide also predicts such a risk in this case. Indeed, the model's cycles of escalation and retreat have characterized the risk profile of ethnic Haitians in the Dominican Republic. The model can therefore be viewed as applicable to this case study as well.

The Wider Applicability of the Temporal Model

Within the limitations of the brief investigations above, it thus appears reasonable to conclude that the temporal model of the risk factors for genocide has a broad applicability to historical and contemporary cases of genocide. Perhaps one limitation of the model is that it also appears to highlight nations at risk of ethnic cleansing as well as genocide. Potentially, this is due to the often similar nature of these events, and the similar processes that lead to them.[64] In numerous instances, such as in Bosnia and Darfur, such massive violence has contained elements of both. Additionally, there is considerable evidence that the ideologies and routes decided upon by perpetrator regimes can be modified considerably by external influences and processes of cumulative radicalization, even as massive violence is underway. For example, as late as 1940 the Nazi regime was primarily focussed upon removal of the Jews from its empire—through the Lublin reservation and Madagascar plan—rather than their outright extermination. Aside from this qualification, however, the case studies of Darfur and the Dominican Republic support the validity and wider applicability of the temporal model of the risk factors for genocide. This suggests it can be a powerful new tool to aid in the understanding of how the risk of genocide progresses over time.

Notes

1. G. Prunier. 2005. *Darfur: The Ambiguous Genocide*, Ithaca, NY: Cornell University Press, 76.
2. Ibid., 90, 156.

3. A. de Waal. 2007. 'War in Darfur and the Prospects for Peace', lecture given at Melbourne Law School, University of Melbourne, 4 April 2007; L. Polgreen. 2006. 'Rwanda's Shadow, from Darfur to Congo', *The New York Times Week in Review*, 23 July 2006, 3.

4. Prunier, *Darfur*, 4–5.

5. R. Iyob and G. Khadiagala. 2006. *Sudan: The Elusive Quest for Peace*, Boulder, CO: Lynne Rienner, 134.

6. J. Flint and A. de Waal. 2005. *Darfur: A Short History of a Long War*, London: Zed Books, 48; M. Daly. 2007. *Darfur's Sorrow: A History of Destruction and Genocide*, Cambridge: Cambridge University Press, 243.

7. Ibid.; Flint and de Waal, *Darfur*, 49, 51.

8. Ibid., 56.

9. Human Rights Watch. 2004. *Darfur in Flames: Atrocities in Western Sudan*, Washington, D.C.: Human Rights Watch, 2. Retrieved 10 September 2007 from http://hrw.org/reports/2004/sudan0404/3.htm

10. Flint and de Waal, *Darfur*, 28.

11. Ibid.

12. Prunier, *Darfur*, 153.

13. Ibid., 154.

14. Flint and de Waal, *Darfur*, 58.

15. Prunier, *Darfur*, 86.

16. Daly, *Darfur's Sorrow*, 268.

17. Flint and de Waal, *Darfur*, 69.

18. United Nations. 2005. *Report of the International Commission of Inquiry on Darfur to the United Nations Secretary-General*, Pursuant to Security Council Resolution 1564 of 18 September 2004, Geneva, 25 January 2005, 22–23.

19. Prunier, *Darfur*, 154.

20. Human Rights Watch, *Darfur in Flames*, 10.

21. Prunier, *Darfur*, 97; A. Natsios. 2006. 'Moving Beyond the Sense of Alarm', in S. Totten and E. Markusen (eds), *Genocide in Darfur: Investigating the Atrocities in the Sudan*, New York: Routledge, 31.

22. Prunier, *Darfur*, 106.

23. Flint and de Waal, *Darfur*, 106.

24. D. Bloxham. 2005. *The Great Game of Genocide: Imperialism, Nationalism, and the Destruction of the Ottoman Armenians*, Oxford: Oxford University Press, 69.

25. Prunier, *Darfur*, 97–98; R. Collins. 2006. 'Disaster in Darfur: Historical Overview', in Totten and Markusen, *Genocide in Darfur*, 20.

26. Ibid.

27. Prunier, *Darfur*, 101.

28. *Al-Anbaa*, 13 January 2004, quoted in Prunier, *Darfur*, 110.

29. Collins, 'Disaster in Darfur', 11.

30. Prunier, *Darfur*, 99.

31. Ibid., 100.

32. Natsios, 'Moving Beyond', 33.

33. Ibid., 36.

34. Daly, *Darfur's Sorrow*, 286.

35. Ibid.

36. O. Degomme and D. Guha-Sapir. 2010. 'Patterns of Mortality Rates in Darfur Conflict', *The Lancet* 375(9711), 294–300; E. Reeves. 2012. 'Evil and Ignorance: The Case of Darfur', *Dissent Magazine*, 26 January. Retrieved 10 April 2013 from http://www.dissentmagazine.org/online_articles/evil-and-ignorance-the-case-of-darfur

37. Prunier, *Darfur*, 102.
38. Human Rights Watch, *Darfur in Flames*, 10.
39. E. Paulino. 2006. 'Anti-Haitianism, Historical Memory, and the Potential for Genocidal Violence in the Dominican Republic', *Genocide Studies and Prevention* 1(3), 281.
40. M. Wucker. 1999. *Why the Cocks Fight: Dominicans, Haitians, and the Struggle for Hispaniola*, New York: Hill and Wang, 95.
41. J. Diamond. 2005. *Collapse: How Societies Choose to Fail or Survive*, Melbourne: Penguin, 356; D. Howard. 2001. *Coloring the Nation: Race and Ethnicity in the Dominican Republic*, Oxford: Signal Books, 153.
42. Paulino, 'Anti-Haitianism', 269.
43. R.L. Turits. 2002. 'A World Destroyed, A Nation Imposed: The 1937 Haitian Massacre in the Dominican Republic', *Hispanic American Historical Review* 82(3), 599.
44. Ibid.
45. Ibid., 604–5.
46. Ibid., 604–5, 612.
47. Ibid., 605.
48. Ibid., 608, 610; R. Turits. 2003. *Foundations of Despotism: Peasants, The Trujillo Regime, and Modernity in Dominican History*, Palo Alto, CA: Stanford University Press, 159.
49. E. Roorda. 1998. *The Dictator Next Door: The Good Neighbour Policy and the Trujillo Regime in the Dominican Republic, 1930–1945*, Durham, NC: Duke University Press, 131.
50. Turits, 'A World Destroyed', 589–91; Diamond, *Collapse*, 356; Turits, *Foundations of Despotism*, 161.
51. Turits, 'A World Destroyed', 614.
52. Ibid., 621.
53. Ibid., 623.
54. Ibid., 591.
55. Ibid., 630, 635.
56. Ibid., 622.
57. M. Midlarsky. 2005. *The Killing Trap: Genocide in the Twentieth Century*, Cambridge: Cambridge University Press, 335.
58. Paulino, 'Anti-Haitianism', 265; Minorities at Risk. 2004. *Assessment for Haitian Blacks in the Dominican Republic*, College Park, MD: Center for International Development and Conflict Management, University of Maryland. Retrieved 15 September 2007 from http://www.cidcm. umd.edu/mar/assessment.asp?groupId=4201
59. P.S. Miguel. 2005. *The Imagined Island: History, Identity and Utopia in Hispaniola*, trans. Jane Ramírez, Chapel Hill: University of North Carolina Press, 57–58.
60. Howard, *Coloring the Nation*, 162–63.
61. Ibid., 153.
62. Human Rights Watch. 2002. *Dominican Republic: "Illegal People": Haitians and Dominico-Haitians in the Dominican Republic*, Washington, D.C.: Human Rights Watch, 16. Retrieved 15 September 2007 from http://www.hrw.org/reports/2002/domrep/
63. Ibid., passim; Minorities at Risk, *Assessment for Haitian Blacks*, passim.
64. For a more comprehensive discussion of what constitutes the 'spectrum' of ethnic cleansing, see N. Naimark. 2001. *Fires of Hatred: Ethnic Cleansing in Twentieth-Century Europe*, Cambridge, MA: Harvard University Press, 2–5.

'WE ARE ALL BROTHERS'
The Temporal Model and Genocide Prevention

This book began with a single quest: to understand why genocides occur when they do. That is, why did genocide erupt in Rwanda in 1994, and not 1964, or, for that matter, in 1974 or 1984? How can we explain the timing of the Armenian genocide, some twenty years after the Hamidian massacres, and only seven years after Armenians were granted equal citizenship rights for the first time in the history of the Ottoman Empire? Is there a predictable pattern in how risk factors for genocide develop over time? In order to address these questions, two detailed investigations were conducted, examining how and when risk factors emerged in the ultimately genocidal societies of Rwanda and Ottoman Turkey. Through examining each society from the emergence of minority identity as an issue to the outbreak of genocide, it was possible to explore how the risk of genocide waxed and waned in each society over time. Such an approach offered valuable insight not only into the core concern of the book—understanding the timing of genocide—but additionally into pregenocidal massacres and the role of constraints in inhibiting genocide.

What I have called the temporal model of preconditions for genocide has been extrapolated from the results of these investigations. Whereas previous models have identified the necessary and sufficient preconditions for genocide, they have proffered little information on how these prerequisites emerge over time. The temporal model, by contrast, is the first model of the preconditions of genocide that incorporates temporal development as an intrinsic component. The eight key stages of the model work both individually and as a whole to provide a greatly improved understanding of how factors that influence the risk of genocide operate over time. Crucially, this model deals not only with predisposing factors, but also with the role of precipitants and constraints in the process. It has identified and examined the key role of perceptions of the outgroup as posing an existential threat to the dominant power in the risk escalation process. It has explored the cyclic process of risk escalation and retreat in societies at risk of genocide. Furthermore, the latter stages of the model offer some real predictive capacity in determining the likely onset of genocide.

These research findings also offer fresh insight into the burgeoning field of genocide prevention. In the wake of the massive mortality from genocide in recent decades—despite the international commitment to 'prevent and to punish' the crime in the Genocide Convention—this area has received renewed scholarly and international attention. In 2004, the UN established the Office of the Special Adviser on the Prevention of Genocide. At the World Summit in 2005, the international community unanimously endorsed the 'responsibility to protect' principle, highlighting the national and international responsibility to protect populations from genocide and mass atrocities.[1] Internationally, more effort and resources are being dedicated to genocide prevention than ever before. Alongside this effort has been the growth of the field of genocide studies, with a growing scholarship specifically focussed on genocide prevention. The temporal model offers a valuable contribution to this field. The following section will briefly explore how the model both highlights some of the shortcomings associated with previous attempts to prevent genocide, and suggests potentially more effective approaches. Ultimately, a greater understanding of the path that leads to genocide can contribute to preventing this catastrophic outcome.

Preventing Genocide through Early Intervention and Promoting Resilience

Potentially genocidal crises commonly only attract substantial international attention when they are already well advanced. If one examines previous attempts at intervention to prevent the outbreak of genocide, typically such intervention occurs at stage seven or eight of the temporal model—when the society is right on the cusp of a genocidal outbreak. By this stage, however, the would-be perpetrators have invested heavily in a genocidal strategy. They are resistant to negotiated solutions. They have calculated that they possess sufficient power to conduct genocide. The population of the nation has been radicalized through massive propaganda, and the situation is inherently unstable. And, in the recent cases of Bosnia, Rwanda and Darfur, the conflicting interests and general self-interest of United Nations Security Council members have prevented the massive interventions that would be required to forestall an imminent genocidal outbreak. The key constraint of international factors is often rendered inoperable by realpolitik. The temporal model confirms the lessons of the 'century of genocide'—that an approach to genocide prevention reliant on intervention on the cusp of genocide is fraught with risk of failure.

While the temporal model highlights the risks of a late-stage approach to intervention, it also identifies earlier intervention as a potentially more effective approach. As the model demonstrates, there are markers that clearly identify societies at risk of genocide well before that risk is imminent. It is here that the best opportunities for preventive action exist. Crucially, early-stage approaches to genocide prevention usually require far less political will than late-stage approaches—a vital advantage given the failure of international political will associated with major instances of genocide in the past fifty years. Furthermore, at this early stage preventive actions can often be undertaken cooperatively with the at-risk nation.

The investigations into the Armenian and Rwandan genocides appear to suggest that governments are much more likely to accept—and even seek—peaceful solutions to perceived problems with 'outgroups' prior to the stage of radicalization. As discussed earlier, for example, in the immediate wake of the revolution in which the Young Turks swept to power, they actively sought reconciliation and a new basis for interaction with the Armenian minority. 'We are all brothers . . . under the same blue sky', declared Enver Pasha.[2] Similarly, the Kayibanda government in Rwanda expressed a desire for peace and tolerance in Rwanda only six months after the Bugesera invasion of December 1963. The Habyarimana government, too, was initially sufficiently pro-Tutsi that Rwanda expert René Lemarchand could comment in 1975 that 'the prospects of a Hutu-Tutsi *rapprochement . . .* have never been brighter'.[3] Indeed, if the central goal is that of genocide prevention, it must be considered of great significance that in 1909 Enver Pasha—later a key leader of the Armenian genocide—referred to minorities in Turkey as 'brothers', and Habyarimana was popularly considered 'the protector of the Tutsi' for much of his rule.[4] This history suggests that genuine opportunities for peaceful and effective intervention exist prior to the stage of radicalization. Had Rwanda's request for international and United Nations assistance with the Tutsi refugee problem in 1964 received an effective international response, for example, the chain of events that led to the 1994 genocide may never have occurred.

An important finding of the temporal model is that early stages of risk of genocide are likely to exist for decades in an at-risk nation. This longevity provides excellent opportunities for programs to mitigate such risk. Many of the strategies proposed for early preventive action are relatively long-term strategies. The temporal model suggests this may not reduce their potential. Educational programs promoting intergroup tolerance and acceptance, for example, may take a generation to take full effect. It may take years for domestic or regional human rights mechanisms to be strengthened, or for domestic laws guaranteeing equal rights to an outgroup to be successfully introduced. Yet relatively long-term time frames should not be a barrier, given the longevity of risk and the important protective contribution of such measures. At the same time, however, the temporal model also testifies to the resilience of preconditions. They can continue to exist despite regime change, ideological change and other profound societal upheavals. The serious challenge of deconstructing preconditions should not be underestimated. Furthermore, the model demonstrates the potentially very rapid processes of risk escalation that can occur in at-risk nations. Preventive programs should always be a priority to reduce the risk of such escalation.

Finally, the temporal model also draws attention to the importance of a multifaceted approach to genocide prevention. Risk of genocide is determined not only by the presence of preconditions but the interplay of preconditions, precipitants and constraints. Preventing genocide, therefore, requires an approach that recognizes opportunities not only for deconstructing preconditions (which may not always be possible) but also to counter their effect through a balance of constraints. For example, the presence of an 'outgroup' can be a particularly persistent feature of a society, with deeply entrenched prejudices and discriminatory practices. It can be extremely difficult to break down historical grievances, myths and stigmas associated with minority groups. Attempts to deconstruct this precondition might include presenting positive publicity about the minority, granting the minority legal equality and providing equitable access to resources. Alongside this, however, should be efforts to counterbalance lingering prejudices through mechanisms that inhibit the possibility of risk escalation. Empowering the minority through access to legal services to protest discrimination, for example, or ensuring defamatory comments specifically targeting the group do not gain traction in the media, may have significant protective value. At later stages of the model, ensuring risk is counterbalanced through the presence of protective factors may be at least as effective as attempts to deconstruct preconditions. This might incorporate strong international oversight in at-risk nations, promoting the protective role of an affine nation or promoting democratic reform to reduce the capacity for extreme violence. While many of these activities already take place in an ad hoc manner, the temporal model highlights the value of concerted analysis and a multifaceted response to all levels of risk.

Conclusion

The death toll from genocide in the twentieth century is some 250 million, according to one estimate.[5] More people have died from genocide than AIDS, breast cancer, tsunamis or terrorism. Many millions of dollars are spent on these latter causes, there is extensive international cooperation to address them and they receive massive amounts of attention from the media and politicians alike. The field of genocide studies, by contrast, attracts much less publicity and funding. And yet, if just a fraction of the funding and international cooperation above were devoted to genocide prevention, there would be a very real prospect of change. Undoubtedly, a concerted program to reduce the risk of genocide in at-risk nations would be complex, expensive and difficult. Yet the cost of inaction is incalculable. As this book has demonstrated, genocide is fundamentally preventable. The path that leads to genocide is complex, but not inexorable. The challenge remains to prevent this 'odious scourge'.[6]

Notes

1. United Nations General Assembly. 2005. '2005 World Summit Outcome', A/RES/60/1, 16 September, 30.
2. G.S. Graber. 1996. *Caravans to Oblivion: The Armenian Genocide 1915*, New York: J. Wiley, 45.
3. R. Lemarchand. 1975. 'Recent History' in section on 'Rwanda', in *Africa South of the Sahara, 1974*, London: Europa Publications, 660, quoted in M. Mamdani. 2001. *When Victims Become Killers: Colonialism, Nativism, and the Genocide in Rwanda*, Princeton, NJ: Princeton University Press, 140.
4. Graber, *Caravans to Oblivion*, 45; Mamdani, *When Victims Become Killers*, 142.
5. E. Richter et al. 2007. 'The Precautionary Principle: Environmental Epidemiology's Gift to Genocide Prevention', poster distributed at Seventh Biennial Meeting, International Association of Genocide Scholars, 9–13 July 2007, Sarajevo, Bosnia and Herzegovina.
6. United Nations. 1948. Convention on the Prevention and Punishment of the Crime of Genocide.

BIBLIOGRAPHY

Adelman, H. and A. Suhrke (eds). 1999. *The Path of a Genocide: The Rwanda Crisis from Uganda to Zaire.* New Brunswick, NJ: Transaction Publishers.

Adeney, H. 1963. *Only One Weapon: Facing Difficulty and Danger with Christ in Troubled Rwanda.* London: Ruanda Mission, C.M.S.

African Rights. 1995. *Rwanda: Death, Despair and Defiance,* rev. ed. London: African Rights.

Ahmad, F. 1988. 'War and Society under the Young Turks, 1908–18'. *Review: Fernand Braudel Center* 11(2), 265–86.

Akçam, T. 2007. *A Shameful Act: The Armenian Genocide and the Question of Turkish Responsibility.* London: Constable.

Alker, H., T. Gurr and K. Rupesinghe (eds). 2001. *Journeys through Conflict: Narratives and Lessons.* Lanham, MD: Rowman and Littlefield.

Anderson, M. S. 1966. *The Eastern Question 1774–1923: A Study in International Relations.* London: Macmillan.

Andreopoulos, G. (ed.). 1994. *Genocide: Conceptual and Historical Dimensions.* Philadelphia: University of Pennsylvania Press.

Astourian, S. 1990. 'The Armenian Genocide: An Interpretation'. *The History Teacher* 23(2), 111–60.

Atterbury, M. 1970. *Revolution in Rwanda,* Occasional Paper 2. Madison: African Studies Program, University of Wisconsin.

Barnett, M. 1997. 'The UN Security Council, Indifference, and Genocide in Rwanda'. *Cultural Anthropology* 12(4), 551–78.

Bauman, Z. 1991. *Modernity and the Holocaust.* Ithaca, NY: Cornell University Press.

Belgian government. 1961. *Rapport sur l'administration belge du Ruanda-Urundi pendant l'année 1960.* Brussels: Fr. Van Muysewinkel.

Belgium, Service de l'information du Ruanda-Urundi. 1960. *Rwanda: Le problème des réfugiés et sinistrés après les troubles de 1959–1960.* Brussels: Service de l'information du Ruanda-Urundi.

Berry, J. A. and C.P. Berry (eds). 1999. *Genocide in Rwanda: A Collective Memory.* Washington, D.C.: Howard University Press.

Bey, S. 1898. *Islam, Turkey and Armenia and How They Happened.* St. Louis: C.B. Woodward.

Bhattacharyya, J. 1967. 'Belgian Administration in Ruanda during the Trusteeship Period with Special Reference to the Tutsi-Hutu Relationship'. Ph.D. diss., University of Delhi.

Bliss, E. 1896. *Turkey and the Armenian Atrocities.* Boston: H.L. Hastings.

Bloxham, D. 2005. *The Great Game of Genocide: Imperialism, Nationalism, and the Destruction of the Ottoman Armenians.* Oxford: Oxford University Press.

Brain, J. 1973. 'The Tutsi and the Ha: A Study in Integration'. *Journal of Asian and African Studies* 8(1–2), 39–49.

Braude, B. and B. Lewis (eds). 1982. *Christians and Jews in the Ottoman Empire: The Functioning of a Plural Society*, vol. 1, *The Central Lands*. New York: Holmes and Meier Publishers.

Bryce, J. 1896. *Transcaucasia and Ararat: Being Notes of a Vacation Tour in the Autumn of 1876*, rev. 4th ed. London: Macmillan.

Bryce, J. and A. Toynbee. 2000. *The Treatment of Armenians in the Ottoman Empire, 1915–1916*, uncensored ed., reprint edited and with an introduction by Ara Sarafian. Princeton, NJ: Gomidas Institute. Originally published 1916.

Burdett, A. (ed.). 1998. *Armenia: Political and Ethnic Boundaries 1878–1948*. Chippenham, UK: Archive Editions.

Burnet, J. 1998. 'The Search for a Middle Ground in a Country Divided: The Production of Ethnic Identity and Violence in the Rwandan Genocide'. Master's thesis, University of North Carolina at Chapel Hill.

Buxton, N. and H. Buxton. 1914. *Travel and Politics in Armenia*. New York: Macmillan.

Carr, R.H. and A.H. Halsey. 1999. *Land of a Thousand Hills: My Life in Rwanda*. New York: Viking.

Chaliand, G. and Y. Ternon. 1983. *The Armenians: From Genocide to Resistance*. London: Zed Press.

Chalk, F. and K. Jonassohn (eds). 1991. *History and Sociology of Genocide*. New Haven, CT: Yale University Press.

Charny, I. (ed.). 1984. *Toward the Understanding and Prevention of Genocide*. Boulder, CO: Westview Press.

———(ed.). 1999. *Encyclopaedia of Genocide*. Santa Barbara, CA: ABC-CLIO.

Chirot, D. and C. McCauley. 2006. *Why Not Kill Them All? The Logic and Prevention of Mass Political Murder*. Princeton, NJ: Princeton University Press.

Chirot, D. and M. Seligman (eds). 2001. *Ethnopolitical Warfare: Causes, Consequences, and Possible Solutions*. Washington, D.C.: American Psychological Association.

Chorbajian, L. and G. Shirinian (eds). 1999. *Studies in Comparative Genocide*. Houndmills, UK: Macmillan Press.

Church, J. 1966. *Forgive Them: The Story of an African Martyr*. London: Hodder and Stoughton.

Claessen, H.J.M. and P. Skalnik. 1981. *The Study of the State*. The Hague: Mouton Publishers.

Codere, H. 1962. 'Power in Ruanda'. *Anthropologica* 4, 45–85.

———. 1973. *The Biography of an African Society, Rwanda 1900–1960: Based on Forty-Eight Rwandan Autobiographies*. Tervuren, Belgium: Koninklijk Museum Voor Midden-Afrika.

Dadrian, V. 1986. 'The Naim-Andonian Documents on the World War I Destruction of Ottoman Armenians: The Anatomy of a Genocide'. *International Journal of Middle East Studies* 18(3), 311–60.

———. 1989. 'Genocide as a Problem of National and International Law: The World War I Armenian Case and Its Contemporary Legal Ramifications'. *The Yale Journal of International Law* 14(2), 221–334.

———. 1994. 'A Review of the Main Features of the Genocide', *Journal of Political and Military Sociology* 22(1), 1–28.

———. 1995. *The History of the Armenian Genocide: Ethnic Conflict from the Balkans to Anatolia to the Caucasus*. Providence, RI: Berghahn Books.

———. 1998. 'The Armenian Genocide and the Legal and Political Issues in the Failure to Prevent or to Punish the Crime'. *University of West Los Angeles Law Review* 29, 43–78.

———. 1998. *Warrant for Genocide: Key Elements of Turko-Armenian Conflict*. New Brunswick, NJ: Transaction Publishers.

———. 2004. 'Patterns of Twentieth Century Genocides: The Armenian, Jewish, and the Rwandan Cases'. *Journal of Genocide Research* 6(4), 487–522.

Daly, M. 2007. *Darfur's Sorrow: A History of Destruction and Genocide*. Cambridge: Cambridge University Press.

Davies, J. and T. Gurr (eds). 1998. *Preventive Measures: Building Risk Assessment and Crisis Early Warning Systems*. Lanham, MD: Rowman and Littlefield.

Davison, R. 1948. 'The Armenian Crisis, 1912–1914'. *The American Historical Review* 53(3), 481–505.

————. 1954. 'Turkish Attitudes Concerning Christian-Muslim Equality in the Nineteenth Century'. *The American Historical Review* 59(4), 844–64.

Degomme, O. and D. Guha-Sapir. 2010. 'Patterns of Mortality Rates in Darfur Conflict'. *The Lancet* 375(9711), 294–300.

Des Forges, A. 1999. *"Leave None to Tell the Story": Genocide in Rwanda*. New York: Human Rights Watch.

Destexhe, A. 1995. *Rwanda and Genocide in the Twentieth Century*. New York: New York University Press.

Diamond, J. 2005. *Collapse: How Societies Choose to Fail or Survive*. Melbourne: Penguin.

Dobkowski, M. and I. Wallimann (eds). 1998. *The Coming Age of Scarcity: Preventing Mass Death and Genocide in the Twenty-first Century*. Syracuse, NY: Syracuse University Press.

'Documents: The State Department File'. *Armenian Review* 37(1), Spring 1984, 60–145.

Duarte, M. 1994. 'Education in Ruanda-Urundi, 1946–61'. *The Historian* 57(2), 275–84.

Dubb, A. 1960. *Myth in Modern Africa: The Fourteenth Conference Proceedings of the Rhodes-Livingstone Institute for Social Research*. Lusaka, Northern Rhodesia: The Rhodes-Livingstone Institute.

Fein, H. 1978. 'A Formula for Genocide: Comparison of the Turkish Genocide (1915) and the German Holocaust (1939–1945)'. *Comparative Studies in Sociology* 1, 271–93.

————. 1979. *Accounting for Genocide: National Responses and Jewish Victimization During the Holocaust*. New York: The Free Press.

Flint, J. and A. de Waal. 2005. *Darfur: A Short History of a Long War*. London: Zed Books.

France, Ministère des Affaires Étrangères. 1897. *Documents diplomatiques: Affaires arméniennes: Projets de réformes dans l'empire ottoman, 1893–1897*. Paris: Imprimerie Nationale.

Gaidzakian, O. 1898. *Illustrated Armenia and the Armenians*. Boston: n.p.

Gatwa, T. 2005. *The Churches and Ethnic Ideology in the Rwandan Crises 1900–1994*. Milton Keynes: Paternoster.

Gellately, R. and B. Kiernan (eds). 2003. *The Specter of Genocide: Mass Murder in Historical Perspective*. Cambridge: Cambridge University Press.

Germany, Turkey and Armenia: A Selection of Documentary Evidence Relating to the Armenian Atrocities from German and Other Sources. 1917. London: J.J. Keliher & Co., Ltd.

Ghazarian, V. (ed.). 1997. *Armenians in the Ottoman Empire: An Anthology of Transformation 13th–19th Centuries*. Waltham, MA: Mayreni Publishing.

Gibbs, Jr., J.L. (ed.). 1965. *Peoples of Africa*. New York: Holt, Rinehart and Winston.

Golde, P. (ed.). 1986. *Women in the Field: Anthropological Experiences*, 2nd ed. Berkeley: University of California Press.

Goose, S. 1994. 'Arming Genocide in Rwanda'. *Foreign Affairs* 73(5), 86–96.

Graber, G.S. 1996. *Caravans to Oblivion: The Armenian Genocide 1915*. New York: J. Wiley.

Greene, F. 1896. *Armenian Massacres or The Sword of Mohammed*. n.p.: American Oxford.

Habyarimana, J. 1981. *Discours, Messages et Entretiens: 5 juillet 1973—décembre 1974*. Kigali: ORINFOR.

————. n.d. *Discours, Messages et Entretiens: Édition 1980*. Kigali: ORINFOR.

Hairapetian, A. 1984. '"Race Problems" and the Armenian Genocide: The State Department File'. *Armenian Review* 37(1–145), 41–59.

Harff, B. 2001. 'Could Humanitarian Crises Have Been Anticipated in Burundi, Rwanda, and Zaire?' In H. Alker, T. Gurr and K. Rupesinghe (eds), *Journeys Through Conflict: Narratives and Lessons*. Lanham, MD: Rowman and Littlefield, pp. 81–102.

————. 2003. 'No Lessons Learned from the Holocaust? Assessing Risks of Genocide and Political Mass Murder since 1955'. *American Political Science Review* 97(1), 57–73.

————. 2012. 'Assessing Risks of Genocide and Politicide: A Global Watchlist for 2012' [electronic version]. In J.J. Hewitt, J. Wilkenfield and T.R. Gurr (eds), *Peace and Conflict 2012*. Boulder, CO: Paradigm. Retrieved 12 October 2011 from http://www.gpanet.org/webfm_send/120

Harris [Mayersen], D. 2001. 'Defining Genocide: Defining History?' *Eras Online Journal* 1(1). Retrieved 2 October 2007 from http://www.arts.monash.edu.au/eras/edition_1/harris.htm

Harris, J.R. and H. Harris. 1897. *Letters from the Scenes of the Recent Massacres in Armenia*. London: n.p.

Harroy, J.-P. 1984. *Rwanda: Souvenirs d'un compagnon de la marche du Rwanda vers la démocratie et l'indépendance.* Brussels: Hayez.

Henderson, G., R. Lebow and J. Stoessinger (eds). 1974. *Divided Nations in a Divided World.* New York: David McKay.

Hepworth, G. 1898. *Through Armenia on Horseback.* New York: E.P. Dutton.

Hintjens, H. 1999. 'Explaining the 1994 Genocide in Rwanda'. *The Journal of Modern African Studies* 37(2), 241–86.

Hinton, A. 1996. 'Agents of Death: Explaining the Cambodian Genocide in Terms of Psychosocial Dissonance'. *American Anthropologist* 98(4), 818–31.

———. 1998. 'A Head for an Eye: Revenge in the Cambodian Genocide'. *American Ethnologist* 25(3), 352–77.

———. 2005. *Why Did They Kill? Cambodia in the Shadow of Genocide.* Berkeley: University of California Press.

Hodgetts, E.A.B. 1896. *Round About Armenia: The Record of a Journey across the Balkans through Turkey, the Caucasus and Persia in 1895.* London: Sampson Low Marston.

Horowitz, I.L. 1976. *Genocide: State Power and Mass Murder.* New Brunswick, NJ: Transaction Publishers.

Hovannisian, R. 1967. *Armenia on the Road to Independence, 1918.* Berkeley: University of California Press.

———(ed.). 1986. *The Armenian Genocide in Perspective.* New Brunswick, NJ: Transaction Publishers.

———(ed.). 1992. *The Armenian Genocide: History, Politics, Ethics.* New York: St. Martin's Press.

———(ed.). 1997. *The Armenian People from Ancient to Modern Times,* vol. 2, *Foreign Dominion to Statehood: The Fifteenth Century to the Twentieth Century.* New York: St. Martin's Press.

Howard, D. 2001. *Coloring the Nation: Race and Ethnicity in the Dominican Republic.* Oxford: Signal Books.

Howard, W. 1896. *Horrors of Armenia: The Story of an Eye-witness.* New York: Armenian Relief Association.

Hubert, J. 1965. *La Toussaint Rwandaise et sa répression.* Brussels: Académie Royale des Sciences D'Outre-mer.

Human Rights Watch. 2002. *Dominican Republic: "Illegal People": Haitians and Dominico-Haitians in the Dominican Republic.* Washington, D.C.: Human Rights Watch. Retrieved 15 September 2007 from http://www.hrw.org/reports/2002/domrep/

———. 2004. *Darfur in Flames: Atrocities in Western Sudan.* Washington, D.C.: Human Rights Watch. Retrieved 10 September 2007 from http://hrw.org/reports/2004/sudan0404/3.htm

Institute for Armenian Studies (ed.). 1987. *The Armenian Genocide: Documentation,* vol. 1. Munich: Institute for Armenian Studies.

———(ed.). 1991. *The Armenian Genocide: Documentation,* vol. 8. Munich: Institute for Armenian Studies.

Iyob, R. and G. Khadiagala. 2006. *Sudan: The Elusive Quest for Peace.* Boulder, CO: Lynne Rienner.

Jackh, E. 1944. *The Rising Crescent: Turkey Yesterday, Today and Tomorrow.* New York: Farrar and Rinehart.

Jensen, S. (ed.). 2003. *Genocide: Cases, Comparisons and Contemporary Debates.* Copenhagen: Danish Centre for Holocaust and Genocide Studies.

Jones, A. 2006. *Genocide: A Comprehensive Introduction.* London: Routledge.

Jones, B. 1999. 'Civil War, the Peace Process, and Genocide in Rwanda'. In A. Taisier and R. Matthews (eds), *Civil Wars in Africa: Roots and Resolution.* Montreal: McGill-Queen's University Press, pp. 53–86.

Kamukama, D. 1997. *Rwanda Conflict: Its Roots and Regional Implications,* 2nd ed. Kampala, Uganda: Fountain Publishers.

Kayibanda, G. 1973. 'Message presidential de pacification', Kigali, 22 March. *Remarques Africaines* 419 (1–15 April), 7–8.

Kiernan, B. 2007. *Blood and Soil: A World History of Genocide and Extermination from Sparta to Darfur.* New Haven, CT: Yale University Press.

Kirakossian, A. (ed.). 2004. *The Armenian Massacres 1894–1896: U.S. Media Testimony*. Detroit: Wayne State University Press.

Krain, M. 1997. 'State-Sponsored Mass Murder: The Onset and Severity of Genocides and Politicides'. *Journal of Conflict Resolution* 41(3), 331–60.

Kuper, L. 1975. *Race, Class, and Power: Ideology and Revolutionary Change in Plural Societies*. Chicago: Aldine.

———. 1977. *The Pity of It All: Polarisation of Racial and Ethnic Relations*. London: Duckworth.

———. 1981. *Genocide: Its Political Use in the Twentieth Century*. New Haven, CT: Yale University Press.

Lambrecht, F. 1991. *In the Shade of an Acacia Tree*. Philadelphia: American Philosophical Society.

Lang, D. 1981. *The Armenians: A People in Exile*. London: George, Allen and Unwin.

Latham-Koenig, A.L. 1962. 'Ruanda-Urundi on the Threshold of Independence'. *The World Today* 18(7), 288–95.

———. 1964. 'Attempted Genocide in Ruanda'. *The World Today* 20(3), 97–100.

Lemarchand, R. 1966. 'Political Instability in Africa: The Case of Rwanda and Burundi'. *Civilisations* 16(3), 307–37.

———. 1966. 'Power and Stratification in Rwanda: A Reconsideration'. *Cahiers D'Études Africaines* 6, 592–610.

———. 1970. *Rwanda and Burundi*. New York: Praeger Publishers.

———. 1995. 'Rwanda: The Rationality of Genocide'. In O. Igwara (ed.), *Ethnic Hatred: Genocide in Rwanda*. London: ASEN Publications, pp. 59–70.

———. 2006. 'Unsimplifying Darfur'. *Genocide Studies and Prevention* 1(1), 1–12.

Lemkin, R. 1944. *Axis Rule in Occupied Europe: Laws of Occupation, Analysis of Government, and Proposals for Redress*. Washington, D.C.: Carnegie Foundation for International Peace.

Lepsius, J. 1897. *Armenia and Europe: An Indictment*. London: Hodder and Stoughton.

———. 1987. *Rapport secret sur les massacres d'Arménie (1915–1916)*. Paris: Payot. Originally published 1918.

Leurquin, P. 1960. *Le Niveau de vie des populations rurales du Ruanda-Urundi*. Louvain: Éditions Nauwelaerts.

Levene, M. 2000. 'Why Is the Twentieth Century the Century of Genocide?' *Journal of World History* 11(2), 305–36.

———. 2005. *Genocide in the Age of the Nation-State*, vol. 1, *The Meaning of Genocide*. London: I.B. Tauris.

Licklider, R. 1995. 'The Consequences of Negotiated Settlements in Civil Wars, 1945–1993'. *American Political Science Review* 89(3), 681–90.

Linden, I. 1977. *Church and Revolution in Rwanda*. New York: Manchester University Press.

Longman, T. 1997. 'Rwanda: Democratization and Disorder: Political Transformation and Social Deterioration'. In J. Clark and D. Gardinier, *Political Reform in Francophone Africa*. Boulder, CO: Westview Press, pp. 287–306.

MacColl, M. 1895. *England's Responsibility Towards Armenia*. London: Longmans, Green.

Mamdani, M. 2001. *When Victims Become Killers: Colonialism, Nativism, and the Genocide in Rwanda*. Princeton, NJ: Princeton University Press.

Maquet, J. 1961. *The Premise of Inequality in Ruanda: A Study of Political Relations in a Central African Kingdom*. London: Oxford University Press.

Maquet, J.-J. and M. d'Hertefelt. 1959. *Les Élections en société féodale: Une étude sur l'introduction du vote populaire au Ruanda-Urundi*. Brussels: Académie Royale des Sciences Coloniales.

Marcus, D. 2003. 'Famine Crimes in International Law'. *American Journal of International Law* 97(2), 245–81.

Mayersen, D. 2007. 'Intermittent Intervention: Europe and the Precipitation of the Armenian Massacres of 1894–1896'. In S. Koehne and B. Mees (eds), *Terror, War, Tradition: Studies in European History*. Unley: Australian Humanities Press, pp. 247–70.

———. 2010. 'On the Timing of Genocide'. *Genocide Studies and Prevention* 5(1), 20–38.

Mazian, F. 1990. *Why Genocide? The Armenian and Jewish Experiences in Perspective*. Ames: Iowa State University Press.

McCall, D., N. Bennett and J. Butler (eds). 1969. *Eastern African History*, Boston University Papers on Africa 3. New York: Frederick A. Praeger.

McCullum, H. 1995. *The Angels Have Left Us: The Rwanda Tragedy and the Churches.* Geneva: WCC Publications.

Melson, R. 1992. *Revolution and Genocide: On the Origins of the Armenian Genocide and the Holocaust.* Chicago: University of Chicago Press.

———. 1996. 'Paradigms of Genocide: The Holocaust, the Armenian Genocide and Contemporary Mass Destructions'. *Annals of the American Academy of Political and Social Science* 548, 156–68.

Melvern, L. 2000. *A People Betrayed: The Role of the West in Rwanda's Genocide.* London: Zed Books.

———. 2006. *Conspiracy to Murder: The Rwandan Genocide,* rev. ed. London: Verso.

Midlarsky, M. 2005. *The Killing Trap: Genocide in the Twentieth Century.* Cambridge: Cambridge University Press.

Miguel, P.S. 2005. *The Imagined Island: History, Identity and Utopia in Hispaniola,* trans. Jane Ramírez. Chapel Hill: University of North Carolina Press.

Miller, D. and L.T. Miller. 1993. *Survivors: An Oral History of the Armenian Genocide.* Berkeley: University of California Press.

Minorities at Risk. 2004. *Assessment for Haitian Blacks in the Dominican Republic.* College Park, MD: Center for International Development and Conflict Management, University of Maryland. Retrieved 15 September 2007 from http://www.cidcm.umd.edu/mar/assessment.asp?groupId=4201

Missakian, J. 1950. *A Searchlight on the Armenian Question, 1878–1950.* Boston: Hairenik.

Morgenthau, H. 2000. *Ambassador Morgenthau's Story.* Ann Arbor, MI: Gomidas Institute. Originally published 1918.

Naimark, N. 2001. *Fires of Hatred: Ethnic Cleansing in Twentieth-Century Europe.* Cambridge, MA: Harvard University Press.

Nalbandian, L. 1963. *The Armenian Revolutionary Movement: The Development of Armenian Political Parties through the Nineteenth Century.* Berkeley: University of California Press.

Newbury, C. 1988. *The Cohesion of Oppression: Clientship and Ethnicity in Rwanda, 1860–1960.* New York: Columbia University Press.

Niyonzima, M., G. Kayibanda, C. Ndahayo, I. Nzeyimana, C. Mulindahabi, G. Sentama, S. Munyambonera, J. Sibomana and J. Habyarimana. 1957. *Manifesto of the Bahutu: Note on the Social Aspect of the Indigenous Racial Problem in Ruanda.* In United Nations, *Visiting Mission 1957,* Annex I.

Nkundabagenzi, F. (ed.). 1961. *Rwanda Politique: 1958–1960.* Brussels: Centre de Recherche et d'Information Socio-Politiques.

Nyrop, R., L. Brenneman, R. Hibbs, C. James, S. MacKnight and G. McDonald. 1969. *Area Handbook for Rwanda.* Washington, D.C.: U.S. Government Printing Office.

Organization of African Unity. 2000. *Rwanda: The Preventable Genocide.* Retrieved 12 April 2013 from http://www.africaunion.org/official_documents/reports/report_rowanda_genocide.pdf

Papazian, B. 1918. *The Tragedy of Armenia: A Brief Study and Interpretation.* Boston: Pilgrim Press.

Paulino, E. 2006. 'Anti-Haitianism, Historical Memory, and the Potential for Genocidal Violence in the Dominican Republic'. *Genocide Studies and Prevention* 1(3), 265–88.

Pears, E. 1911. *Turkey and Its People.* London: Methuen.

Pierce, J. (ed.). 1896. *Story of Turkey and Armenia: With a Full and Accurate Account of the Recent Massacres Written by Eye Witnesses.* Baltimore: R.H. Woodward.

Polgreen, L. 2006. 'Rwanda's Shadow, from Darfur to Congo'. *The New York Times Week in Review,* 23 July 2006, 3.

Power, S. 2003. *"A Problem from Hell": America and the Age of Genocide.* London: Flamingo.

Prunier, G. 1995. *The Rwanda Crisis: History of a Genocide.* New York: Columbia University Press.

———. 2005. *Darfur: The Ambiguous Genocide.* Ithaca, NY: Cornell University Press.

Ravitch, N. 1981. 'The Armenian Massacre'. *Encounter* 57(6), 69–85.

Rawson, D. 1966. 'The Role of the United Nations in the Political Development of Ruanda-Urundi, 1947–1962'. Ph.D. diss., American University.

Redgate, A.E. 1998. *The Armenians*. Oxford: Blackwell Publishers.

Reed, W.C. 1996. 'Exile, Reform, and the Rise of the Rwandan Patriotic Front'. *The Journal of Modern African Studies* 34(3), 479–501.

Reeves, E. 2012. 'Evil and Ignorance: The Case of Darfur'. *Dissent Magazine*, 26 January 2012. Retrieved 10 April 2013 from http://www.dissentmagazine.org/online_articles/evil-and-ignorance-the-case-of-darfur

Richter, E., R. Blum, J. Lindert, T. Berman, C. Soskolne and G. Stanton. 2007. 'The Precautionary Principle: Environmental Epidemiology's Gift to Genocide Prevention'. Poster distributed at Seventh Biennial Meeting, International Association of Genocide Scholars, 9–13 July 2007, Sarajevo, Bosnia and Herzegovina.

Riemer, N. 1998. 'Protection against Genocide: Towards a Global Human Rights Regime'. In S. Feinstein, K. Schierman and M. Littell (eds), *Confronting the Holocaust: A Mandate for the 21st Century, Part Two*. Lanham, MD: University Press of America, pp. 297–308.

Rittner, C., J. Roth and J. Smith (eds). 2002. *Will Genocide Ever End?* St. Paul, MN: Paragon House.

Rolin-Jaequemyns, M.G. 1891. *Armenia, The Armenians, and the Treaties*. London: John Heywood.

Roorda, E. 1998. *The Dictator Next Door: The Good Neighbour Policy and the Trujillo Regime in the Dominican Republic, 1930–1945*. Durham, NC: Duke University Press.

Rotberg, R. and A. Mazrui (eds). 1970. *Protest and Power in Black Africa*. New York: Oxford University Press.

Rummel, R.J. 1984. *Death by Government: Genocide and Mass Murder since 1900*. New Brunswick, NJ: Transaction Publishers.

———. 1995. 'Democracy, Power, Genocide, and Mass Murder'. *Journal of Conflict Resolution* 39(1), 3–26.

Rwanda, High Council of State. *Statement of Views (Mise au Point)*. In United Nations, *Visiting Mission 1957*, Annex II.

Rwanda, Ministère des Affaires Étrangères. 1964. *Toute la vérité sur le terrorisme "Inyenzi" au Rwanda: Une mise au point du Ministère des Affaires Étrangères du Rwanda*. Kigali: Services d'information.

'Rwanda.—Raids by Watutsi Refugees on Rwanda—Mass "Reprisal" Killings of Resident Watutsi—U.N. Investigation in Massacres'. *Keesing's Contemporary Archives*, vol. 10, May 1964, 20085.

Rwanda, Service de l'Information (ed.). 1963. *Le Président Kayibanda vous parle*. Kigali: Service de l'Information.

Sayinzoga, J. 1982. 'Les Réfugiés Rwandais: Quelques repères historiques et réflexions socio-politiques'. *Journal of the Swiss Society of African Studies* 20(1), 49–72.

Sazonov, S. 1928. *Fateful Years: 1909–1916: The Reminiscences of Serge Sazonov*. London: Jonathan Cape.

Segal, A. 1964. *Massacre in Rwanda*, Fabian Research Series 240. London: Fabian Society.

———. 1964. 'Rwanda: The Underlying Causes'. *Africa Report* 9(4), 3–6.

Simsir, B. (ed.). 1990. *British Documents on Ottoman Armenians*, vol. 3. Ankara: Turk Tarih Kurumu Printing Office.

Smith, R. 1994. 'Introduction: The Armenian Genocide: Perpetration, Denial, Documentation'. *Journal of Political and Military Sociology* 22(1), iii–ix.

Stanton, G. 1998. *The Eight Stages of Genocide*. Washington, D.C.: Genocide Watch. Retrieved 4 October 2007 from http://www.genocidewatch.org/aboutgenocide8stages.htm

———. 2004. 'Could the Rwandan Genocide Have Been Prevented?' *Journal of Genocide Research* 6(2), 211–28.

———. 2005. 'Early Warning'. In D. Shelton (ed.), *Encyclopedia of Genocide and Crimes Against Humanity*. Detroit, Mich.: Macmillan Reference, pp. 271–73. Retrieved 4 October 2007 from http://www.genocidewatch.org/aboutus/stantonearlywarningarticle.htm

Staub, E. 1989. *The Roots of Evil: The Origins of Genocide and Other Group Violence.* Cambridge: Cambridge University Press.

Stead, W. (ed.). 1896. *The Haunting Horrors in Armenia.* London: 'Review of Reviews' Office.

Suny, R. 1983. *Armenia in the Twentieth Century.* Chico, CA: Scholars Press.

Surbezy, F. 1911. 'Les Affaires d'Arménie et l'intervention des puissances européennes (de 1894 a 1897)'. Ph.D. diss., Université de Montpellier.

Tabara, P. 1992. *Afrique: La face cachée.* Paris: La Pensée universelle.

Ternon, Y. 1981. *The Armenians: History of a Genocide.* Delmar, NY: Caravan Books.

———(ed.). 1985. *The Armenian Genocide: Facts and Documents.* New York: Diocese of the Armenian Apostolic Church of America.

Totten, S. 2006. 'The US Investigation into the Darfur Crisis and the US Government's Determination of Genocide'. *Genocide Studies and Prevention* 1(1), 57–78.

Totten, S. and E. Markusen (eds). 2006. *Genocide in Darfur: Investigating the Atrocities in the Sudan.* New York: Routledge.

Townshend, A.F. 1910. *A Military Consul in Turkey.* London: Seeley.

Turits, R.L. 2002. 'A World Destroyed, A Nation Imposed: The 1937 Haitian Massacre in the Dominican Republic'. *Hispanic American Historical Review* 82(3), 589–635.

———. 2003. *Foundations of Despotism: Peasants, The Trujillo Regime, and Modernity in Dominican History.* Palo Alto, CA: Stanford University Press.

Twagilimana, A. 2003. *The Debris of Ham: Ethnicity, Regionalism, and the 1994 Rwandan Genocide.* Lanham, MD: University Press of America.

Üngör, U.U. 2012. *The Making of Modern Turkey: Nation and State in Eastern Anatolia, 1913–1950.* Oxford: Oxford University Press, 51.

'The United Nations' Findings on Rwanda and Burundi: A Summary of Reports Made by Max H. Dorsinville on His Two Missions to Rwanda and Burundi as the United Nations Secretary General's Special Representative'. 1964. *Africa Report* 9(4), 7.

United Nations. 1948. *Convention on the Prevention and Punishment of the Crime of Genocide.*

———. 1957. *United Nations Visiting Mission to Trust Territories in East Africa, 1957, Report on Ruanda-Urundi.* T/1346, 6 December.

———. 1959. *Conditions in the Trust Territory of Ruanda-Urundi: Report of the Drafting Committee.* T/L.928, 21 July.

———. 1959. *Communication from the Hutu Social Party (APROSOMA) Concerning Ruanda-Urundi.* T/COM.3/L.30, 7 November.

———. 1960. *Petition from the Chairman of the Interim National Committee of the "Union Nationale Ruandaise" Concerning Ruanda-Urundi.* T/PET.3/L.19, 10 May.

———. 1960. *Petitions Concerning Ruanda-Urundi: Observations of the Belgian Government as Administering Authority.* T/OBS.3/26, 27 May.

———. 1960. *Visiting Mission to Trust Territories in East Africa, 1960: Report on Ruanda-Urundi.* T/1538, 3 June.

———. 1960. *Petition from H.E. Monsignor Perraudin, Archbishop of Kabgayi, Ruanda, concerning Ruanda-Urundi.* T/PET.3/L.35, 22 June.

———. 1960. *Petition from J.B. Kigeli Ndahindurwa, Mwami of Ruanda, Concerning Ruanda-Urundi.* T/PET.3/L.39, 24 June.

———. 1960. *Petition from the Chairman of the Provisional National Committee of the "Union Nationale Ruandaise (UNAR)" Concerning Ruanda-Urundi.* T/PET.3/L.44, 29 June.

———. 1960. *Question of the Future of Ruanda-Urundi: Statement Made by the Representative of Belgium at the 1065th Meeting of the Fourth Committee on 25 November 1960.* A/C.4/460, 25 November.

———. 1960. *Question of the Future of Ruanda-Urundi: Statement Made by the Representative of Belgium at the 1077th Meeting of Fourth Committee,* A/C.4/462, 15 December.

————. 1960. *Question of the Future of Ruanda-Urundi: Written Statement by Kigeri V. Mwami of Ruanda.* A/C.4/467, 19 December.

————. 1961. *Question of the Future of Ruanda-Urundi: Statement Made by the Representative of Belgium at the 1108th Meeting of the Fourth Committee on 20 March 1961.* A/C.4/473, 20 March.

————. 1961. *Question of the Future of Ruanda-Urundi: Note from the Aprosoma and Parmehutu Parties Concerning the Coup d'État at Gitarama on 28 January 1961.* A/C.4/477, 4 April.

————. 1961. *Question of the Future of Ruanda-Urundi: Report of the United Nations Commission for Ruanda-Urundi.* A/4994, 30 November.

————. 1962. *Question of the Future of Ruanda-Urundi: Statement Made by Mr. Max H. Dorsinville, Chairman of the United Nations Commission for Ruanda-Urundi, at the 1258th Meeting of the Fourth Committee.* A/C.4/518, 16 January.

————. 1962. *Question of the Future of Ruanda-Urundi: Statement Made by Mr. P. H. Spaak, Vice Prime Minister, Minister of Foreign Affairs of Belgium, at the 1259th Meeting of the Fourth Committee, on 16 January 1962.* A/C.4/519, 16 January.

————. 1962. *Question of the Future of Ruanda-Urundi: Statement Made by Mr. E. Gassou, United Nations Commissioner for Ruanda-Urundi, at the 1264th Meeting of the Fourth Committee.* A/C.4/524, 19 January.

————. 1962. *Question of the Future of Ruanda-Urundi: Statement Made by Mr. Majid Rahnema, United Nations Commissioner for Ruanda-Urundi, at the 1265th Meeting of the Fourth Committee.* A/C.4/525, 23 January.

————. 1962. *Question of the Future of Ruanda-Urundi: Report of the United Nations Commission for Ruanda-Urundi Established under General Assembly Resolution 1743 (XVI).* A/5126, 30 May.

————. 1999. *Report of the Independent Inquiry into the Actions of the United Nations during the 1994 Genocide in Rwanda.* S/1999/1257, 16 December.

————. 2005. *Report of the International Commission of Inquiry on Darfur to the United Nations Secretary-General.* Pursuant to Security Council Resolution 1564 of 18 September 2004, Geneva, 25 January.

————. 2005. '2005 World Summit Outcome'. A/RES/60/1, 16 September.

Uvin, P. 1996. 'Tragedy in Rwanda: The Political Ecology of Conflict', *Environment* 38(3), 6–15, 29.

Veenhoven, W. et al. (eds). 1976. *Case Studies on Human Rights and Fundamental Freedoms: A World Survey,* vol. 4. The Hague: Martinus Nijhoff.

Verwimp, P. 1999. 'Development Ideology, the Peasantry and Genocide: Rwanda Represented in Habyarimana's Speeches', Working Paper 13. New Haven, CT: Yale University Genocide Studies Program.

Wagoner, F. 1968. 'Nation Building in Africa: A Description and Analysis of the Development of Rwanda'. Ph.D. diss., American University.

Walker, C. 1980. *Armenia: The Survival of a Nation.* New York: St. Martin's Press.

Wallimann, I. and M. Dobkowski (eds). 1987. *Genocide and the Modern Age: Etiology and Case Studies of Mass Death.* New York: Greenwood Press.

Webster, J. 1966. *The Political Development of Rwanda and Burundi,* Occasional Paper 16. Syracuse, NY: Syracuse University Maxwell Graduate School of Citizenship and Public Affairs, Program of Eastern African Studies.

Weitz, E. 2003. *A Century of Genocide: Utopias of Race and Nation.* Princeton, NJ: Princeton University Press.

Williams, A.W. and M.S. Gabriel. 1896. *Bleeding Armenia: Its History and Horrors Under the Curse of Islam.* New York: Publishers' Union.

Winter, J. (ed.). 2003. *America and the Armenian Genocide of 1915.* Cambridge: Cambridge University Press.

Woods, H.C. 1911. *The Danger Zone of Europe: Changes and Problems in the Near East.* Boston: Little, Brown.

Wucker, M. 1999. *Why the Cocks Fight: Dominicans, Haitians, and the Struggle for Hispaniola.* New York: Hill and Wang, 1999.

INDEX

CPSIA information can be obtained at www.ICGtesting.com
Printed in the USA
BVOW08*0022020215

385841BV00003B/28/P